Rereading the Rabbis

Rereading the Rabbis

A WOMAN'S VOICE

Judith Hauptman

WestviewPress
A Division of HarperCollins*Publishers*

Copyright © 1998 by Judith Hauptman

Published in 1998 in the United States of America by Westview Press, 5500 Central Avenue, Boulder, Colorado 80301-2877, and in the United Kingdom by Westview Press, 12 Hid's Copse Road, Cumnor Hill, Oxford OX2 9JJ

Library of Congress Cataloging-in-Publication Data
Hauptman, Judith.
  Rereading the rabbis : a woman's voice / Judith Hauptman.
    p. cm.
  Includes bibliographical references and index.
  ISBN 0-8133-3400-4
  1. Women in rabbinical literature. 2. Talmud—Criticism,
interpretation, etc. 3. Talmud—Feminist criticism. I. Title.
BM509.W7H38 1998
296.1'206'082—dc21   97-18281
                                                      CIP

The paper used in this publication meets the requirements of the American National Standard for Permanence of Paper for Printed Library Materials Z39.48-1984.

10   9   8   7   6   5   4   3   2   1

In memory of Judy Hurwich,
miyakirei Yerushalayim

Contents

Acknowledgments

I am deeply thankful to have had the opportunity to write this book while living in Jerusalem for a year. Spending time in Israel was spiritually satisfying and intellectually stimulating. Unfortunately, many catastrophic events took place during that year, including the assassination of a peace-seeking prime minister and a series of bus bombings that killed innocent people. As far away as the ultimate resolution of the conflict seems, I would like to believe that day by day, however imperceptibly, it grows closer.

Many people generously gave of their time to read and critique this manuscript. The following brief statements hardly reflect the intensity of my gratitude to them. Robert Brody, associate professor of Talmud at the Hebrew University, read and commented on the entire manuscript; Rabbi Shmuel Sandberg, formerly a professor of English at the City University of New York, did the same, while also paying attention to felicitous expression; Susan E. Shapiro, assistant professor of Jewish Thought and Philosophy of Religion at Columbia University, read the greater part of the manuscript, discussed it with me at length, and made many important suggestions for its improvement; Noam Gavriely, a physician and head of the Pulmonary Physiology Unit at Rambam Hospital/Technion, read much of the manuscript and commented on it from a medical and humanist perspective; Lippman Bodoff, an attorney, brought to a number of chapters his legal sensibility and training; Shaye J. D. Cohen, professor of Judaic Studies at Brown University, made many helpful comments on the chapter on *Niddah*; Shamma Friedman, distinguished service professor of Talmud at the Bet Midrash in Jerusalem and the Jewish Theological Seminary in New York, and Athalya Brenner, professor of Bible at the University of Amsterdam, spent time discussing various issues with me.

The manuscript also benefited from the editorial advice of Ellen Frankel of the Jewish Publication Society, from extensive editorial attention by Beth Berkowitz, and from the research assistance of Naomi Lubarr, Avigayl Young, and Orit Kent.

I am also indebted to Marian Safran at Westview Press for her excellent comments. She brought this entire manuscript to a higher level of clarity, consistency, and pleasing expression. I wish to thank Fern Zekbakh for the fine indices.

I would also like to thank the Stroock Foundation for its fellowship assistance.

My husband, Milton Adesnik, and my three teenage sons, Ariel, Moshe, and Hillel, not only supported my project in general, but also expressed interest in every detail, often debating subtle points of Talmudic logic with me and stopping me from drawing unwarranted, although highly appealing, conclusions.

While in Israel, I spent Sunday nights teaching a women's Talmud class and discussing different parts of the manuscript with the class. Their collective insight has woven itself into much of the textual analysis. I thank all of these women.

I am dedicating this book to Judy Hurwich, of blessed memory, a legendary Jerusalemite, in whose home, or more accurately, salon, these Talmud sessions took place. It was she who initiated the study group and energetically and enthusiastically kept it going. Her death on the road in August 1996 saddened us all. Like the rabbis of the Talmud who appear in this book, she tirelessly sought and even fought to improve women's status in ritual and law. Also like them, she was torn between her loyalty to the texts and practices of the past and her unwavering commitment to the ethical stances of the present. May we be inspired by her life.

The practice of Judaism in the United States today, and also around the world, differs greatly from what it was as little as twenty years ago. Much of this change was spurred on by the emergence in the early 1970s of a feminist critique of Judaism. Whereas at that time female rabbis, cantors, and Talmud teachers and students were unheard of or scarce, today they abound. As more and more talented individuals—men and women alike—devote themselves to the spread of Jewish ideas and practice, they contribute to the continuing appeal and viability of the Jewish heritage. This book attempts to present the Talmudic basis for welcoming women into the full-fledged membership ranks of the Jewish people.

Judith Hauptman
New York, New York

Note to the Reader

The translations of rabbinic texts are my own. The bracketed words are explanatory insertions.

The term rabbis refers, in most instances, to the rabbis of the Talmud, the majority of whom flourished from about 1 to 500 C.E.

The expression "Said Rabbi X said Rabbi Y" means that Rabbi X transmitted what he had heard from Rabbi Y.

When a reference is to the Mishnah as an entire work, the "M" is uppercase. When a reference is to one paragraph within the larger work (*mishnah*), the "m" is lowercase and the word is italicized.

The collective name for the rabbis of the first 200 years of the rabbinic period is Tannaim, and for the rabbis of the next 300 years, Amoraim. A citation introduced by two single dashes (– –) is a statement attributed to an Amora; a citation introduced by two double dashes (==) is a statement attributed to the anonymous, post-amoraic editors of the Talmud. Statements without special designation are tannaitic.

God is occasionally referred to in the masculine for reasons of style only.

Unless stated otherwise, the volume of the Mishnah that I refer to when citing the work of Hanokh Albeck is Nashim, the Division of Women.

The Tosefta is cited, where possible, from the Lieberman edition.

The references to the Talmud Yerushalmi (Palestinian Talmud) are presented in two ways. The first is by chapter and paragraph (*halakhah* or *mishnah*) and the second by page and folio. The second reference is keyed to the standard one-volume Venice edition of this Talmud.

Talmudic references are to the Bavli (Babylonian Talmud) unless they are identified as to the Yerushalmi.

Abbreviations and Acronyms

AZ	Avodah Zarah
b., b'	Heb., *ben* or *bar,* son of
BB	Baba Batra
BM	Baba Mezia
BK	Baba Kama
BT	Babylonian Talmud
Deut.	Deuteronomy
Exod.	Exodus
Ezek.	Ezekiel
Gen.	Genesis
Lam.	Lamentations
Lev.	Leviticus
M	Mishnah
Num.	Numbers
1 Cor.	1 Corinthians
Ps.	Psalms
PT	Palestinian Talmud
R.	Rabbi
RH	Rosh Hashanah
T	Tosefta

Introduction

The past isn't dead. It isn't even past.
—*William Faulkner*

LIKE THE BIBLE, THE TALMUD IS A compendium of Jewish law, ethics, and culture. Even more than the Bible, the Talmud shapes the contours of Jewish life today. In a formal sense, it is an expansion of the legal portions of the Pentateuch, the first five books of the Bible. In an informal sense, it is a wide-ranging series of inquiries into how a Jew should live his or her life. For hundreds of years Jews have devoted long hours to studying the Talmud. Its terse but dense style, mixture of Aramaic and Hebrew, intricate logical arguments, and hard-to-unravel textual history have given it a mystique of its own.

Until recently, it was almost exclusively men who pored over the Talmud and wrote commentaries on it. Women neither studied it nor played any role in interpreting it. This difference is not surprising: Judaism, like most ancient religions, placed key religious tasks in the hands of men only. Today, with women's growing interest in their past and desire to use the past to reshape the present, these texts need to be looked at afresh.

This book will read Talmudic texts from a woman's perspective. Therefore, the choice of texts and the questions asked of them derive from a wish to determine how the Talmud sees and treats women. The core of each chapter is composed of the texts themselves, which I will cite in translation and interpret according to standard techniques of Talmudic analysis. Unlike other books that present texts shorn of context, this book will locate and then read the key texts in a sustained fashion, in their own context, and in a rich context of closely associated materials. The point of doing so is to arrive at as accurate an interpretation as possible, not reading meaning into the text, but eliciting meaning from it.

Let me begin with an illustration drawn from the aggadic (nonlegal) material in the Talmud.

1

An apostate [כופר][1] once came before Rabban Gamliel and said,
"Your God is a thief. He stole a rib from Adam when he was asleep."
Rabban Gamliel's daughter[2] [was sitting nearby and] said, "Let me
answer him" [whereupon she began to act as if a calamity had be-
fallen her] and asked to summon a policeman. When queried as to
what had taken place, she said that thieves had broken into her apart-
ment the night before and taken her silver goblet but left a gold one in
its place. The apostate then chimed in, "[But how can you call that an
act of theft if they left you, in place of what they took, something of
greater value?] Would that such thieves come upon us often!" ["That's
precisely the point,"] she said, "Was it not to Adam's benefit that God
took his rib but left him in its place a handmaiden to serve him
[שפחה לשמשו]!" (BT Sanhedrin 39a)

On one level, this anecdote shows, like the many others with which it is
grouped in context, that the claims of scoffers can be rather easily refuted;
that no matter what their argument, it can be rebutted. But on another
level, this story is about women and rabbinic attitudes toward them. Had a
man, let's say a son of Rabban Gamliel, responded to the apostate, the sense
of the story, in addition to repudiating the claim, would be that the rabbinic
view of women is that they were created to serve men. However, since it is a
woman who makes this point about women, we must think further.

The question is, how are we to read the parable posed by the daughter of
Rabban Gamliel? Is she saying that women's role in life is to be subservient? Or is she saying that women are beings of independent value and
substance, and that it is only for the sake of her didactic analogy that she
first downgrades them, which gives her the opportunity to upgrade further
the value of God's replacement object? For of what benefit to Adam would
be the gift of a woman in place of a rib unless the woman were there to
serve him?[3] Note that her metaphor arouses no objection from the men
present.

The irony here is that the daughter of Rabban Gamliel[4] is not a self-
effacing maidservant but a self-confident, intelligent, and aristocratic
woman. What she is and what she stands for are diametrically opposed to
what she says women are meant to be. It is even possible that she has in
mind the now-famous contradiction about the nature of woman found in
the first two chapters of Genesis: In chapter 1, woman is portrayed as
equal to man; in chapter 2, she is created from his rib, as secondary.

It seems to me that the rabbis who told this story, who reported her
words, were ambivalent in their attitudes toward women, viewing them on
the one hand as lowly creatures, to be controlled, cared for, and used for
men's own purposes and pleasure, and on the other as essentially as human
as men, not physically and mentally immature like children and not chattel

like slaves.[5] This point is supported by the fact that the parallel versions of the story place the provocative question in a woman's mouth and the clever answer in a man's.[6] By reversing these roles, the Babylonian Talmud displays its attitude toward women: smart but subordinate.

What I have just demonstrated is how to read a text from a woman's perspective. The salient feature of this approach is looking below the surface message, in this case theological, in order to dig out information about how men and women viewed each other and themselves and the nature of their relationship during the Talmudic period. When texts that have been looked at by so many for so long are examined from new angles, it should not surprise us that they yield new information.

We can easily deduce that Talmudic law and the biblical law upon which it is based mandate a patriarchal social order. The following representative examples will suffice to prove the point: Men may have more than one wife, but women may have only one husband; men take women in marriage and may divorce them at will, but women neither take men in marriage nor may they dismiss them; women inherit from neither a father nor a husband, but men inherit from both a mother and a wife (as well as from a father); women's religious vows may be canceled by either a husband or a father, but men's vows may not be canceled by either a wife or a mother. The male bias of these rules is evident.

It is all too easy, as sensitive human beings, to grow angry each time we come across yet another example of a blatantly patriarchal law. But that, to my mind, is not the only or even the most reasonable response. It is entirely predictable that when judging rabbinic law from the perspective of our own recently developed egalitarian stance, we will find the treatment of women unacceptable and even morally offensive. Today, we can no longer justify assigning second-class status and fewer rights to an entire category of human beings for no reason other than their gender.

Were the Talmud simply an arcane body of ancient texts, we would not find ourselves troubled upon reaching such a conclusion. But there is much more at stake here: The rabbis' literary and legal legacy rests at the foundation of Judaism as it is practiced today. We therefore have a problem: How can we continue to adhere to Jewish observance today in the face of a conflict between it and our modern sense of social justice?

One solution is simply to recognize that the rabbis were products of their times. Since the ancient world (and even much of the modern world until recently) subscribed to a patriarchal worldview, they did too. Although such a relativist perspective in no way diminishes the religious authority of the rabbis, neither does that perspective properly recognize their real accomplishments, even in their own time and place.

I am, therefore, suggesting that we devise a different standard by which to evaluate what the rabbis achieved. One possibility is to investigate how the rabbis' legal thinking compares to that of their Greco-Roman counter-parts. Since the rabbis were familiar with the Roman law of their day and incorporated some of its principles and even specific institutions into their own legislation, such as a gift in contemplation of death, how does the rab-bis' treatment of women compare to that of the Roman legislators?[7] As in-teresting as it would be to draw these kinds of comparisons, and I will do so from time to time, this is not the best question to ask. A religious legal system, much more than a secular one, is bound by a commitment to main-tain continuity with the practices of the past and accept the authority of the texts of the past. It ascribes a divine origin to these practices and texts.

I therefore propose that we evaluate the rabbinic system from a dynamic rather than a static perspective. Since the rabbis make it clear that the Torah undergirds their legislation, the questions that merit investigation are the following: In comparison to the Torah, which the rabbis accepted as holy, God-given, and hence immutable, how does their own legislation treat women? Without violating the letter of the law, were they seeking to accord them more rights and a higher status than that accorded them by the Torah? Or were they introducing new stringencies that would make women's lives more difficult? In general, in what direction was their legisla-tion concerning women headed? Furthermore, do the legislators openly re-veal their own sense that women are discriminated against in key areas of Jewish law? Is there any evidence that they are uncomfortable with their patriarchal privilege? Do they allow women, whose voices they occasion-ally include in the text, to express dissatisfaction, even opposition, to the way things were?

My answer, stated succinctly, is that the rabbis upheld patriarchy as the preordained mode of social organization, as dictated by the Torah. They thus perpetuated women's second-class, subordinate status. They neither achieved equality for women nor even sought it. But of critical importance, they began to introduce numerous, significant, and occasionally bold cor-rective measures to ameliorate the lot of women. In some cases, they elimi-nated abusive behaviors that had developed over time. In others, they broke new ground, granting women benefits that they never had before, even at men's expense. From their own perspective, the rabbis were seeking to close the gap that had developed over time between more enlightened social thinking and women's more subordinate status as defined by the re-ceived texts, biblical and rabbinic, without openly opposing such texts. In almost every key area of law affecting women, the rabbis introduced signif-icant changes for the better. We cannot be sure that the rabbis themselves conceived of the notion or initiated the trend of improving women's lives— such ideas could have come from the surrounding culture or from previous generations—but we can find clear evidence that the rabbis endorsed this position of their own free will.[8]

This conclusion should not surprise us. Law tends to develop over time in the direction of more humane treatment of the underprivileged. In the past several centuries, the move in many parts of the world from hierarchy to democracy is paralleled in the ancient rabbinic world by a move toward a modified, benevolent patriarchy and even a modified hierarchy. And this expansion of "rights" for women applied, albeit on a lesser scale, to other groups, such as non-Jewish slaves. Thus, the rabbis' growing sympathy for women is not out of line with broad legal developments in other areas of Jewish law.

But did the rabbis go far enough? Could we have expected more from them? I tend to think they accomplished what they could. Although they reacted with leniency to the excessive stringencies of the Dead Sea sects that preceded them, for instance in the realm of ritual purity, and though they did not embrace the rampant misogynism of Philo, the first-century Hellenistic Jewish philosopher, neither did they adopt some of the more advanced provisions of Roman law. They cannot, therefore, be called feminists. More accurately, we can regard them as helpful to women.

I am troubled by the contemporary assumption that the presence of patriarchy necessarily precludes the possibility of those within it acting on women's behalf. When scholars find evidence of proto-feminist action, they consider it an aberration, the expression of a dissident voice. I am not so sure. It is also possible to conclude that absolute patriarchy is only a theoretical projection, a construct, not a reality. Careful examination of rabbinic texts has led me to believe that rabbinic sympathy for women is not an expression of dissidence but rather reflects a more nuanced patriarchy than is generally assumed. Recent research in the Bible[9] and my own evaluation of the Talmud suggest that rabbinic society is more accurately characterized as a "benevolent patriarchy." Even though it placed men in charge of women, it also permitted men to make changes that benefited women and that showed concern for women in general and even respect for individual women of accomplishment (as measured in male terms).

A number of books have already appeared that deal with women in rabbinic texts. They fall into two broad categories: those that analyze what these legal texts have to say about men, women, society, and culture; and those that try to reconstruct women's history in the Talmudic period, based on passages found in the rabbinic corpus and elsewhere. I will briefly mention some of the more important ones. Jacob Neusner and Judith Wegner, in their systematic, detailed studies of the Mishnah, find extensive evidence of women's second-class status. According to both authors, the rabbis view women as morally lax temptresses from whom men must protect themselves.[10] Daniel Boyarin and Shulamit Valler, in their close readings of legal and aggadic materials, identify multiple rabbinic outlooks on women, ranging from the more indifferent to the more empathetic.[11] Tal Ilan, in her historical work on women's status in the early rabbinic period, notes the vast differences between rabbinic pronouncements and real women's lives.[12] Miriam Peskowitz, upon reading rabbinic texts in the context of Greco-Roman legal and literary texts, gender theory, and material evidence, demonstrates that the tannaitic statements about women's work constitute a theory of masculinity and femininity.[13]

Those six books have all made significant contributions to our understanding of how the Talmud addresses the topic of women. Although this book will also read texts closely and arrive at some shared conclusions with the above authors, the question that drives this research is different, as is the methodology.

What I am *not* trying to do in this book is to present the basics of Jewish law, from the Bible until today, as it affects women, as does Rachel Biale.[14] Rather, I have selected for consideration those matters that best illustrate that the law, in general, was in the process of change. There are many issues that I do not deal with at all, such as levirate marriage, and others that I do not deal with in full, like testimony. I build my case by analyzing only ten topics in detail, although not exhaustively.

What I am also *not* trying to do in this book is to write social history. Historians often find themselves using law to write history, and Talmudists, using history to understand law. Both of these approaches are faulty. Historians cannot assume that all or even most people followed the law. Similarly, Talmudists cannot assume that sociohistorical realities are accurately reflected in the law. As hard as it will be to restrain myself from seeing the law as a representation of social reality, I will try to do so. What I am interested in is a history of the law, not a history of people. Although it is likely that what jurists see around them dictates their choice of cases to deal with and focus on, we cannot know that for sure. Since all cases could be hypothetical constructs, we cannot deduce social realities from legal preoccupation with certain issues.

The question is, how does one read an ancient text to arrive at the truth, at the author's intended meaning? Plucking statements from different works, written in different time periods by different authors, weaving them together into a unified whole, and then claiming that they represent the rabbinic view on a particular topic is deceptive. Each text must be examined on its own; the interplay of voices over time and between texts should not be muted.

To write a credible book on the subject of Talmud and women requires that we read the texts as objectively as possible, not arriving at interpretations dictated by preconceived conclusions. In order to avoid this pitfall, I have developed the following method for reading texts: First, for each topic under consideration, I go to the loci classici, the places in the Torah and the Talmud where that topic is discussed initially and/or fully and extract the main ideas. For the Torah, that usually involves several verses. For the Talmud, that can be an entire volume, a chapter, or just one passage. Note that by so doing I am not making any choices as to which material to examine but am merely analyzing the rabbis' principal statements on a subject. I then compare the biblical and rabbinic statements in order to see if the rabbis have made any significant changes.

Second, because I assume, as noted above, that literary and legal contexts influence meaning, I then read each paragraph of the relevant Mishnah, also called a *mishnah,* in the light of the surrounding cluster of *mishnah*s. Third, I read the mishnaic passages in the context of related rabbinic texts, from both the same time period and later. By thus seeing the full range of views on a subject, we can understand more accurately and precisely the meaning of each view articulated. Also, by noting the field of choices open to each rabbinic speaker, we can assess the relative stringency or leniency of the view he chose to adopt.

To illustrate by way of example: The Mishnah sharply reduced the number of cases in which a rapist had to pay the biblically prescribed fine to a young victim's father—he was obligated only if he raped her when she was between twelve and twelve and one-half years old. This ruling might lead us to conclude that the early rabbis make light of the crime of rape. But by means of a contextual reading, we learn that the Mishnah replaced the fixed fine *(kenas)* with a variable one *(pegam),* to be paid in all cases without exception and able to exceed the fifty silver shekels stipulated by the Torah. From this fine we realize that the rabbis were taking rape *more* seriously rather than less. In this way, we see how a richer contextual reading yields a more nuanced interpretation.

The Rabbinic Texts

The key rabbinic text, the touchstone of all subsequent rabbinic commentary, is the Mishnah (M), the first canonical and reasonably comprehensive compilation of Jewish law to follow the Bible. It is written in Hebrew and arranged topically into six major divisions, called orders, which are each subdivided into tractates (volumes), named accordingly. One of the six divisions is called Nashim, meaning women or, more likely, married women.[15] Most texts we will examine in this book derive from that order.

Much of the material in the Mishnah is anonymous, but about one third to one half is attributed to specific individuals, called Tannaim. Although some material precedes the common era, such as that attributed to Hillel and Shammai, the vast majority dates from the first two centuries of the common era. It is easy to see that the Mishnah developed in layers over time, each generation of rabbis adding its thoughts to those of the previous ones. Rabbi Judah the Prince, usually referred to merely as Rebbe, is credited with the final redaction of the Mishnah in about the year 200. Whoever the redactor was, it is clear that an editorial hand imprinted the entire work with a consistency of style, syntax, and even legislative outlook.[16] It is therefore legitimate to ask, with respect to most topics, what the broad legislative goals of the redactor of the Mishnah were.

The Tosefta (T), also written in Hebrew and organized just like the Mishnah, with the same major divisions and subdivisions, is a companion volume to the Mishnah, dating from the same period of time and presenting the views of many of the same rabbis. It seems more a compilation and compendium than a thoroughly redacted work. It is intimately related to the Mishnah, even beyond its organization, in that paragraph by paragraph it supplements, disputes, and illustrates passages of the Mishnah. But what is the relationship of these two works to each other?

It is standard scholarly opinion that the Tosefta postdates the Mishnah and is a commentary on it, in fact, the very first commentary. But this statement does not give the complete picture. For although the Tosefta contains much material posterior to the Mishnah, it contains anterior material as well. Careful comparison of passages in the Mishnah and Tosefta shows that many mishnaic rules are based on and constitute a reworking, often very subtle, of the parallel Tosefta passage. It is likely that the redactor of the Mishnah changed the earlier formulation of the rule in order to have it conform to his view on a particular subject. By examining the roads not taken by him, by seeing which of the many options he selected and which he rejected, we can better understand his legislative approach and goals, as well as those of his contemporaries. Comparison of two similar but slightly different formulations of the same rule makes it possible, again, to see in what direction the law was headed and what were the legal concerns of the day. The striking fact that the views of the Tosefta are often more lenient, and hence beneficial to women, than those of the Mishnah, suggests that the redactor of the Mishnah had a more conservative bent than some of his colleagues.[17]

The Babylonian Talmud, known as the Bavli, is the great commentary on the Mishnah, produced in Babylonia from about 200 until 750 C.E., and written in both Hebrew and Aramaic. In today's printed texts of the Talmud, each passage from the Mishnah is followed by the associated Gemara, that is, the analysis of the *mishnah* drafted by the Tannaim and Amoraim, the latter being the collective name of rabbis of the post-mishnaic period. The earliest form of the Gemara on a given *mishnah* consisted of a string of tannaitic and amoraic statements, the tannaitic ones commenting directly on the *mishnah* and the amoraic ones both on the *mishnah* itself and on the related tannaitic comments. These tannaitic materials, called *baraitot*, external teachings—because they remained outside of the Mishnah—are often the same passages that appear in a parallel place in the

Tosefta. They prove extremely useful when one is deciphering the meaning of cryptically worded *mishnah*s.[18]

Like the Mishnah, the Bavli developed in layers, each generation adding its thinking on the matters under discussion to that of the previous one. Unlike the Mishnah, it does not seem to have been redacted by one individual, although tradition claims that R. Ashi (d. 425 C.E.) was a principal redactor.[19] The Bavli also contains an extensive layer of anonymous commentary, called *stama d'gemara,* the anonymous voice of the text. It does not express independent opinions of its own but rather weaves together the tannaitic and amoraic materials into a unified whole. There is general scholarly consensus that this commentary, without which it would be almost impossible to understand the interrelationship of the earlier materials, was composed between approximately 500 and 750 C.E. Because of its subsidiary nature, I will pay less attention to it and more to the tannaitic and amoraic dicta themselves. The Talmud also cites, with reasonable frequency, anecdotes and courtroom cases that relate to the law under discussion. Since no women functioned as Tannaim or Amoraim, it is in these materials, which often feature women, that we find what appear to be historically reliable data about women, what concerned them, how they articulated their ideas before the rabbinical judges, and how the judges responded to them. Whenever relevant, I will cite this material.

The last major text under consideration is the Palestinian Talmud, known as the Yerushalmi, an analogue of the Bavli, written at approximately the same time, but in the land of Israel. It, too, is a commentary on the Mishnah, composed of tannaitic passages, amoraic sayings, and interwoven anonymous commentary. It was completed in the early part of the fifth century C.E., much before the Bavli.

Of these four texts, only two are studied with regularity today, the Mishnah and the Bavli. The other two, the Tosefta and the Yerushalmi, were not regarded by the codists as the basis for fixing Jewish law and have been routinely neglected, probably for that reason. For the purposes of this inquiry—and for the satisfaction of general intellectual curiosity—these works are extraordinarily useful.

The Plan of the Book

Throughout this book, I limit myself to consideration of halakhic texts and ignore aggadic (i.e., nonlegal and homiletical) ones because I am interested in the development of law—not attitudes—over time. Some of the aggadic statements praise women, and others exhibit deep misogyny. Since almost every aggadic statement can be offset by another that says just the opposite, all that we can conclude by collecting many examples of any one view is that it existed, not necessarily that it dominated. However, even if I fail to show that misogyny did not predominate, I still hope to show that it stayed in the realm of theory and was not incorporated into the law. This is a point worth emphasizing.[20]

Each chapter of this book strives to accomplish two goals: one, to tell the "story" of one aspect of Jewish law—how it changed over time— through close readings of texts; two, to dispel some well-established myths about what these texts mean. Chapters 1 and 2 of this book, "Sotah" (wayward wife) and "Relations Between the Sexes," illustrate the contextual method of reading rabbinic texts and provide background material for the rest of the book. Both deal with the rabbis' perception of men's and women's sexual nature and the implications of this outlook for social and religious life. The next five chapters, "Marriage" (3), "Rape and Seduction" (4), "Divorce" (5), "Procreation" (6), and "*Niddah*" (menstruants) (7), all deal with aspects of marital life. The reason that a discussion of sex crimes against women follows a discussion of marriage is that, according to the Bible, the simplest solution for the victim's predicament was marriage to the aggressor. Chapter 8, "Inheritance," follows, because a woman's dowry upon marriage is the share she receives from her father's estate. "Testimony" and "Ritual," Chapters 9 and 10, deal with women interacting with men in a court of law and in the performance of religious ritual, at home or in the synagogue. Note that since each chapter tells its own "story," each may be read independently of the others. Also note that each chapter is designed for all readers, Talmudic novices as well as veterans. Both groups will find material to ponder.

Two populations may object to the conclusions reached in this book. First, some Jews will not grant that the rabbis made any changes in the law to improve women's status because the law in its entirety was all there in the Torah to begin with. Since they posit the transcendent value of Torah and its non-time-bound system of ethics, then, even that which is not made explicit in the Torah is still embedded in the words and is waiting to be discerned by the reader at the appropriate time. This view is a matter of belief; I cannot dispute or disconfirm it.

I see things somewhat differently. If the Torah is silent and the rabbis speak up—for instance, if the Torah describes marriage as the purchase of a young woman from her father, and the rabbis later portray it as a "social contract"—then I will credit them with adapting the older rules to the more progressive social thinking and altered social configurations of their day. I am not thereby casting aspersions on the Torah. Rather, I am suggesting that in some cases what was appropriate at an earlier time was no longer perceived of as ethical by later generations. There is ample precedent for such legislative evolution in the ancient world. For example, research on the Dead Sea Scrolls has shown that many of them rework biblical texts in order to accommodate these texts to the outlook of the scroll's author. Scholars consider that an early form of exegesis. I am making the same claim for the Talmud. It, too, is a work of exegesis in that it bases itself on the Torah but, at the same time, alters those rules that do not sit well with its own contemporary sensibilities.

The second population that may challenge my conclusions is the feminist one. In light of my reasonably positive evaluation of rabbinic behavior toward women, some feminists may label this reading thinly veiled apologetics. I would counter by arguing that my approach represents a "contextualized feminism." It demonstrates that patriarchy was the dominant form of social organization in the rabbinic corpus and only identifies improvements in women's legal status within such a framework. It also seeks to determine what role notions of gender play in men's thinking on a variety of subjects affecting women and also their attitude toward women. In a broader sense, it is feminist in that I show, as does Ilana Pardes[21] and others for the Bible, that some of the rabbi-legislators themselves, and occasionally some women, put forth countervoices, calling into question the patriarchal basis of Jewish law.[22]

It is unfortunate that so little feminist Bible research focuses on biblical *law*. Some researchers who study the biblical women, like Tikvah Frymer-Kensky, claim that the social status of women devolved over time, from the biblical to the Talmudic period, in particular in response to Hellenism and its misogynies.[23] If such studies focused on biblical law, however, they would show that the *legal* status of women improved over time. Just as so many feminist studies are recovering the Bible for women, identifying the feminist countertraditions, reading the stories about major and also minor female characters through feminist eyes, and reaching the conclusion that the Bible speaks to feminist women and men today, I will, in a general way, do the same for Talmud. I do not believe that it is possible to depatriarchalize the Talmud, but I will show that, within its patriarchal framework, not only is sympathy expressed for women, as already noted by Valler and Boyarin, but, even more important, resolute action taken on their behalf.[24]

I will not try to fit my conclusions into the framework of any particular feminist theory. Nor will I dismiss the rabbinic corpus merely as the thinking of men about women, not women about women. I read and analyze these texts both from the perspective of a feminist consciousness and from the perspective of the Talmudist that I am trained to be. These qualifications, I hope, have predisposed me neither to put the rabbis on a pedestal nor to ignore their limitations. I place before the reader all the texts and my methods of analysis. The words will speak for themselves.

Notes

1. The standard printed edition of the Talmud reads, "an apostate." Other editions read, "the Caesar," meaning the Roman emperor.

2. According to the editions that have "the Caesar" rather than "an apostate," it may be the emperor's daughter, not Rabban Gamliel's daughter, who responds to the challenge. Also, according to the standard reading of this text, one could say that it is not Rabban Gamliel's daughter but the apostate's daughter who answers him. But whichever way we read these phrases, since it is the men of the Talmud who are telling this story about women, the broad implications remain the same whether the woman who speaks is Jewish or not.

3. In the two parallel versions of this story, in *Bereshit Rabbah* 17 (Theodor and Albeck ed., 158) and *Aboth de Rabbi Nathan B*, chap. 8 (Schechter ed., 23), no mention is made of woman as a handmaiden to serve man. The main point is that a woman is gold in comparison to a man's rib, which is clay *(Aboth de Rabbi Nathan)* or that a woman is a pound of silver in comparison to a man's rib, which is an ounce of silver *(Bereshit Rabbah)*. In these two stories it is a *matrona*, a Roman woman, who claims that God is a thief. A rabbi (R. Yossi or R. Joshua) answers her. See previous notes and Tal Ilan's comments on the *matrona* in *Jewish Women in Greco-Roman Palestine: An Inquiry into Image and Status* (Tübingen: J.C.B. Mohr, 1995).

4. Since most of the women who appear in Talmudic anecdotes are close relatives of rabbis, they are identified as the daughter of Rabbi X, the sister of Rabbi X, the wife of Rabbi X, and sometimes even the mother of Rabbi X. Only on rare occasions are they identified by their own name.

5. Cf. Daniel Boyarin, *Carnal Israel: Reading Sex in Talmudic Culture* (Berkeley: University of California Press, 1993), 108: "This ironic double stance of both genuine empathy for women and rigid hierarchical domination is endemic in the Talmudic discourse."

6. See note 3.

7. The gift in contemplation of death is treated in Chapter 8. On the subject of rabbinic knowledge of Hellenistic law, see Saul Lieberman, "How Much Greek in Jewish Palestine," in *Texts and Studies* (New York: Ktav, 1974), 216–234, in particular, 225–228. For an analysis of broader cultural influences, see Lieberman, *Greek and Hellenism in Jewish Palestine* (Jerusalem: Bialik, 1962).

8. See Judith Plaskow, *Standing Again at Sinai* (San Francisco: Harper and Row, 1990), who recognizes that the rabbis were disturbed by women's implied absence from Sinai and therefore "read women's presence into the text" (27). But she goes on to say that they do this "despite the fact that in their own work they continually reenact that absence." I understand the rabbinic texts somewhat differently.

9. See Athalya Brenner, ed., *A Feminist Companion to Wisdom Literature* (Sheffield: Sheffield Academic Press, 1995). Brenner's comments (in "Some Observations on the Figurations of Woman in Wisdom Literature," 85–97) on the unnamed queen who shames her husband and is the only intelligent and calm person around, as well as Valler's comments (in "Who Is *Eshet Hayil* in Rabbinic Literature?" 65) on the rabbinic concept of "a woman of valor" reveal that the women of the Bible and Talmud are not the docile, submissive helpmates that patriarchy implies and that a patriarchal text would be expected to portray.

10. Jacob Neusner was the first to engage in a systematic reading of rabbinic texts from a feminist perspective. He develops a theory in a wide variety of publications, and in particular in *Method and Meaning in Ancient Judaism*, Brown Judaica

Series, no. 10 (Missoula, Mont.: Scholars Press, 1979), 79–100, about how the rabbis defined the essential nature and character of women and men. Because of women's unruly sexual potential, lying just below the surface, it has been necessary for men to exercise control over women. Surveying all the volumes of Mishnah that treat women, he shows that the rabbis are especially interested in the moments when women are transferred from one man to another because those times pose the greatest dangers.

Judith Wegner, in *Chattel or Person? The Status of Women in the Mishnah* (New York: Oxford University Press, 1988), examines, from the perspective of today's jurisprudential standards, the vast body of mishnaic law dealing with women. She finds that in some areas, such as those relating to a woman's sexuality and reproductive capacity, the woman is treated as chattel; in all others, she is treated as person.

11. Boyarin, in *Carnal Israel*, identifies two phenomena relevant to the focus of this book: the rabbis' empathetic thinking about women, and the existence of women on the margins who engaged in actions that the culture highly valued, such as the study of Torah. He concludes that although such empathetic thinking did not overturn the male-dominated hierarchy, the texts in which men oppose the dominant ideology imply the participation of a dissident, proto-feminist voice.

Shulamit Valler, in *Women and Womanhood in the Stories of the Babylonian Talmud* (Tel Aviv: Hakibbutz Hameuchad, 1993), analyzes in detail five clusters of halakhic anecdotes relating to women. She finds that the rabbis abandoned the stringencies that they themselves had developed and decided cases that came before them in a more lenient manner, one that displayed sensitivity toward women.

12. Tal Ilan, in *Jewish Women in Greco-Roman Palestine: An Inquiry into Image and Status*, a historical work, asks what was the exact social status of women in the period beginning 332 B.C.E., the time of Alexander's conquest of Palestine, and ending 200 C.E., close to the time of the Mishnah's publication. She concludes that only a small segment of the Jewish population, in particular the upper classes, lived according to tannaitic prescriptions.

13. Miriam Peskowitz, *Spinning Fantasies* (University of California Press, forthcoming). In "Engendering Jewish Religious History," in *Judaism Since Gender*, Peskowitz puts forward the theory that the study of "women in rabbinic Judaism" or "women and rabbinic Judaism" is no longer appropriate because it implies that women are separate from and marginal to Judaism. In the same volume, Judith Baskin responds that there still is a need to conduct these kinds of studies. In exploring images of women, she claims, we find evidence of multivocality, of minority views that are sometimes more enlightened than those of the dominant view of women's essential difference from and inferiority to man. We can thus learn "important things about how Jewish knowledges are engendered" ("Rabbinic Judaism and the Creation of Woman," 125–130).

14. Rachel Biale, *Women and Jewish Law: An Exploration of Women's Issues in Halakhic Sources* (New York: Schocken, 1984).

15. I prefer this translation because women are dealt with in virtually every volume of the Mishnah. Married women and a variety of marital institutions are dealt with primarily in the tractates of Nashim.

16. Jacob Neusner, ed., *The Study of Ancient Judaism*, pt. 1 (New York: Ktav, 1981), 18ff.

17. Judith Hauptman, "Pesiqah L'humra B'mishnat Gittin," *Proceedings of the Tenth World Congress of Jewish Studies,* August 1990; "Women's Voluntary Performance of Commandments from Which They Are Exempt" (in Hebrew), *Proceedings of the Eleventh World Congress of Jewish Studies,* Jerusalem, 1994; Shamma Friedman, "Tosefta Atikta . . . " *Tarbiz* 62, no. 3 (5753/1992–93).

18. It is especially common for the Amoraim of the two Talmuds to interpret a *mishnah* in the light of the parallel paragraph in the Tosefta. In so doing they often read back into the *mishnah* a line of thought that the redactor of the Mishnah had decided to reject. In this way the Amoraim are able to reclaim discarded points of view, ones that they may find more to their liking than that of the redactor of the Mishnah. See my book *Development of the Talmudic Sugya: Relationship Between Tannaitic and Amoraic Sources* (Lanham, Md.: University Press of America, 1988), chap. 3.

19. See David Goodblatt, "The Babylonian Talmud," in *The Study of Ancient Judaism,* pt. 2, ed. Jacob Neusner (New York: Ktav, 1981), 170–177.

20. Tikvah Frymer-Kensky, in her chapter on biblical women (in *Feminist Perspectives on Jewish Studies,* ed. Lynn Davidman and Shelly Tanenbaum [New Haven: Yale University Press, 1994]), notes that "much of the patriarchy that we associate with the Bible and all of its misogyny has been introduced . . . by later generations of readers" (26). Although I find extensive evidence of a patriarchal so- cial order in biblical laws, I agree with Frymer-Kensky that misogyny is not the driving force.

21. Ilana Pardes, *Countertraditions in the Bible: A Feminist Approach* (Cam- bridge: Harvard University Press, 1992), 4, 144–145. Pardes finds remnants of fe- male voices in the biblical texts that speak out against patriarchy, that put forth truths other than the predominant patriarchal ones. Although suppressed, those remnants were nonetheless included in the canon.

22. The redactor of the Talmud, by including these male voices, and occasional women's voices that also speak out against rabbinic patriarchy, is himself express- ing some doubts about the appropriateness of its male bias. For women's voices, see, for example, BT Yevamot 34b and PT Ketubot 2:5; 26c. These texts are dis- cussed in Chapter 6 and the Conclusion.

23. Frymer-Kensky, *Feminist Perspectives,* 26. The same point is made by S. D. Goitein, in "Women as Creators of Biblical Genres," *Prooftexts* 8, no. 1 (January 1988): 29. Goitein, in this article, analyzes women's poetry, not laws of personal status.

24. I disagree with Rosemary Ruether ("Feminist Interpretation: A Method of Correlation," in *Feminist Interpretation of the Bible,* ed. Letty M. Russell [Philadelphia: Westminster Press, 1985]), who claims that the Bible becomes the authoritative source for justification of patriarchy in Jewish and Christian society (116). Since Jews today read the Bible and practice its teachings through a rabbinic filter, it is more accurate to say that the Bible and Talmud justify, not patriarchy per se, but a modified, benevolent patriarchy, as explained above. Ruether's interpre- tive, redemptive strategy is to focus on the prophetic traditions that destabilize the ideologies supporting the male-dominated social order.

1

Sotah

Sотан (WAYWARD WIFE) IS A TRACTATE at war with itself. Based on a chapter of Bible, it describes in grim and sometimes lurid detail how a woman who is only suspected by her husband of infidelity may be subjected by him to the ordeal of the bitter waters. In between the laws, the redactors insert lengthy harangues against the woman in question, deriding her behavior in extreme terms and seeking to use her public humiliation to deter other women from promiscuous behavior. But the careful reader will find this tractate somewhat schizophrenic: At the same time that it regards the suspected adulteress with such contempt, it sets up legal procedures that virtually guarantee that the ordeal of the bitter waters will never be implemented, or if implemented, that its results will be ambiguous and hence useless. As prominent as are the numerous passages that lay out the details of the ritual, surrounding and throttling them are many others that place unrealistic restrictions on their implementation.

How are we to understand this phenomenon? The rabbis' aversion to capital punishment stems, apparently, from a reasonable fear of putting an innocent person to death. However, since the *sotah's* punishment is determined by the waters, not the judges, and only the guilty will be punished, the rabbis had no reason to fear judicial error and its consequences. It therefore seems that at least part of what animated the rabbinic revolt against this ordeal was a desire to treat women fairly, to eliminate a practice that confounded their notions of justice and morality.

Biblical Basis for Sotah and Problems

Numbers 5:11–31 is one of the more perplexing sections of the Bible. It describes the case of a woman straying from the right path and engaging in sexual relations with a man other than her husband. If a fit of jealousy

sweeps over a man and he suspects his wife of errant behavior, even though
there are no witnesses to her act, he may take her to the Temple and make
her undergo the ordeal of the bitter waters. As part of the ritual, she has to
drink a potion made of water, earth from the Temple floor, and ink dissolved into the water from a parchment on which were written the curses
of this very chapter. If she is innocent, the waters will not hurt her; if guilty,
they will cause her serious physical harm.

This chapter of Torah gives the reader pause for several reasons: First,
the Torah is sanctioning trial by ordeal, albeit only here and only for this
suspected transgression. Elsewhere, the Torah sets a protocol for justice: It
is to be dispensed in the courtroom, by judges, and based on the testimony
of witnesses. Here, since there are no witnesses, there is, theoretically, no
basis for a trial. Nevertheless, the Torah requires the woman to undergo
this trial by ordeal. We should recognize that the ordeal described here,
where there must be divine intervention in order for the benign potion to
do damage, is an improvement over others of the Ancient Near East, where
the accused was thrown into a river and if innocent was assumed to be able
to find his way out. Still, the Torah deviates from its own protocol to order
for the *sotah* a trial by ordeal, not by judges.

Second, a man suspected by his wife of exactly the same kind of behavior cannot be taken to the Temple and subjected to the ordeal of the bitter
waters. This asymmetry points to the underlying extreme patriarchy: She is
his property, intended for his exclusive use, and must therefore conform to
the behavioral standards he sets for her; he is not her property and so she
can make no demands of him.

In a patriarchal society, a sexual act between a man and a woman is
viewed as adulterous only if the woman is married to another man; if the
man is married to another woman, that is of no consequence. Therefore, a
married woman is allowed to have sex with her husband only, but a married man is permitted to have sex with his wife and other women as well,
provided they are not married. His wife has no sexual monopoly on him.
Thus a woman who commits adultery seems to be perceived as a greater
disruption of the social order than a man who does the same. Society
frowned upon her misconduct more than his because she betrayed not only
God but also her husband, whereas a man's extramarital sex is not considered a betrayal of his wife.[1]

Third, if the woman under suspicion was, in fact, unfaithful to her husband, she would be punished by the waters; but the man with whom she
committed this act would go free. It does not seem right to us today that if
the two of them committed exactly the same sin, together, that only one
gets punished and the other does not.

Not only do we today find these to be serious inequities, but the rabbis
of the Talmud did as well. If we examine closely their interpretation of the

verses, as found in Tractate Sotah, we will see that they struggled with every one of these issues. Sometimes, what appear to be expansions and clarifications of Torah and nothing more are, in reality, rabbinic responses to complicated and troubling problems.

Of the nine chapters of Tractate Sotah, only the first six address the topic of the *sotah*. Beyond that there is one key comment in chapter 9. I have selected five topics for close reading.

The Warning and the Seclusion

Tractate Sotah opens with several statements about warning and seclusion, topics that have no obvious biblical referent.

> If a man issues a warning to his wife [**המקנא לאשתו**]:

> R. Eliezer says: He must do so in the presence of two witnesses. [Should she violate the terms of the warning and seclude herself with the forbidden man], her husband can subject her to the ordeal of the bitter waters on the basis of the testimony of one witness or even his own testimony.

> R. Joshua says: He must warn her in the presence of two and can subject her to the ordeal only on the basis of two [witnesses to the seclusion]. (M Sotah 1:1)

> How does he warn her? If he says to her, in the presence of two [witnesses], do not speak with that man, and she spoke with him, she is still permitted to her husband [lit., her house] . . .

> If she secluded herself with him [**נכנסה עמו לבית הסתר**] and remained there long enough to have defiled herself, she is forbidden to her husband. . . . (1:2)

This passage allows a husband to subject his wife to the ordeal of the bitter waters only if he had issued a warning to her not to talk to a particular man and she then went and secluded herself with him long enough to have had sexual relations with him. Both the warning and the seclusion have to have been witnessed for them to have legal ramifications.

These opening paragraphs, although they appear matter-of-fact, are in many ways astonishing. First, the rabbis interpret the Hebrew root K-N-A to mean "warn," even though in the Torah in general and in this chapter in particular this verb means to "suffer a fit of jealousy, to be wrought up over." Second, the rabbis interpret S-T-R[2] to mean "closeting" herself with the specified man, not "hidden," which is what the root means in the Bible—in the sense that her sexual improprieties did not become known.[3]

Why did the rabbis retain these biblical roots, yet stray so radically from their accepted definitions? I think they are deliberately and consciously preserving the sacred text but, at the same time, infusing it with new meaning. Upset that this section deviates from the standard procedures of justice, they attempt to make it conform: They say that the only circumstance in which a husband has the right to force his wife to submit to the ordeal is if he had warned her in advance—in the presence of two witnesses—not to have any contact with a particular man and then two witnesses, or only one witness, or only the husband himself saw her closet herself with that very man long enough to have had sexual relations with him. Delimiting this time span gives rise to much dispute (T Sotah 1:2; BT Sotah 4a), but even the most lenient opinion allows for no more than a few minutes. As the Talmud notes, each rabbi defined the duration of intercourse according to his own experience (4b).

Since witnessing the seclusion is not tantamount to witnessing the sexual act itself (in which case one must testify that he saw "the painting stick inserted into the tube" [Makkot 7a]), such testimony could not normally stand up in a court of law, but here it does raise serious doubts about the behavior of the woman in question. According to these rabbinic rules, only those women who aroused their husband's suspicion, were publicly warned by him, and then deliberately violated his word in the presence of others could be dragged by him to the Temple for the ordeal. This series of events is a far cry from the Torah's mere "fit of jealousy." The intention of the rabbis was to sanction administering the bitter waters only to women who were highly likely to be guilty of what their husbands suspected them of. Most fits of jealousy could not lead to further action on the part of the husband, however, for they involved neither prior warning nor seclusion in the presence of witnesses.

The rabbis sharply reduced the number of instances in which a man could subject his wife to the ordeal of the bitter waters because they recognized that, by their standards, this section of the Torah treats women unfairly. Those who agree that the rabbis reinterpreted the Torah may disagree, however, that their motivation was a concern for women. Some may argue, for instance, that the rabbis' concern was for justice, a cause they pursued with a passion. I would answer that these concerns are essentially the same. If, as I will show, in case after case in which biblical law treats women inequitably in comparison to men, the rabbis rework it so that women are treated fairly, then differentiating between one motivation and another loses its importance.

One might also argue that the rabbis suppressed this ritual out of their embarrassment over what they perceived as a primitive, barbaric rite within the Jewish legal system. However, were this so, I do not think that they would have made reference, as we will see later, to the paramour's punishment and to the husband's possibly spotty past vitiating the results of the test, both of which address the specifically moral problems created by the ritual. When this tractate is read as a whole, we can discern how bothered the rabbis are by the immorality and discriminatory nature of the ordeal, not its barbarism. That latter aspect they almost seem to relish.

Despite the Talmud's reinterpretation of Torah to make it fairer to women, we cannot fail to notice the considerable residual patriarchy in the way that the Talmud presents the husband-wife relationship. That a husband could warn his wife not to talk with a specific man implies that he had extensive control over her ordinary, day-to-day activities. Although the contextual reading of these paragraphs explains why the rabbis proposed this warning—for her good, not his—even so, we must consider what the passage says about social relationships. A key statement on this topic is found in T Sotah (5:9), the companion volume to the Mishnah dating from the same period of time. I will cite the passage and then spell out its implications.

> R. Meir says that just as men differ in their taste for food, so they differ in their taste for women.
>
> 1. There are some men who, if a fly alights on the rim of the cup, cannot drink what is inside. This is a bad lot for a woman because a husband like this will decide to divorce her [if she has any contact at all with another man].
> 2. There are men who, if a fly enters the cup, will discard the fly but still not drink what is inside. Such a man is like Pappas b. Judah, who would lock the door on his wife [so that she could not converse with a man] and go out.
> 3. And then there are men who, if a fly falls into the cup, will discard the fly and drink what is inside. This is the way most men are: He sees his wife talking to her [male] neighbors and relatives and leaves her alone.
> 4. Finally, there are men who, if a fly falls into the tureen, will take it, suck out [the liquid], and throw it [the fly] away. So an evil man behaves: He sees his wife going out with her head uncovered, scantily clad, . . . spinning in the marketplace, and bathing and sporting with any and all men [and does nothing about it]. This kind of woman one should divorce.

First, note that this passage is about problems with men's behavior, not women's. Its main point is that a man should be neither too accepting nor too suspicious of his wife's behavior: He who is finicky is derided (1, 2), as is he whose sexual pleasure is enhanced by his wife's promiscuity (4). The proper way for a man to behave is to tolerate reasonable social contact between his wife and other men (3).

That this passage originates in Sotah suggests that the husband can also be at fault, unlike the title of the tractate, which implies that the wife is always at fault. The husband's fit of jealousy can be triggered from within, not just without. Here the rabbis critique themselves, namely men, and implicitly, given the context of this passage, the entire ordeal.

Second, what can we learn from this passage about social relations between men and women in the Talmudic period? In a sex-segregated society, as indicated in Pirkei [= Mishnah] Avot, just conversing with the opposite sex seems to have been an erotic activity. The warning "Do not talk excessively with women . . . lest it take time away from Torah . . . and lead you to Gehenna" (M Avot 1:5) does not imply that women are considered intellectually inferior but that men who have casual social relations with women are easily aroused, as the parallel statement in BT Nedarim 20a adds, "lest talking with women lead a man to adulterous behavior." It is for this reason that a husband would suspect his wife of inappropriate behavior if she engaged in conversation with a man who was neither a neighbor nor a relative, for he knew that the man would have been aroused by the encounter. This passage also creates the impression that the force at greatest odds with the desire to study Torah was the desire for sex. We will return to this subject later.

As for marital relationships, this passage suggests that a husband can legally limit his wife's social contacts and can even force her to stay at home. Such potential control is clear evidence of the patriarchal construction of Jewish marriage, as is his right to divorce her for any reason. But note that the very source that acknowledges the possibility of despotic control over a wife also denounces it.

The Ordeal in Detail

After reading the first several paragraphs of Mishnah Sotah and noting their essentially enlightened implications, we are rather disturbed to read what follows—a detailed description of a gruesome ordeal.

The first mention of the ordeal itself appears in 1:4–7. After a number of homilies intervene, the description of the ordeal continues at the beginning of the second chapter, and again, after a break, at the beginning of the third. The Mishnah adds many details to the core ritual presented in the Torah.

> They would bring her to the Great Court in Jerusalem and attempt to intimidate her, saying: My child, wine brings one to sin; so too do frivolity, immaturity, and evil neighbors. [Confess] for His great

name's sake, that is written in holiness, so that it will not be dissolved in the water. (M Sotah 1:4)

. . . they would bring her to the Eastern Gate . . . and a *kohen* would grab hold of her garments and rip them until he uncovered her heart (bosom) and then he would let down her hair . . . (1:5)

He would clothe her in black . . . and remove her jewelry in order to disfigure her. And then he would bring a rope and tie it above her breasts [to keep her garments from slipping down]. And all those who wanted to see could come and see . . . (1:6)

One pays back a person measure for measure: Since she dressed herself up for sin, God will undress her; since she exposed herself to sin, God will expose her to all . . . (1:7)

Her husband would bring her *minhah* sacrifice in an Egyptian basket and rest it on her hands in order to tire her . . . . Rabban Gamliel says: Just as she behaved like an animal, so her offering will be [brought from] the food of an animal [barley flour]. (2:1)

If the words of the scroll had already been dissolved in the water and she then said, "I will not drink," they would pour the liquid down her throat . . . (3:3)

Immediately upon drinking her face would turn yellow . . . (3:4)

The harshness of these statements is appalling. They unquestionably reflect deep rabbinic contempt for a suspected adulteress. At the same time, the details of the ritual seem to have sexual overtones. Ripping off her clothes to partially expose her body is both strange and suggestive. It feeds the sexual fantasies of the bystanders, in particular the young priests (T Sotah 1:7). It is also reminiscent of the treatment of adulterous women by other cultures, who would strip them naked in public, a custom already documented in Hosea 2:5. The *mishnah* notes the logic of this practice: Since she broke the rules by showing her body to her paramour, she will now be forced to reveal herself to all, a kind of perverted measure for measure. The problem, of course, is that at this stage she is only accused, not yet proven guilty.

How does this description mesh with the sympathetic treatment of women in the opening *mishnah*s of the tractate? It seems to me that the ordeal represents an older strand of material, very callous and offensive to women, which was later framed by more reasonable statements that reflected a growing dissatisfaction with the ordeal. A fairly standard editorial principle in tannaitic literature is to bracket the earlier layer with a later one, rather than simply to present the sources in chronological order. The strategic advantage of this alternate scheme is that it forces one to read the older sources, which appear second, in light of the newer ones, which appear first. In this tractate, we read about the ordeal only *after* being informed that the circumstances for carrying it out could almost never arise.

Merit and Its Protection

Immediately upon drinking the water, her face would turn yellow, her eyes would bulge, and her veins would swell. . . . If she had merit, it would protect her [from the effects of the water]. Some merit protects for one year, some for two, and some for three.

From here Ben Azzai learned: A man is obligated to teach his daughter Torah so that if she should drink these waters, she would know that merit will protect her [שאם תשתה תדע שהזכות תולה לה].

R. Eliezer says: Anyone who teaches his daughter Torah teaches her lewdness.

R. Joshua says: A woman prefers one measure of lewdness to nine measures of separation. . . . (M Sotah 3:4)

R. Simon says: Merit does not protect [from the effects of] the bitter waters. . . .

Rebbe [R. Judah the Prince] says: Merit protects [from the effects of] the bitter waters. (3:5)

After describing the immediate yellowing of the *sotah*'s face and bulging of her eyes upon drinking the potion, the *mishnah* (3:4) goes on to limit the cases in which these changes occur: Accumulated merit could protect her and defer the physical devastation for one, two, or even three years. Before assessing the considerable implications of this statement, I will examine the one that follows, surely one of the most memorable in the entire Talmud.

Ben Azzai presents the reason a man is obligated to teach his daughter Torah (and this has to mean Torah in the broad sense, with tannaitic commentary): Should she be warned by her husband not to talk to a particular man, then go and closet herself with him, and be dragged to the Temple and forced to drink the bitter waters, and should she be guilty as suspected, she should know that if she had amassed a record of good deeds, they would delay the harmful effects of the water. Stated succinctly: If she studies Torah, she will know that if she commits adultery, her punishment will be postponed because of the good deeds she has done in the past. It is hard to imagine a more absurd rationale for teaching women Torah![4]

I find it remarkable that Ben Azzai is concerned with the mental state of even those women who commit adultery, who, one might argue, deserve to fear for their future. But why is his attitude to them so different from the contemptuous one demonstrated by his colleagues? It is doubtful that he is more forgiving of adultery. More likely, his statement indicates his repudiation of the entire Sotah ritual. Not only does merit protect, as already stated, but a woman should be entrusted with this knowledge in advance in order to alleviate her fear of what Ben Azzai considers to be an excessively harsh ritual.

Interpreted in this way, Ben Azzai's statement is yet another example of the rabbis' ability to reflect and comment upon women's unfair lot in life. He seems to say that this ritual is such a travesty of justice that the only way to rectify matters is to teach women Torah, so that they know that nothing will happen to them for a long time if they drink the water, even if guilty. He thus not only denies the potency of the water to punish sinners, as mentioned without attribution earlier in this passage, but also claims that women, for this immoral and profoundly demeaning way of treating them, must be compensated with Torah study, an activity at the other end of the continuum, one that evinces great respect for the student. That is not surprising coming from a man whose desire is only for the study of Torah, not for women (T Yevamot 8:4).

The mishnaic passage continues with R. Eliezer's dissenting opinion: One who teaches his daughter Torah is teaching her *tiflut,* lewdness. This is an almost equally absurd statement. One possible interpretation is that knowledge is dangerous: If a woman knows that the accumulation of good deeds can defer the punishment, she will be tempted to engage in forbidden sexual acts (as if ignorance of this fact were the only deterrent!). Another possible interpretation is that a woman's inferior intellect will only allow her a limited understanding of Torah, which may then innocently, or even otherwise, lead her astray. Since this same rabbi is reported in the Yerushalmi *(ad locum)* to have said that it is better to burn the words of Torah than to hand them over to women—a deeply misogynistic sentiment—it is likely that his statement in the Mishnah is to be best understood as a condemnation of women's intellectual capacities. R. Eliezer would thus be in direct conflict with Ben Azzai, who views women as competent. But why an inferior mind would misunderstand Torah in a way that leads to sexual impropriety is still not clear. R. Joshua, the next speaker in the Mishnah, provides an answer: Were a woman confronted with the choice of more frequent (marital) sex and a lower income or less frequent sex and a higher income, she would choose the former.[5] The context shows that R. Joshua means to say that women are incapable of applying themselves to the serious endeavor of Torah study because of their preoccupation with sex and their great sexual appetite.[6]

It is quite astonishing that the only place in the Mishnah where the issue of educating women is raised directly is in this context of women's inappropriate sexual behavior. I, therefore, think it possible that the Mishnah here hints, below the surface, that the reason a man should not teach a woman Torah, or that men and women may not study Torah together (and it is well known that the disciple circles were composed of men only), is not a woman's intellectual insufficiency but rather a man's sexual proclivities: When with women, he will find himself unable to observe the boundaries of acceptable social intercourse. What we see here, it seems, is the displacement of great and uncontrollable interest in sexual activity from men to women. It is not she who will be led astray by learning Torah, but he: In the course of teaching it to her he will find himself sexually distracted.

As we will see in Chapter 2, "Relations Between the Sexes," the Mishnah assumes that men who spend time with women are likely to be aroused by them and may not be able to stop themselves from initiating some kind of sexual involvement (M Kiddushin 4:12). This would be even more likely were the setting deep intellectual exchange. As stated in BT Berakhot 24a, men are aroused by the sight of a woman, any exposed part of her body, and even the sound of a woman's voice. This assessment supports what was stated above—that talking with women was considered an erotic activity. Note that the same kinds of statements are not made about women. They are portrayed as easily seduced, what the Talmud calls "light-minded" (BT Kiddushin 80b), but not as seducers. Therefore, men's ideal conditions for Torah study are apart from women. Given all this, it is not surprising that men need to deny that women are intellectually capable.

Mishnah 5, an apparent continuation of the discussion of the ability of merit to protect, cites two more views. R. Simon (b. Yohai) proposes that merit does not protect—if it did, aspersions would be cast on all the innocent women who already submitted to the ordeal and suffered no adverse consequences. Rebbe (R. Judah the Prince) responds that merit does protect—a guilty woman can be distinguished from an innocent one by how she dies, even though she will have continued to live a long time unharmed. The guilty, ultimately, will die a *sotah*'s death, characterized by slow physical deterioration.

When the redactor of the Mishnah surveyed the views of these rabbis and others found in parallel passages in the Midrash Halakhah,[7] he took a stand on several disputed matters: (1) merit does protect; (2) it protects for a long time, even three years, not just for three months, nine months, or one year, as suggested by the others. In this way the redactor rendered the ordeal of no use at all. What would a husband gain from having his wife drink the waters if they would not immediately prove her guilt or innocence? The point of the ritual, according to the Torah, was to calm his jealousy if she were innocent and punish her if she were guilty. The minute the notion of deferred punishment is introduced, the ordeal neither punishes her nor yields the information sought to pacify him.

In terms of the Mishnah's structure, this section, in its redacted form, upholds the outlook of the opening paragraphs of the tractate and goes one step further. Even in the unlikely event that all the conditions for administering the ordeal, set forth at the beginning of the tractate, were fulfilled, this section would destroy all reason to implement a test from which nothing would be learned.

The Paramour

Just as the waters test her, so too they test him, as it says (vv. 24, 27), "and they shall enter," "and they shall enter."

Just as she is forbidden to her husband, so too she is forbidden to the paramour, as it says (vv. 27, 29), "she was defiled," "and she was defiled." (M Sotah 5:1)

Chapter 5 of Sotah opens with a statement about the paramour, whose potential existence, until now, has been largely ignored. The Mishnah considers that the superfluous appearance of the phrase "and they shall enter" implies that the waters will test not only the woman who is forced to drink them but also the paramour, wherever he is, by adversely affecting him in the same way as her. This symmetry suggests that the rabbis found it morally unacceptable for only one of two partners in crime to be punished. If she has sinned and is consequently harmed seriously by the waters, then he, too, who would never be charged, should and will, they assert, suffer a similar punishment. (According to Maimonides [*Mishneh Torah*, Hilchot Sotah 3:17], he will die the same death that she dies, at the very same moment!)

The Mishnah goes on to say that just as she is forbidden to her husband until she drinks the bitter waters and even afterwards if she is guilty, so too she is forbidden to the paramour. Should the opportunity arise for her to reconnect with the paramour, because of the death of the husband or divorce, or a delay in punishment for her, the rabbis feel that it would not be right for her to do so. If it were allowed, then this tractate would be teaching a woman how to jettison one man for another: Have an adulterous relationship with the man to whom she took a fancy, arouse her husband's suspicion, bring it about that he divorce her, and then be free to continue the relationship with the paramour. In fact, the rabbis in M Nedarim 11:12 (and elsewhere) express their fear that women will do exactly that. Note the symmetry in this *mishnah*: The rabbis speak of two situations, one in which a woman and another in which a man (the husband of an adulteress) is treated unfairly in their eyes, even though the rules of the Torah are followed. Presenting these two situations together, and casting them in the same literary/midrashic form, suggests that the authors were finding fault with the water ordeal in toto, pointing out its pervasive absurdities, and not just tinkering with it to make it more fair.

Abolishing the Ordeal

The last powerful critique of the ordeal of the bitter waters appears in chapter 9. After discussing the rules of breaking the neck of a calf if a corpse is found near a city (*eglah arufah,* Deuteronomy 21:1–9), the Mishnah says:

> When the number of murderers grew large, they stopped performing the *eglah arufah* ritual; ... when the number of adulterers grew large, the bitter waters stopped, and it was R. Yohanan b. Zaccai who stopped them, as it says, "I will not punish their daughters for fornicating, nor their daughters-in-law for committing adultery, for they [themselves turn aside with whores ...]" [Hosea 4:14]. (M Sotah 9:9)

According to a midrash appearing in both Talmuds (BT Sotah 47b, PT Sotah 9:9; 24a), this *mishnah* is saying that once sexually immoral behavior becomes standard, the waters will no longer be able to test wives: The husbands of many of these women will be guilty of the same act themselves and therefore ineligible to invoke the test. The midrash derives the need for guiltless men from the concluding verse of the Sotah section (Numbers 5:31), which says that "the man shall be clear of guilt," implying that only men who are themselves clear of guilt may test their wives. In other words, this ritual was discontinued because of its inherent unfairness: It punished women but not men who committed the very same crime, and who were, themselves, the ones who initiated the test for the women. But the Tosefta (14:2) interprets the *mishnah* differently. It says that when adultery became common and hence public knowledge, they (the authorities) could no longer administer the bitter waters because the test works only in a case in which there is a doubt and in so many of these cases the transgression was certain.[8]

These different approaches suggest that there are two interpretive stages: The older approach, represented by the Mishnah and the Tosefta, treats the abolition matter-of-factly. According to the *mishnah,* because there was a backlog of cases, a long line of angry husbands waiting to test their wives, the time-consuming ritual had to be abolished, just like the *eglah arufah* ritual. The *mishnah*'s verse from Hosea, supporting the notion that adultery had become rampant, singles out women as adulterers and says that, despite their sin, God would not punish them—an apt prooftext. Note that the verse describes men's sin as seeking out prostitutes, not adultery. The Tosefta's tradition, attributed to R. Yohanan b. Zaccai, a Tanna who lived at the end of the Temple period, gives a rationale that is an alternative to the *mishnah*'s backlog of cases, but still offers no moral critique of the ordeal. However, the later rabbis and also the redactors of the Bavli and Yerushalmi felt the need to explain the Mishnah's abolition in a different way altogether, as a response to the hypocrisy of a ritual that permitted guilty but unpunished husbands to punish a guilty wife. As time passed, moral instincts seem to have prodded rabbis into explaining the abolition as a moral necessity.

Was this ritual ever carried out? Need one take this line of the Mishnah at face value? There is no obvious answer. Only one mention is made in rabbinic literature of the actual subjection of a woman to this ordeal (Mishnah Eduyot 5:6; PT Sotah 2:5; 18b). We read, however, in Mishnah Yoma 3:10, that Helene, the queen of Adiabene who converted to Judaism in the time of the Second Temple, made several generous donations to the Temple, among them a golden tablet on which were inscribed the verses of Sotah. The purpose of this tablet, presumably, was to make it easier for the *kohanim* to prepare the Sotah's scroll. I find it ironic, and a bit too didactic, that a woman would make a gift to the Temple to be used to test women for sin.[9]

Conclusions

What has this holistic study of Mishnah Sotah yielded? To begin with, we saw that the tractate begins on a note that radically transforms Torah, requiring a husband to warn his wife about a particular man and then, only if she paid no attention to the warning and secluded herself with that man in front of witnesses, allowing him to subject her to the ordeal. Whereas the Torah prescribes the ordeal for instances in which there are no witnesses, the rabbis inject witnesses, thus ensuring that the administration of the waters will be permitted only in cases where the man's jealousy is reasonably justified. So, the tractate opens with a rabbinic rendition of this institution that does not deviate as much from the rules of due process as one may at first think.

Then, in the course of reading through the tractate, we hear the message loud and clear: First, the rabbis are interested in limiting the implementation of this ordeal to the extent that they can; second, they believe that with divine intervention, the paramour, too, if there was one, will be punished exactly as she is; third, they believe that a history of good deeds on her part will postpone the implementation of the punishment; and, finally, because so many men were committing adultery with so many women, they abolish the ordeal of the bitter waters altogether.

This tractate, although it presents a detailed, gruesome description of the ritual, bordering, one might say, on the pornographic, at the same time suppresses this hostile and offensive core by the later addition of the elements mentioned above. When we read this tractate, we get the impression that overriding the disdain and even disgust the rabbis feel for a woman who may have been extramaritally involved is the even greater dislike they had for the ritual itself, probably because of its inherent injustice: An innocent woman could be humiliated, whereas a guilty man could be neither humiliated nor punished. On the surface, this tractate appears to endorse and develop the ritual of the bitter waters as set down by the Torah, but in reality, in all of its elaborate expansion, the rabbis eliminate this ancient ritual, paragraph by paragraph, until, almost anticlimactically, at the end of the volume, they supply a historical note, that the waters were, in fact, abolished by R. Yohanan b. Zaccai.[10]

All of this change notwithstanding, the image of marriage presented in this tractate and related rabbinic materials is one of a dominant husband and subordinate wife. As in other tractates, marriage is constructed here as a patriarchal institution: Men take women to be their wives, may dismiss them at will, and may deny them the compensation set forth in the *ketubah* if they have transgressed the rules of Jewish marriage, such as the requirement of fidelity. Although the rabbis do give a man these rights, they warn him time and again not to exercise absolute control over his wife.

It seems to me that the major achievement of the rabbis of the Talmud with regard to women, in this tractate and also in general, was significantly to improve their status in a variety of important areas. Since by the rabbis' own account, the ordeal of the bitter waters was abolished in the last days of the Temple, and thus was completely inoperative for most of the rabbinic period, this entire tractate may be seen as a lengthy statement of rabbinic dissatisfaction with patriarchy as they knew it. Moreover, since the men in this tractate were not, in fact, yielding any new rights to women or making any concessions in their comments, which almost explicitly reject the ordeal, they probably intended to show that rabbis take action when they see unjust treatment of women. Such action does not mean that they granted women full equality with men, such as the ability to make demands of marital fidelity on a husband, but that, within a patriarchal framework, they took steps to reduce women's legal disabilities.

Throughout this chapter we have read the Bible through the eyes of the rabbis, noting how they adapted a single biblical institution to their more progressive social outlook. It is noteworthy that a similar claim has been made by Bible scholars about the biblical institution of Sotah itself. As grossly unjust as Sotah may seem to the uninitiated reader of the Bible, when read in the context of Ancient Near Eastern literature, the ritual appears to have been reworked by the priestly legislators "in order to protect a suspected but unproved adulteress from the vengeance of an irate husband or community by mandating that God will decide her case."[11] Strange as it may sound, the point of the biblical reworking of the ordeal, according to Jacob Milgrom, is to improve women's lives. Just as Milgrom has read Bible in its ancient setting—literary, legal, and social—so have I attempted to read Talmud. And it has yielded similar results: although Tractate Sotah seems sexist on the surface, a contextualized reading shows that the underlying intent of the rabbis is to erase the inequities of the ritual and thereby diminish, although not eradicate, its patriarchy.

Notes

1. Cf. *The JPS Torah Commentary, Deuteronomy,* 206–207. Tigay writes that in the Ancient Near East, adultery by a woman was viewed as an offense solely against the woman's husband. In the Bible, it is viewed as a sin against God, as well as the husband, since God has forbidden adultery.

2. M 1:2, *bet haSeTeR;* also, M 6:1, *v'niSTaRah.*

3. New Jewish Publication Society (hereafter, NJPS) translation: "she *keeps secret* the fact that" (Num. 5:13). Ibn Ezra, a medieval exegete, comments, "She did not reveal the matter." Albeck, 227.

4. An alternative explanation is that if she is guilty as suspected and finds that the waters do not harm her, she will know that it is her good deeds that have postponed the waters' taking effect, not their inherent inefficacy. But that, too, is a strange reason to teach women Torah.

5. Or, according to the version of the text quoted above, a woman likes sex a lot more than abstinence.

6. See Chapter 7 for further comments on this *mishnah.* See also Daniel Boyarin, *Carnal Israel* (Berkeley: University of California Press, 1993), 174–180.

7. *Sifrei Bemidbar,* 8 (p. 15, Horovitz ed.).

8. Cf. Judith Wegner, *Chattel or Person?* (New York: Oxford University Press, 1988), 54.

9. Cf. Ilan, *Jewish Women,* 137.

10. A very brief version of this chapter appears in my article "An Assessment of Women's Liberation in the Talmud," in *Conservative Judaism* 26, no. 4 (Summer 1972).

11. *The JPS Torah Commentary, Numbers,* 354.

2

Relations Between the Sexes

THE PICTURE THAT EMERGES from many Talmudic passages is that society in the rabbinic period was both sex-segregated and patriarchal. Was it permissible, in such a society, for men and women to engage in social and intellectual exchange of ideas? The answer is no.

A close reading of the key texts on the subject of relations between the sexes will show that the reason for this ban was that men found themselves easily aroused in the presence of women and therefore did not trust themselves to be alone with them. It is hard to say whether such a low threshold of sexual arousal is the result of living in a society in which dealing with women was sufficiently rare that it heightened their sexual attraction for men, or whether just the opposite obtained: Because of men's sexual nature, it was necessary for them to live their lives, not with women, but parallel to them.

As much as we will try to understand what these texts have to say on the subject, we must recognize that the conditions of life in the rabbinic period were so different from those of today, the lack of privacy being just one example, that we cannot be sure that we are properly understanding the nature of men's and women's relationships. Even today, relationships between the sexes differ so greatly in the West and East that it is hard for someone in one culture to understand properly human relations in another.

The theory proposed—that men recognized that their own sexual nature makes social interchange with women impossible—is at odds with much current thinking on gender relations in rabbinic culture. Jacob Neusner suggests that men view women as anomalous, dangerous, dirty, and polluting, and in possession of an unruly sexual potential that is lying there just below the surface.[1] Judith Wegner says that rabbis ascribe to women moral laxity.[2] David Biale writes that according to the rabbis, women are "incapable of willed sexual restraint."[3] Leonie Archer claims that the rabbis consider women to be insatiable sexual aggressors.[4] Michael Satlow says that although men and women were both thought to be sexually desirous, only men were thought capable of controlling their desire.[5] According to all of these authors, men, rather than accepting responsibility for their own sexual misbehavior, blame women for instigating it. These theories fit in with, or are the consequence of, these authors' general sense that men viewed women as Other.

I have no quarrel with the fact that men in ancient societies, and even today, view women as Other. But that does not necessarily imply that they impute evil or depravity to women. On the contrary, I find in the Talmudic sources three general principles or observations that recognize the complexity of sexuality: (1) as already noted, men are easily aroused sexually by being in the presence of women, looking at them, dressed or undressed, or even just thinking about them; (2) women, in general, do not actively try to entice men; (3) sexual attraction in and of itself is considered to be normal and natural but, because it demands resolution, can easily lead to violation of social and religious norms.[6] I will try in the course of this chapter to show that these principles emerge when we read in entirety a rabbinic unit on sexual relations between men and women and compare the views of the Mishnah, Tosefta, Bavli, and Yerushalmi to each other. Only when these materials are examined out of context does it become possible to reach other conclusions. To their credit, the rabbis seem to be aware of some aspects of their own psychological makeup.

The subject not addressed in these passages is what women feel about sex. Although women are central to this material in that they are the source of sexual tension for men, their own opinions are not recorded. Nor do men have much to say about women's sexuality except to acknowledge that women, too, have a need for sexual satisfaction. The halakhic corollary is that since women are subordinate to their husbands and hence not free openly to seek satisfaction, the rabbis require men to meet their wives' sexual needs.

One other point to keep in mind as we read through this material is that just as the chapters in the Bible on forbidden sexual liaisons (Leviticus 18 and 20) place a man at the center and proceed to list the women with whom he may not enter into sexual contact, the Mishnah too, when discussing sexual matters, looks at the world with a man's eyes. Similarly, just as laws affecting women in the Bible are, for the most part, a derivative of laws affecting men, so too in the Mishnah rules affecting women must be derived from those affecting men.

Men and Women Alone Together

The key set of statements on the topic of relations between the sexes appears in chapter 4 of Tractate Kiddushin. After dealing with lineage and with appropriate and inappropriate marital unions, the Mishnah moves on to another topic altogether, relationships between men and women who are not married to each other.

> A man may not be alone with two women [neither of whom is married to him], but a woman may be alone with two men [neither of whom is married to her].
>
> R. Simon says: A man may even be alone with two women, as long as his wife is with him, and he may sleep with them at an inn, because his wife watches over him [and will not allow him to engage either of the two women who are not married to him in sexual relations].[7]
>
> He [i.e., any male] may be alone with his mother and his daughter and lie in bed with them in physical contact. Once they grow up [the boy who lies in bed with his mother or the girl who lies in bed with her father], she must sleep in her garment [כסותה] and he in his [but they may still lie in the same bed]. (M Kiddushin 4:12)

The first part of the *mishnah* states the well-known rule that men and women may not be alone together, but it distinguishes between prohibiting one man from being alone with several women and permitting one woman to be alone with several men. If we read this part of the *mishnah* independently of its context, at least two reasons for the distinction come to mind: Either men need to be protected from being seduced by women, or women need to be protected from being seduced by men. In order to find out which of these explanations is right, we need to read these rules in the context of those that follow.

The second clause of the *mishnah,* about relations between family members, makes the assumption that a father is not aroused sexually by sleeping naked in the same bed as his young daughter, with their bodies touching, that a young boy is not aroused by sleeping together with his mother, nor, we may assume, is a mother aroused by her young son. That is, immature bodies do not bring about sexual arousal in others or experience it themselves. But once a man matures physically, he will experience involuntary sexual arousal if he is in close physical contact with either his mother or a physically mature daughter. Therefore, although they may still sleep in the same bed, they may not do so naked, but each wrapped in his or her own garment.

This second part of the *mishnah* sheds light on the first. In this second case, the father, mother, son, or daughter is not intent on enticing anyone to engage in a sexual act. The *mishnah* is dealing with a situation, in this case a family bed, in which a man will, *without intending to,* find himself sexually aroused by sleeping in bodily contact with a naked woman, even his own mother or daughter. The *mishnah*'s law offers advice on how to avoid such arousal: Have each of them wrap themselves in his or her own blanket-like garment.

It follows that the first part of the *mishnah*, men and women finding themselves alone with each other, is also describing a situation in which men are not actively trying to entice women, nor are women actively trying to entice men. Even so, men will find themselves aroused sexually simply by being secluded with women. To guard a man from interacting sexually with an unattended woman, a likely outcome of their being alone together, the *mishnah* recommends that he make sure another man or else his own wife is present. The juxtaposition of these two sections within one *mishnah* makes it very unlikely that in the first part women are actively trying to seduce men whereas in the second men are trying to contend with involuntary sexual arousal. Since, in addition, the second part of the *mishnah* uses the same key term as the first part—"to be alone with" [להתייחד עם]—they constitute one literary unit on the topic of seclusion, involuntary sexual arousal and its routine consequence, illicit sexual activity.

Note that this *mishnah* is written with a man's concerns in view. It is he who will find himself unable to resist sexual temptation when in the presence of an unattended woman or women. For the *mishnah*, sexual arousal in these circumstances is natural, uncomplicated, involuntary, and perceived of as bad only if it leads a man into sexual transgression. To prevent him from engaging in a sexual act when alone with a woman, the *mishnah* forbids a man from allowing himself to be found in such a situation.[8]

The reason that two men may be alone with one woman but two women may not be alone with one man has to do with a man's controlling his instincts: In both cases a female presence excites a man, but in the first instance, the presence of someone else like himself will inhibit him from pursuing gratification, whereas in the second, in the presence of women only, he will not be embarrassed to carry out his sexual design. We will return to this subject later.

The next *mishnah* continues to deal with the subject of involuntary sexual arousal:

> A bachelor may not train to become a Bible teacher for children nor may a woman train to become one. R. Eliezer says: Even a man who does not have a wife [living with him] may not train to become such a teacher.[9] (M Kiddushin 4:13)

No reason is given for why an unmarried man may not teach young children. The simple explanation, raised and then immediately rejected by both Talmuds (BT Kiddushin 82a; PT Kiddushin 4:11; 66c), is that an unmarried man's pent-up libido may lead him to molest the students sexually.[10] As close to the meaning of the words as this explanation is—exploitation of schoolchildren is a problem to this very day—it would force us to say, in parallel fashion, that a woman, unmarried or *even married,* is similarly suspect. Since no statistics support the notion that women are *more* frequent sexual offenders of children than men, that is not likely to be the view of women's sexual nature that the rabbis are expressing in these texts.

The two Talmuds propose instead that unmarried men may not serve as teachers because of the mothers who accompany young students to school, and women, unmarried or even married, may not serve as teachers because of the fathers who accompany young students to school.[11] This means that an unmarried man may not be a teacher of young children because he will come into contact with a student's mother, become aroused by her, and commit a sexual violation. Overpowered by him, she will be unable to say no. The rule about women serving as teachers does not make reference to marital status because the rabbis think that any woman, married or unmarried, will arouse a man. They are not saying, therefore, that the female teacher will attempt to seduce the student's father but only that he will attempt to seduce her. This alternate interpretation, which focuses on adults and not children, is reasonable in light of the topic of the entire section—a man's low threshold of arousal and lack of control in subduing it. If a man does not have a sexual outlet, the chances of involuntary arousal followed by sexual transgression are even higher. I think it possible that the *mishnah* at some point in time referred to child abuse, in at least the first clause about men. But from the time of the Talmud and on—and maybe even earlier—the interpreters saw it as referring only to the behavior of adults among themselves.[12]

> R. Judah says: A bachelor may not pasture cattle nor may two bachelors sleep in one tallit [a blanket-like garment]; but the Sages allow [these activities]. (M Kiddushin 4:14)

In this next *mishnah,* R. Judah seems to be worried about involuntary sexual arousal or illicit sexual activity when an unmarried man is in close physical contact with another man or even, as offensive as this sounds to us today, with cattle. The rabbis disagree with him, apparently because they think that such behavior is not prevalent among Jews, as they say explicitly in T Kiddushin 5:10 (לא נחשדו ישראל על כך, Jews are not suspected of that).

The *mishnah* continues:

> Anyone whose business is with women should not let himself be alone with them [לא יתיחד עם הנשים]. And a man should not teach his son a trade that will make him go among women.

This passage again suggests that when a man spends time alone with women, he will be sexually aroused, leading him to engage in forbidden sexual acts. As noted above, she is likely to be overpowered by him and unable to resist. I do not see any suggestion here that the women are actively tempting him or that women are to be looked upon as evil and conniving or even morally lax. Rather, this *mishnah* is a straightforward and almost matter-of-fact presentation of the pitfalls of men's physical responses to being with women, and for some men to being with other men or even cattle, in the event that a man does not have a licit sexual outlet. By mentioning that he is a bachelor, the *mishnah* puts the onus on him. It is he who, because of his suppressed libido, finds himself more easily aroused involuntarily by close contact with women, other men, or even animals.

The *mishnah* here accepts what it perceives as men's sexual nature and tries to restrain it. Just as the rabbis tell people to avoid any actions that may lead them to violate the Sabbath,[13] so too do they tell men to stay away from women because of the likelihood of attraction, arousal, and the likely result, sexual activity. There is no suggestion here that the women themselves are deliberately trying to entice men, as the Mishnah elsewhere suggests about women who bare their arms in the marketplace, engage men in conversation, and bathe publicly with them, all activities the Mishnah perceives to be clearly designed to lure men into sexual activity (M Ketubot 7:6 and T Sotah 5:9). Here it is the men who seem unable to control themselves in the presence of women and who need other men to inhibit them from unacceptable sexual activity.

It is remarkable that the Mishnah considers a wife to be an appropriate guardian of her husband's chastity, since, in most cases, she could not restrain him physically. But the assumption seems to be that she has a vested interest in keeping him away from sexual encounters with other women. Therefore, she will see to it, probably in subtle or morally admonishing ways, that he will not find himself aroused or, at least, not able to act on such arousal.

The parallel passages in the Tosefta sharpen our understanding of these *mishnah*s.

> A woman may be alone with two men, even if both of them are Kutheans, even if both are slaves, even if one is a Kuthean and one is a slave, except [if one of the two is] a minor, because she is not embarrassed to engage in sexual relations in the presence [of a minor, שאינה בושה לשמש כנגדו]. . . .
> But she may not be alone with pagans, even if one hundred of them are present. (T Kiddushin 5:9, 10b)

According to the beginning of this statement, even men who are not fully Jewish, such as Kutheans and pagan slaves,[14] may be alone with a Jewish woman. From this we can conclude that the rabbis did not fear that women would seduce men, for if they did, why would they distinguish between one man, fully Jewish, and another, not fully Jewish—all would be equally vulnerable to her initiatives. On the contrary, this statement implies that as long as a man has some connection to Judaism, he can be trusted not to force himself on her in the presence of another man. As for mature pagan men, she cannot be alone even with one hundred. Why? I do not think the rabbis fear that she would seduce one after the other of these more seducible pagan men. More likely, the rabbis' concern is that no matter how many of them there are, they will shamelessly engage in sexual activity with her, even in the presence of ninety-nine others, without a single one of them interfering with the seduction or, more accurately, the rape.

The above passage also says that a woman may not be alone with one man and a minor because *she* would not be embarrassed to have sexual relations with the mature man in the presence of a minor. This can be understood as saying that it is not men who actively seduce women but women who actively seduce men.[15] But given the immediately preceding and following statements about men who either can or cannot restrain themselves from engaging an unattended woman in sexual activity, I think such an interpretation is not likely. What the passage may be saying is that a grown man will become sexually aroused when with a woman and that the presence of a minor will not deter him or *even her* the way the presence of an adult male would. Minors do not count. According to this interpretation, the passage assumes that she engages in sex consensually.

> His sister, his mother-in-law, and *all* the other women forbidden on the basis of consanguinity, as mentioned in the Torah, he should not be alone with them except if two [i.e., at least one other] are present. (T Kiddushin 5:10a)

It goes without saying that a man may not be secluded with only one woman because of the opportunity they would have to engage in sexual relations, but one might still think that he could be alone with a female relative. However, the Tosefta says that seclusion with *any* female relative is not allowed. Another adult must be present. This law could be seen as a direct contradiction of the *mishnah* that says that he may be alone with his mother when he is young, or with his daughter when she is young, and even sleep with them in the same bed. But there is no necessary conflict. Either this rule already assumes and accepts the exceptions listed in the *mishnah* and talks about other female relations, not mentioned in the *mishnah,* or else this rule is older than the related *mishnah* and the *mishnah* comes to relax its restrictions somewhat. The *mishnah*'s rationale seems to be, as noted above, that it is hard to imagine sexual arousal between a father and a young daughter and a mother and a young son. Furthermore, it would be hard to prohibit parents and children from being alone together, given that they live under the same roof.[16]

The Tosefta continues:

> R. Judah says, a bachelor may not pasture small cattle [e.g., sheep, goats], nor may two bachelors sleep in one tallit.
> But the Sages say, Jews are not suspected of that.

If we assume that these passages from the Tosefta were known to the redactor of the *mishnah* we looked at above (4:14), we can see that he changed these statements slightly. He simply said that the Sages allow such seclusion, thereby implying, without saying so explicitly, that, according to them, Jews do not engage in homosexual behavior or bestiality.[17]

But note that what we are talking about here, it seems, is involuntary arousal. The *mishnah*'s statement that the Sages allow two unmarried men, those with no licit sexual outlet, to sleep together in one tallit implies that the Sages do not fear involuntary homosexual arousal and, its likely consequence, homosexual relations.[18] R. Judah disagrees: Whether the two men chose to sleep this way for warmth or for sexual arousal, it is not allowed because of the possible outcome of sexual relations. The Tosefta's wording of the Sages' statement—that Jews are not suspected of "that," of homosexual or even homoerotic behavior—means that according to the Tosefta the Sages recognize the possibility that the reason that two pagan men may choose to sleep in one tallit is to arouse themselves sexually; Jewish men, they feel, would not do so and hence may sleep in close physical contact.[19]

The Tosefta's last statement on the subject of relations between the sexes upholds the points made above.

> Whoever plies a trade among women should not be alone with them. Such as the net makers, the men who sell combed wool and flax, the weavers, the peddlers, the tailors, the barbers, the launderers, the mill repairmen. (T 5:14)

To stray from the subject for a moment, this passage of the Tosefta, which also appears in the Bavli (Kiddushin 82a), paints an interesting picture of a woman's life in Talmudic times, similar in many ways to that of the Roman matron. This passage presents a list of the kind of men who went from house to house to peddle their services or their wares.[20] Were these men in a fixed place of business, one would not say that their business was with women; if they sold flax and wool in the marketplace, they would sell to all. Rather, it seems that many of these people performed their work at the home of the client or else made a series of visits to the home to check on the progress of their handiwork. For that reason, that they could find themselves in a woman's home alone with her, the Tosefta issues a warning that they should avoid doing so.

This source suggests that the concepts of private and public domains were blurred in those days.[21] The home was not a private place in which a woman was sequestered. There appears to have been a constant stream of people passing through.[22] In addition, male and female servants worked in the home and were supervised by the mistress of the household. With respect to the public sphere, many sources indicate that women shopped in the market, went to the baths, visited friends and relatives,[23] and showed up at court and public lectures.[24] I am not suggesting that men and women engaged in the same kind of work—women were more domestic and men were engaged in agriculture or commerce, and, of course, there were significant differences resulting from social class—but that women's work, although at home, did not isolate them in the way a woman who works at home today is isolated. The distinction between public and private meant something different in Talmudic times than it does today. It is therefore incorrect to talk about women's private role as opposed to men's public one, a favorite theme of much recent literature on life in the Talmudic period.

To return to the topic at hand: What emerges from all of this material is a sense that men are easily aroused by women and that they will follow through with sexual activity, even engage in forbidden sexual liaisons, unless restrained by the presence of others. We can generalize and say that men are not calm in women's presence; that there is always a degree of sexual tension. It is for this reason that the rabbis decided to legislate against their being alone together.

We will now turn to the Talmudic commentary on these tannaitic passages. Following the halakhic discussion, a string of anecdotes will draw connections between law and life, thus further supporting the conclusions we reached above.

==What is the reason [that according to the *mishnah* a man may not be alone with two women]?

Tanna d'vei Elijah: Because women are light-minded [הואיל ונשים דעתן קלות עליהן]. (BT Kiddushin 80b)

The light-mindedness referred to here is not intellectual but sexual. This statement, ostensibly a tannaitic source,[25] is saying that each of the two women will allow herself to be seduced by the man with whom she finds herself, despite the presence of another woman. It does not mean that each of them will attempt to seduce him, as the later discussion makes clear. Unfortunately, this statement has been widely quoted as evidence that the rabbis disparaged a woman's intellectual capabilities. Although the words themselves may suggest that, and it would be hard to argue that this quote could not aptly be put to that use, for the record, one should note that in this context its meaning is sexual. "Light-mindedness" here means lacking a strong enough will to resist that which one is being pressed into doing.[26] She did not say no, in their opinion, because of her own shortcomings, not because of the hard-to-withstand pressure a man placed on her.

Even if this passage does not mean that women actively entice men, as I argue, it does seem to represent a partial shifting of responsibility from men to women for sexual misadventure. That is possibly an expression of men's sentiment, or wishful thinking, that they would not have sinned had the women only resisted the advances.

The Gemara continues with a scriptural derivation in support of sex segregation:

> ==From where in Scripture does this principle emerge?
> – –Said R. Yohanan in the name of R. Ishmael: A hint of the prohibition of being alone with a woman is found in the Torah. Where? "If your brother, the son of your mother, should entice you [to sin]" [Deuteronomy 13:7]—Does a brother on the mother's side entice, but not a brother on the father's side? [Since both are likely to do so in equal measure, this verse must have something else in mind.] It comes to teach that a son may be alone with his mother but not with any of the other women who are forbidden to him.[27]

This statement of R. Ishmael contradicts the *mishnah* that allows a man to be alone not just with his mother but also his daughter, and even to sleep together with them, in physical contact, until the time of physical maturation (of the boy who sleeps together his mother or the girl who sleeps together with her father). The existence of a tannaitic dispute on this subject suggests that it was undergoing debate and change.

Starting with the following text, the Gemara openly subscribes to the notion that men's ease of involuntary sexual arousal is the primary reason for the social separation of the sexes.

> We learned in a *baraita*: For the first thirty days [after birth, if a child dies] it is carried out in its mother's bosom and buried by one woman and two men. But not with one man and two women. Abba Saul says: even with one man and two women.
> ==One can even say that the *mishnah* agrees with Abba Saul, for when a man is in deep mourning his sexual inclination is subdued. . . .
> "But a woman may be alone with two men."
> – –Said R. Judah said Rav: They only spoke of fit men [that she may be alone with two of them]; as for promiscuous men, she may not be

alone even with ten of them. [This same point has already been made in the Tosefta, if we understand that pagans are in the category of promiscuous men. R. Judah is here expanding the rule to include all promiscuous men, not just pagan ones.]

--There was an instance in which ten men carried out a woman on a bier [and then each had sexual relations with her].

--Said R. Joseph: One should note that ten [men] join to steal a beam and are not ashamed [to do so] in the presence of each other.

R. Joseph's remark about men as partners in crime suggests, yet again, that it is men's shame in the presence of each other that restrains them from having sexual relations with the women among them. For certain transgressions, such as stealing, the shame can be suppressed. "Fit" men, however, will refrain from engaging in sexual relations in the presence of another man. Note that it is not a man's sense of violation of Jewish law that stops him from committing the act, but his sense of shame in front of someone else. Were he totally alone with the woman, nothing, probably not even her saying no, would stop him. A social-status argument can be suggested even here: The reason for the difference in ruling in the two clauses of the *mishnah*—that one man may not be alone with two women but one woman may be alone with two men—is that a man is embarrassed to breach conventions of proper behavior in the presence of fit men, his social equals, but not in the presence of women, his social inferiors.

Let me point out once more that these observations could only be made if we read these sources in context. If we examine the first two clauses of the *mishnah* independently, we could conclude that the reason for the differential ruling is that women actively seek to entice men; it is only when another man is present that each can protect the other from her sexual advances. As absurd as I think such fear of women sounds in a patriarchal setting, nevertheless, one cannot properly refute the notion until one reviews the broad literary and legal context of this *mishnah*. Such a reading shows that the rabbis are not worried about active enticement on anyone's part; rather, they are worried about men's inability to control themselves once they are aroused involuntarily.

The Gemara continues with a series of anecdotes about rabbis and sexual arousal.

--Rav and R. Judah were walking on a road and there was a woman walking in front of them. Said Rav to R. Judah: Step lively before Gehenna, [i.e., let us pass her and not be sexually aroused—consumed by Gehenna—by looking at her body from behind]. Said R. Judah: But you are the very one who said that a woman alone with fit men [כשרים] is all right! Said Rav: I did not mean fit men like you and me.

==But like whom?
==Like R. Hanina bar Pappi and his colleagues [who withstood the sexual advances of a Roman matron (BT Kiddushin 39b)].[28] (81a)

This story, like the others that will follow, makes it abundantly clear that ordinary men and even rabbis, who are ordinary men but are assumed to be more in control of themselves because of their commitment to mitzvot, are not immune to visual stimulation. They, too, need to remove themselves from the situation in which they find themselves, *even if Jewish law allows it.* Despite the *mishnah*'s ruling, the presence of a second man seems to be no guarantee that the first will not attempt to pursue and seduce an unattended woman, even if he is an individual who takes the rules seriously, such as the very rabbi who formulated them. Sexual temptation and arousal overtake even men like that. The best advice, they say about themselves, is to avoid compromising circumstances. Note that the woman in this story is not paying them any attention but merely going on her way. It is they who inadvertently approach her from behind and find themselves vulnerable to sexual arousal.

After some discussion of related matters, the Gemara continues:

--There were a number of women captives who, upon being redeemed, came to Nehardea and were housed [in an upper chamber at the home of] R. Amram the Pious.[29] They[30] removed the ladder [to deny access to the women. It happened that] when one of them passed by [the opening to the lower story], light fell from the opening [and R. Amram found himself sexually aroused]. He took the ladder, which was so heavy that ten men could not lift it and, all by himself, positioned it below the upper chamber and began climbing. When he was halfway up, he stopped himself and cried out: Fire at R. Amram's! The rabbis came [running but, upon realizing the sexual nature of the fire, chided him, saying] you have shamed us. He said to them, better that you are shamed by me in this world than in the world-to-come. He then adjured [Satan, the embodiment of the sexual urge] to leave him. And Satan issued forth in the shape of a pillar of fire. R. Amram said to him: You are fire and I am flesh and yet I am stronger than you.

In this story, as in the others, a rabbi who is loyal to Jewish law finds himself sexually aroused, burning with passion, simply by seeing the shadow of one of the women in his upper chamber. His desire is so overpowering that he is able to execute a superhuman feat in seeking to satisfy it. But in attempting to regain control of himself when halfway to his destination, he summons help. The presence of others stops him from sexual transgression. This point merits attention. As strong as sexual desire is, it is immediately extinguished, or at least suppressed, when others appear. It was not knowledge of the law, respect for it, or fear of punishment in the world-to-come that enabled him to accept frustration of desire. He required the presence of other men to do so.

Note that this story demonizes the sexual urge, portraying it as an independent being that has invaded the body of the rabbi and is later forced to leave. Rather than view his sexuality as a natural part of himself, to be satisfied in appropriate circumstances, he fears it and wants to be rid of it.[31]

Two stories about Tannaim follow. The issue in these is not the seclusion of men with women but the ease with which men are sexually stimulated and goaded into action. This unit of commentary opened with the statement that women are easily seduced, but the anecdotal material that follows ironically indicates just the opposite, that it is men who are easily aroused and single-minded in pursuing release.

> R. Meir used to make fun of sinners. One day Satan appeared to him as a woman on the other side of the river. There was no ferry [at the time]. So he seized the rope and began to cross [on his own]. When he was halfway there, he [Satan] let him go, saying: Had they not announced in Heaven, beware of R. Meir and his Torah, I would have valued your life at [only] two ma'ahs [small coins; i.e., I would have allowed you to sin and thus made your life worthless].
>
> R. Akiva used to make fun of sinners. One day Satan appeared to him as a woman at the top of a palm tree. He took hold of the palm and began to climb. When he was halfway up, Satan let him go, saying: Had they not announced in Heaven, beware of R. Akiva and his Torah, I would have valued your life at two ma'ahs.

Written in Aramaic, these two stories are probably an amoraic retelling or reshaping of older, tannaitic material. As in the story about R. Amram, here, too, rabbis are easily aroused by the sight of a woman and unable to withstand temptation. But in these instances the rabbi is stayed, not by his own hand, but by Satan's. Once Satan shows them that they are like all men in their inability to resist, he does not let them break the rules but merely chastises them for having succumbed. He teaches the rabbis that rather than mock others for their inability to avoid sin, they should be sympathetic because they themselves are no different.

These anecdotes have far-reaching implications. That Satan stops tormenting the two men because of their amassed merit of Torah study implies that such study has cumulative protective power. This notion allows us to return to a *mishnah* treated in Chapter 1 and interpret it differently. M Sotah 3:5 says that if a woman who drank the bitter waters possessed accumulated "merit," then that merit would postpone the onset of punishment. We can now suggest that the merit in question is that of Torah study: Just as here it protected the two rabbis from sexual sin and punishment, so too, with respect to the *sotah,* the *mishnah* is saying that if she studied Torah, that fact would postpone the onset of the punishment (if she had, in fact, sinned). There does not seem to be any reason that the protective powers of Torah study would be limited to men.[32] Now we can understand Ben Azzai's statement that follows, obligating a father to teach his daughters Torah, so that they know that if they ever have to drink the bitter waters their "merit" will postpone punishment. Ben Azzai must mean that their accumulated merit of Torah study will protect them.[33] In both of these cases—M Sotah and the anecdotes here—the (purported) sin is sexual and the protection from sin or from punishment comes from the study of Torah. For men such an opportunity exists, according to these anecdotes in tractate Kiddushin; for women, only according to Ben Azzai in tractate Sotah.[34]

The next page of Talmud (81b) presents yet another story about men's complacency. It too mocks men who believe themselves to be above temptation.

--R. Hiyya bar Ashi made it a practice that when he fell down prostrate [at the end of the morning prayers], he would ask God to save him from his evil inclination [a reference to the sexual urge]. One day his wife overheard him and mused, but it is already several years that he has separated himself from me; why, then, does he find it necessary to keep making this supplication? Once, when he was studying in the garden, she disguised herself as a prostitute and paraded back and forth in front of him. He asked her: Who are you? She answered: I am Haruta and have returned today. He propositioned her. She said to him: First bring me the pomegranate from the top of the tree. He jumped up and went and got it for her. When he came home [after his sexual encounter], his wife was lighting the oven. He went and sat inside [or on] it [in order to punish himself]. She said to him: What is this? He told her what had happened. She said to him: But it was I. He paid her no attention until she brought [him] proof [the pomegranate]. [But he refused to be comforted] because he said that his intent, nonetheless, had been to commit a prohibited act. He tormented himself and fasted regularly until he died.

This story, more than the others, drives home the point that even the most pious and learned of men are involuntarily aroused when they gaze upon a woman. It also shows that the Talmud strenuously objects to sexual asceticism. This particular sage, who seemed to think that sexual relations in and of themselves were bad, had ceased sexual activity with his wife. But when a prostitute showed an interest in him, he immediately succumbed, even, remarkably, abandoning the Torah that he was studying. That is, what distracts men from Torah study is sexual thoughts or fantasies. This association, again, helps us understand why the discussion of women and the study of Torah appears in the context of a discussion of women and sexual transgression (M Sotah 3:5). We may now conclude that, according to most Tannaim, it is not knowledge of Torah that will lead a woman astray, as claimed by R. Eliezer—who says that teaching a woman Torah is teaching her lewdness—but rather the opposite: that Torah offers those who study it a refuge and respite from their consuming sexual drives.[35] And also, as noted above in the stories about R. Akiva and R. Meir, the very study of Torah will protect them in the future from contemplated sexual misadventure.

This story is different from the others in that a woman speaks up about her sexual desires and needs. R. Hiyya bar Ashi's wife says, apparently in a tone of regret and wistfulness, that he has not engaged in sexual activity with her for several years. She then devises a way to satisfy herself and also, at the same time, find out if he still possesses the sexual impulses from which he keeps asking God to protect him. In addition to saying that women want sex, this story also teaches that women are not, for the most part, evil temptresses, but devoted, long-suffering wives, and even wise, resolute, and appropriately assertive women. In the course of praising women, the Talmud, as is its wont, discredits a man, in particular, his renunciation of sexual activity. R. Hiyya is a hypocrite: He shuns sexual activity for a long period of time, thus ignoring his wife's needs and rights; he throws himself on the ground each day to ask for God's protection from sexual sin, implying that he was sexually active even though he was not; as soon as a woman shows interest in him, he falls prey to temptation. This story is thus about vanity just as much as it is about sexual desire.

Note also the biblical echoes of this episode. In Genesis 38, after Judah refuses to arrange a levirate marriage with his third son for Tamar, his twice widowed, childless daughter-in-law, he himself engages in sexual relations with her, thinking her a prostitute. She first secures from him several personal items for future use. When her resulting pregnancy becomes known, he orders her burnt at the stake. She then sends him back his seal and cord to show him that it was he who impregnated her. This biblical narrative is possibly a sophisticated spoof of the biased sex laws of the Ancient Near East: Men may engage with impunity in sexual encounters with women to whom they are not married, but women may not do the same with men to whom they are (apparently) not married. Tamar has clearly outsmarted Judah tactically, and he praises her for her clever and resolute action. In the Talmud account, R. Hiyya bar Ashi's wife outsmarts him tactically,[36] but he never regains equanimity after having his hypocrisy exposed. The fact that women test men in these two episodes does not suggest that women, in general, are temptresses. In each of these cases a woman chastises a man for unethical behavior: Judah, in that he let Tamar languish, and R. Hiyya, in that he denied his wife sexual satisfaction.

I also suspect an element of male fantasy. Many men are likely to dream that a sexually exciting woman will appear from nowhere, take a fancy to them, and satisfy them in ways that they have not been satisfied before. In this story, the shame at being caught in the realization of such a fantasy, even though, ironically, the prostitute was none other than his own wife, consumed this man to such an extent that he ultimately died. In another well-known Talmudic anecdote, a man who paid a prostitute her steep fee in advance, changes his mind about securing her services at the last moment, when already in bed with her. She is so impressed with his self-restraint that she follows him back to the land of Israel, converts to Judaism, and marries him (BT Menahot 44a). It is hard to imagine a better example of male sexual wish fulfillment.

Having completed its discussion of the first part of M 4:12, the Gemara now cites the second part, on the subject of a man and his female relatives, and proceeds to discuss it.

"A man may be alone with his mother."

--Said R. Judah said R. Assi: A man may spend time alone [מתיחד] with his sister but even live [alone] with his mother and his daughter [but not with his sister].

--When he recited this in the presence of Samuel, he said: It is forbidden for a man to be alone with *any* of the consanguineous women.

. . .

==But we learned in the Mishnah that a man may be alone with his mother and daughter and sleep with them in physical contact.

==This is a challenge to Samuel. . . . (BT Kiddushin 81b)

This section of Talmud bears out what we saw above: There is a wide range of views on the subject of being alone with one's female relatives. These are the women with whom a man was likely to find himself alone and, therefore, the women by whom he would be sexually aroused. The many views on this topic and the plethora of anecdotes—not all cited here—lead me to believe, as stated above, that sexual arousal by female relatives was a controversial and real issue for the rabbis.

The Talmud then defines the *mishnah*'s statement that a child who matures physically may no longer sleep in bodily contact with a parent of the opposite sex.

==And at what age [does this prohibition take effect]?

--Said R. Adda b. R. Azza said R. Assi: a girl, nine years and a day; a boy, twelve years and a day. Some say: a girl, twelve years and a day;

a boy, thirteen years and a day. For the following must be true: breasts have appeared and [pubic] hair has grown . . . [Ezekiel 16:7]. . . .

The discussion of sexual arousal by female relatives ends with an anecdote:

--R. Aha b. Abba visited his son-in-law R. Hisda and took his young granddaughter to bed with him. [Alternate version: put her on his lap.[37]]

--He [R. Hisda] said to him [his father-in-law]: Does it not occur to you that she may be betrothed [and therefore taking her to bed is inappropriate]?

--He said: But then you have violated Rav's dictum, that one should not betroth a young girl until she is old enough to say, "He is the man I want."

--But, sir, you have violated Samuel's dictum, one may not make use of a woman.

--I agree with Samuel's other dictum, all may be done for the sake of Heaven [Rashi, I have no sexual intentions; I only mean to show her affection].

We see here an amoraic move away from the permission the *mishnah* gives to sleep in the same bed as young female relatives. R. Aha b. Abba's action is permitted by the *mishnah*[38] if we assume that his granddaughter had not yet matured physically, and yet it deeply disturbs her father, R. Hisda. R. Hisda, in fact, expresses this concern elsewhere, saying that a man is no longer allowed to sleep in physical contact with his daughter once she reaches three years and one day.[39] He politely criticizes his father-in-law but to no avail. The parallel discussion in the Yerushalmi (later in this chapter) similarly lowers the age of children sleeping with parents naked.

When read independently of context, this anecdote seems to say that someone accused of inappropriate behavior can gamely deflect all charges against him by finding a reasonably relevant tradition or text. The old rabbi has the last word, and also, it would seem, his granddaughter in bed with him. But when read in context, it makes the almost frightening point that the grandfather is sexually exploiting or abusing the little granddaughter, using her to "warm himself up," as did Abishag the Shunamite for King David in his old age (1 Kings 1:1–4). R. Hisda—who says elsewhere that he prefers daughters to sons (BT BB 141a), and he had both—is agitated, it seems, and rightfully so. It is hard to say whether the narrator sides with R. Hisda or not. He appears to be portraying the grandfather in negative terms, but one cannot be sure. It would seem, however, that with the passage of time the need arose to restrict the *mishnah,* to lower the age of permitting children and parents to sleep in the same bed naked. Since the discussion of family sleeping habits ends with this anecdote, the narrator seems to endorse restricting the *mishnah,* which would mean he agrees with R. Hisda and disapproves of the father-in-law's behavior.

The disagreement here and elsewhere about the age at which a young person's body can create involuntary arousal, with a total of four different views expressed, again suggests that the rabbis were actively dealing with the subject. The *mishnah,* in its simple presentation, considers puberty to be the limit. But the rabbis in Babylonia and Palestine, with the exception of one anonymous view, lower it. This legal change probably reflects a shift in social standards, a move from a more relaxed attitude about nakedness and physical contact to a less relaxed one. This redefinition can also be seen, certainly in terms of results and maybe even in terms of intention, as an attempt to legislate protection for children—for girls from grown men and also for boys from grown women.

The Yerushalmi commentary on this *mishnah* is much more limited than that of the Bavli.

> "A man should not be alone with two women . . . ."
> – –Said R. Abun: To what does this refer? To fit men. As for promiscuous men, she should not be alone with even one hundred. (PT Kiddushin 4:11; 66c)

This same statement appeared in the Bavli in the name of R. Judah, who said it in the name of Rav. Although it is similar to the Tosefta's statement that she may not be alone even with one hundred pagans, it is different in that it refers to Jewish men who, like the stereotypical pagan,[40] are promiscuous and know no shame.

Like the Bavli, the Yerushalmi cites the *baraita* in which Abba Saul and the Sages disagree about whether two women and one man may bury an infant, as well as the comment that one need not fear sexual arousal in a cemetery. It then talks about sexual arousal within the family unit.

> A man may be alone with his mother and live with her. [He may be alone] with his daughter and live with her. [He may be alone] with his sister but may not live with her.
> "And he may sleep with them in physical contact."
> It was taught by Tannaim: R. Halafta b. Saul [said], a daughter may [sleep] with a father until three years and one day. A son may [sleep] with a mother until nine years and one day.
> "Once they grow up, each sleeps in his or her own garment."
> It was taught by Tannaim: If two were sleeping in one bed, each covers himself with his own garment and reads Shema. If his son and

daughter were still small, it is all right [to be in bodily contact and even so to read Shema].

In this passage the Yerushalmi presents views like those in the Bavli but at variance with those in the Mishnah and Tosefta. The Mishnah stated that a man may be alone with his mother and daughter and, we may surmise, live with them. By implication, the *mishnah* forbids him to seclude himself with other female relatives. The Yerushalmi, however, comments that he *may* spend time alone with a sister, although he may not live with her. This rule is more lenient than the Mishnah and Tosefta, which explicitly forbade even being alone with a sister. The Yerushalmi then restricts a father to sleeping in physical contact with his daughter until she reaches the age of three, and a mother with her son until he is nine, even though the simple meaning of "*higdilu*," as used in the Mishnah, is puberty. This is an example of an amoraic stringency, found in both the Bavli and Yerushalmi. As already noted several times, the appearance of this topic in both Talmuds, as well as in the Mishnah and Tosefta with variations in each of these major rabbinic works, creates the impression that it was very much a live issue at the time.

Before I summarize all these materials, it should be noted that throughout this entire discussion, beginning with the Mishnah and ending with the Yerushalmi, the matter of sexual arousal is looked at from a man's perspective only. It is men who find themselves sexually aroused when seeing or being with women. Whether there is reciprocal arousal on the part of women is not openly considered.

The message of this extended Talmudic discussion is that men and women were not allowed, in contemporary parlance, to develop friendships, enter into social contact with each other, or engage in exchange of ideas because men are understood, first, to be sexually aroused just by the sight of a woman and, second, to be unable to hold themselves back from seeking release. The men most criticized are those who place themselves above others, claiming that they are able to withstand temptation. The only successful strategy is to avoid putting oneself at risk, and that means to avoid the company of women.

Note that this material does not imply that men fall prey to their sexual urges because women deliberately excite them. I find it important to dwell on this point because one can all too easily make the woman the culprit in these situations, in that she entices him to sin. That is precisely what many have written about the rabbinic perception of women, as we have noted.[41] But I think that this extensive commentary makes it clear beyond the shadow of a doubt that, according to the Gemara, women do not seek to snare men, but rather men, in the presence of women, lose control of themselves, even or especially if they are generally pious rabbis, and even if the women are close relatives. Taking the attitudes of someone like Ben Sira or

Philo, who describe women as deliberately trying to entrap men, and reading their misogyny into this text would be incorrect.[42] Rabbinic patriarchy had common features with the other patriarchal cultures of the times, but it was not necessarily identical to them.

I also do not think that these texts portray men as sexual predators. These passages reflect the rabbis' attitude toward human nature: It is good when restrained. It should also be noted that the outcome of separation is beneficial not only to men but also to women. To the extent that in the ancient patriarchal world women are socially and physically more vulnerable than men, they would, if these rules became normative, find themselves less harassed. Of course, separation from men also disadvantaged women by limiting their opportunities for active participation in so many matters that affected them.

We find earlier in Kiddushin, 39b–40a, a set of three anecdotes that portray men very differently from the way they are portrayed above. In all three stories, a woman called a *matrona,* suggesting perhaps that she is a non-Jewish woman of the aristocracy, summons a man to engage in sexual relations with her. In all three cases, the men successfully resist her advances, one preferring to attempt suicide rather than succumb. He is saved by Elijah.

The context of these stories is being rewarded, even with a miracle, for keeping the mitzvot of the Torah. Unlike the men in the other set of stories, who cannot resist temptation, these men actively attempt to extricate themselves from the sexual situation in which they find themselves, even at serious risk to their lives. As a reward, they are saved from the *matrona's* overtures and, in the last case, also from the poverty that had initially placed the man at risk.

How can one reconcile these stories with the others? The *mishnah* in chapter 1 of Kiddushin talks about people who do good deeds and receive rewards for them, and the associated *gemara* brings the above set of stories in which men are portrayed as morally strong. The *mishnah* in chapter 4 of Kiddushin talks about men who should not be alone with women, implying that men cannot control their libido, and the *gemara* brings stories about men who succumbed to sexual temptation. Where, then, does the truth lie? Are men weak or strong in resisting sexual temptation? It seems to me that the *mishnah* that addresses the topic of relationships between the sexes, and its associated commentary, is the material to which we should turn for the rabbis' perception of men. The other set of passages describes unusual, heroic men. They are not to be confused with the majority.

Attitudes to Sexual Sin

R. Simon bar Rebbe says: Behold it says, "Restrain yourselves and do not eat the blood because the blood is the life . . . " (Deuteronomy

12:23). Just as in an instance of refraining from eating the blood, which a man finds repulsive, if he abstains he is rewarded, so too in an instance of appropriating the property of others and engaging in illicit sexual acts, *which a man is attracted to and lusts after* [מחמדתן], if he abstains—how much the more so should he merit [a reward] for generations to come! (M Makkot 3:15)

This source, which does not address relationships between men and women in a direct fashion, as does Kiddushin chapter 4, but is instead providing moral preaching at the end of a tractate, incidentally reveals social and psychological truths. Misappropriating the property of others and having sexual relations with the women forbidden to a man by the Torah are tempting acts because they speak to his deepest instincts. These are the activities that a man craves. The term *meHaMDatan* reminds us of the last of the ten commandments: "Do not lust *(lo taHMoD)* after a woman . . . or any [other] property belonging to someone else" (Exodus 20:17). Although rewards are usually given for actions that we take, in this case, simply not yielding to the ever-present desire to commit these illicit acts is grounds for reward, according to this rabbi. This moralistic *mishnah*, I think, sums up the rabbis' attitudes to relations between the sexes: No social relations between men and women are possible because men are preoccupied with sex. A man who seeks the companionship of women will merely be putting himself in a trying situation.

This passage accords well with the statements in Pirkei Avot and BT Nedarim, quoted in the discussion of the *Sotah*, that men should not talk much with women because it leads, unavoidably, to forbidden sexual liaisons. *Sihah*, which means banter or friendly chitchat, will lead to friendly feelings, which will lead, ultimately, to sexual activity. It seems to me that women's exclusion from the study of Torah with men is not linked to their intellectual level or their educational background or their penchant for sin. Rather, in a sex-segregated society, permitting women to interact freely with men would surely lead to sexual intimacy.[43]

Another telling text appears in the Tosefta.

> . . . R. Yosseh said in the name of Rabban Gamliel: Any man who has a trade, to what may he be compared? To a woman who has a husband: Whether she dresses herself up or not, no one will gaze upon her; and if she does not dress herself up, she should be cursed. A man who does not have a trade, to what may he be compared? To a woman without a husband: Whether she dresses herself up or not, everyone will gaze upon her; and if she does dress herself up, she should be cursed.[44] (T Kiddushin 1:11)

This statement, uttered incidentally in the context of a legal obligation, also gives us a sense of the social realities of the times. A woman was considered fair game if she did not have a man to protect her. Her behavior, modest or immodest, did not much matter. She would be gazed upon and would likely fall prey to sexual exploitation by men, regardless of her manner of dress, if she did not have a husband. It is not what is right or wrong that matters to men but what is possible and what is not, according to the rabbis here. Theirs is a rather pessimistic evaluation of men's predispositions. Only the protective presence of another man, the woman's husband, will stop men from acting on their base instincts. Note, also, the touch of irony: Despite the possible pitfalls involved—drawing the attention of other men—a husband expects his wife to dress up, to make herself as attractive as possible in order to maintain his sexual interest in her. This theme repeats itself in so many rabbinic texts that its general acceptance in those days is beyond question.[45] It seems to be a standard feature of a patriarchal culture: Those who are dependent on the patriarch must seek to please and satisfy him. Note the underlying message that the rabbis view marital sexual activity positively.

Men's Perception of Women's Sexuality

And the following women leave their husbands but are not given their marriage settlement: the ones who violate Mosaic or Jewish practice.

What constitutes [violation of] Mosaic practice? Feeding her husband untithed food, having sex with him while a *niddah* [a menstruant], not separating hallah, and taking a vow but not keeping her word.

What constitutes [violation of] Jewish practice? A woman who goes out to the market with her head uncovered, who spins in the marketplace, who engages in conversation with any man. . . . (M Ketubot 7:6)

The parallel passage in the Tosefta elaborates on this behavior:

If a husband took a vow that his wife give everyone a taste of the food [that she burnt],[46] or that she fill up and spill out on the dunghill [apparently a reference to nonprocreative sex], or that she speak to everyone of intimate matters between him and her, he must divorce her and pay the marriage settlement, because he has not treated her *according to Mosaic and Jewish practice.*

And similarly, if she goes out with her head uncovered, or goes out
with her clothing baring [parts of her body], if she has no modesty in
the presence of her male and female[47] servants or her neighbors, if she
goes and spins in the marketplace, or if she bathes herself and others[48]
[רוחצת ומרחצת במרחץ עם כל אדם] in the baths, she must leave without a *ketubah* because she has not behaved toward him *according to
Mosaic and Jewish practice*. (T Ketubot 7:6)

These passages accuse a woman of immodest, even sexually provocative
behavior, of deliberately trying to entice men to become sexually involved
with her. But such a woman is portrayed as one who strays from the right
path, who is not like most others. Considering her behavior egregious and
calling for divorce imply that most women, in the opinion of the rabbis, do
not behave in this way, despite their need for sexual satisfaction.

The passage from the Tosefta is remarkable in that it creates a symmetry
between men and women. Both of them can be accused of violating Jewish
practice, "dat moshe v'yisrael," although the *mishnah* calls it "dat moshe
v'yehudit," an older version of the same term. And each list of violations,
for him and for her, involves sexual misbehavior. His is forcing her, by
means of a vow, to share sexual intimacies with others, apparently in order
to heighten his sexual pleasure or to deliberately avoid procreative sex.[49]
Hers, as already mentioned, is immodest dress and behavior, bordering on
deliberate enticement.[50]

Elsewhere the Mishnah talks about the sexual needs of the average
woman:

If a husband takes a vow that he will not have sex with his wife: Bet
Shammai says, two weeks; Bet Hillel says, one week. (M Ketubot 5:6)

This passage says that if a man vows to deny his wife sexual activity for
one week, according to Bet Hillel, or two, according to Bet Shammai, he
must divorce her. This clear statement that women have conjugal rights in
marriage indicates that the rabbis recognized that women too, and not just
men, are desirous of sex.

The mishnah goes on to prescribe conjugal frequency for men engaged in
a variety of occupations.

Students may leave home without permission of their wives for up
to thirty days. Workers may leave for up to one week.

The conjugal duties prescribed by the Torah are: men of leisure,
every day; workers, twice a week; donkey drivers, once a week; camel
drivers, once in thirty days; and sailors, once in six months. This is the
opinion of R. Eliezer.

This passage is hard to understand. Were it not for men's expending energy on the job, and sometimes having to leave home for a period of time, the *mishnah* suggests that they would be sexually obligated to their wives every single day. But the Bavli interprets part of this passage from the *mishnah* in a way that virtually empties it of meaning. Saying that this view is R. Eliezer's only, as the *mishnah* itself states, the Bavli goes on to present the view of the Sages that a Torah scholar may leave his wife, *without* permission, for up to two or three years. The stories that follow, however, suggest that he will be sorry if he takes advantage of this leniency.[51]

> --Said Rava: Any scholar who makes use of this ruling takes his life in his hands. Like the case of R. Rehumi, a student of Rava's in Mehoza, who used to come home [from a long stay away] on the eve of Yom Kippur. One such day, he found himself very engrossed in his studies. His wife, looking forward to his return, kept saying, "Now he is coming, now he is coming." But he did not come. She lost hope and began to cry. He was sitting at that moment on a balcony. It collapsed from under him, he fell down, and he died. (BT Ketubot 62b)

Although R. Rehumi had permission to stay away for long periods of time, his absence was still considered by the rabbis to be abusive of his wife. When he reached the point of not even going home for a brief stay over the holidays, he gave up his right to life. This anecdote is perhaps more sympathetic to women than almost any other found in the Talmud: Even though the majority of rabbis give a scholar permission to favor the study of Torah over affording his wife (or even himself) sexual gratification, he will pay with his life if he chooses to ignore her human needs. Although not formally obligated to engage her sexually for years at a time, he is encouraged to do so as a decent and sensitive human being. He is in control of her: Although he can leave her to study and either come back or not, she has to stay at home. When in this dominant position, says Rava, he had better not forget about her or favor Torah study over her company.[52]

What is the difference, then, between men's and women's sexual nature and behavior in these rabbinic portrayals? The argument from silence is that women, in general, are *not* easily aroused by looking at men or being in their company; the sources indicate men *are* easily aroused by looking at women or being in their company. A woman will not, according to the rabbis, find herself involuntarily drawn to sexual transgression and fail to stop herself from seeking gratification. Women, as Samuel says (BT Ketubot 64b), keep their sexual urges within themselves, whereas men cannot contain them. All of the cited material indicates that only the unusual woman solicits a man for a sexual encounter. One should not assume that the rabbis thought that women lacked libido, however, simply because they did not imagine most women actively seeking sexual gratification. Women are, indeed, understood to possess libido, but given their subordination to men, they are not allowed the freedom to exercise it. In a patriarchal society, men could satisfy themselves as they saw fit, but women, whom they controlled and over whom they had a sexual monopoly, could not. That is, what may in fact be biological differences between men and women are aggravated by men's control over women. Note that these are men's views about what women want and how they behave; they do not, necessarily, reflect rabbinic reality.

Conclusions

The sources we have considered were written by men and for men. They make a very simple point: Seeing and being with women arouses men sexually. Often, the woman who arouses a man is forbidden to him. Since his arousal demands resolution, it is better for him not to put himself in circumstances in which arousal is likely. To that end, he should not spend time talking to women or being alone with them, even female members of his own family. This last category, which includes mothers, sisters, and daughters, leads the reader to believe that the Mishnah speaks of involuntary sexual arousal. It is hard to imagine, even in circumstances very different from our own, that a normal man would solicit his mother or daughter for sexual activity or that she would solicit him. We should also note that the effect of separation in a patriarchal social configuration was to protect women and children from sexual exploitation.

Nowhere have we seen a sense of women, in general, as responsible, through deliberate actions that they took, of tempting men to sin. It is only individual women about whom such reports appear. But note that it is men, in general, who succumb to sexual arousal with ease. This conclusion challenges those scholars who picture women as temptresses; they reach their conclusion by weaving together scattered aggadic passages, not by reading key halakhic passages in context.

Women's sexual arousal does not receive much commentary, although women's right to sexual gratification is dealt with extensively. The rabbis understood that women have sexual needs, dependent for satisfaction on the men who marry and control them. Recognizing the power that a husband has over his subordinate wife, the rabbis spell out in detail his obligations to her, above and beyond sex for the sake of procreation. There is no frequency of obligation on her part to him, most likely because initiating sexual activity was considered his prerogative. Even if she was also an initiator, his sexual rights did not need the same kind of protection that hers did.

Although we see here an accepting attitude toward sex, with the passage of time and possibly under the influence of foreign ideas, we can trace a less accepting attitude toward sex creeping into the rabbinic mind, as evidenced by some of the later stories. However, even when we look at the texts that view sex favorably, we find them demanding very modest public behavior. The rabbis expected women to cover themselves when they went out in public. A woman who bared her head or her arm was considered to be engaging in sexually provocative behavior, as was a woman who conversed freely with men, or who, in an even more extreme case, sported with them in the public baths.

And, finally, the linkage of sex and Torah came up once again: Sex is seen as a distracting force from Torah study, and conversely, Torah study is seen as a means of taking one's mind off sexual impulses. All these sources lead to the conclusion that the rabbis, like ordinary men, were engaged in a continuous battle with their libido. They were hoping that the intellectual and spiritual side of them would triumph over the physical. The material above does not lead us to think that they fully accomplished this goal.

Notes

1. Jacob Neusner, *Method and Meaning in Ancient Judaism*, Brown Judaica Series, no. 10 (Missoula, Mont.: Scholars Press, 1979), 97.

2. Wegner, *Chattel or Person?* (New York: Oxford University Press, 1988), 159–162.

3. David Biale, *Eros and the Jews* (New York: Basic Books, 1992), 57.

4. Leonie Archer, *Her Price Is Beyond Rubies: The Jewish Woman in Graeco-Roman Palestine,* Journal for the Study of the Old Testament Series, 60 (Sheffield: Sheffield Academic Press, 1990), 105.

5. Michael Satlow, *Tasting the Dish: Rabbinic Rhetorics of Sexuality* (Atlanta, Ga.: Scholars Press, 1995), 158.

6. It does seem to be the case, though, that over time, some rabbis began to display a negative attitude to the sexual urge, particularly in that it competed with the desire to study Torah. See further discussion.

7. See Albeck (415) for a slightly different interpretation of this *mishnah*. See Tosafot, s.v. *R. Simon*.

8. Since the Mishnah allows no seclusion of men with any women at all, even unmarried, it is concerned not just about the violation of Jewish law by men with married or consanguineous women but also about promiscuous behavior of men with unmarried women.

9. See Albeck (415) for an analysis of the phrase *yilmad soferim*. See also T AZ 3:2 (and next note).

10. T AZ 3:2 fears such sexual molestation if a gentile teacher is hired for a Jewish child. Kutheans are not suspected of such behavior (T AZ 3:1).

11. BT Kiddushin 82a; PT Kiddushin 4:11; 66c. The Bavli offers symmetrical explanations for male and female teachers; the Yerushalmi only explains why men may not serve as teachers. This possibly means that the Yerushalmi discounted the notion of women not teaching children.

12. Wegner (*Chattel or Person?* 160) cites BT Kiddushin 82a and says that the presence of a child will not discourage a woman or a man from fornicating with each other. Because women are viewed as morally lax, the *mishnah* does not distinguish between married and unmarried women. Ilan (*Jewish Women in Greco-Roman Palestine* [Tübingen: J.C.B. Mohr, 1995], 193) also interprets the *mishnah* according to the Talmud (PT Kiddushin 4:11; 66c).

13. An example would be reading by the light of an oil lamp, which may lead someone inadvertently to tilt the lamp to get it to burn more brightly and thereby kindle a flame on the Sabbath. See T Shabbat 1:12, 13.

14. Pagan slaves are regarded by the rabbis as individuals who are on their way to becoming Jewish. The rabbis required the owners of slaves to circumcise the males and obligated all slaves to observe all mitzvot except for the time-bound positive ones. Upon manumission a slave attained not just freedom but also Jewish status. Kutheans are people whose Samaritan ancestors converted to Judaism not on principle but out of fear. See 2 Kings 17:24ff. They are regarded by the rabbis as neither fully Jewish nor fully pagan.

15. Wegner (*Chattel or Person?* 160) comments: "The sages' androcentric perspective blames the dangers of private encounters between the sexes on women's moral laxity rather than on men's greater susceptibility to arousal." I disagree.

16. Samuel, as quoted later in the Gemara, does not make *any* exceptions to the rule of men not being alone with women, even relatives. He may derive his view from a literal understanding of this passage in the Tosefta.

17. M AZ 2:1 says, "One may not leave cattle in the inns of pagans because they are suspected of bestiality. Similarly, a woman may not be alone with non-Jews because they are suspected of sexual transgression." See also T AZ 3:2.

18. The possibility of self-gratification by means of masturbation is not raised here or anywhere else. The rabbis banned such behavior. See M Niddah 2:1, BT Niddah 13a-b, and PT Niddah 2:1; 49d. See a full discussion of this matter by Michael L. Satlow, "'Wasted Seed,' The History of a Rabbinic Idea," *HUCA* 65 (1994).

19. See Satlow, *Tasting the Dish*, 208–209.

20. Susan Treggiari, in *Roman Marriage: Iusti Coniuges from the Time of Cicero to the Time of Ulpian* (Oxford: Oxford University Press, 1991), 421, says that the Roman *matrona* could receive visitors during the day in the atrium, where she sat in a chair and supervised the work of the household. These visitors included tradesmen to whom she had given commissions, peddlers who laid their wares at her feet, men and women asking for favors, her own servants, and so on.

21. See the comments on this issue by Miriam Peskowitz, in her forthcoming book *Spinning Fantasies*. See also my chapter "Feminist Perspectives on Rabbinic Texts," in *Feminist Perspectives on Jewish Studies*, ed. Lynn Davidman and Shelly Tanenbaum (New Haven: Yale University Press, 1994), 45.

22. Tal Ilan, in "A Window onto the Public Domain—Jewish Women in the Time of the Second Temple," in *Eshnav Lehayeihen Shel Nashim B'Hevrot Yehudiot,* ed. Yael Azmon (Jerusalem: Mercaz Shazar, 1995), 47–62, says that rabbinic literature prescribes absolute separation of the sexes but that the picture that emerges from historical texts is different and is class based. Upper-class women behaved according to their own set of more-secluding norms, and poor women ac-

cording to more-relaxed norms. There is thus much variety in the lives of Jewish women in the land of Israel at that period of time.

23. Supporting this notion are the *mishnah*s in the sixth chapter of Shabbat that talk about jewelry and related items that a woman may and may not wear out into the street on the Sabbath. This implies that women dressed up and walked about in the public domain on the Sabbath.

24. Treggiari, *Roman Marriage* (423), says that the social activities of an upper-class matron included frequenting galleries, colonnades, temples, synagogues, theaters, the circus, the games, triumphs, and resorts outside Rome. Women played dice. Married women went out to visit their friends, met them at the baths, strolled with them in places of public resort, and so on.

25. The collection *Seder Elijah* is actually post-Talmudic. Individual passages like this one were probably circulating in the Talmudic period.

26. In its one other usage in the Bavli, this phrase makes reference to the belief that women, when tortured, will reveal secret information (BT Shabbat 33b). The phrase *kalei da'at*, with the two Hebrew words reversed, also appears in *Sifrei Bemidbar*, 103 (p. 102, Horowitz ed.), in association with the term *hedyotot*, simple people. It thus seems to have had two related but different meanings. *Kalut rosh*, also light-headedness, is a term that appears in BT Succah 51b, to describe the immodest behavior of women and men in the Temple on the holiday of Succot, during the feast of the water libation. Cf. Rashi (BT AZ 18b, s.v. *v'ikka d'amrei*), who says that Beruriah ridiculed the rabbis for saying that women were light-headed, in the sexually seducible sense.

27. The Gemara itself recognizes that this is far from the simple meaning of the verse.

28. Rav could not have known about R. Hanina b. Pappi, who lived several generations later. This appears to be a later addition. See discussion of this kind of heroic behavior further on in the chapter.

29. Note that his honorific was most likely conferred after, not before, this event. Cf. the story about (Rabbi) Elazar b. Durdaia, who lived his entire life dissolutely but repented at the end and was awarded the title Rabbi after he died (BT AZ 17a).

30. It is not clear who did so—household attendants or the people who brought the women to R. Amram's home.

31. Is this story a turning point in terms of how people view their innate sexual nature? Can we say that in the tannaitic period they accepted their sexual selves as a normal part of their being but that later, in the amoraic period, they were beginning to fight against and suppress their sexuality?

32. The Gemara (BT Sotah 21a) actually raises but then rejects this interpretation.

33. Some say that Ben Azzai wants them to learn Torah, i.e., to learn that merit protects an unfaithful wife, so that should they sin and drink and not immediately suffer punishment, they will understand that it is not that the waters are not effective but that their own accumulated merits are giving them a period of grace. See Kiddushin 30b, where the study of Torah is the antidote to the evil inclination. Torah, here, is not just knowledge but knowing that knowledge protects.

34. See Daniel Boyarin's fascinating analysis of this *mishnah* and its associated interpretation in the Bavli and Yerushalmi, in *Carnal Israel* (Berkeley: University of California Press, 1993), 174–180).

35. See BT Yoma 35b. The question addressed to an evil man, when he comes to judgment after death, is: Why didn't you spend time studying Torah? The Gemara answers that if he says, "Because I was handsome and had to attend to my sexual needs [נאה הייתי וטרוד ביצרי] [and this left me no time for Torah study]," then say to him, "Were you more handsome than Joseph? . . . "

36. A standard Talmudic technique is to use a smart woman to shame a silly man. See my chapter, "Images of Women in the Talmud," in *Religion and Sexism*, ed. Rosemary Ruether (New York: Simon and Schuster, 1974), 202–203.

37. The expression in the Talmud is, he put her in his *kanaf*. In the Bible, this term has sexual connotations, e.g., in Deut. 23:1. The context of the story clearly dictates that the grandfather's action should be interpreted sexually, but the commentators, apparently unable to address that rather unpleasant possibility, suggest it means his bosom or lap. Rashi is silent. Tosafot R'Y Hazaken, *ad locum*, says: He slept with her in bodily contact, meaning he put her inside his bedclothes [שהניחה תחת בגדי מטתו].

38. I am assuming that this permission extends to young granddaughters, too.

39. R. Hisda's statement is in BT Berakhot 24a: "If his children were still small, it is permitted [to recite Shema in bed with them naked, without a tallit separating them].

=="Until what age?

– –"Said R. Hisda: a girl, until three years and a day and a boy until nine years and a day.

– –"Some say: a girl, eleven years and a day and a boy, twelve years and a day." See also the section "Sex with a Minor," in Chapter 4.

40. M AZ 2:1, 2.

41. See the views cited in the opening paragraphs of this chapter.

42. See Amy-Jill Levine, Introduction, *"Women like This": New Perspectives on Jewish Women in the Greco-Roman World,* ed. Amy-Jill Levine (Atlanta, Ga.: Scholars Press, 1991), 22. Levine writes that Ben Sira's belief about the indiscriminate sexuality of women is typical of men in Mediterranean culture. See also Judith Wegner's "Philo's Portrayal of Women—Hebraic or Hellenic?" in the same volume.

43. As we see elsewhere (BT Ketubot 13a), speaking with a woman can serve as a euphemism for sexual relations with her. Still, in this case, the verb "to speak" seems to have been intended literally.

44. This is the reading of the text that Lieberman prefers (*Tosefta Kiddushin*, 280), as it appears in the Erfurt ms.

45. See, for example, BT Ta'anait 23b, the statement by Abba Hilkiah and the discussion between R. Mani and R. Yitzhak b. Elyashiv. See also "Self-examination and Sexual Relations" and "R. Akiva's Intentional Leniencies," in Chapter 7.

46. Lieberman, *Tosefta Ketubot,* 80.

47. Lieberman prefers the Erfurt manuscript's version of this line that does not include "female servants" (ibid.).

48. The Erfurt ms. does not include the word *"marhezet"* (she bathes others).

49. It seems to me that having others taste her food is also a sexual reference. The common thread of most violations in the Tosefta is sexual. Lieberman (*Tosefta Ketubot,* 80) holds otherwise.

50. The Tosefta makes it clear that men and women alike can behave immodestly. When the Mishnah redacted this same *halakhah,* however, it did not call the men's actions a violation of sexual norms, as it did women's provocative behavior, but simply listed two out of three of these items, ruling that in such cases he must divorce her and pay the marriage settlement (M 7:5). That is, the Mishnah does not make the point that men, too, can violate "dat moshe v'yisrael" or "yehudit": Even though it does not legally tolerate these same behaviors, it does not call them by the name that it calls women's sexual immodesty. The Mishnah also redefines "dat moshe v'yehudit" for women, separating it into two types of behavior, with the first being a new category of unacceptable behavior: She deceives him regarding her performance of mitzvot that he relies on her to perform, when he has no way of knowing whether she did what was expected of her or not. The second is sexually provocative behavior, as already described by the Tosefta. This phrase is part of the ancient betrothal formula. It is appropriated by the Tannaim as a behavioral standard. See Chapter 5, note 23.

51. See Shulamit Valler, *Women and Womanhood in the Babylonian Talmud* (Tel Aviv: Hakibbutz Hameuchad, 1993), 56–80, for an analysis of this entire section. See the rest of her book for other examples of the discrepancies between prescriptive law and rabbinic decisions in specific cases.

52. See Boyarin's analysis of this episode, *Carnal Israel,* 146ff.

3

Marriage

SINCE MOST ANCIENT SOCIETIES were patriarchal in structure, it is not surprising to discover that rabbinic society was patriarchal as well. In the rabbinic conception of marriage, a man took a woman to be his wife and could dismiss her at will. He managed all the finances and could, if he wished, cancel, or annul, her vows and even bar her from talking to other men or going out of the house.

But throughout the rabbinic period changes were taking place. By the time it ended, women had acquired many more rights. They occupied a new status, one closer to men's. Although in certain areas they were more equal to men and in others less, in no marital area were women treated merely as chattel or fully as equal.[1]

Nearly every one of the biblical institutions relating to marriage was maintained by the rabbis but radically transformed. It is impossible to know if these transformations were the consequence of rabbinic invention or the infiltration of new ideas from other cultures. Or maybe they were the formal record of what had already been established generations earlier. Whatever the case may be, we find in the rabbinic materials a wholehearted endorsement of these changes and, possibly even more important, justification of these changes by means of legal arguments or scriptural interpretation.

The main change we shall observe is that marriage evolved over time from the purchase of a woman from her father to a kind of "social contract" entered into by a man and a woman, albeit with him dominant and her subordinate. The critical difference between her old status in marriage as chattel-like and her new status as "second-class citizen" is that she acquired, in exchange for sexual and other service to her husband, a wide array of rights and protections.

The Framework of Jewish Marriage

The first topic we will examine is the marriage document, or *ketubah*. Some have called it one of the most progressive pieces of rabbinic legislation.[2]

The principal provision of the *ketubah* is that the husband or his estate will pay a stipulated amount of money to the wife upon dissolution of the marriage by death or divorce. She will be allowed no other claims on him or his estate. In Roman marriage, an institution familiar to the rabbis, a woman did not receive this type of payment. Rather, a wife whose Roman marriage was dissolved retrieved only the dowry that she brought into it.[3] Unlike the husband of the rabbinic marriage, who was required to pay out of his pocket the amount he promised in the *ketubah*, the husband in a Roman marriage made no additional payments from his own resources. Mishnah Ketubot opens with a discussion of the statutory amount of the marriage settlement.

A virgin, her *ketubah* is 200 [zuz] and a widow [or any previously married woman or a non-virgin], hers is 100. . . . (M Ketubot 1:2)

The difference in "price" between the virgin and the previously married woman, which appears throughout the legislation about marital matters, is not explained or derived from verses but presented as a given. A premium on a virgin was commonplace in the ancient world and continues today in many places. It tells us that one way of looking at marriage is the acquisition of a woman by a man for the purpose of sexual gratification. The rules reflect a male perspective: He is most pleased if the woman he acquires for himself has not previously known, in a sexual sense, any other man. He will be the first. Making the amount of the marriage settlement vary so significantly with the presence or absence of virginity says, in very clear terms, that her sexual status is a major factor in his choice of a wife. Elsewhere we learn that her lineage also matters.[4]

This opening *mishnah* of tractate Ketubot sets the stage for the discussion of marriage. Other *mishnah*s later in the tractate address various aspects of the marital relationship. Beyond making herself available to him sexually, the wife is expected to perform the basic household tasks.

These are the chores that a woman performs for her husband: She grinds [the grain], bakes, and launders; she cooks and nurses her child; she makes his bed and works in wool. (M Ketubot 5:5)

The passage goes on to allow her to assign these jobs to others, as long as she makes sure that they are fulfilled.

As for his obligations to her:

A father has the right to betroth his daughter . . . and he is entitled
to whatever she finds or earns; and he may cancel her vows . . . but he
is not entitled to the income of her assets in her lifetime. When she
marries, her husband has more rights and privileges [than her father]:
He is also entitled to the income of her assets, even in her lifetime; he
is obligated to support her, to redeem her [if taken captive], and to
bury her. . . . (M Ketubot 4:4)

If he appoints a third party to manage his financial obligations to
his wife, . . . he must give her a *kippah*(!)[5] for her head, a belt for her
waist, shoes on the holidays, clothing valued at 50 zuz each year . . .
spending money. . . . (M Ketubot 5:8, 9)

Notice that his financial outlay for support and other payments is offset
by his right to the usufruct of her assets and to any other moneys that she
earns or anything she finds.

All these rules describe a situation in which she enters his home, provides a wide variety of service to him, has all her needs met by him, and is
even promised a lump sum payment by him upon dissolution of the marriage. But the arrangement is rather uneven: He controls her time, her activities, and her money; she does not control his. For this reason she, but
not he, needs a guarantee of basic rights. The general social construction of
Jewish marriage in the Bible and Talmud is, thus, sexist in the extreme.
This is not surprising for the ancient world. What is surprising, however,
are the rules the Mishnah institutes to modify this state of affairs. As we
examine selected passages on marriage, we will see in each case how its
sexist bias was altered but not eradicated.

The Marriage Contract: From Bride-Price to Ketubah

The changes that took place in the payments associated with marriage are
probably the best indication of an evolving rabbinic perception of the nature of marriage. The following derivation, although rather intricate,
makes a simple point: The *ketubah* is based on Scripture. The verses about
rape and seduction that will be cited are the only legal passages in the
Pentateuch that make explicit reference to the exchange of marital moneys.

. . . Have we not learned in a *baraita*: "He [the seducer] shall weigh
out silver according to the bride-price of virgins" (Exodus 22:16).
[This implies] that the [fine of the seducer] should be like the bride-
price of virgins [paid by the groom,[6] an amount of fifty shekels] and
the bride-price of virgins should be like this [like the fine of the seducer, paid in silver shekels]. From here the rabbis learned [מכאן

סמכו חכמים[7]] that the *ketubah* was stipulated by the Torah. R. Simon b. Gamliel says: The *ketubah* was not stipulated by the Torah but by the rabbis [מדברי סופרים]. (BT Ketubot 10a)

According to the first view expressed in this passage, the words "the bride-price of virgins," that is, the fifty silver shekels that the husband paid to the father of the bride (Deuteronomy 22:29) in normal circumstances, not just following rape or seduction, imply the establishment of the *ketubah*. But the *ketubah* is not a bride-price. On the contrary, the differences between the two are so great that it is at first hard to understand how anyone could see those words as the scriptural basis for the *ketubah*. The bride-price of virgins is paid to the father by the husband at the time of marriage, whereas the *ketubah* is paid to the woman herself, upon the dissolution of the marriage by death or divorce. That is, it is paid at the end, not at the beginning; it is paid to her, not to her father. Therefore, one can only argue that the *ketubah* is Torah mandated in the broad sense of a marriage payment. The following passages clarify this matter by pinpointing the "historical" reasons for this change.

> . . . And a man may not say to his wife [upon betrothal]: Behold, your *ketubah* is on the table. Rather, all of his assets are responsible for the payment of her *ketubah*. (M Ketubot 8:8)

This *mishnah,* and even more so the *baraita* that follows, imply that it used to be the case that a man could acquire a wife by putting her *ketubah* moneys on the table, that is, paying for her in advance. But this practice was later outlawed. Instead, the man had to create a lien on all of his assets and make them responsible for the payment of the *ketubah*. Should he die leaving insufficient funds for the payment of the *ketubah*, she could seize properties purchased from him by others after he married her. She was first creditor on his estate.

The Gemara gives a fuller account of this transformation.

> --R. Judah said: At first they used to write[8] for a virgin 200 zuz and for a widow 100. And the [men] would grow old and not marry. Until Simon b. Shetah came and enacted that all of his [the groom's] assets are responsible for the payment of the *ketubah*.
>
> It was also taught thus in a *baraita:*
>
> At first they used to write for a virgin 200 zuz and for a widow 100. And they, [the men], would grow old and not marry.
>
> So the rabbis instituted [a change]: They would place it in her father's home. But still, when he would grow angry with her, he would say, go [home] to your *ketubah*.

So they instituted [a further change]: They would put it in her father-in-law's home. Rich women would fashion it into baskets of silver and gold and poor women into brass tubs. And still, when he grew
angry with her, he would say, take your *ketubah* and leave.

[This obtained] until Simon b. Shetah came and instituted that he
write for her that all of his assets are responsible for the payment of
the *ketubah*. (BT Ketubot 82b)

This text is hard to understand. First, what is the relationship between
the statement of R. Judah—the Amora, not the Tanna—and the older passage, the *baraita*, that follows? They seem to be saying the same thing in
the same words. Why would an Amora repeat verbatim the first and last
clause of a *baraita*? Second, and even more serious, parts of the *baraita*
make no sense.

R. Judah says that men did not marry because they could not afford to
put either 200 or 100 zuz on the table at the outset of the marriage. At that
early period in their lives they were not in a position to make such a large
outlay of cash to the father of the bride. The *baraita* begins by repeating
the first part of R. Judah's statement verbatim. It continues and says that
they would put the *ketubah* in her father's home in order to solve the problem. How the new location solves the problem of a young man's inability
to give up such large sums in cash is not at all clear. However, if we over-
look this difficulty, we see that this "solution" created a new problem: It
made divorce too easy. Since no financial outlay was required for divorce,
if a groom lost his temper, he could simply ask his bride to leave.
Therefore, to promote the stability of marriage, the rabbis decreed that the
ketubah be placed in the marital home, that of the groom's father, where
the bride could then turn the moneys into silver or gold or brass utensils.
But since divorce still required no financial outlay, the groom could easily
dismiss her along with the utensils that she had fashioned from the money.

Marriage was stabilized only with the advent of Simon b. Shetah, who
arranged for the groom not to lay out the money in advance, upon taking a
wife, but to defer payment until the dissolution of the marriage. This defer-
ral solved two problems at once: one, young men's inability to part with
large sums of cash at the time of marriage; second, men's impulsive divorce
of their wives. Not only did Simon b. Shetah's solution encourage a man to
marry, but it also discouraged him from divorce, which became too costly:
He would have to liquidate assets in order to pay the marriage settlement.
Since the husband could no longer simply send his wife out with the *ketubah* utensils in hand, many a marriage could be saved. By the time the
husband was able to raise the money that he needed to pay her settlement,
he had calmed down and come to the realization that he did not want to
divorce her.

According to this source, the monetary arrangements in effect before the time of Simon b. Shetah were akin to the bride-price of the Bible, money paid up front. Simon b. Shetah transformed marital moneys owed by the husband from a prepayment into a deferred payment, thereby creating the *ketubah* as we know it. We thus find that both the Sages and R. Simon b. Gamliel, mentioned earlier, are right: The origin of the *ketubah* as we know it is both biblical and rabbinic.

The above *baraita,* which, as we noted, seems illogical, is actually the conflation of two distinct sources—the preceding amoraic statement by R. Judah, which looks at the change from a male perspective, and Simon b. Shetah's rather radical change in practice, which looks at the issue from a woman's perspective or at least from the point of view that women, in general, do not want to be summarily dismissed by their husbands. R. Judah read the tannaitic source, which also appears in slightly different form in both the Tosefta and the PT:[9] Those passages talk about the need to stabilize marriage to benefit women but make no reference to men's hardships at that period of time. R. Judah added that, in his opinion, this change benefited men too by putting marriage within the reach of most of them, rich or poor. Over the course of time, his statement, which appeared in the Bavli text right before the *baraita* because it was based on it, was assimilated by the *baraita,* probably because the two statements were, in many ways, similar. As a result, the *baraita* became hard to understand and his statement became superfluous.[10]

The image of men in this *baraita* is not flattering. A husband's decision to divorce did not follow a lengthy period of introspection and deliberation but was based on a whim: For some reason, most likely slight, he grew angry with his wife and decided to send her away. Only later did he realize that his hasty actions would hurt him as well as her. In fact, this image of impulsivity reappears in many different places in the Talmud, in particular with respect to *kohanim,* who, if they divorce a wife in a fit of pique, are not allowed to take her back.[11] The Talmud makes the standard assumption that one cannot trust men to act rationally when embroiled with their wives over some matter, large or small. When Bet Hillel says, at the end of Mishnah Gittin, that a man is within his rights to divorce his wife even if the only unseemly thing she did was burn the food (M Gittin 9:10), they are probably making reference to this same emotional instability.[12] R. Judah, by explaining the transformation of the *ketubah* from prepayment to deferred payment in terms of men's financial straits and not their hotheadedness, as does the *baraita,* redeems their image.

This transformation of the *ketubah* from bride-price to marriage settlement benefits women. Although the price structure did not change—virgins were still valued more than nonvirgins—the woman was paid the money directly, at a time when she needed it, in between marriages or facing years to come as a widow. In addition, she may have benefited from the obstacles that paying this money placed in the way of a quick and easy divorce. Couples in marital trouble may have remained together because of the difficulties of getting divorced.

The question now arises: Once the *ketubah* was transformed into a terminal payment, a way of providing a woman with some assets to tide her over into her next marriage, then why was the *ketubah* of a virgin twice the amount of the *ketubah* of a previously married woman or nonvirgin? The *ketubah*, as a deferred payment, was no longer a gauge of her sexual intactness.

The distinction seems to be a carryover from the bride-price era. It was not discarded because the notion that "unused" women are worth more and are more desirable than "used" women still resonated deeply within the (male) population. If nothing else, this distinction was an incentive to women to remain virgin, in anticipation of an easier "retirement" at the end of marriage. But it is also true that this distinction paled in significance once the rabbis had instituted a voluntary payment called "*tosefet ketubah*," additional moneys written into the *ketubah*, to be paid upon dissolution of the marriage. These did not vary with a woman's sexual history. As M Ketubot 5:1 states, "If he wishes to obligate himself to an additional 10,000 zuz, he could do so." It would seem, then, that the *ketubah* monetary stipulations varied with the economic status of the husband and did not reflect, for the most part, the virginal or nonvirginal state of the bride. So, although the 200 and 100 zuz payments appear frequently in rabbinic literature and suggest that virgins were treated differently from nonvirgins, those sums were only a starting point, not the actual price agreed on. The difference between virgins and nonvirgins thus appears to have lost much of its financial significance no later than the time of the Mishnah.[13]

What we have seen so far does not yet qualify the *ketubah* as one of the "most progressive pieces of rabbinic legislation," even though the document, as it was written then and as it is still written today, does enable her to collect a stipulated amount from his estate and receive her dowry intact upon dissolution of the marriage. We must also look at other rules associated with the *ketubah* that were not necessarily included in writing but were obligatory nonetheless. They are called "stipulations of the court" [תנאי בית דין] because they could be upheld in a court of law. It is the combined set of written and unwritten benefits that allows the *ketubah* to be properly considered a landmark document.

The additional stipulated benefits are as follows:

1. If she is taken captive, he will redeem her and take her back as his wife, even if she was raped in captivity. This rule does not hold for the wife of a *kohen*, who promises only that he will return her to her home, not that he will resume his marital relationship with her.[14] A *kohen*, according to

the rabbis, may not live with a wife who had sex with someone else while married to the *kohen*, even if the sex was not consensual (M Ketubot 4:8).

2. If she falls ill, he must provide her with medical care (M 4:9).

3. If she predeceases her husband, her sons—and not his sons from other wives—inherit the *ketubah* money that her husband never had to pay out to her, as well as her dowry (M 4:10).

4. If she outlives her husband, her daughters will be able to continue to live in the same house and receive support from his estate until they marry (M 4:11).

5. If she outlives her husband, she has the right to remain in his house and maintain herself from his assets for as long as she lives there (M 4:12).

In a sense, this is a complete insurance policy. She will be provided for if catastrophe strikes during the marriage. She will be provided for after she is widowed. Her children will be provided for after the death of her husband: Her sons will inherit his estate as well as hers and her daughters will be maintained by it.

Having reviewed these laws, we must now ask again: What does the *ketubah* tell us about social structures? We learn from it that a married woman is dependent upon her husband and needs to have her rights protected. No *ketubah* is written for him, not because he had fewer rights, but because he had, in the past, *all* the rights and resources. He alone makes promises to her, whereas she makes none to him. So even though the *ketubah* guaranteed many rights that women would not have had otherwise, still, the married woman's need to have a *ketubah* drawn up for her indicated, very clearly, that she was under her husband's thumb: He controlled all the financial assets of the family and could dole them out to her as he saw fit.

We thus see that as enlightened a document as the *ketubah* is, it was necessary only because the society in which women lived and the laws that that society developed were patriarchal. Since the *ketubah* consolidates some basic rights for women, even though it leaves patriarchy in place, it was an improvement over what was the case prior to the time it was instituted, the bride-price. But this transformation of the bride-price into the *ketubah* benefited women not only for the reasons stated in the *baraita*. By deferring the *ketubah* payment to the end of the marriage, the nature of marriage could no longer be described as the purchase of a bride from her father. As long as the bride-price was paid at the outset, marriage had to be looked upon as a purchase. But from the time that the *ketubah* was paid at the end, the arrangements at the beginning of the marriage are more correctly termed negotiation rather than purchase. I think the importance of this paradigm shift for women cannot be overestimated. The patriarchal construction of marriage, although certainly not dismantled with the development of the *ketubah*, was significantly altered. Marriage became a relationship into which two people entered. Even though the man and woman were not on equal footing, they worked out the details between themselves, as we will now see.

A look at betrothal procedures will provide further evidence of this trend toward greater women's participation.

The Betrothal:
From Purchase to "Social Contract"

Chapter 1 of Tractate Kiddushin opens with the basic rules of betrothal.

> A woman is acquired in three ways and buys herself [back] in two ways. She is bought by money, a document, or sexual intercourse.
>
> By money: Bet Shammai says with a dinar or something worth a dinar; but Bet Hillel says, with a perutah [copper coin of least value] or something worth a perutah. . . .
>
> And she buys herself back with a *get* or by means of the death of her husband. (M Kiddushin 1:1)
>
> A Hebrew [Jewish] slave is bought by money or a document. And he buys himself [back] with years [that is, the end of his period of indenture], the jubilee [which sets him free], or paying [back] the difference. . . . (M 1:2)
>
> A Canaanite slave is bought by money, a document, or being taken possession of. . . . (M 1:3)
>
> A large animal is bought by handing it over. . . . (M 1:4)
>
> Real estate is bought by money, a document, or being taken possession of. . . . (M 1:5)

This chapter deals with how a person/man buys various kinds of property, both animate and inanimate. The wife's position at the head of the list indicates that she is the most important and precious kind of property, but property nonetheless. Moreover, the means listed for buying women are virtually identical to the means listed for acquiring other items. Note also that acquiring a woman by sexual intercourse is parallel to taking possession [הזקה] of a slave or field. That is, in this context, sex is something that he does to her to demonstrate that he owns her and wields power over her. Not an uncommon feminist observation in the contemporary world as well.

But more subtle points are being made here. If we move beyond the remarkable similarities between buying women and buying fields, we see that there are equally remarkable differences. The amount paid for fields corresponds to their value, as does the amount paid for the other items listed. The amount paid for a woman may be minimal. It can be described in no way other than symbolic: The perutah and the dinar (zuz) are the smallest units of currency, the first in copper and the second in silver. These legal differences show that acquiring a woman may be identical *in form* to acquiring a variety of other objects, but it is not similar *in content*. The form of purchasing a woman has been maintained over time, even to this very day in traditional circles, but the essence of the transaction changed. Notice also that the money for betrothal, or the object worth money, such as a ring, is presented to the object of betrothal herself, the woman, who is the focus of the first *mishnah,* and not to a third party, as is the case with the purchase of a slave and as used to be the case with women.

This first *mishnah* of the chapter, therefore, when it lines up betrothal with all the other salable items and the rules of how they are acquired, makes it look like a purchase. And that is what it used to be. But the difference in the rules for buying women and all other items indicates that acquiring a wife was no longer simply a purchase but a negotiated contract. According to this *mishnah,* marriage occupies a mediate place on the continuum: It is neither a purchase of chattel nor a relationship between equals. It is somewhere in the middle.

The move away from marriage as a purchase is borne out by the *mishnah*'s terminology. The term *kinyan* (purchase) in relationship to marriage appears here and in several other places,[15] but it is superseded in most instances by the term *kiddushin,* the name of the tractate, the root of which is K-D-SH, meaning holy or set aside. Marriage is an arrangement in which a man sets aside a woman to be his wife. She does not set him aside to be her husband, for he may marry more than one woman. Despite this imbalance, the standard rabbinic term for betrothal, *kiddushin,* unlike its biblical equivalent, *erusin,*[16] suggests that marriage has now been infused with a sense of sanctification.

Chapters 2 and 3 of Kiddushin deal with standards for the betrothal formula and moneys, as well as stipulations that accompany the betrothal and the need for there to be no misunderstanding or deception on the part of either side as to what he or she is getting in a mate. If there is, the transaction is invalidated. The importance of these rules for our inquiry is that they affect the bride in the same way that they affect the groom, thus providing another indication of the changing nature of betrothal. The fourth and last chapter deals with lineage and the need for a groom to check a bride's background before betrothing her. She need not check his, however.

Consent to the Betrothal

The Tosefta introduces yet another matter that supports the distinction between marriage and purchase.

[If he said,] "Be betrothed to me with this sela [coin, worth 4 zuzim]," and if, when she took it out of his hand, she threw it into the ocean or into a river, she is not betrothed.

"Be betrothed to me with a maneh [100 zuz]," and she said to him, "give it to so-and-so," she is not betrothed. "That so-and-so accept it on my behalf," she is betrothed. . . . (T Kiddushin 2:8)

If he is counting [out the coins] and dropping them into her hand, one by one, she may change her mind until he finishes. (T 2:9)

Implicit in a number of these statements is the notion that a woman's consent is necessary for betrothal. That is, if she flings the betrothal moneys he presents to her into the ocean, she is making a clear statement that she is rejecting him. But if she accepts the tokens of betrothal, she indicates her consent. Similarly, if, when he offers her the betrothal object, she asks him to give it instead to a third party, that again indicates that she is turning him down. But if she asks him to give the object to someone who will accept it for her, then she indicates acceptance of his offer. Finally, if it takes time for him to transfer the full sum of the betrothal money to her, she may retract up until the moment that he hands her the last coin. This statement makes it almost explicit that a woman must consent to the betrothal for it to be valid. Any indication on her part that she refuses his proposal prevents the betrothal from taking effect. Consent, in all of these instances, is indirect.

Elsewhere the Tosefta notes that betrothal takes effect—allows the groom to *purchase* the bride—only if both of them consent (T Yevamot 2:1).[17] But a woman's *consent* to be *purchased* in marriage makes little sense. It seems that the language of purchase, which was an accurate representation of the transaction in the Bible, has become standard terminology for marriage, even as the nature of the marital transaction was undergoing significant change. This supports the point made above that the Mishnah's (1:1) occasional use of the verb K-N-H, to purchase, in describing betrothal, does not necessarily imply that the substance of the transaction tallied with its descriptive term.[18]

Direct negotiation with the woman herself is how most of the *mishnah*s and *baraita*s picture the betrothal. If we add to that the requirement that she give her consent, which would not have been the case if her father betrothed her, we see a move in the direction of transforming a betrothal from a purchase into a "social contract." Note, however, that although the Tosefta, Bavli, and Yerushalmi all require that a woman consent to an offer of betrothal, the Mishnah does not. This may be evidence of a more conservative point of view of the redactor of the Mishnah, a stance he espoused in reference to other issues as well.[19]

The Bavli brings, in conjunction with its citation of a variation of one of the cited *baraita*s (T 2:8), a number of related amoraic questions, all with the purpose of establishing boundaries for consent. No one suggests that a woman be required to say aloud that she consents to the marriage, as is standard in most secular wedding ceremonies today. Rather, the rabbis discuss different ways in which consent can be demonstrated.

> ––A man was selling strings of [glass] beads. A woman came by and said to him, "Give me one strand." He said to her, "If I give it to you, will you marry me?" She said, "Give, give." Said R. Hama: A statement like "give, give" has no legal validity.
> ––A man was drinking beer in a store. A woman came in and said to him, "Give me a drink." He said, "If I do so, will you marry me?" She said, "Give me a drink." Said R. Hama, a statement like "give me a drink" has no legal validity.
> ––A man was throwing [down] dates from a palm tree. A woman came by and said, "Throw me [down] two dates." He said to her, "If I do so, will you marry me?" She said, "Throw, throw." Said R. Zevid: A statement like "throw, throw" has no legal validity. (BT Kiddushin 9a)

In each of these cases the question that the rabbi must address is whether the woman's response to the man's proposal constitutes consent. In all three the decision is that it does not. She wanted what she wanted, but it was not marriage. The three stories give the impression that this exchange between him and her is innocent banter. We see a woman who is flirting with a man in the public domain—a market, a store, or a palm tree somewhere—and in response to his rather flippant betrothal offer, simply reiterates what she said in the first place. She is playing a game with him, as is he with her. She initiates the conversation in what appears to be a mildly provocative manner, he intensifies it with a betrothal offer, and she dodges the question in response. This is about as contemporary as a Talmudic anecdote can get. The rabbi in each case understands that this is not a proposal of marriage followed by an acceptance.

All those decisions taken together, most of which rule that the woman's response does not indicate consent, show that the Bavli sees betrothal as something that he offers to her, but to which she, either explicitly or implicitly, must give consent.[20] These rulings narrow the definition of consent, clearly benefiting women. If she were thought to be consenting when she was not, she would need a *get* from, or be forced to live with, a man she did not want. I think that the requirement of consent puts to rest the concept of marriage as a purchase.

Women's Initiation of Betrothal

Another development favoring women is the discussion of their initiation of and participation in the betrothal ceremony by giving the betrothal gift. To the extent that she plays a role in the betrothal process, she is functioning more as partner to her husband and less as subordinate. In this instance we will see change and development within the Talmudic period itself.

The Tosefta restricts a woman from participating in any way in the betrothal ceremony.

> How does a man betroth a woman with money? If he gives her money, or something worth money, and he says to her, "Behold you are betrothed to me" . . . , she is betrothed. But if she gives him money or something worth money and says, "Behold I am betrothed to you," . . . , she is not betrothed. (T Kiddushin 1:1)

It is interesting that the Tosefta felt it necessary to raise the possibility of a woman's initiating the betrothal procedure. By way of comparison, when discussing divorce, no one suggests that a woman write a bill of divorce for a man. It is, therefore, tempting to conclude that a woman betrothing a man was thinkable in the ancient, rabbinic world. I say this because the Bavli, in its commentary on this very *baraita*, explores this possibility (5b). At first, it rules out women's participation, deciding that if a man issued the betrothal statement but a woman gave the betrothal gift, that there is "doubtful betrothal": She is not his wife, but even so she may not become betrothed to someone else until this man writes her a bill of divorce. This implies that her participation may have had legal standing. A little later in the discussion, Rava, a prominent Amora, presents several unusual cases of betrothal with the participation of a third party. He brings his sequence to a climactic conclusion by asking about women who propose to men and actively participate in the betrothal proceedings.

> – –Rava said:
> 1. [If a woman says to a man,] give 100 zuz to so-and-so, and I will become betrothed to you, she is betrothed [if he does so]. . . .
> 2. [If a man says to a woman,] here is 100 zuz and be betrothed to so-and-so, she is betrothed [if she accepts it]. . . .
> 3. [If a woman says to a man,] give 100 zuz to so-and-so and I will become betrothed to him, she is betrothed [if he does so and the designated husband accepts it]. . . . (BT Kiddushin 6b–7a)

In two out of these three cases a woman initiated the betrothal ceremony and requested that a sum of money be given either by the groom to a third party or by a third party to the groom. We assume, in all of these instances, that the groom then recited the betrothal formula to her.[21] Betrothals like these, in which either the woman does not receive betrothal money or the man does not give it, or both, are valid, says Rava. Weaving these cases together, he then asks:

4. [If a woman says,] here is 100 zuz and I will become betrothed to you, what is the law?
--Said Mar Zutra in the name of R. Pappa: She is betrothed.
--Said R. Ashi to Mar Zutra: If so . . .
--He responded: . . . We are dealing here with a man of means. With the pleasure she receives from his accepting the betrothal gift from her, she consents to the betrothal [that is, he gives her pleasure worth a penny and in this way the betrothal, although initiated by her, has been performed by him: He recites the betrothal formula and gives her a betrothal gift—pleasure worth a penny].

Rava has constructed a remarkable set of cases. After establishing several legal principles in cases involving three people—the bride, the groom, and a third party—he collapses the three-person scenario into a two-person one, and asks what the law is in a case in which she makes the betrothal presentation to him. The answer flows logically from his previous statements: The betrothal is valid. Furthermore, he seems to have constructed his previous three statements for the express reason of arriving at the fourth—which goes beyond the first three—the initiation of betrothal and the presentation of betrothal moneys by a woman to a man. Given the skill with which Rava drafted the first three cases, Mar Zutra's immediate response is unsurprising: In such a case, the betrothal is valid. But, in the following generation, R. Ashi voices an objection based on a technicality and Mar Zutra finds it necessary to restrict his position: A woman may initiate betrothal proceedings and make the betrothal gift only when the man in whom she is interested is a man of means, whose acceptance of her offer will give her pleasure worth a penny, which can then be considered the man's betrothal gift to her.

We thus see that the extent of women's involvement in initiating and performing the betrothal ceremony expanded over time. First raised and rejected by the Tosefta, it becomes permissible, within limits, in the later amoraic period. Notice that the amoraic case is not just the offering of a betrothal gift by a woman to a man, but the initiation by her of a particular match. Did this reflect social realities of women proposing betrothal to men? That could very well be so, because we find several instances in tannaitic literature in which women choose husbands.[22] Note, also, the changing model of marriage. Although we began with women being married off by their fathers and then moved on to women needing to consent to the betrothal offer, we have now reached the opposite end of the continuum, women themselves initiating the betrothal and actively participating in it.

Conclusions

This selection of passages dealing with marriage shows us that there were, over time, significant changes in how it was contracted. The father recedes as a key player and the woman, who will be taken in marriage by the man, approaches center stage, becomes the focus of attention. Her consent is required; she may even initiate the betrothal discussions and present the groom with the betrothal moneys. Most important, the bride-price of virgins, which used to be paid in advance, was turned into a lien on the husband's real assets and deferred to the time of dissolution of the marriage by death or divorce. That, probably more than any of the other changes, transformed marriage from a purchase of "chattel" into a negotiated relationship between a woman who is subordinate and a man who is dominant. Note that it is only she whose rights have to be guaranteed in a *ketubah*.

This study is not intended to cover all aspects of marriage as presented in the Talmud. Instead, I have attempted to show, through selection of topics within the general category of marriage, that this institution was undergoing extensive, and perhaps radical, change in the rabbinic period. Although we cannot say that the change approximated treating women equally with men (which is probably the goal of much legislation within Jewish circles today, particularly in the area of marital law), the inescapable conclusion is that the general thrust of rabbinic legislation regarding marriage still seems to have intended to confer, or at least had the effect of conferring, more rights and benefits on women and on men at the same time. This is not a circumstance in which the more they give the woman, the more they deny the man, but rather one in which the more she gains, the more he gains.

Notes

1. Judith Wegner (*Chattel or Person?* [New York: Oxford University Press, 1988], 19) maintains that women are treated as chattel with respect to any matter affecting a man's proprietary interest in their sexuality or reproductive abilities and as person with respect to all others. However, the details do not tally with this theory. For example, in sexual areas she was not chattel, since she had conjugal rights (see Chapter 2); in civil areas she was not equal, because as long as she was married to him she had no right to dispose of any of her property (M Ketubot 8:1).

2. Jacob Neusner, *Judaism: The Evidence of the Mishnah* (Chicago: University of Chicago Press, 1982), 191.

3. Susan Treggiari, *Roman Marriage* (Oxford: Oxford University Press, 1991), 323ff.

4. Chapter 4 of M Kiddushin deals extensively with investigating a prospective wife's lineage.

5. There are a number of references to the fact that women wore *kippot* (skull-caps) on their heads in the Talmudic period, not necessarily identical to the *kippot* that Jewish men wear today. See also M Zavim 4:1; T BK 11:5.

6. Or by the rapist.

7. The verb *samchu* implies that they did not literally derive the *ketubah* from the verse but found that the verse supports their legislative enactment.

8. The text says "write," but other texts make it clear that "write" also means "give." See Chapter 8. Note, however, that if all he had to do was promise payment (write), and not actually pay (give), then it would *not* have been difficult for men to marry. Or if the reference is to a *ketubah* without guarantees, as suggested by Rashi (s.v. *hayu kotevin*), it would be hard to understand why that was ever acceptable to women. Such a *ketubah* would have been a meaningless piece of paper if, during the course of the marriage and prior to divorce, he alienated his property and used up his money.

9. T Ketubot 12:1; PT 8:11; Ketubot 32b, c.

10. See my book *Development of the Talmudic Sugya*, 146–157. The early commentators on the Talmud solve all of these difficulties but in ways that seem more forced.

11. BT BB 160b.

12. Treggiari (*Roman Marriage*, 440) makes similar comments about Roman husbands who uttered the divorce formula in the heat of the moment and then regretted it.

13. The standard *ketubah* in use today requires that the groom stipulate an amount to be added to the basic 200 or 100 zuz.

14. M Ketubot 2:9. The rabbis interpret the *"zonah"* of Lev. 21:7 as a woman who had sex with a man forbidden to her.

15. See, for instance, M Ketubot 1:6 and 7:7, where reference is made to a mistaken purchase *(mekah ta'ut)*. See also the *baraita* in BT Ta'anit 31a in which women use the term purchase *about themselves* when talking to men about marriage. See also T Yevamot 2:1, cited in the next section.

16. *Erusin* and *kiddushin* are synonyms. Each refers to the first stage of marriage, called in English "betrothal." This state can only be dissolved by divorce.

17. The Hebrew text reads: הקדושי׳ אינן קונין באשה אלא מדעת שניהם ....

18. See Tal Ilan (*Jewish Women in Greco-Roman Palestine* [Tübingen: J.C.B. Mohr, 1995], 88–89). David Weiss Halivni writes that the root K-N-H "is ill-suited for normal use in connection with regular marriage because of its predominant connotation of purchase" ("The Use of קנה in Connection with Marriage," *Harvard Theological Review*, 1964, 244–248). He is referring to biblical usage, as well as rabbinic. I find his view problematic because the use of K-N-H in conjunction with marriage is only one reason, among many others, such as the use of the root L-K-H (to purchase) to describe marriage (see note 15, this chapter), that leads to the conclusion that marriage in ancient Israel was a purchase, albeit of a special kind (see the preceding section). See Y. N. Epstein, *Mevo'ot Lesifrut Hatannaim* (Jerusalem: Magnes Press, 1957), 52–53, who writes that a woman used to be bought, just like a slave.

19. See Chapter 8, "Disposition of a Mother's Estate." See also Chapter 5, "The World of Divorce According to R. Meir."

20. The anonymous voice of the text upholds the requirement of consent in a lengthy discussion of related matters in BT Kiddushin 44a and also BT Yevamot 19b. The Yerushalmi (Yevamot 5:4; 7a) cites a *baraita* in which Rebbe says that betrothal can only be effected with consent.

21. Rashi understands this to be so, that the groom recites the formula. It is also possible to construct a case in which an explicit betrothal declaration is not necessary. See BT Kiddushin 6a.

22. See Ilan (*Jewish Women*, 80ff). See, for example, BT Ketubot 22a.

4

Rape and Seduction

SEX CRIMES AGAINST WOMEN is a topic of dispute between the sexes. Men rape and seduce women but, when charged, not only deny having committed the act but even doubt that there is such a thing as forced sex. Women invite sexual attention, men say, but if the women are not satisfied with the outcome, contend they were coerced.

Even the Torah expresses skepticism about some claims of forced sex. Several passages in Deuteronomy (22:23–27) suggest that rape in a city is not possible, for if the victim cries out, she would be saved because her cries would be heard. Outside the city, rape is possible because a victim's cries would not be heard. Should rape occur, punish the rapist but not the victim(!), because he is like one who murders by ambush, whereas she is blameless (v. 26). Since disbelief about these crimes persists to this very day, with special rules of rape corroboration only now being removed from the books in American and English law, we should note that such doubt is absent from the rabbis' discussion of this matter. They understand the Torah's city versus open country opposition metaphorically, distinguishing instead between those instances in which a woman objected but was overcome ("open country") and those in which she did not object ("city").[1]

The reason that the rape and seduction of an unbetrothed virgin—seduction being the act of enticing a woman to unlawful sexual intercourse without the use of force—are presented by the Bible as aspects of marital law is that the preferred resolution of these cases is marrying off the victim to the aggressor. This means that rape and seduction, according to the Bible, were primarily crimes against the young woman's father, for he would lose the anticipated income from his daughter's virginity. However, by arranging for the seducer or rapist to marry her and pay the father a bride-price for his now not-so-eligible daughter, the matter is fully resolved. Even so, the rabbis introduced far-reaching legislative change, transforming rape and seduction from crimes against a woman's father into crimes against a young woman herself. The motivation for these changes, although not stated explicitly, is likely to be society's altered perception of the status of women, the nature of marriage, and women's role in negotiating it.

By introducing the requirement that the victim consent to marriage with the rapist, the rabbis give her a measure of control over her own future. She can choose either to marry him or not to marry him. This means that rape or sex does not make a marriage, as it did in the Bible. The rabbis thus turn rape into a crime against women, with marriage no longer the only outcome, but one possible outcome. Similarly, by discussing women's pain in rape, although mediating it through men's eyes, the rabbis are saying that rape has consequences for women other than lowering their value on the marriage market and limiting their marital prospects.

The issue of consent also underlies the passages that deal with sex with a minor. Since consent has virtually no meaning when speaking of sex between adults and children, it follows that all sex with a minor is forced. The rabbis discourage such activity, such as a father's marrying off a young daughter, but still find it necessary to discuss the legal consequences of such acts. They go on to say that consent can only be given when one reaches intellectual maturity, not before. For this reason, they make a woman legally independent when she reaches physical and mental maturity *(bogeret)*. By creating this new category, the *bogeret,* the rabbis say in a very clear way that women may—and perhaps should—make their own decisions about marriage, that they have the power to choose with whom to live and with whom to engage in sex. This is a far cry from a woman's being handed over in marriage by her father to her husband.

Rape and Seduction in the Torah

> If a man seduces an unbetrothed virgin and has sexual relations with her, he shall pay the bride-price and marry her. If her father refuses to give her to him, he will weigh out silver like the bride-price of virgins. (Exodus 22:15–16)

This set of verses is rather puzzling. In all cases of seduction, the seducer has to pay the bride-price of virgins to the father of the girl he seduced, but not in all cases will he get a bride. It depends on how her father feels about the match. If he refuses to give his daughter in marriage, he still deserves to be paid because, as a nonvirgin, she is worth less to him on the marriage market. That she was taken advantage of and shamed is not addressed. These verses suggest that a daughter is seen as the property of her father, almost as a part of him, so that it is he, not she, who suffers as a result of her exploitation. Or, more accurately, she does not suffer independently of him. The individual is not viewed so much as an individual but as a member of a family.[2] The seducer must therefore make amends to the collective body, in particular to the head of the household, but not to the girl herself.

We find a similar outlook and legal resolution of the related crime of rape, dealt with only in Deuteronomy.

> If a man finds an unbetrothed virgin and forces her to engage in sexual relations with him, and they are found out: The man who had sex with her has to give her father fifty silver [shekels] and she will be his wife, because he forced her [תחת אשר ענה[3]], he may not dismiss her ever. (Deuteronomy 22:28, 29)

Here, too, the sexual crime that is committed against the daughter is analyzed in terms of its economic effect upon the father. He is paid fifty silver shekels, the equivalent of a bride-price.[4] But in this instance the Torah also shows its concern for the young woman by assigning the rapist to her as a husband, for as long as he lives, with the stated rationale "because he forced her." This phrase expresses sympathy for the young victim: She now has a husband for good who may not fabricate a reason to divorce her. But why would she find it acceptable to marry the rapist? It seems that a girl who was raped could not easily be married off, as we will see with Tamar. Since ancient expectations of marriage had more to do with financial and social security and the opportunity to raise children than a loving relationship, the girl who was raped might not look all that askance upon the prescribed union. In addition, the Torah seems to regard the marriage to his victim as a penalty for the rapist. She becomes an albatross around his neck; he must provide for her forever. So the Torah is punishing the rapist much more severely than it punished the seducer. Since his crime was worse, in that her consent was not sought, his punishment, long-term economic obligation to his victim, without any possibility of divorce, is greater.

In a preceding verse (25), the Torah says that if a man raped a betrothed virgin, his penalty is death. But why such a vast difference between the two punishments—marriage for the rape of an unbetrothed young woman and a death penalty for the rape of a betrothed young woman? Her suffering is identical in both instances. This forces us to conclude that the rape of a woman who already belongs to a man is a far more serious breach of the social order than the rape of a woman not yet purchased in marriage. The purported victim of the rape of a betrothed young woman is her husband. His virgin bride-to-be has been violated; therefore, the rapist, like the adulterer, has to die.[5]

It is even possible to argue that the Torah does not describe two different crimes against unbetrothed women, seduction in Exodus and rape in Deuteronomy, but only one, seduction. The author of the Temple Scroll, one of the Dead Sea documents, dating from sometime after 120 B.C.E., cites the Torah's "rape" verses from Deuteronomy almost verbatim but substitutes the verb "seduce" for "rape."[6] Since he prescribes for seduction the same punishments that the Torah prescribes for rape—forced marriage, no divorce, payment of fifty silver shekels to the father—he may be suggesting that he sees both sets of Torah verses as portraying only one crime, seduction. In his opinion, there is no such thing as rape, that is, nonconsensual sex on her part. With the appropriate blandishments, women succumb.[7]

It is interesting that in the two famous rape cases in the Bible, that of Dinah by Shechem (Genesis 34) and Tamar by Amnon (2 Samuel 13), the resolution differs from the recommendations made by the verses in Deuteronomy. In both instances, the brother(s) of the rape victim, in a devious manner, kill the rapist (and his family, in the first instance). The reason for their intense anger, as stated in reference to both episodes, is that "such a thing is an abomination [נבלה], something not done in Israel" (Genesis 34:7; 2 Samuel 13:12). We thus see that no marriage took place, in either case, between victim and rapist. Note further that neither victim ever married. Following the rape, Tamar lived in her brother's home for two years, in a state of severe depression (2 Samuel 13:20).[8]

The Rabbinic Paradigm Shift:
From Crime Against Father to Crime Against Daughter

Unlike the author of the Temple Scroll, the rabbis posit the existence of two different sex crimes against unbetrothed women, seduction and rape. They use a new Hebrew term for rape, *ones* [אנס],[9] and view all cases of forced sex as rape, without regard to where the act took place.[10] Even more important, they transform seduction and rape from mainly monetary crimes against the girl's father to cases of assault and battery against the girl herself. In no instance is either the father or the victim herself forced to agree to marriage with the perpetrator of the crime. It follows that not only do the rabbis view girls as separate entities from their fathers, but as shown in earlier chapters, they no longer consider marriage a purchase, or, at least, they no longer think that such a purchase can be enacted through rape.

> . . . The seducer pays for shame and injury [בשת ופגם], and a fine; in addition to these, the rapist pays for pain; the rapist must pay [all] immediately; as for the seducer: when he divorces her, he pays her for shame, injury, etc.; the rapist must drink from his flowerpot [that he "watered" with his seed, i.e., marry her]; the seducer may choose to divorce her. (M Ketubot 3:4)

The same is true for the rapist and the same is true for the seducer: Either she or her father can withhold consent, as it says, "if her father

refuses" [Exodus 22:16], ". . . and she will become his wife"
[Deuteronomy 22:29]—only with her consent [מדעתה]. (T Ketubot 3:7)

In the first source above, a *mishnah,* the rabbis institute a new set of payments, shame and injury, for both rape and seduction, and also pain for
rape, based on what the victim of the crime—*the woman*—suffered.[11]
Unlike the biblical fine of fifty shekels, which is fixed, these vary from case
to case. This legal innovation represents considerable social progress. Rape
is now dealt with as a case of assault and battery, compensation for which
is documented elsewhere, in M Baba Kama 8:1.[12] Although the *mishnah* in
Baba Kama lists five different payments for standard cases of assault, only
the three mentioned above apply routinely to seduction and rape.

The second source, a *baraita,* is strikingly innovative: Despite explicit
statements in the Torah to the contrary, no marriage between victim and aggressor is required, neither in a case of rape nor in a case of seduction. Not
only the father, but *even the young victim* may refuse the match. In the associated Gemara (BT Ketubot 39b), the Amoraim struggle, after the fact, to
base each one of these new rules on scriptural phrases, as does the above
baraita in a rather cryptic manner. These belabored efforts underscore the
fact that this set of rules was generated, not by the Torah, but by the rabbis,
most likely out of their desire to right a wrong to women: In the Talmudic
period, automatic marriage to a rapist or seducer was no longer considered
an appropriate solution to a young girl's predicament. No one presumed
that he was the man she wanted to marry. It is hard to understand, however,
why the Mishnah makes no reference to this rule of refusal. The Tosefta,
where it originates, and the Bavli, which accepts it, appear to be more concerned with her psychological welfare than the Mishnah.[13]

The Mishnah further explores forced marriage resulting from rape.

How is he forced to "drink from his flowerpot"? [He must marry
her] even if she is lame, or blind, or covered with boils. . . . (M
Ketubot 3:5)

This passage seems to be providing a rationale for the Torah's forcing a
raped woman to live with the man who raped her. The rabbis are saying
that a man who takes advantage of a physically handicapped woman, who
is more vulnerable to rape and less marriageable than others, is punished
by having her "foisted" on him for the rest of his life, as repulsive as he
finds her.[14] Such a punishment may benefit the woman who was his victim
in that it provides her with a husband. When her lack of virginity was
added to her physical disability, finding herself a mate, in a patriarchal society, would have been difficult.

We also see that marital suitability in this passage is viewed strictly from
a male perspective: The more physically blemished she is, the less appealing

she is to him and other men, the more important, therefore, for him to have to marry her. It is even possible to suggest that this passage is homiletical: It informs men that rape may give short-term pleasure, but warns them that the price they pay may be long-term suffering; no matter how unsuitable and unappealing she may be to him, he will have to live with her for the rest of his life. How attractive he is in her eyes and her opinion of him as a mate are of no relevance for this *mishnah,* however. It assumes that women, especially those whose marital prospects are limited, prefer any man to no man at all.[15]

From Fixed to Variable Fine

If he raped the following girls [נערות, those between the ages of twelve and twelve and one-half] he pays the [50 shekel] fine ... but if he raped these other girls, he does *not* pay a fine. ... (M Ketubot 3:1, 2)

... A girl [who has not yet turned twelve] *may* be sold as a maidservant; a fine is *not* paid by the man who rapes her. A girl between twelve and twelve and one-half may *not* be sold as a maidservant; a fine *is* paid by the man who rapes her. An independent young woman may *not* be sold as a maidservant; a fine is *not* paid by the man who rapes her. (M 3:8)

At first reading, these *mishnah*s surprise us: they exempt many men from paying a penalty for rape or seduction, even though explicitly mandated by the Torah. Moreover, as shown by a parallel statement in the Tosefta (3:8),[16] the redactor of the Mishnah has codified the more restrictive view of R. Meir instead of the dissenting view of the Sages, who impose a fine in most cases of rape of a young girl. Some have claimed that this *mishnah* is evidence that the rabbis downplayed the gravity of sex crimes against women.[17] But if we read these *mishnah*s in the context of the entire chapter, we see that the Mishnah's aim is very specific: to limit sharply the circumstances in which it will be necessary for the rapist or seducer to pay the fine. But why would the rabbis wish to do that? That they impose restrictions in other cases, such as implementation of the death penalty and remission of debts in the sabbatical year, is understandable, given the obvious broad social benefits of interpreting those institutions out of existence. But why would they limit the scope of cases in which the rapist must pay a fine, in addition to damages, for the crime he committed? The fine, punishment above and beyond damages, makes this case different from others of personal injury. Releasing a man from paying it almost implies that he was not guilty of the crime of rape or seduction, only of damages that were incidental to the sexual act.

If we backtrack for a moment and remind ourselves that the "fine," a rabbinic term for the fifty silver shekels of the Torah, was paid to compensate the father for the loss of anticipated income from his daughter's virginity, we realize that the fine had nothing to do with the criminality of the act. Therefore, the rabbis' restriction of the fine should not be understood as overlooking her as victim, since the fine, like the other payments, was given not to her but to her father. In their eyes, payment of such a large amount to the father for a crime committed against the daughter must have seemed a travesty, especially since the bride-price was no longer paid, as already noted. If we read the other *mishnah*s of this chapter and the first *mishnah* of the next, we begin to notice that the fine was not eliminated but replaced by an alternative payment, *pegam*, and, perhaps even more important, that all rape and seduction payments were in the process of being reassigned from the father to the daughter.

> What is the amount of payment for shame? It all varies with the [status and circumstances] of the one who inflicts shame and the one who suffers it.
>
> *Pegam* [payment for personal injury]? We look upon her as a slave woman on sale in the marketplace; how much was she worth [as a virgin] and how much is she worth now [and he pays the difference].
>
> The fine *(kenas)* is the same in every case. Any payment stipulated by the Torah is the same in all cases. (M Ketubot 3:7)

Before the broad implications of this passage are examined, the statement about how to assess the *pegam* payment requires explanation. In determining the amount to be paid for injury in a standard case of assault and battery, the rabbis say that the injured man (or woman) should be viewed as if for sale on the slave market. The amount to be paid corresponds to the difference in purchase price between a wholly intact individual and a handicapped or impaired one (M Baba Kama 8:1). Similarly here, to establish the "value" of a woman's virginity, its differential price on the slave market has to be established. This does not imply that women are slaves to their husbands, in the sexual sense or in any other.

Pegam, payment for personal injury, is almost always coupled with shame and appears in rabbinic literature almost exclusively in connection with seduction and rape.[18] It is interpreted by the Amoraim as payment for the loss of virginity, the critical injury suffered in these cases.[19] But if that is what it means, it is a different name for the fine, which also compensated the father for the loss of virginity. So why are two payments made for the same virginity? *Pegam*, as noted by the *mishnah*, is not fixed like the Torah's fine, but variable, like the payment for shame. The level of payment varies with the victim's socioeconomic circumstances. As the rabbis imply in M Arakhin 3:4, a fixed payment of fifty shekels can lead in some cases to paying too much, if she is of poor lineage and standing, and in others to paying too little, if she is of high social standing. So the rabbis, by virtually eliminating the fixed fifty-shekel fine and replacing it with their own variable payment, *pegam,* which can either exceed fifty or else go below it, show just how seriously they take the payments for rape and seduction: They insist that the payments correspond to the damage done, as is the rule in all cases of assault and battery. I must note, however, that allowing compensation for shame and loss of virginity to vary with family background is a concept that is foreign to most people today.[20]

Furthermore, the rabbis begin to transfer sex crime payments from the father to the victim herself.

> If a young woman [נערה] was seduced, the payment for shame and injury, and the fine, go to her father. And also the payment for pain if she was raped.
>
> If she stood trial before her father died [to collect payment from the rapist or seducer], they [the moneys] are his. If the father then died, they go to her brothers.
>
> If she did not stand trial before her father died, **they go to her.**
>
> If she stood trial before becoming a *bogeret* [an independent young woman], they go to the father. If the father then died, they go to her brothers.
>
> But if she did not stand trial before becoming a *bogeret,* **they go to her.**
>
> R. Simon says: If she did not collect payment before her father died, **they go to her.**
>
> [Earnings from] the work of her hands and what she finds, even if she has not yet collected [payment], if the father died, go to the brothers [because these moneys were due her when her father was still alive, they thus now go to the brothers]. [The Gemara adds (43a) that anything she finds after her father dies is hers, and similarly anything she makes and sells after her father dies belongs to her and not her brothers.] (M Ketubot 4:1)

The rule that this *mishnah* seeks to establish is that in certain circumstances the rapist or seducer pays damages to her and not to her father or to her brothers who are his heirs. If she went to court as a *bogeret,* an independent young woman, twelve and one-half years old or more, or if her father dies before the trial begins,[21] the payments are made to her. We further learn that all moneys earned by or due her after she reaches maturity, either physically or because of her father's death, accrue to her and no one else.

It therefore seems to me that the rabbis, without their saying so explicitly, have made a significant statement about crimes against women: The woman is the victim and she deserves compensation. The value of a human being as a person independent of her family seems to have gained currency by the rabbinic period. Her consent is sought for marriage to the rapist. He is no longer, automatically, her husband. Payments that go to the father, which imply that he is the victim, and not she, are in the process of being eliminated, and payments for what she suffered are in the process of being developed and transferred to her. Moreover, by eliminating the fine from most cases of rape and seduction, the rabbis are saying that this fixed, biblically prescribed payment no longer makes legal sense: The new payments, for shame, pain, and personal injury, not referred to in the Torah in this context, are the ones that they are interested in establishing firmly. Less obvious, the rabbis understand that rape is something a man does to a woman, uninvited and hurtful. When these passages are read in context, they show that the rabbis have gone a long way to rectify the no-longer-appropriate indifference of the Bible to the young woman as victim.

Men's Understanding of Women's Pain

The Bavli's commentary on M Ketubot 3:4, which introduces the payment for pain, is an attempt by men to grasp a woman's experience in being raped.

==What pain [does the *mishnah* refer to when it says that the rapist pays for pain]?

‑‑Said the father of Samuel: that he threw her down on the ground [שחבטה על גבי קרקע].

‑‑R. Zera attacked the logic [of this answer]: Does this mean that if he threw her down on silk [cushions, instead of on the ground], he would be free from paying for pain?!

And should you say that is so, have we not learned in a *baraita* [that he does pay for pain in all cases]: R. Simon b. Judah said in the name of R. Simon, A rapist does not pay for pain because this is what awaits her in the future from her husband [i.e., upon marriage, she will have her hymen torn, causing her pain, שסופה להצטער תחת בעלה]. But they said to him: There is no comparison between engaging in [a first sexual act] willingly and unwillingly [and the rapist *does* have to pay for the pain of the forced sexual act]! . . . (BT Ketubot 39a, b)

Samuel defines the pain payment of the *mishnah* as a reference to the pain suffered by the victim in being forced to submit. R. Zera expands it to include the pain of the forced sexual act itself. He relies on the view of the rabbis who disagree with R. Simon. In his cynical statement, R. Simon characterizes women's pain in rape as not much different from the pain they suffer in the course of a consensual first sexual encounter. This means that, for him, forced and consensual sex are the same, that a virgin's pain in rape is limited to the tearing of her hymen. His colleagues sharply rebuke him.

Before examining the rest of the unit on pain, we will look at the parallel section in the Yerushalmi. It cites the same *baraita* to make the point that the Mishnah is *not* in accordance with R. Simon. That is, the Yerushalmi notes that the redactor of the Mishnah ignored R. Simon's dismissive view of women's pain in rape, accepting, instead, the Sages' more sympathetic approach.

> The *mishnah* is not in agreement with R. Simon, for R. Simon exempts the rapist from paying for pain.
>
> What is the [experience of rape] like, [according to Rabbi Simon]? One who cuts a wart off his friend's foot that his friend was anyway planning to remove. Or one who cuts down his friend's young trees that he was anyway planning to cut down.
>
> They said to him: There is no comparison between engaging in sex by force and doing so willingly. There is no comparison between engaging in sex on a dunghill and engaging in sex in the bridal chamber.[22] (PT Ketubot 3:5, 27c)

R. Simon, in this version of the *baraita*, justifies his omission of a pain payment not only by pointing out that discomfort is inevitable in a first sexual encounter but also that—even in rape—it is negligible. The rabbis chide him for missing the point that, in addition to rupturing a hymen, there are other kinds of suffering that a raped virgin endures, including the psychological pain of degradation.[23]

This discussion by men of women's pain in rape is of interest to women, in particular, since men, in many cultures, are skeptical about rape, not believing that women suffer during rape and not believing that women play no role in instigating this kind of abusive sexual attention. Here we find that the majority of rabbis understand that women suffer pain in rape. The point that rape is an act perpetrated on her against her will is summed up nicely in the following rather extreme statement:

> ––Rava said: If it began as a forced sexual act but ended as a consensual one—and even if she says, "Let him be, for if he had not accosted me, I would have paid him money to do so,"—[she only said so] because she was sexually aroused [יצר אלבשה]. She is therefore permitted [to resume marital life with her husband because such an act is classified as rape, *not* as consensual sex and hence adultery]. (BT Ketubot 51b)

According to this Amora, rape is rape, even if at some point it appears to be sanctioned by her, a conclusion diametrically opposed to the one reached by the author of the Temple Scroll, as mentioned above. Her alleged pleasure, despite the conditions of fear and brutality, does not mitigate, in any way, the fact of rape. Pleasure does not imply consent.

The Bavli continues its discussion of women's pain in rape:

> – –Rather, said R. Nahman said Rabbah b. Abuha: The pain [referred to in the Mishnah is not the pain of being thrown down but the pain] of having her legs forced apart. . . .
> ==If so, the seducer also [should have to pay for pain and yet the *mishnah* says that he does not]!
> – –Said R. Nahman said Rabbah b. Abuha: I will give you a parable. It [seduction] is like a person who says to someone else, rip my silk and I will not hold you responsible [i.e., she waived her right to payment for pain because she *chose* to have sex].
> =="My" [silk]? But it belongs to her father!
> – –Rather, said R. Nahman said Rabbah b. Abuha: The wise women [פקחות] among them say, a woman who is seduced does not suffer any pain(!). [The question was, why not pay the seduced woman for pain since she too must have experienced it, if we accept the last definition of pain? The answer, according to wise women, is that a woman who consents to an illicit sexual act does not suffer any pain.]
> ==But do we not see that she suffered pain [and the seducer should have to pay for it]?
> – –Said Abaye: "Mother" told me that it [the discomfort a virgin feels when engaging in sex for the first time] is like hot water on a bald head.
> – –Rava said: The daughter of R. Hisda told me [i.e., his wife] that it is like the prick of a bloodletter's lancet [Rashi].[24]
> – –R. Pappa said: The daughter of Abba Sura'a [i.e., his wife (Rashi)] told me, like a dry crust on the gums. [Since the pain of consensual sex is so minor, the seducer need not pay for it.] (BT Ketubot 39b)

In this last section, men try to understand what women experience in their first sexual encounter when it is *not* forced upon them. Each of the rabbis quotes a woman, two their wives and one a nursemaid (whom he refers to as "Mother"). The pain described by all three women is minor and is expressed in terms that speak to men's experience, too. By quoting women only, men recognize that the pain is real but that they cannot adequately describe it because they are men. The Bavli also reports, in the name of women but transmitted by a man, that a seduced woman does not suffer pain, which explains why the seducer does not pay for pain. This statement preaches: Since she "asked" for it, she deserves to suffer and we cannot show any sympathy for her. The women who say so are called "wise." They appear to have internalized patriarchal values and, as a result, fail to recognize that seduction is a crime by men against women even if women, at some point, give their consent.

Creation of a New Legal Category: The Bogeret

The Bible never refers to a *bogeret,* an independent, physically mature young woman.[25] It consistently assumes that a girl who reaches puberty is married off by her father and passes from his authority to her husband's without an interim period of independence.[26] The rabbis present, or possibly invent, a third category: a girl who is under neither her father's nor her husband's authority. Today we call women (and men) who are in this category "single." A distinguishing feature of the *bogeret,* as we will soon see, is that she has reached the age of consent. Her father may no longer arrange a marriage for her. She has to function on her own.

> The Sages gave an analogy for women: *pagah, bohal, tzemel* (three stages in the growth of a fig); *pagah,* she is still a child; *bohal,* these are the days of her youth; during both of these periods her father is entitled to what she finds and what she earns and may cancel her vows; *tzemel,* once she reaches full physical maturity,[27] *her father no longer has authority over her.* (M Niddah 5:7)
>
> If a young woman is seduced, the payments for shame and injury belong to her father, and also [the payment for] pain if she was raped
> . . .
> If she did not stand trial until after her father died, they belong to her. . . .
> If she did not stand trial until after she reached maturity [עד שבגרה], they belong to her. . . . (M Ketubot 4:1)

Before drawing any legal conclusions, we must note the legal/literary dissonance in the first *mishnah.* A woman's physical and sexual development is compared to that of a fig, the obvious underlying metaphor being that she ripens at puberty and is ready to be picked and eaten. A passage like this sees women as objects, not persons. But note that it is precisely at this point in her life that the Sages confer independence on her, making her responsible for her own sexuality. I cannot go so far as to call this move feminist, because she loses her new status as soon as she marries, but for the rabbis to make her independent just when she reaches sexual "ripeness" is remarkable.

The principle emerging from these two *mishnah*s is that a girl is legally emancipated in two ways—by the death of her father or by reaching the age of physical maturity. When she reaches the age of twelve and one-half, she keeps the proceeds of her handicrafts, what she finds, and any payments due her, for instance from winning a court case. Also, since M Kiddushin 2:1 says that a father may betroth his daughter when she is a *na'arah* (between twelve and twelve and one-half), it implies that he may no longer do so when she passes that age.[28] Nor may he sell her as a maidservant even prior to that time, from twelve on (M Ketubot 3:8). Finally, if a girl is raped or seduced after twelve and one-half, the aggressor does not pay a fine. The reason given by the Gemara is that her hymen disappears on its own after she reaches physical maturity.[29] This means that she is legally no longer a virgin, even though she has never engaged in sexual relations. All these rules suggest that a woman is in control of her own affairs when she reaches maturity, provided she is not married.[30]

Why did the rabbis create such a category, that of a young woman who is capable, upon reaching full physical and mental maturation, of functioning on her own? Granting an unmarried *bogeret* such extensive rights makes the important point that the reason she loses most of them upon marriage is not that she is not capable but that she comes under the aegis of a man. She remains competent but must cede all control to him; it is he who functions as sole head of household. Even so, the creation of such a category in a patriarchal society is a step in the direction of viewing women, although not wives, as independent legal personalities.

Sex with a Minor

Contemporary readers are accustomed to linking the topic of sex crimes against women to the topic of sex between men and girls. In fact, the Talmud gives attention to relations both beween men and girls and between women and boys. I will first consider the case of marital sex between an adult man and a girl less than twelve, sometimes even as young as three. Consent has no real meaning in such a case. The man's behavior may appropriately be described as an act of forced sex. The Talmud makes a number of references to this kind of sexual connection and, at first reading, could be interpreted as condoning such behavior on the part of the man. But when we read those same statements in context, we see that they do not mean that the rabbis tolerated such relations. There is no one place in the Talmud that could be considered the locus classicus for a discussion of the topic of sex with a minor. The following set of sources, however, should provide us with some sense of the rabbis' thinking on the subject. The main point we will glean from these texts is that one cannot deduce merely from the fact that a passage addresses the issue of sex between adults and minors that the particular passage or the Talmud in general sanctions such activity. As always, we will pay particularly close attention to the anecdotes interwoven among the prescriptive passages.

> We learned in a *baraita*: R. Simon bar Yohai says, a girl who converted under three years and a day is fit to marry a *kohen* [גיורת פחותה מבת שלש סנים ויום אחד כסירה לכהונה]. As it says, "All female children [among the Midianites] who have *not* engaged in sexual relations, you may keep alive for yourselves [the soldiers]" (Numbers 31:18), and surely Phineas the *kohen* was among them. (BT Yevamot 60b)

This passage appears to be permitting—and even encouraging—a *kohen* to marry a very young girl, ostensibly because one can safely assume she is still a virgin. But the halakhic issue is not virginity per se. According to the rabbis, a woman who has sex with a man who is forbidden to her, such as a gentile, is called a *zonah* (not to be confused with the modern Hebrew word for prostitute), and is forbidden in marriage to a *kohen*. But several distinctions have to be made: If the sex act took place before she was three, it is of no lasting halakhic consequence because a hymen that was ruptured at such a young age, according to the rabbis, would repair itself.[31] Therefore, if she converts to Judaism *before* the age of three, then even if she had sex forced upon her as a very young child, prior to conversion, she is *not* considered a *zonah* and may marry a *kohen*. If she converts *after* she reached three, she is ineligible to marry a *kohen,* ever, because the rabbis assume she was sexually molested or active prior to conversion, when she was older than three, and hence a *zonah*. These are the rules that R. Simon deduces from Scripture. When understood in this way, this passage does not encourage marriage between *kohanim* and little girls. It merely notes the difference in marital eligibility to a *kohen* between girls who converted at a very young age and girls who converted a little later.

The Bavli's discussion of the topic ends with the following anecdote:

> --A certain *kohen* married a convert less than three years and one day old. [ההוא כהנא דאנסיב גיורת פחותה מבת שלש סנים ויום אחד] R. Nahman b. Isaac said to him [critically]: What have you done? He answered: R. Jacob b. Idi said in the name of R. Joshua b. Levi, the *halakhah* is like R. Simon bar Yohai [and she is a fit wife for a *kohen*]. He said: Go, dismiss her. If not, I will pull R. Jacob b. Idi out of your ear(!).[32] (BT Yevamot 60b)

The wording of this passage gives the impression that it can be interpreted in two ways. One possibility is that a *kohen* married a very young girl and R. Nahman b. Isaac severely reprimanded him for doing so.[33] If so, the Amora adamantly opposes marriage with a minor. Alternatively, and more accurately, the passage is saying that a *kohen* married a woman who herself converted to Judaism before the age of three (and married him at some later time) and thus was not of Jewish stock on either her father's or mother's side. R. Nahman b. Isaac criticized the *kohen* for not going beyond what the law requires of him and marrying a woman with at least one Jewish parent. That the issue is lineage, not age, is supported by statements elsewhere in the Bavli and by a similar anecdote in the Yerushalmi.[34] But either way we interpret the incident, we cannot find in it rabbinic approval of marriage with a very young girl.

Another text that appears to address the topic of sex with a minor is a *mishnah* in Niddah.

> A girl who is three years old and one day may be betrothed by sexual intercourse; if her *levir* has sex with her, he has acquired her; any man [other than her husband who has sex with her] is guilty of adultery; . . . if she marries a *kohen*, she is entitled to eat *terumah* (priestly dues); if a man unfit for her to marry has sex with her [before she is married], she is forbidden to marry a *kohen*; if someone forbidden to her by the Torah [i.e., a close relative] has sex with her [consensually(!)[35]], he is subject to capital punishment but she is exempt [because of her youth]; if a man has sex with a girl who is less than three years and one day, it is like putting a finger in the eye [and has no legal significance]. (M Niddah 5:4)

This *mishnah* discusses the legal consequences of sex with minors, of different ages and marital states, but does not sanction either marriage or sex with a very young girl. It says that until the age of three there is no legal outcome at all because the hymen returns and thus cancels the significance of the sex act. Putting a finger in the eye hurts and triggers tearing but does not usually cause permanent damage. After three, if a man has sex with a girl, not only does he cause her to lose her virginity permanently, but also—and precisely because of this—the sex act has a variety of legal consequences for both of them: for him, if she were forbidden to him, he will be punished in the same way as if she were a mature woman; for her, if the sexual relations were for the sake of marriage, they will make her a married woman. Just as forbidden sexual relations are not being encouraged by this *mishnah,* so, too, marriage to a minor is not being encouraged. In all instances, the consequences of such acts are the issue.

The aim of this *mishnah* is to establish standards against which one can judge cases that arise. This *mishnah* is *not* saying that since an incestuous relationship with a girl over three is punishable by death[36] but under three is not, men should limit their sexual attention to girls under three. On the contrary, all it is saying is that should any of these acts have taken place—for example, betrothal of a minor by means of sex or an act of incestuous or adulterous sex with her—since she had already reached the age of three, the act has legal consequences. The fact that the return of virginity delegitimizes prior acts of sex is clear evidence of a patriarchal outlook: A man can only establish "ownership" of a woman if he leaves his mark on her. Since sex acts prior to three are not traceable, a man cannot lay claim to a young girl.

If we examine this *mishnah* in context, we see that in the preceding and following ones, the same kinds of topics arise, namely, what are the legal consequences of reaching different ages, such as one day for a boy or girl, three years for a girl, nine for a boy, twelve for a girl, thirteen for a boy, and so on. Just as the age of three is a turning point for a girl's sexual status, so is nine for a boy.

> A boy of nine who engages in sexual relations with his deceased brother's wife [in order to fulfill the levirate requirement] has acquired her; but he may not issue a *get* until he grows up [i.e., reaches puberty]; . . . if he has sex [consensually] with a woman forbidden to him by the Torah, she is subject to capital punishment but he is exempt. (M Niddah 5:5)

This *mishnah* parallels the preceding one in many ways. Again, sex with a minor is not being promoted here. All that is being said is that the sexual actions of a boy less than nine have no legal significance but that those of a boy over nine do, presumably because starting from that age and on he can maintain an erection and is thus capable of insemination. He is not encouraged to have sex with a woman who is forbidden to him; on the contrary, if such a woman has sex with him, she is subject to the same punishment as if she had committed an act of incest or adultery with a grown man.

The Bavli's discussion of the mishnah about a three-year-old girl ends with two anecdotes that indicate that sex with minors was not unknown in the ancient world.

> We learned in a *baraita:* It once happened that Justinia, the daughter of Aseverus b. Antoninus, came before Rebbe [R. Judah the Prince] and said to him: Rabbi, at what age may a woman marry? He answered: at three years and one day. And at what age can she get pregnant? He said to her, twelve years and a day. She said to him: I married at six and gave birth at seven.[37] I regret the three years that I lost while still in my father's home(!). . . .

> We learned in a *baraita:* A woman came before R. Akiva and said to him, I had sex before the age of three. Am I fit to marry a *kohen* [be-

cause it is possible that she had intercourse with a man unfit for her or
forbidden to her, such as her father?[38]] He said to her: You are fit. She
said to him: Let me draw an analogy. To what is this similar? To a
child whose finger was dipped into honey. The first and second time he
gets angry; the third time, he sucks it. He said to her: If so, you are *not*
fit to marry a *kohen*. He then saw his students looking at each other
[in astonishment] and said to them, why do you find my decision difficult? They said to him: Just as the entire Torah is law given to Moshe
at Sinai, so too, [the rule that] a girl under three who had sex is still fit
for a *kohen* is a law given to Moshe at Sinai. R. Akiva only issued this
ruling to sharpen the minds of his students. (BT Niddah 45a)

In both of these anecdotes women speak positively about the sex that
they had while still very young, in the first case at the age of six and in the
second before the age of three. The first woman is an aristocratic Roman
and the second Jewish. In the second instance, the woman suggests that she
was forced into a sexual act as a very young child but, after experiencing it
several times, came to like it. It goes without saying that the men who had
sex with her did so of their own free will and derived pleasure from it.

Is the Talmud, by means of these anecdotes, sanctioning sex with minors? The first is typical of rabbinic literature in that it attributes a strong
libido to non-Jews and also upholds what the rabbis say about them in
many different places, that they behave promiscuously and that one may
assume that a non-Jewish girl over the age of three is sexually experienced.
The unique aspect of this passage is that the woman herself reports that her
sexual encounters as a young girl were pleasurable. But this anecdote does
not necessarily have implications for Jews.

The second story is much more striking and even chilling. It seems to be
saying that even under conditions of near rape, a very young girl can learn
to enjoy sex. Nonetheless, I do not think that this anecdote is promoting
sex with children. It is raising the possibility that exploitative sexual relations, such as those between an adult and a child, can still be, on a physical
level, pleasurable to the child. The point remains, however, that, unlike the
first story in which the girl wishes she had sought sex at a very young age,
in the second instance, the woman who reports the incident does not appear to be advocating it, only remarking upon it. As noted earlier in this
chapter, there are men who hold that women, despite the presence of force
and intimidation, may derive physical pleasure from rape (Rava, BT
Ketubot 51b). That is not an endorsement of rape by men (or women).

The woman in this second anecdote seems to be mocking the rabbis,
claiming that their standard of a three-year-old girl's sexual readiness for
marriage is meaningless. This is like the Roman woman's challenging the
rabbis' assertion that pregnancy cannot be achieved until a girl reaches

twelve. The Jewish woman's almost seductive use of the "finger in honey" metaphor—and "finger" in this very tractate is used to denote the male sexual organ—paints her as someone who virtually flaunts her lack of inhibition in both discussing sex and engaging in it. A likely reason she came to them and divulged the details of her sexual past was to challenge them and their pedantic analysis of topics that they are removed from and that she is, regrettably, caught up in. If so, she is saying that they have no understanding of the cruel facts of her childhood and, presumably, that of many other women. While she was suffering repeated acts of forced sex at the hands of men, other men were convening and dispassionately analyzing the legal consequences of the rapists' actions.[39]

In all, we will see four stories in which rabbis issue pronouncements about women's biology—two here in Niddah and two more in Yevamot 34b, where the rabbis say that a woman who abstains from sexual activity for ten years will not be able to achieve pregnancy—and in which the women themselves demonstrate the falseness of these assertions. The women's attitude to the rabbis in all four anecdotes is derisive in varying degrees. Since men told these stories about women to other men and the redactor of the Talmud included them in the corpus, I think we can say that they represent a "countertradition":[40] They show opposition by women—and men—to the regnant patriarchal order, at least in the sense that women are telling men that they do not fully understand women's bodies and biology, although the men think they do.

The second part of the story is also hard to understand. Why does R. Akiva change his halakhic decision in response to the woman's admitting that she enjoyed sex as a young child? Why would her pleasure play a role in determining whether or not she is later fit for a *kohen,* since her ruptured hymen will repair and she will no longer be a *zonah* by the time she is ready for marriage? Does he think that sex accompanied by pleasure taints her for future marriage to a *kohen,* even if she is technically no longer a *zonah?* And why do his students respond so strongly to his decision, claiming that this rule, that a girl under three who had sex is still fit for a *kohen* once she returns to a virginal state and cannot, therefore, be considered a *zonah,* is an ancient Jewish law, just like the rest of the Torah? They seem extraordinarily protective of a *kohen's* freedom to marry a woman whose sexual past, prior to the age of three, is unknowable. It is the hymen that counts, not the girl's sexual history. These rabbis appear to deny the existence of that which they cannot know.

We also find references to women and sexual activity with young boys. A *baraita* on this topic appears in the Tosefta, the Bavli, and the Yerushalmi.

If a woman plays lewdly [*mesalelet*[41]] with her young son and [it happened] that he came into genital contact with her [but did not ejaculate], Bet Shammai declares her unfit to marry a *kohen* [on the grounds of having been sexually involved with a male who is forbidden to her] but Bet Hillel declares her fit [because this act of sexual contact does not count]. (T Sotah 5:7)

This same *baraita* appears in the Yerushalmi (PT Gittin 8:10, 49c) in the context of a *mishnah* that reports a dispute between Bet Shammai and Bet Hillel about a woman's eligibility to marry a *kohen*: Bet Shammai says that even if all a man did was prepare a *get* for his wife but not deliver it, she is not fit to marry a *kohen* should her husband then die. Bet Hillel says she is. The Yerushalmi then brings the same baraita as above, replacing the word *meSaLeLet* with *meSaLeDet*.[42] The debated point is similar to the one in the *mishnah*: Does an incomplete sexual act disqualify her in the same way that a complete act does? Is genital contact with a male who is forbidden to her to be considered equivalent to sexual relations with him? The second part of the *baraita* in the Yerushalmi, which does not appear in the Tosefta, speaks of women who mutually arouse each other, *meSoLeLot*—the same verb as in the first part of the *baraita*—and addresses the question of their being fit to marry *kohanim*.[43] The issue is similar: Does a woman's sexual act with another woman, that is, an incomplete act from a man's point of view, have legal standing? Does it disqualify her from marrying a *kohen* the way sex with a man forbidden to her would? Bet Shammai says that it does, and Bet Hillel says that it does not.[44]

Finally, the same *baraita* appears in the Bavli, in conjunction with a discussion of the rebellious son.

> We learned in a *baraita*: If a woman plays lewdly *[mesolelet]* with her young son, Bet Shammai declares her unfit to marry a *kohen*. But Bet Hillel declares her fit.
> – –Said R. Hiyya the son of Rabbah b. Nahmani said R. Hisda, and some say, said R. Hisda said Ze'iri: All agree that sexual relations with a boy of nine and one day are legally significant [ביאתו ביאה]; but with a boy under eight are not. They disagree with respect to a boy of eight, Bet Shammai says that we learn from the early generations [that a boy of that age could cause conception[45]] and Bet Hillel says we do not. (BT Sanhedrin 69b)

The rabbis who speak up in all of these passages take no stand on the situations that they describe. They indicate neither approval nor disapproval of women who play lewdly with their sons or with each other. The only issue for them is the consequences for marital eligibility. Note that even the Amoraim who directly address the issue of sexual relations with a boy of eight make no comment on their attitude to such behavior by women. We can find aggadic statements that disapprove of these acts, such as "those who sport with children delay the messiah" (BT Niddah 13b), but no halakhic ones. It is tempting to say that the practices described in these passages, lesbian sex and sex with minors, are so clearly viewed by the rabbis with contempt that there is no need for the halakhic passages to say so explicitly. But that might be considered an argument from silence. We could also say that it is not the role of Halakhah to exhort but to examine the outcome of actions.

We have not exhausted, in this brief survey, the sources that address the topic of sex with minors, but we have seen enough samples of rabbinic legislation to grasp that statements about the legal consequences of such activity are not to be understood as condoning it. Similarly, just because the Torah resolves an incident of rape with the marriage of the girl to the rapist, we should not conclude that the Torah sanctions forced sex.

A law code needs to address the issue of sexual activity of adults with children. Such abusive acts occurred then and occur to this very day. Since marriage in the Talmudic period appears to have taken place around the time of puberty, sex with a young boy or girl was not a concept as foreign and offensive to the rabbis as it is to us today. Sex with a very young child, however, was. My basis for this assertion, in addition to the aggadic passage quoted above, is that the Mishnah (Kiddushin 4:12) bans parents and children of the opposite sex who have already reached puberty from sharing the same bed and lying next to each other naked but allows parents and young children of the opposite sex to do so. This means that the rabbis did not regard sexually immature bodies as capable of causing arousal in *normal* adults.[46] Furthermore, their recommendation that girls and boys be married off close to puberty[47]—and not before—suggests that, according to them, one does not put a young man and woman into a sexual situation until they are sexually mature.[48]

Conclusions

All these sources indicate that the rabbis moved beyond the Torah in their legislation for rape and seduction. They shift the sex crime paradigm from an outrage against a woman's father to an act of assault and battery against her, begin to transfer the payments from her father to her, and also indicate that they have some sense of the trauma that she suffers, both the exertion of force in general and the forced sex in particular. Moreover, they legislate that she will not be forced into marrying either the seducer or the rapist, even though according to the Torah her opinion about this match is not sought. Either her father or she herself can refuse the overly ardent suitor. Note that this is yet another way in which the rabbis seem to view marriage differently from the Torah: The man who raped or seduced a

woman is not necessarily the right husband for her. She can choose to reject him. She will be able to find another. In short, the rabbis recognize that
rape and seduction are crimes against women as individual women and not
just women as part of a collective family unit. Furthermore, creation of the
category of the independent young woman, who is in charge of her own
marital and financial affairs, reflects the changing rabbinic perception of
women and of marriage. They no longer see daughters as their father's
property and marriage as a purchase. Finally, the emerging importance of
gaining a woman's consent to marriage means that the rabbis opposed
marrying off children who, by definition, were too immature to be able to
give their consent. Even so, the manifold legal consequences of sex with a
minor had to be addressed.

We may want to criticize the rabbis for not prescribing a criminal punishment for someone who rapes or seduces an unmarried woman, a glaring
deficiency from a contemporary point of view. Although they did, with little fanfare, introduce major changes in the biblical legislation, all of which
move in the direction of placing her and not her father at the center of their
inquiry, they left an important question unanswered: How does one deal
with the rape of an *un*betrothed *non*virgin, such as a widow or divorcee?
Will she receive payment for pain and shame even though there is no loss
of virginity?[49] Their silence on this topic suggests that despite all their progressive thinking, they had not yet completely abandoned the idea that the
rape and seduction of a virgin is more a marital matter than a criminal one.

Notes

1. See Menahem Elon, *Jewish Law, History, Sources, and Principles* (Philadelphia: Jewish Publication Society [hereafter, JPS], 1994), 1030–1031, and his references to Philo, who lived in the first half of the first century, and to *Sifrei
Devarim*, Ki Tetzei, sec. 243, ed. Finkelstein and Horowitz (273). See further discussion.

2. We still hear today about traditional Middle Eastern families killing a young
female member because her immodest sexual behavior "stained the family honor."

3. The Hebrew root ענה apparently means to exert force. It does not necessarily
mean that he afflicted and tormented her in the course of the rape.

4. Jeffrey Tigay (*JPS Torah Commentary, Deuteronomy*, 208) writes that the
fifty shekels may represent a combination of an average bride-price and also puni-
tive damages.

5. Tigay (ibid., 207–208) writes that raping an engaged virgin is a capital crime
because it is adulterous but raping an unengaged virgin is not a capital crime because it is not adulterous. This distinction is correct. However, since he offers no
explanation as to *why* the rape of an unbetrothed virgin is viewed as a far less serious offense, even though the victim suffers in an identical manner, he conceals the
sexist bias of these laws.

6. *The Temple Scroll*, ed. Yigael Yadin (Jerusalem: Israel Exploration Society/ Institute of Archaeology of the Hebrew University of Jerusalem, 1977–1990), col. 66, ll. 8–11, pp. 209–210.

7. Lawrence H. Schiffman, in "Laws Pertaining to Women in the *Temple Scroll*" (*The Dead Sea Scrolls: Forty Years of Research*," ed. Devorah Dimant and U. Rappoport [Leiden: E. J. Brill, 1992]), compares rape and seduction in the Torah, the Temple Scroll, and tannaitic literature. He concludes that since the Temple Scroll does not mention a bride-price, only a fifty-silver-shekel payment to her father, the author of the scroll considers it a penalty, like the Tannaim who will later call it *kenas*, not a compensation to the father for the loss of his daughter's virginity (224). The author, he says further, "seeks to restore the moral balance and order." I am not convinced by his argument.

Moshe Weinfeld (*Deuteronomy and the Deuteronomic School*, [Oxford: Oxford University Press, 1972], 283–287) suggests that the Torah deals with only one case, seduction. The laws as they appear in Deuteronomy pay more attention to the victim of "rape" because the Deuteronomic author is more humanistic. He takes the seduction laws of Exodus and rewrites them according to his own outlook.

It seems to me that there is only one sex crime presented in the Bible: It is neither rape nor seduction, as we know them today, but something in between—part forced and part consensual. The Torah's skepticism about rape, combined with its two different terms to describe the same act, lead me to believe that it recognizes the use of force by the man but also imputes some sexual interest to the woman.

8. The Hebrew expression for depression is "ותשב תמר [ושממה]." No husband is ever reported for Dinah.

9. The only time that this word appears in the Bible is in Esther 1:8, "no one was to be forced" [to drink], [והשתיה כדת] אין אנס]. According to the NJPS translation, "No restrictions!"

10. The rabbis, utilizing the word *"moshi'a"* in v. 27, also require an innocent bystander to prevent the rape of a betrothed young woman, even if it means killing the man who is about to attack her (M Sanhedrin 8:7). The theory is let him die innocent rather than guilty. The penalty for the rape of a betrothed young woman is execution.

11. Should one argue that the shame spoken of here is that suffered by her father, because the verb "to suffer shame" is in the masculine מתבייש, I would respond that this formulation is borrowed from M BK 8:1 where it refers to the victim, male or female. Furthermore, M Ketubot 6:1 and T BK 9:14, when speaking of an assault on a woman that was committed in private, or on a concealed part of her body, either by her husband or by others, assigns part of the shame payment to her (two-thirds) and part to her husband (one-third). This source makes it clear that the primary one who suffers the shame is the victim, even though the payment is split between her and her husband, because he suffers shame secondarily. Cf. Judith Wegner, *Chattel or Person?* (New York: Oxford University Press, 1988), 26 and n. 53.

12. M BK 8:1 lists five payments for damages—loss of limb, pain, medical costs, unemployment, and shame. Here we find only injury, pain, and shame—because the other two, medical costs and unemployment, do not always apply to rape. However, if the woman suffered injuries in the course of the forced sex act, they do. Three of these payments derive from the Torah—loss of limb, medical costs, and

unemployment—and the other two, pain and shame, are rabbinic in origin. It is remarkable that Maimonides, in *Mishneh Torah,* Hilchot Hovel Umaziq 1:7, deduces the payment for pain (in a general case of injury) from the phrase "because he forced her." This means that Maimonides acknowledges that women suffer pain in rape. The Gemara derives the pain payment from a different verse. See BT BK 85a.

13. The Yerushalmi does not mention the possibility of refusal by the girl herself.

14. The only women he is not forced to marry are those of inappropriate lineage (e.g., a *mamzeret,* born of an incestuous or adulterous union). The rabbis will not force a violation of their own marital rules, even in a case of rape. The Temple Scroll already states that a rapist can marry his victim only if she is fitting for him according to the law. It then lists a variety of forbidden consanguineous relationships.

15. See Chapter 6 and Chapter 7 for a further expansion of this idea.

16. "A girl from the age of one day until [she shows the first signs of] puberty may be sold as a maidservant but *no* fine is paid by a man who rapes her. . . . The opinion of R. Meir. . . . But the Sages say: A girl from the age of one day and until the age of independence [full physical maturity, twelve and one-half], a fine *is* paid by the one who rapes her" (T 3:8). Rape penalties and the proceeds of the sale of a daughter as a maidservant are linked in that both are sums that the father receives for the "use" of his daughter.

17. Rachel Adler, "I've Had Nothing Yet So I Can't Take More," *Moment* 8 (September 1983): 22–26, writes that the rabbis neglect to ask how to hold the rapist of a little girl morally responsible for his behavior and how to compensate the young victim. The important question, she says, is how such things could happen. She further says that in a legal system in which a woman's sexuality belongs to her father, such questions cannot arise. I disagree. The texts analyzed in this chapter indicate a growing rabbinic awareness of the suffering of the victim of rape and seduction.

18. One exception is M Ketubot 6:1. Another can be found in PT Ketubot 5:5; 30a: "If one cuts off the hand of someone else's slave, his master takes [from the one who did so] payment for injury, pain, shame, and *pegam.* . . . "

19. −−"Said the father of Samuel: We estimate the difference between what a man would pay to have sex with a virgin slave and with a nonvirgin slave" (BT Ketubot 40b).

20. Chapter 3 of M Arakhin reviews the various fixed payments prescribed by the Torah and examines those cases that lead to paying either more or less than the circumstances required. It seems that the rabbis, in general, opposed stipulated payments, which do not take socioeconomic standing into consideration, despite the democratic nature of such payments. Although in a number of *mishnah*s the rabbis themselves seem to say that all Jews are equally precious in God's eyes (M BK 1:6), the other view, that social standing matters in assessment of damages, takes precedence.

21. The Hebrew phrase is "if she stood trial" [עמדה בדין], which could be taken as saying that she, not he, is on trial. The suit is named for her because she brings it, not because she is tried.

22. See M Ketubot 7:5, where pouring out onto a dunghill is a euphemism for coitus interruptus or an immediate attempt on her part to thwart a possible pregnancy.

23. The last part of the Yerushalmi *sugya* pursues R. Simon's thinking further:

"How does R. Simon understand the biblical phrase תחת אשר ענה [which implies that she suffered pain]?

--R. Hisda refers it [R. Simon's statement, ותפתר] to a case in which he came upon her [sexually] on thorns [meaning that in such a case, according to R. Simon, he pays for the pain of the thorns but not for the pain of the first sexual act itself]."

We thus see that the Yerushalmi is shocked that R. Simon can assert that there is no pain associated with rape of a virgin, since the Torah explicitly says that there is. R. Hisda therefore comments that according to R. Simon the verse must be referring to the pain of the force he exerted in getting her to submit, throwing her down on a bed of thorns.

24. Cf. BT Niddah 66b, where this phrase is cited as an example of a substance—namely, a scab—that does not interpose between the woman who immerses and the waters of the *mikveh,* and thus the immersion remains valid.

25. I strongly disagree with Wegner, *Chattel or Person?* (14), who asserts that the Bible acknowledges such a status.

26. In the Bible she went from being a daughter in her father's home, an unbetrothed young woman (Exod. 22:15; Deut. 22:28), to a betrothed young woman (Deut. 22:23, 25), to a wife in her husband's home. Some *mishnah*s paint the same picture, e.g., Ketubot 4:5, but posit marriage prior to the time of physical maturity.

27. These terms seem to refer to different stages in the development of breasts. See Albeck, *Niddah,* 392.

28. M Ketubot 4:4 says that a father is entitled to his daughter's betrothal, be it by money or any other means. The commentators explain this to mean that he gets the betrothal money only for a girl that he is permitted to marry off, namely a *na'arah* (between twelve and twelve and one-half), but not for a *bogeret* (over twelve and one-half).

29. BT Yevamot 59a, פרט לבוגרת שכלו לה בתוליה . . . [except for a mature woman whose hymen disappears].

30. There is one more way to achieve independence from her father at an even earlier age, and that is to have been married and then divorced (M Ketubot 4:2; see also 3:3, the opinion of R. Akiva).

31. I know of no scientific basis for this assertion.

32. The meaning of this colorful phrase is not clear.

33. If she were very young, her father would have to give her in marriage. It is not clear that he could do so even if he converted at the same time that she did.

34. See BT Kiddushin 78b and PT Bikkurim 1:5; 64a. The Bavli passage deals with the issue of a *kohen* marrying a Jewish woman, both of whose parents are converts, and decides that, like the view of R. Yossi in M Kiddushin 4:7, it is acceptable. R. Nahman comments:

--"Huna said to me that if a *kohen* comes to ask for advice, one should recommend that he adopt a personal stringency, as suggested by R. Eliezer b. Jacob [and only marry a woman who has at least one parent of Jewish stock]; if he had already married, we do not force him to divorce her, in accordance with R. Yossi."

35. Of course, consent has no meaning at this young age.

36. Or *karet* (see Chapter 7), depending on the precise relationship between the two participants.

37. This may be the basis for the statement by the *stama d'gemara*, in BT Sanhedrin 69b, that Bat Sheva gave birth to Solomon when she was very young, possibly eight or even six years old.

38. According to some rabbis, e.g., the Tanna R. Elazar, any incident of sexual relations of an unmarried woman, irrespective of the identity of the man, makes her into a *zonah* and hence forbidden in marriage to a *kohen*. See BT Yevamot 61b.

39. Cf. Judith Plaskow (*Standing Again at Sinai* [San Francisco: Harper and Row, 1990], 69), who says that "the delights of legal argumentation can lead to a certain distance from the concrete world of people and things."

40. As defined by Ilana Pardes, *Countertraditions in the Bible* (Cambridge: Harvard University Press, 1992). See Introduction herein, note 21.

41. This is the reading of the Vienna ms. The Erfurt ms. reads המסלסלת. See next note.

42. This verb appears differently in the various texts. Either it changes so often because it is not commonly used and was therefore unrecognizable to the transmitters or else the action described is so abhorrent to the transmitter that he alters the text somewhat. The root S-L-L means to rub. The root S-L-D means to shrink back, sometimes in disgust.

43. It does not seem that the *baraita* speaks of lesbians but of women, perhaps married, who sport with each other for pleasure.

44. Cf. BT Yevamot 76a, where R. Huna says that women who engage in this kind of sexual activity (*meSoLeLot*) are unfit to be married to a *kohen*. See also BT Shabbat 65a.

45. See the lengthy midrashic discussion of this point in the continuation of the Gemara.

46. See a full discussion of this passage in Chapter 2, in the first section.

47. BT Kiddushin 41a; BT Yevamot 62b. The same view is held by Paul. See 1 Cor. 7:36. Cf. Tal Ilan (*Jewish Women in Greco-Roman Palestine* [Tübingen: J.C.B. Mohr, 1995], 65–69), who concludes that there is no firm indication that girls were married off at twelve. Women as old as twenty were still viewed as desirable brides.

48. We should also remember that in a society that valued virginity, sex with a young girl would not be tolerated by her father. It would diminish her marital prospects.

49. Tigay speculates (*JPS Torah Commentary, Deuteronomy*, 208) that the Bible does not discuss the rape of a married woman, since engaged and unmarried girls "were less likely to have deliberately sought sexual experience than were married women, who were more sexually mature." The younger women, he says, were more likely to have been forced. In my opinion the explanation lies with men's sexual nature, not women's maturing sexuality: The rape of younger women was more likely because they appeared more attractive in the eyes of the male perpetrator and were probably more vulnerable.

5

Divorce

*I*T IS VERY TEMPTING TO DISMISS Mishnah Gittin as the volume that places men squarely in control of women's marital availability—in that only men may dissolve a marriage—and therefore responsible, to this very day, for women's suffering serious disabilities under Jewish divorce law. However, if we look at the tractate as a whole and ask ourselves what it is trying to accomplish, we will discover that the answer is more complicated. For the goal of this tractate, as we will see, is to ensure that the *get,* the instrument of divorce, is above reproach, and therefore fully protects women and children from unscrupulous men who would challenge its validity. Of course, the rabbis accepted the patriarchal construction of marriage, but within this framework they sought to improve the lives of the women governed by their laws. We cannot construe their end product as egalitarian; the right to issue a bill of divorce remains, even today, in the hands of men. But the introduction of a forced *get* and marriage annulment gave women seeking to extricate themselves from marriage options they never had before. Before examining these provisions in detail, we will first look at the tractate as a whole in order to gain insight into the rabbi's mindset about divorce. Unlike today, when divorce is most typically an indicator of the breakdown of marriage, divorce in the rabbinic period was often pictured as a consequence of forced, geographical separation of husband and wife.[1] Also unlike today, when the knottiest divorce problem among Jews is the spiteful, recalcitrant husband, in the tannaitic period the most commonly cited problem is the former husband who tries to reclaim his divorced, remarried wife.

The Biblical Basis of Divorce Law
and Grounds for Divorce

Deuteronomy 24:1–4 says that if a man takes a wife and then discovers that she no longer finds favor in his eyes because he has found some unseemly thing in her, he may write her a bill of divorce, put it in her hand, and send her out of his house. It further says that if she remarries and is then divorced or widowed by the second husband, her first husband may not take her back; such an act would be an abomination.

These verses imply that a woman may neither initiate divorce nor resist it. All marital decisions are in her husband's hands. But the Torah requires him to have grounds for divorce. As it says, she no longer pleases him because he has found in her "an *ervat davar.*"[2] This expression is enigmatic. The first word, a construct of *ervah,* meaning nakedness, has stark sexual overtones. This same word appears in the Torah's list of forbidden sexual liaisons (Leviticus 18). The association would imply that he dismisses her because he finds her sexually promiscuous.[3] But the phrase could also mean "obnoxious thing," as it does elsewhere (Deuteronomy 23:15),[4] and not necessarily refer to something sexual.

Other rules of the Torah enhance our understanding of the legal and also, perhaps, social realities of divorce in the biblical period. A priest, a *kohen,* may not marry a divorced woman, apparently because repudiation by her first husband has stigmatized her (Leviticus 21:7). In fact, because a priest should have the best, and a high priest, the very best, the latter cannot even marry a widow (21:14).[5] Moreover, unlike a wife or daughter, whose vows may be canceled by either a husband or a father, when a divorcee makes a vow, she must keep her word (Numbers 30:10): She is not subordinate to any man in her life who would have the power to cancel it. In this way a divorcee has more control over her religious life than a married woman.[6]

It is surprising that although the Torah stipulates that a husband must find in his wife an "unseemly thing" in order to divorce her, the rabbis nevertheless debate whether there need be any grounds for divorce at all.

> Bet Shammai says: A man should not divorce his wife unless he has found in her some kind of promiscuous behavior, as it says, "because he found in her some unseemly thing [with the focus on "unseemly," in the sexual sense]" (Deuteronomy 24:1).
>
> But Bet Hillel says: even if she burned his food, for it says, "because he found in her some unseemly thing" [with the focus on "thing," understood as anything at all].
>
> R. Akiva says: even if he found another more pleasing than she, as it says, "and should she no longer find favor in his eyes" (24:1). (M Gittin 9:10)

We see here a three-way dispute: Bet Shammai morally justifying divorce only for a serious cause, such as adultery; Bet Hillel for any reason whatsoever, even her burning the food just once; and R. Akiva, for no cause at all, merely his infatuation with another woman. R. Akiva and even Bet Hillel deliberately read the verse *not* according to its simple meaning, reaching a conclusion opposite to the Torah's intent of divorce for a good reason only. Although it is true that these rabbis seem to threaten a woman's domestic position, almost sanctioning divorce for the most minor of infractions or even none at all, that may not be the correct interpretation of their views. Do they imply so great an asymmetry in the relationship that she is like a slave whose place in the household can be guaranteed only by means of continuous, outstanding service?

A plain sense reading of the words of the *mishnah* suggests precisely that, but I think that a deeper reading yields a different message. Several clues take us below the surface. First, this *mishnah* is the concluding paragraph of the tractate, and tractates often close with an aggadic, homiletic flourish, not a point of *halakhah*. Second, this last paragraph does not connect thematically to the ones that precede it in the chapter. Nowhere else in Gittin is there a discussion of grounds for divorce, except in this *mishnah,* at the very end. Third, as we learn from M Ketubot, divorce poses enormous financial challenges. A husband who divorces his wife without good reason must liquidate assets in order to pay her the amount he promised her at the time they married, 100 zuz for a previously married woman, 200 for a virgin, or more if he chose to stipulate an additional amount *(tosefet ketubah).* In fact, when the rabbis joke about a bad wife, several say that it is one whose *ketubah* is large (BT Ketubot 63b).[7] In addition, as we learn from all nine chapters of this tractate, because of the attention that must be paid to detail, the execution of a bill of divorce is far from quick and simple. All these factors suggest that the final *mishnah* was placed here by the redactor not to examine the issue of legitimate grounds for divorce, not to teach that a man can discard his wife as easily as an old shoe, as proposed elsewhere,[8] but rather to make a closing, morally charged statement on the topic of divorce. It was appended here to warn men that despite the enormous power resting in their hands, the difficulties of *get* preparation and *ketubah* payment should make them think twice before acting without good cause.

A survey of grounds for divorce, as they are presented in M Ketubot, will support the suggestion that the concluding *mishnah* is merely exhortatory. A cluster of *mishnah*s (7:1–5) discusses at length the topic of the breakdown of marriage and gives examples of situations in which divorce is recommended or required. The question in such cases is whether the wife is entitled to collect her marriage settlement, as stipulated in the *ketubah.* For instance, if a husband takes a vow that his wife may derive no benefit from any of his assets, that is, that he will not support her, then he must divorce her after a short period of time and pay her the *ketubah.* Similarly, if he forbids her to eat certain foods or wear certain clothes, he must divorce her. In yet another case, if he forbids her to visit her family or go to houses of mourning or weddings, he must divorce her and pay her the *ketubah* "because he locks her up." As we saw in Chapter 1, it is clear that he has the right to control her comings and goings. However, these laws in Ketubot go so far as to tell a husband that if he abuses this privilege and denies his wife a social context altogether, the rabbis will come to her defense, forcing him to divorce her with payment of the *ketubah*.[9]

M Ketubot goes on to list grounds for divorce that result from women's misbehavior:

> These women leave without a *ketubah*: . . . If she feeds him food from which she has not separated tithes, or engages in sex with him when a *niddah* (menstruant), or does not separate hallah, or takes a vow and does not keep her word. . . .
>
> If she goes out without covering her head, spins in the marketplace, speaks with any man. . . . (M Ketubot 7:6)

Finally, the Mishnah lists a wife's grounds for divorce that derive from her husband's physical attributes (M 9–10). If a woman tells a rabbinical court that she cannot tolerate her husband's blemishes, the *mishnah* dictates that the court assist her in obtaining a divorce. Legitimate complaints include boils, a polyp on the nose, or an unpleasant odor, such as from a husband who is a tanner. In such cases the court forces him to divorce her [כופין אותו להוציא] and pay the *ketubah* in full.

M Ketubot thus sets forth the relative rights of the husband and wife to end their marriage: He may divorce her for serious cause, with the benefit of not having to pay the marriage settlement; she may "divorce" him for cause, without suffering any financial penalty. By implication, he may even divorce her without good reason, but he will have to pay in full.[10] She may not do the same to him.

Although this list tilts toward him, it clearly discourages the husband from divorce on a whim: If he dismisses his wife with only flimsy grounds or without any grounds at all, although within his rights, he will suffer serious financial setback. T Ketubot (12:1) says that the *ketubah* payment was instituted to inhibit impetuous divorce. Moreover, divorcing on impulse is not easy, given all the rules of *get* preparation. When we read the final *mishnah* of Gittin against this background, remembering that it is isolated thematically from the rest of the tractate, we find that, rather than expanding men's options for divorce and threatening women with unstable marriages unless they toe the mark, the redactor seems to suggest (but does not say so explicitly) that exercising one's rights for no good reason is likely to cause a man more pain than relief. Not a bad concluding homily.

Standardization of the Get
and Comparison with the Writ of Manumission

According to M Gittin, a woman's bill of divorce and a slave's writ of manumission are two variations of the same institution. The word *get* merely means document, not instrument of divorce.[11] The term for a bill of divorce is *get ishah* and for a writ of manumission, *get shihrur*. Just as an emancipated slave needs a document to prove his status as a freedman, so does a woman need a document to prove her marital availability, not just when she gets remarried but also later on to defend herself against possible challenge. By discussing these bills in tandem and according them similar names and rules, the Mishnah is suggesting that divorce of a wife by a husband is like manumission of a slave by a master: Divorce "frees" a woman from a marital relationship in which he is dominant and she subordinate.

Since the *get* and the writ of manumission are given for the good of the recipient, so that he or she has proof of dissolution of prior "ownership," the attempt to standardize these documents is intended to benefit the recipient, not the donor. If a woman remarries and only later discovers that her *get* was flawed, Jewish law will view her second marriage as an adulterous relationship and her children from her second "husband" as *"mamzerim,"* of impaired lineage and maritally ineligible to anyone other than another *mamzer*.[12] In order to protect a woman and her offspring from ever acquiring such status, the rabbis spend much time laying down rules for the *get*. These rules are not meant to be burdensome but to set standards against which to judge a *get*. If it conforms, it will be above reproach.

After chapter 1 of M Gittin discusses the special rules that apply to a *get* sent from abroad to the land of Israel, chapters 2 and 3 present the basic rules for preparing a *get*.

> One may write *with* anything: ink, arsenic, red chalk, gum, sulphate of copper, and anything else that lasts. One may not write with drinks, fruit juice, or anything that does not last.
>
> One may write *on* anything: an olive leaf, a horn of a cow and he must give her the cow, a hand of a slave and he must give her the slave. R. Yossi says: One may not write on anything animate or on food. . . . (M 2:3)

> All are fit to write the *get*, even a deaf-mute, a mentally impaired person, and a minor. . . .
>
> All are fit to bring the *get* [from one place to another for delivery to the wife], except for a deaf-mute, a mentally impaired person, or a minor. (2:5)

> Any *get* that was not written expressly for the woman [to be divorced] is not valid. (3:1)
>
> One who prepares divorce documents must leave room for the name of the man, the woman, and the date. (3:2)

It is not hard to see that the rabbis are striving in these paragraphs to produce a *get* that a woman will be able to present at any time in the future in order to validate her status. For this reason they require ink that lasts and paper that will not disintegrate. No restrictions at all are placed on the scribe, for the written word counts, not who writes it. In addition, since many *gittin* discussed by this tractate are brought from abroad to the land of Israel, the bearer must be someone who is capable of giving testimony that it was written and signed in his presence. If anyone then appears and challenges its validity, the bearer can testify that the *get* is valid (and his testimony will be sufficient, that is, will be considered as the testimony of two) even though the witnesses to the *get* are abroad. Those who are not of sound mind are excluded, since they would be unable to testify. Elsewhere in the tractate, rules are presented about the attestation of the *get* itself and its delivery.

The text of the *get* does not appear until the very last chapter of the tractate. It is written partly in Hebrew and partly in Aramaic.

> The text of the *get*: Behold you are permitted [in marriage] to any man. R. Judah says: And this will be to you from me a document of severance, certificate of leaving, and a writ of dismissal, that you may go and marry any man whom you wish.
>
> The text of the writ of manumission: Behold you are a free woman,[13] behold you are on your own. (M Gittin 9:3)

Here, at the end of the tractate, where the two kinds of documents are once more dealt with side by side, the reader is again forced to confront the similarity of the two situations: Just as a slave is owned by the master and then set free, so, too, is a wife dominated by her husband and then set free, which means, in her case, able to enter into another marital relationship. In each of these instances one person, the husband or master, is relinquishing control over another, the wife or slave. In each of these cases it is not a declaration but a document that severs the relationship and will safeguard the newly won status of its recipient.

The essential similarities of these two institutions also draws attention to their differences. As tempted as we may be to call marriage slavery, we may not do so for a number of reasons. A woman always owns herself, her physical being. She cannot be passed along from one "master" to the next.

She may own property even when married. She has a right to part of her husband's estate upon dissolution of the relationship through divorce or death. She may make demands of him. He has an obligation to support her. None of this is true in reference to slaves. Whereas we may draw the inference that the means of divorce, like the means of betrothal, preserve the older purchase-of-a-wife model of marriage—she is bought like a slave and also dismissed like a slave—nevertheless, the essence of the marriage, as refashioned by the Mishnah, is significantly different from slavery. Although the husband is dominant and the wife subordinate, it would be wrong to equate subordination with slavery.

The aim of the standardization of the *get,* as noted, is to protect the woman from a challenge to its validity. The Mishnah, as early as chapter 1:3, makes reference to the possibility of such a challenge. But who is likely to question the validity of the *get* and thereby wreak havoc on her life? R. Hisda says that it is her first husband, the man who wrote the *get* and sent it from abroad, who is now trying to hurt her.[14] Perhaps he left home against his will, for fear of persecution by a hostile government, or went on a business trip and decided to stay abroad and start a new life. Should he find his way back home, he may be displeased to discover that the wife he divorced is living with some other man, her new husband, and in a fit of jealousy may try to undermine the validity of the *get* that he himself sent. If he were believed, the children of her second husband would be *mamzerim* and she would have to leave him without receiving a *ketubah.* She would also be forbidden to resume life with her first husband.[15]

Recurrent Themes: The Vacillating Husband and Compatible Divorce

Since the Mishnah is usually studied one paragraph at a time, the larger issues—those that the Mishnah returns to again and again—often elude the eye of the reader. But it is precisely the recurrent themes that point us to legal truths, if not social ones as well. The matters that especially interest legislators are likely to be those that speak to their contemporary situation. By identifying these motifs, we can better comprehend the rabbis' mindset about divorce. This comprehension will lead, in turn, to a more precise understanding of their legal pronouncements.

In many different passages throughout the tractate, in five out of the nine chapters, M Gittin portrays the divorcing husband as a man who decides one day to divorce his wife but on the next changes his mind.

> If a man says [to a messenger], "Give this *get* to my wife or this writ of manumission to my slave," if he wishes to **retract** in both of these

cases he may, [provided the *get* has not yet reached the wife or the slave]. This is the opinion of R. Meir. . . . (M Gittin 1:6)

. . . If a man prepares a *get* for his wife and then **changes his mind** [and decides not to divorce her], and someone else whose wife has the same name [wishes to use the *get*,] he may not do so [because a *get* must be written expressly for the woman who is to be divorced]. (M 3:1)

If he sends a *get* to his wife via messenger and he then overtakes the messenger, or if he sends a second messenger after the first, and says to him, "The *get* that I gave you is **canceled**," it is canceled. If he reaches his wife before the *get* does or if he sends a [second] messenger to his wife and says, "The *get* I sent you is **canceled**," it is canceled. But once the *get* reaches her hand, he may no longer cancel. . . . (M 4:1)

If he says [to a messenger], "Accept this *get* for my wife," or "Take this *get* to my wife," if he wishes to **change his mind**, he may do so [as long as the *get* has not yet reached his wife]. If the wife says [to her messenger, "Go and] accept this *get* on my behalf," if the husband wants to **change his mind** . . . (M 6:1)

If he wrote a *get* for his wife and then **changed his mind**, Bet Shammai says . . . but Bet Hillel says . . . (M 8:8)

The repeating image of vacillation throughout this tractate suggests that, in the eyes of the rabbis, divorcing husbands, or perhaps men in general, are emotionally unstable, one moment so angered that they decide to divorce, as evidenced by Bet Hillel's example of burnt food (M Gittin 9:10), and the next sufficiently calm that they regret their decision. Rather than point out women's emotional or behavioral flaws, these laws highlight men's. In other words, the blame for the breakdown of the marriage is placed not on women but on men.

Another repetitive theme is the divorce that results, not from incompatibility, but from the exigencies of life. The many references to a *get* that one sends from abroad suggests that men, through no fault of their own, were forced to live abroad for a while, or at least in a different province in ancient Israel. In these situations, it must have seemed reasonable for a man to divorce his wife, even though he was at peace with her, so that she could live out her life, remarry, and have children with another man. Divorce terminates his obligations to support her. We also read of men about to be executed or die from an illness who save their wives from levirate marriage—if a man died childless, the Torah mandates the marriage of his widow to his brother (Deuteronomy 25:5–9)—by issuing a divorce before they die (M 6:5,6; T 5:1). We similarly find men who leave town and intend to come back, but even so give their wives a conditional divorce, one that will take effect only if they do not return by the stipulated date (M 7:7). In this way they ensure that their wives will never be anchored to a man who is not living with them and possibly not even alive.

The repeated references to men in dire straits and to the arrival in ancient Israel of *gittin* sent from abroad leads me to believe that these laws were written in response to harsh economic and political realities. Although it is generally not wise to draw conclusions about social realities from a legal text, in this instance it seems warranted.

All in all, the husband described in many *mishnah*s in this tractate is not a man who is holding back a *get* in order to spite a wife with whom he did not get along or press her for concessions—the children were his (BT Ketubot 59b),[16] as was true in most systems of ancient law,[17] and he owed her nothing but the *ketubah*. Rather, he does not necessarily want to let go of the woman to whom he is married, although he, for now, is unable to live with her. This tractate paints a rather poignant portrait of men who divorce their wives under duress, probably for the benefit of the wife. In cases like these, I think it important to note, divorce is not an act of anger but an expression of kindness.

Annulment of Marriage

As much as a man's predicament may arouse our sympathy, it is also necessary to look at divorce law from a woman's perspective. And this is precisely what one *mishnah* does, with far-reaching consequences.

> At first, a man would convene a court in a different location [from where his wife was living] and cancel the *get* [he had sent and not inform her of his actions]. Rabban Gamliel the Elder passed a law prohibiting men from doing so, in order to repair the social order [מפני תקון העולם]. (M Gittin 4:2)

By restricting a man's freedom of action, by requiring him to inform his wife that he canceled the *get* he sent her, Rabban Gamliel repaired the social order, which meant, in this case, improving the lot of women and children. Until that time, a woman could receive a *get* that looked perfectly valid, remarry, and only afterward, most likely by chance, find out that her husband had canceled it. In such a case her second union would be adulterous and the children of that union *mamzerim*.

In this passage, Rabban Gamliel essentially closed the gap that was developing between law and ethics. Allowing a husband to cancel a *get* after it was drawn up and dispatched but before it was delivered was reasonable, but it would be unreasonable and unfair if he were not required to inform his wife of the cancellation. So, even though divorce was exclusively in a man's hands, Rabban Gamliel placed limits on him.

The Gemara comments:

> ==What does "for the sake of repairing the social order" mean?
> – –R. Yohanan said: [He made] this enactment [to reduce the number] of *mamzerim*.
> – –Resh Lakish said: [He made] this enactment [to reduce the number] of *agunot*. (BT Gittin 33a)

These two Amoraim disagree about which social wrong Rabban Gamliel was trying to repair. R. Yohanan holds that Rabban Gamliel's enactment was intended to reduce the number of instances in which the news will *not* reach the wife's ears and she will remarry and bear illegitimate children before she finds out about her husband's cancellation. Resh Lakish, according to the Gemara, explains the enactment differently. He says that by making a cancellation more difficult to execute, it is unlikely that a man whose only aim is to torment his wife, to keep her tied to him but not live with her, would bother to intercept the messenger. As a result, the number of *agunot*—women anchored to their first husband from whom they are separated—would decrease.

The Yerushalmi's alternative explanation of Resh Laskish's statement on *agunot* is more to my liking.[18] It says that if a man is permitted to cancel a *get* without informing his wife, then a woman who receives a *get* by messenger will worry that it may have been revoked after it was mailed but before she received it and will, therefore, refrain from remarrying, thus becoming a self-imposed *agunah*. She will consider herself tied to a man she is not living with and who has, in fact, divorced her. Once the enactment was made, a woman no longer had to fear that a *get* that looked valid was not.

There is no need for us to choose between the comments of Resh Lakish and R. Yohanan. The two rabbis probably intended to complement each other, as suggested by R. Huna,[19] since the enactment reduces both the number of *mamzerim* and of *agunot*. In either case, Rabban Gamliel's larger point is the unfairness of delivering to a wife a *get* that looks perfectly valid, only to have her discover at a later date that it was a worthless piece of paper. This leads us once more to the main purpose of the entire tractate: the attempt to create standards for the preparation and delivery of the *get* that will make it impossible for it later to be found invalid. Since it is only women who need a *get*, these standards aim to protect them.

Support for this idea can be found in the second part of the very same *mishnah*. It reports that Rabban Gamliel the Elder introduced yet another enactment to repair the social order: that all names by which the husband

and wife are known be entered into the *get* so that there will be no question as to who is divorcing whom. The next *mishnah* (4:3) presents yet two more divorce enactments by Rabban Gamliel, one that made it possible for the woman to collect a marriage settlement upon divorce at a time when many rabbis made it impossible for her to do so, and a second,[20] that the witnesses to the writing of the *get* affix their signatures to it so that verifying its validity in the face of a challenge would be easier. These four changes, all enacted for the sake of *tikkun ha-olam,* to repair the social order, and all obviously intended to aid women, head a long list of other enactments also introduced for the same reason. Some of these improve the lives of slaves, some protect the Jewish ownership of land in Palestine, and the rest address a variety of other issues.

Although this group of laws and the following one, enactments made for the sake of peace, *mipnei darchei shalom* (M 5:8, 9), are well-known collections, little attention has been paid to the fact that changes benefiting women, primarily with respect to the dissolution of marriage, head the list of *tikkun ha-olam* enactments and determine its placement in M Gittin. These new rules make an extraordinarily powerful statement about the rabbis' ability to introduce legislation independent of, and even, as the Gemara will point out, contradictory to Scripture, when acting to restore a stance of social justice to the system. Once more, however, it should be noted that these changes needed to be made only because society, and divorce law in particular, was configured in a patriarchal and hierarchical manner. In contradistinction to the rules of Jewish divorce, Roman law, in the late Republic, allowed either a man or a woman to terminate a marriage, simply by one saying to the other, "Take your things for yourself."[21]

The Gemara continues with a discussion of the broader implications of this change in law:

> We learned in a *baraita* (T Gittin 3:3): If he canceled the *get* [without her knowledge, after Rabban Gamliel the Elder's enactment disallowing such behavior was already in place], it remains canceled. The opinion of Rebbe. R. Simon b. Gamliel says: He may not cancel it . . . for that would undermine the legislative authority of [Rabban Gamliel's] court [and all others].
>
> ==Can it be that, according to the Torah, the *get* is canceled [and the woman, therefore, still married to her husband], but [in order to uphold] the authority of the court, we [i.e., the rabbis] declare a married woman to be available for remarriage?
>
> ==Yes, all who betroth accept upon themselves the rabbinic rules of marriage [אדעתא דרבנן מקדש] and [if they break them] the rabbis [of their day] may annul the betrothal. (BT Gittin 33a)

The opening passage of this unit presents a dispute that appears to be about the cancellation of a *get* without the woman's knowledge but is also, at a deeper level, about the extent and limits of rabbinic authority. Rebbe holds that the freedom that a man has to cancel a *get* without informing his wife can be taken away from him only ab initio, but that, after the fact, such a cancellation is valid. His father, R. Simon b. Gamliel, disagrees, noting that if the husband's obligation to inform his wife of the cancellation were disregarded after the fact, then the ability of rabbis like Rabban Gamliel the Elder, his own great-grandfather, to introduce legislative change would be seriously impaired. The Gemara, in an attempt to push the opinion of R. Simon b. Gamliel to its logical extreme, asks if later rabbis would declare a woman to be available for remarriage if in the eyes of the Torah she was still married to her husband. Such a stand would uphold the authority of earlier rabbis to make a change that they deemed necessary for the sake of social justice, even if it contravened Torah law.

The Gemara answers yes, presumably meaning that later rabbis accept the idea that earlier rabbis have the authority to do so.[22] But the next line implies that this word "yes" is not to be taken literally, for the Gemara goes on to explain that when a man betroths a woman, he does so on condition that he not violate rabbinic marital law.[23] And since one of the rabbinic provisions is that a man not cancel a *get* without his wife's knowledge, any man who does so is violating the stipulations of his betrothal. In such a case, the Gemara continues, the rabbis of his day have the right to annul his betrothal, which means to free his wife to remarry *without a get*.

To my mind, the Gemara has not given a direct answer to the question whether the rabbis have the right to contravene Torah law. It is merely saying that, according to R. Simon b. Gamliel, any man who cancels a *get* without his wife's knowledge has stepped outside the bounds of rabbinic marital law. But since he stipulated upon betrothal that he accepted rabbinic marital law, he has now paved the way for the rabbis of his day to annul his betrothal and declare his wife free to remarry without a *get*. This is the Gemara's interpretation of the words of R. Simon b. Gamliel, but, we should note, it is not an explicit statement that the rabbis have the right to rescind Torah law. All Sages would agree that breaking a stipulation of marriage invites annulment. As long as the matter is cast in this light, no groundbreaking principle emerges from this discussion. But a more subtle principle has been expressed here: When rabbis run amok of Torah, *as they themselves define Torah*—which, in this instance, means a man's unfettered right to cancel a *get* before it reaches his wife—and recognize that by adhering to the written Torah they are promoting injustice to women, then they may in fact, if not in principle, abrogate a rule of the written Torah. In this case, the rabbinic restrictions on a man's right to cancel a *get* are given precedence over the written Torah's more problematic, unrestricted rights.

The practical implications of this discussion are far-reaching. If men accept upon themselves all of rabbinic marital law as a condition of their betrothal, then, if a man cancels a *get* without informing his wife, he makes his marriage subject to annulment. The rabbis of the Mishnah added that rule to the corpus of rabbinic marital law and thus eliminated one form of divorce abuse by husbands. Similarly, rabbis of a different time period could place other rules within the corpus and in this way make a marriage subject to annulment because of those violations as well. They could thus prevent other forms of divorce abuse, such as a husband's refusing to issue a *get* even after a rabbinical court has instructed him to do so. I stress violations by a husband and not by a wife because it is he who is in control of the *get*, and so dissolving or maintaining the marriage is in his hands alone, often to her detriment.

We thus see that the rabbis devised an extraordinarily powerful technique for dealing with husbands who behave in ways that hurt their wives: The rabbinical court, on its own volition or at the wife's request, has the power to step in and dissolve the marriage without his approval or participation. This provision is a move away from patriarchy and toward resolution of marital difficulties in a manner fairer to women. It still falls short of wife-initiated divorce.

Forced Divorce

Although M Gittin contains nine chapters, sixty-six paragraphs in all, only one part of one paragraph deals with the topic of forced divorce.

> . . . A forced bill of divorce—[if executed] by a Jewish [court], it is valid; by a non-Jewish court, it is invalid. And in a non-Jewish court they may beat him [חובטין אותו] and say, do what the Jewish court asks of you, and it [i.e., the *get*] is valid. (M Gittin 9:8)

The simplicity of this passage is startling. Having no connection at all to what precedes or follows it, and coming very close to the end of the tractate, it says that it is acceptable for a Jewish court of law to force a man to write a *get* for his wife. No explanation is given of the circumstances under which a court could issue such an order. Even so, we should not underestimate the revolutionary nature of this brief statement. For more than eight chapters, the tractate has made it abundantly clear that it is men who divorce women and not women who "divorce" men.[24] And this *mishnah* states the opposite, if we assume that it is she who asked the court to assist her in obtaining a divorce from him. At the very least, men are no longer in full control of divorce proceedings. Since the rabbis were aware of the fact that non-Jewish courts enabled women to divorce men,[25] this ruling may have been triggered by a rabbinic desire to make such an option available to Jewish women, who, as we will see, were probably clamoring for it.

Reading this *mishnah* together with another from Yevamot will sharpen our understanding of both.

If a deaf-mute man married a woman who could hear, or if a man who could hear married a deaf-mute woman: if he wishes to, he may divorce [her]; or, if he wishes to, he may remain married to her [thus indicating that a deaf woman may be divorced and a deaf man may give a divorce]. Just as he betroths by [giving] a sign, so he divorces by [giving] a sign.

If a man with normal hearing married a woman with normal hearing and then she lost her hearing, if he wishes to, he may divorce her, or if he wishes to, he may remain married to her. If she lost her mind, he may not divorce her. If he lost his hearing or his mind, he may never divorce.

Said R. Yohanan b. Nuri: *For what reason* [מפני מה] may a woman who lost her hearing be divorced but a man who lost his hearing not give a divorce?

They said to him: A man who gives a divorce is not like a woman who gets a divorce. A woman leaves whether she wishes to or not; a man sends her away only if he wishes to [שהאשה יוצאה לרצונה ושלא לרצונה והאיש אינו מוציא אלא לרצונו]. (M Yevamot 14:1)

This *mishnah* does more than simply record a point of law about men and women who have lost their hearing. There is a debate here about larger halakhic issues. R. Yohanan b. Nuri's query, why the difference in the rights of men and women who have lost their hearing, seems to fall on "deaf" ears. His colleagues respond to him as if he had asked, "Why does this law treat men and women differently?" But their answer—that women may be divorced against their will but men may not give a divorce against theirs—is almost certainly a rule he already knew, since it underlies so much of Jewish divorce law and makes so much sense in a patriarchal society. I therefore think that his question is rhetorical: He is not *asking* "why does this difference exist?" but is *asserting* that this difference in the application of the rules is not fair. R. Yohanan b. Nuri issues a challenge: If you rabbis consider divorce acceptable and even desirable in cases of misfortune like these, then it is not morally right that you allow a hearing husband to cast off a wife who became deaf, but do *not* allow a hearing wife to cast off a husband who became deaf. Having no real answer, his colleagues merely reiterate the well-known rule of unilateral divorce by men only. Note that this is the same R. Yohanan b. Nuri who said to R. Akiva and R. Meir, when they were listing grounds for divorce, such as suckling a baby in public(!), that according to their excessive demands of modesty, no Jewish woman would be able to remain married to her husband (Gittin 89a). We thus find in this *mishnah* one rabbi who was sensitive to women's relative disablement under Jewish divorce law in this particular case—and, it stands to reason, in other cases as well.[26] He critiques Jewish divorce law as a system in which only men can effect divorce.

If we now return to the forced divorce rule of M Gittin 9:8, we can begin to understand it better. It is possible that this rule, which undercuts so much of the legislation in this tractate, is a vestige of a different point of view, similar to R. Yohanan b. Nuri's, that recognized that women, too, should be able to extricate themselves from a bad marriage. The redactor of the Mishnah includes it in the collection of miscellaneous rules at the end of the tractate because he is sympathetic to women's vulnerability to abuse under divorce law and wishes to begin to act on their behalf.

The Mishnah develops further the notion of a forced divorce in a different tractate. When discussing the forced donation of sacrifices to the Temple, M Arakhin says:

> . . . [The verse says, "He shall offer it . . .] willingly" [Leviticus 1:3, לרצונו]! [How is this possible?] They exert force on him until he says, I wish to [make this donation to the Temple of my own free will].
>
> And similarly with bills of divorce: They exert force on him until he says, I wish to [כופין אותו עד שיאמר רוצה אני] [write this *get* of my own free will]. (5:6)

This *mishnah*, strangely enough, seems to undermine the concept of a forced divorce. Once the element of willingness on the part of the husband is introduced into the process of forcing a *get*, execution becomes virtually impossible. Force and free will are contradictory concepts. However, it is possible that the declaration "I do this of my own free will" means that he will, in fact, give the *get* willingly because he wants those who are applying pressure on him to stop doing so. As the Talmud says elsewhere (BT Baba Batra 48a), the result of the application of pressure is that he reconciles himself to his fate and does what is asked of him "of his own free will."[27]

When this same passage appears in the Midrash Halakhah,[28] where it probably originated, it does not make any reference to a *get*, only to the donation of a sacrifice. The midrash, like the Mishnah, derives the requirement that a sacrifice be "of his own free will"—even if forced—from a word in the verse that says that it must be offered voluntarily, *li-retzono*. No such word appears in the verses that speak of divorce. It is therefore tempting to conclude that the clause about the freely granted, yet forced, *get* was added later to the *mishnah* in Arakhin, probably by individuals who wished to make it difficult for a woman to force a man to write a *get*, or even by the redactor of the Mishnah himself, who may have remained ambivalent on the subject. Both references in the Mishnah to a forced *get* seem to be later additions, one expressing sympathy for women and trying to help them, the other hedging this concern.[29] The Yerushalmi raises another interesting possibility—that in certain situations the rabbis should "seduce" (but not force) a man into giving a *get*, convince him, and maybe even pressure him into doing what they think is right. By the time he writes it, it is of his own free will.[30]

The important question is, How did the rabbis of the Talmud respond in theory and in practice to this set of contradictory rules? I find it remarkable that the passage from Arakhin about a man's writing a forced *get* of his own free will seems to have been consistently ignored by the Amoraim or else assumed not to pose a problem. The Gemara's discussion in M Gittin 9:8—about a forced divorce—makes no reference to it, nor do the other discussions of the subject elsewhere in this tractate. The Yerushalmi parallel also makes no reference to it. We will soon see that although forcing a *get* became part of mainstream amoraic practice, requiring the husband to do so of his own free will did not.

> – –Said R. Nahman in the name of Samuel: A *get* compelled by a Jewish court according to the rules is fit; not according to the rules is unfit [and she remains a married woman]; even so, were a woman to receive such a *get* and then, upon the death of her husband, wish to marry a *kohen,* she would not be allowed to do so. . . . A *get* from a gentile court . . .
>
> – –Said R. Mesharshaya: According to the Torah [דבר תורה], a *get* compelled by a non-Jewish court is valid(!). Why did the rabbis go and declare it invalid? To stop each and every Jewish woman from seeking the assistance of a non-Jewish court [to compel a *get*] and thus release herself from the control of her husband [שלא תהא כל אחת ואחת הולכת ותולה עצמה בערכ ומפקעת עצמה מיד בעלה] . . .
>
> ==The statement of R. Mesharshaya was fabricated . . . [בדותא היא] (BT Gittin 88b)

Samuel, a first generation Babylonian Amora, limits the scope of the mishnaic rule by saying that a woman cannot seek the assistance of the court in obtaining a divorce unless she has grounds. What he apparently means by this, as noted by Rashi (s.v. *kadin*), is that she must register one of the claims about which the Tannaim said, "he should dismiss her and pay her the marriage settlement," as discussed above. A court could also force a *get*, according to Rashi, if she were forbidden to him by Jewish law.[31]

Several other instances of acceptable wife-initiated divorce are added by the Bavli and the Yerushalmi: if she wishes to move to Palestine and he refuses to do so, he is forced to divorce her and pay the *ketubah* (Ketubot 110b; PT Ketubot 13:11; 36b); if they have not had any children after ten years of marriage and she wishes to leave him, he is forced to divorce her and pay the *ketubah* (Yevamot 65b; PT Yevamot 6:6, 7d).[32]

If Samuel has cases like these in mind, then he is limiting the scope of a woman's ability to turn to the courts for assistance. He restricts the apparently broad latitude the Mishnah granted a woman to initiate the divorce proceedings herself. But R. Mesharshaya, who lived several generations later than Samuel, says that according to the Torah, even a *get* compelled by a non-Jewish court is valid. However, as a political move—to stop Jewish women from seeking relief from non-Jewish courts—the rabbis decided to rule more stringently than was required and invalidate it.

This last statement is shocking. It suggests that men were so deeply disturbed by women's newly discovered way of extricating themselves from the control of their husbands that they found it necessary to declare a valid document invalid. This is a rather troubling use of legislative power. But why were Jewish women preferring gentile courts to Jewish ones? Was it because Jewish courts were biased against them? Did Jewish courts make it hard for women to produce valid grounds?

The Talmud, perhaps embarrassed by its own callousness, claims that R. Mesharshaya's statement was fabricated.[33] Elsewhere (BT Baba Batra 48a), however, this same statement by R. Mesharshaya is cited without such a disclaimer. This leads me to believe that the statement "it was fabricated" was itself fabricated. We may have historical evidence here of Jewish women turning to non-Jewish courts to protest the discriminatory practices of Jewish law courts.[34] We may even want to view R. Mesharshaya's statement as a countertradition, one that views wife-initiated divorce as a moral necessity, even within a patriarchal social order.

The *sugya* continues:

> – –Abaye found R. Joseph sitting [in court] and compelling [husbands to give] *gittin* [to their wives]. He said to him: But we are [only] lay judges [and hence not authorized to do so]! . . .
> – –He responded: We are deputized by them [the expert judges in Palestine to judge these kinds of cases]. . . . We are thus empowered to decide all matters that frequently come before the courts. . . . (BT Gittin 88b)

This segment concludes the Gemara's commentary on the *mishnah* about compelling a *get*. It points out that the rabbis of Babylonia, like those in Palestine, had the authority to compel a *get* and, moreover, that they were actually doing so. Even more surprisingly, according to the concluding note of the anonymous voice of the text, they were doing so fairly often.[35] This note about frequent coercion appears to be a ringing endorsement of the rule of forcing men to write a *get*. The question that remains is whether the courts were forcing *gittin* because women filed complaints or because the courts opposed certain marriages, such as that between a *kohen* and a divorcee. Although I do not know, I find no reason to think that it was just one case or the other.

There is also evidence that other rabbis, for example R. Sheshet and R. Judah, both early Babylonian Amoraim, were forcing *gittin*. In one of the Gemara's accounts (Gittin 34a), it is reported that R. Judah forced a man to write a *get*, and the man then canceled it. R. Judah forced him to write it again, after which the man canceled it again, upon which R. Judah forced him to write it a third time. It is hard to reconcile these details with the notion of "forcing him until he does so voluntarily" that we saw in M Arakhin. Had he agreed to do it voluntarily, he would not have canceled it immediately twice. This case, as well as the other one cited on the same page, thus suggests that a not unusual response to forcing a *get* was cancellation of a *get*. The existence of such a problem implies a husband who is acting *against* his own free will, not in consonance with it. As soon as the immediate compulsion is removed, his real inclination reasserts itself.

The Yerushalmi's discussion of this topic is, in certain ways, more informative than the Bavli's. Among several statements by Samuel that begin the Palestinian *sugya* is the unexpected one that the only time a court may force a divorce is if the couple violated Jewish law, such as a divorcee who married a priest or a widow who married a high priest. It continues:

> --R. Jeremiah asked R. Abahu: Do we force a divorce if he refuses to support her?
>
> --He responded: If because of [his] bad odor we force a divorce, would we not force a divorce when her very life depends on it?
>
> --R. Hezeqiah came [and reported]: R. Jacob bar Aha ... R. Yohanan said: If a man says, "I refuse to support my wife," we say to him, "Either support her or divorce her." (PT Gittin 9:9; 50d)

Although the Mishnah declares a forced divorce legitimate, it is left to the Amoraim to figure out precisely when this rule could be implemented. Some opinions, it seems, were more lenient in defining the validity of the woman's complaint, and some more stringent, but the focus is on women's needs, not just violation of marital law. After laying out this dispute for the reader, the *sugya* moves toward resolution, offering an extraordinarily powerful logical argument. If a man is forced, according to the Mishnah (Ketubot 7:10), to divorce his wife because she cannot tolerate his odor, certainly he may be forced if he refuses to support her. A statement by R. Yohanan, a giant among Palestinian Amoraim, reiterates this position,

adding that one should first attempt to repair the relationship by request-
ing that he start supporting her. But if he refuses, the court may force him
to divorce her. Again, we note, there is no reference here to forcing him to
divorce "of his own free will."

The Babylonian and Palestinian discussions of the Mishnah create the
impression that recalcitrant husbands and forced divorces had already
made their appearance in the amoraic period. Both Talmuds view legitimate grounds for divorce as a limiting factor on a woman's ability to exercise her right to ask for a forced divorce. But the concept of the forced divorce, although interpreted and restricted, becomes entrenched. Much of
this legal development, it seems to me, is a response to the injustice of allowing men, but not women, to dissolve a bad marriage.

A Husband Who Claims That
He Issued the Get Under Duress

The following difficult passage informs us that even though the courts
forced men to write a *get* "of their own free will," the men devised ways of
thwarting these efforts to help women. Yet another layer of legislation had
to be added to safeguard the validity of the forced divorce.

> – –Said R. Sheshet: He who issues a statement that he is about to be
> forced to give a *get* [מסר מודעא אגיטא], his notification is valid [and
> the *get* that he then gives is not].
>
> ==But that is obvious!
>
> ==No, it needed to be stated for the following case, that they forced
> him [to write a *get*, after he had issued a notification of duress], but by
> the time he wrote it, he did so of his own free will [דעשאוה ואירצי].
>
> ==What erroneous conclusion might we have arrived at [had R.
> Sheshet not issued this statement]? That it stands to reason that he
> canceled the notification of duress prior to writing the *get*. [Therefore,
> R. Sheshet] comes to teach us otherwise: [that although the man is, in
> the end, writing the *get* voluntarily, even so, we must not *assume* that
> he canceled the notification of duress but must require him to do so
> explicitly].[36] (BT Arakhin 21b)

This segment indicates that there was another difficulty associated with
forcing a man to issue a *get:* He could sidestep the pressure by prior notification of duress. According to Jewish law, such notification invalidates the
document that he then writes, be it a bill of divorce or a bill of sale (BT
Baba Batra 48a). A woman who received such a *get* might believe it to be a
valid document, but it was not.

R. Sheshet's statement that a notification of duress is valid, issued in conjunction with the Mishnah's statement (Arakhin 5:6) that a man may be forced to write a *get* but must do so "of his own free will," might appear to undermine the Mishnah, to reject its solution to the problem of a recalcitrant husband. A man had the right to issue a prior notification of duress, according to R. Sheshet, and if he did so, the *get* that they then force him to write "of his own free will" is not valid.[37] However, since R. Sheshet himself is one of the three rabbis reported in the Talmud to have forced men to write a *get* (BT Gittin 34a; 88b), he is not trying to preserve a man's freedom of action to invalidate a forced *get* but, like Rav (as we will see), only trying to anticipate loopholes. It is this same rabbi who requires that cancellation of a *get* be done in the presence of three individuals, not just two, thereby making it somewhat more difficult for a man to cancel a *get* (BT Gittin 32b). The solution to this new problem, as indicated by the anonymous voice (and interpreted by Rashi), is explicit cancellation of the prior notification of duress.

Rav, who lived a generation earlier than R. Sheshet, provided a practical solution to the problem of men's prerogative.

> --Rav would prescribe lashes for anyone who betrothed in the marketplace, or betrothed by means of sexual intercourse [even though permitted by M Kiddushin 1:1], or without *shiddukhin* [prior negotiations], or who canceled a *get*, or *issued a notification of duress.* ... (BT Kiddushin 12b)

Rav's rulings attempt to correct the apparently widespread habit of taking marriage and divorce law lightly. The last two provisions speak to the issue of a man who is unable to make up his mind, who would write a *get* and then cancel it, or who issued a statement that he was going to be forced to write a *get*. Such behavior would seriously harm women: They would discover, at a later date, that the *get* they had received, on the basis of which they had remarried, was not valid. Or they would remain tied to a husband they were not living with in peace. Rav is sympathetic to the injustice of this situation and, perhaps because he could not single-handedly change the law, or because he felt that the law was fixed, sought to discourage these exploitative practices by ordering lashes for a man who engaged in them.

Where does all this Talmudic discussion leave women? To an extent, where they were before, but also somewhat better off. Men are compelled, in certain circumstances, to issue a bill of divorce; they are punished if they issue a prior notification of duress; they can cancel a *get,* but only in ways that do not put a woman at risk; the rabbinical courts can annul a marriage if a man violates any of their marital stipulations. All of this adds up to a reduction of women's disabilities under divorce law.

The World of Divorce According to R. Meir

Chapter 8 of Tractate Gittin, as we will soon see, presents a series of rulings that treat women who have *unwittingly* violated Jewish law with excessive harshness. This is perplexing. How can a tractate that makes the many helpful changes already discussed also include and subscribe to such views?

> If the scribe dated the *get* according to a king who did not rule in that province, or according to a past ruler, . . . , if the scribe was in the east but wrote in the *get* that it was prepared in the west, . . . , a woman [who remarried on the basis of such a *get*] must leave her second husband and also her first . . . (M Gittin 8:5)

In any one of these cases, a woman who remarries suffers a series of punishments, called in the Tosefta "the thirteen things" (6:6, 7, 9). A partial listing is as follows:

> She must leave her first husband [from whom she is not legitimately divorced] and her second husband [to whom she is not legitimately married], and must get a *get* from each one of them; she is not paid her *ketubah,* nor do these men return to her the usufruct [income of her assets] that they collected, nor [do they pay her] alimony. . . . A child born from either one of them is a *mamzer* [from the second husband because she is not married to him, and also from the first—although she is married to him—if she went back to him after leaving the second]. If she dies and the two men are *kohanim,* neither need defile himself in order to bury her [because she is not considered their wife]; neither one of them is entitled to what she finds or what she earns, and neither is able to cancel her vows. . . . (M8:5)

It is particularly troubling that although it was the scribe who made the mistake in preparing the *get,* one that not many people would catch, it is the woman who will suffer as a result. These punishments lead to marital and financial disarray for her, and a serious stigma for her children. The succeeding *mishnah*s prescribe the same punishments for several other instances of divorce irregularity: if he changed his name or she changed hers or the name of the city was changed and the *get* was prepared with the new name only (8:5); if the scribe mistakenly gave the *get* to the woman and the receipt to the man and they then exchanged documents—as was usually the case with a *get* and a receipt—and only some time later did they discover their mistake (8:8); if a "tied" *get,* usually signed by one witness on each of many folds, was one witness short (8:10).

In all, this is a shocking set of rules. In these cases most people would not even know that they were acting in violation of Jewish law and yet they would be held responsible for their behavior, the woman in particular. If the date on the *get,* or the names, or the number of witnesses on a "tied" *get* did not conform to the standards set by earlier rabbis, or if the scribe mixed up the documents, the woman would suffer—with no reprieve possible—whereas the man, who is able to take the *ketubah* moneys back from her because she was living adulterously, would be rewarded.[38]

If we now turn to the Tosefta, we find that some of these very same paragraphs appear there, but with significant differences. First of all, the Tosefta says that if a mistake occurs in the dating of the *get,* it will be declared invalid, but she will not suffer the series of thirteen punishments (T 6:3). In a second and rather amazing paragraph, the Tosefta says that if *gittin* come to Palestine from abroad and the names in them are non-Jewish, they are still valid, because Jews living abroad are known to take non-Jewish names for themselves(!) (T 6:4).[39] This seems to be in outright disagreement with M 8:5, cited previously. The Tosefta also talks about a man with two names and two wives, one in the Galil and another in Judaea, and says that he must divorce each of these wives with the name he is known by in the place where she lives. This paragraph thus provides a solution to the problems generated by men who adopt a new name and then want to send a *get* to a wife who knows them by their old name. Mishnah 4:4 also deals with this problem: it says that if someone changes his name, he should enter any and all names into the *get* so that the wife not suffer from any challenges raised in the future. The Mishnah thus solves in chapter 4 the serious problem it first describes in chapter 8.

The Tosefta, like the Mishnah, then brings other instances in which women suffer a full complement of penalties, but in reference to each it points out that this is the view of two Tannaim only: R. Meir who said it in the name of R. Akiva. In the very last case, that of a "tied" *get* with one witness too few, the stringency is presented as the view of R. Meir on his own.[40] The Tosefta then notes that the Sages disagree with him, which means they do not prescribe penalties in such a case, because they do not hold that the additional witnesses' signatures that are affixed to the "tied" *get*—above and beyond the first two—are critical. They are only a preventive measure to make the *get* easier to validate.

We thus see that for five out of the six cases in which the Mishnah prescribes harsh penalties, the Tosefta either provides a dissenting, more lenient view or else limits the stated, harsh view to R. Akiva and R. Meir alone. This contrast suggests that the Mishnah is far more stringent in these matters than the Tosefta; the redactor could have cited both opinions or, at the very least, listed R. Meir as the author of these extraordinary stringencies. By doing neither, he indicates that he subscribes to these extreme views. But, as we will now see, both Talmuds distance themselves from this set of rules.

. . .

––Said Ulla: Why did they require that a *get* be dated according to the ruling government? For the sake of maintaining good relations with the government.

==Can it be that for the sake of maintaining good relations with the government we force a woman out of a marriage and declare her children to be *mamzerim* [if the scribe wrote the date incorrectly]?

==Yes, R. Meir [who is presumed to be the author of all anonymous *mishnahs*] is consistent with his own reasoning.

––As R. Himnuna said in the name of Ulla: R. Meir used to say that [if a scribe, when preparing a *get*,] deviated from the standards that the rabbis set for drawing up *gittin*, the offspring [of the divorced woman's second marriage] will be considered *mamzerim*. (BT Gittin 80a)

The Bavli, or R. Himnuna, first asserts that the Mishnah is authored by R. Meir and then offers a "noble" rationale for his stringencies: to achieve standardization of the *get*, which, as we noted above, is good for women. The Gemara continues and says:

––Said R. Judah said Samuel: This is the opinion of R. Meir [that the year of the current reign must be mentioned, and if it is not, the *get* is invalid]. *But the Sages say,* even if he only dated the get to the term of office of the city officials, *she is divorced.* . . .

––Said R. Abba said R. Huna said Rav: This is the opinion of R. Meir. *But the Sages say that the offspring is fit.* (80b)

We see here an outstanding and clear-cut instance of Amoraim setting aside an excessively harsh mishnaic ruling by attributing it to one Tanna only. They then say that the Sages ruled far more leniently, as we saw in the relevant Toseftan passages. The Yerushalmi's treatment of these stringencies is no less remarkable.

––R. Huna in the name of Rav: This [entire] chapter is authored by R. Meir, except for "if he changed his name etc." (PT Gittin 8:5; 49c)

R. Huna, in Rav's name, narrows the scope of the problem. He claims that the majority of rabbis would not have punished innocent women in these six cases, but R. Meir alone. One can rule otherwise in these matters.

These liberal amoraic views prod us to ask: Why did the redactor of the Mishnah incorporate R. Meir's view as the dominant one, leaving out all reference to the Sages' leniencies? One answer is that he did so to teach that one must be scrupulously careful when it comes to preparing the *get* because a woman's marital availability depends on it. A document that indicates that her second husband is actually her husband, and her children with him are fit, must be treated with utmost care. But if the gravity of the *get* is the point of these *mishnah*s, it is unfortunate that they make it by presenting rulings that shock and distress the reader.

A second answer is that the redactor accepts R. Meir's and R. Akiva's views and rejects the Sages' more lenient approach to these matters. If so, we find within this tractate, as we did in Sotah, internal struggles and contradictions. On the one hand, the redactor presents a frightening picture of the fate of a woman whose *get* was drawn up with mistakes, but on the other, he talks about the possibility of a woman's initiation of the divorce proceedings. He also presents a whole series of measures taken to repair the social order, the first several of which are adjustments in divorce law. Thus he pits the unusually sensitive enactments of Rabban Gamliel the Elder against the grossly insensitive ones of R. Meir. I would submit that the tractate captures for us a moment in time when rabbis are beginning to think about the differences in status between men and women and are beginning to take tentative steps toward eradicating injustice to women.

Conclusions

On the whole, the development of divorce law reflects a movement from fewer rights for women to more. The Gemara upholds the Mishnah's liberal enactments and sidesteps R. Meir's harsh ones. Moreover, the Gemara gives evidence that perhaps the most important provision of the Mishnah for women—that a court may force a man to give a divorce—was accepted by the Amoraim and applied by them to real instances of recalcitrant husbands. The Gemara's description of men who issued a statement of duress is further evidence that the rabbis were pressuring them to write a *get* against their will, even though the men were trying to avoid it. In addition, the Gemara itself introduces the possibility of annulling a marriage, when it responds to Rebbe's unusually strict legislation that a canceled *get* remains canceled despite the preventive decree established "to repair the social order." Even within the Mishnah itself we see laws passed to benefit women, such as its prescriptions to standardize a *get,* to make every *get* look like every other so that no one could possibly, after a woman's remarriage, challenge its validity. Although the biblical grounds for divorce were given some expansive definitions, especially in the final "glib" *mishnah,* the substantial financial outlay required by divorce, as well as the scrupulous attention to detail that characterized the preparation of a *get,* served as strong barriers to the impetuous initiation of divorce. We also saw that divorce realities in the tannaitic period did not necessarily posit a spiteful husband but one who, in a fit of pique, divorced his wife only to regret it later, or one who divorced his wife out of concern for her welfare, not his.

Even so, there is no real movement in the Gemara in the direction of altering the patriarchal construction of divorce. It is the man who has virtually all the power in this area: He decides to divorce, issues the bill of divorce to the woman—just as one issues a writ of manumission to a slave—and she can neither initiate nor resist. Since she cannot remarry without a *get,* she is dependent upon him for her future marital well-being.

The changes that are made to improve a woman's lot require her to seek the assistance of a court, either to force her husband to write a *get* or to annul her marriage. Despite the improvement, she is still dependent upon others for resolving her marital difficulties. But these others are instructed to function on her behalf. If we judge the rabbis, not in terms of how close they came to eradicating all inequity, but in terms of how they improved the status quo, it is clear that they were aware of women's suffering and were in the process of alleviating it. The meta-message of the tractate is that the rabbis identify problems and provide solutions.

Notes

1. It seems significant that the very first *mishnah* of Gittin, and many subsequent *mishnah*s, talk about a *get* that comes from abroad.

2. The JPS translation of this phrase is "something obnoxious." Jeffrey Tigay (*JPS Torah Commentary, Deuteronomy*, 221) writes that this refers to her conduct, not to a physical trait. Albeck (265) says that as a result of finding an unseemly thing, he comes to hate her, as v. 3 says explicitly, "and her second husband comes to hate her."

3. See Yair Zakovitch ("The Woman's Rights in the Biblical Law of Divorce," *Jewish Law Annual* 14 [1981]: 28–46), who not only says that in the Bible no one could divorce a woman without serious reasons but also that most often that serious reason was adultery. He also suggests that the Bible records instances of divorce by women of men, e.g., if he denies her support or deserts her. See Tigay (*JPS Torah Commentary, Deuteronomy*, 221) for a discussion of the possibility of women divorcing men in biblical Israel.

4. See Tigay, *JPS Torah Commentary, Deuteronomy*, 214.

5. This rule implies that a divorcee is of lower standing than a widow, either because she has been repudiated, or else, since her first husband is likely still to be alive, because of a second husband's anxiety over his sexual performance in comparison to that of the first. See BT Pesahim 112b.

6. The same is true of widows, as noted in the same verse in Numbers.

7. Roman law also recognizes the power of a dowry: "Whatever her legal position, a wife with a big dowry was never really in her husband's control" (Susan Treggiari, *Roman Marriage* [Oxford: Oxford University Press, 1991], 329). "Husbands won over by dowries have to behave like maidservants to their wives"

(330). The point is clear: The way a woman can dominate a man in marriage is to provide him with a large dowry. Note that these statements refer to the dowry a woman brought into the marriage, which must be returned to her upon its dissolution. In Jewish marriage, the money that makes divorce difficult is the amount stipulated in the *ketubah* that the husband promised to pay her out of his own pocket.

8. Wegner (*Chattel or Person?* [New York: Oxford University Press, 1988], 47) considers this *mishnah* to represent the bottom line of the entire tractate, one that underscores its basic premise—that a wife may be discarded at the husband's whim. Although it is true that divorce is unilateral, when this passage is read in conjunction with the rest of the laws of divorce, including payment of the *ketubah,* we see that dissolution of marriage is not easy. Women are not disposed of like chattel.

9. The *mishnah* goes on to say that if he justifies the restrictions by saying that he fears she will be lured into promiscuous behavior, he is permitted to place these restrictions on her (Albeck, 112).

10. Treggiari, *Roman Marriage,* 442. The same used to be true in Roman law. Originally, only the husband could divorce. If he dismissed his wife for an offense, she lost her dowry; if for no good reason, he was penalized.

11. Tigay (*JPS Torah Commentary, Deuteronomy,* 221) writes that *get* is an Aramaic word meaning "legal document," derived from a Sumerian term meaning "oblong tablet." Zakovitch ("The Woman's Rights," 43) notes that in addition to the prescriptive verses from Deuteronomy that mention "a book of severance," there are verses in Isaiah (50:1) and Jeremiah (3:8) that do the same. From this he concludes that bills of divorce were known to Israelite society already in the late days of the Kingdom of Judah. See M Gittin 9:3 and M BB 10:1, 2 for references to the Aramaic text of the *get* in the tannaitic period. Aramaic was the lingua franca in Palestine.

12. See M Kiddushin, chapter 4, for a set of rules on the topic of permitted matches.

13. Most manuscripts read "man." However, for the purposes of comparing the *get* and the writ of manumission, it makes no difference whether the model is that of a man or a woman who is being freed.

14. PT Gittin 1:3; 43c; *stama d'gemara,* BT Gittin 9a.

15. Cf. M Yevamot 10:1–3.

16. The Gemara cites a tannaitic source that says that if he divorces her, he can not force her to suckle his child. But if the child recognizes its mother, the ex-husband can pay her and force her to suckle. This implies that the child is his.

17. See Susan Treggiari, "Divorce Roman Style: How Easy and How Frequent Was It," in *Marriage, Divorce, and Children in Ancient Rome,* ed. Beryl Rawson (Oxford: Clarendon Press, 1991).

18. Gittin 4:2; 45c.

19. PT Gittin 4:2; 45c. R. Huna says that even the Amora who says that Resh Lakish holds that a woman should not "sit and be tied to him" also thinks that Resh Lakish holds that she should not find herself in a situation in which she will give birth to *mamzerim.*

20. Apparently also instituted by the same rabbi (Rashi). His name is not mentioned explicitly in connection with this enactment, but it stands to reason that it is his. See the end of T Gittin (7:13).

21. Treggiari, *Roman Marriage*, 446.

22. There are no variant readings for this line of text.

23. It is for this reason that the betrothal formula today includes the words, "according to the law of Moses and Israel" (Tosafot, s.v. *kol d'mekadesh,* Gittin 33a). It should be noted that this formula, in the form "according to the laws of Moses and Jewish men," was already prevalent in the early tannaitic period and appears in marriage documents from the Bar Kokhba period that were found in the Judaean desert. It is therefore likely that Tosafot is interpreting the standard marriage formula in a way that serves the purposes of the text of the Gemara. This phrase also appears in M Ketubot 7:5, with a different meaning altogether. See Chapter 2, note 50.

24. See note 3.

25. See *Bereshit Rabbah* 18 (Theodor and Albeck ed., 166–167 and notes). See also Lieberman, "How Much Greek in Jewish Palestine?" in *Texts and Studies* (New York: Ktav, 1974), 226. He writes that the rabbis recognized, for gentiles, *divortium* given by men and *repudium* given by women.

26. Note that a woman who lost her mind may *not* be divorced, just as a man who lost his mind may not give a divorce. It could be that that relative equality triggered R. Yohanan b. Nuri's comment.

27. See also BT Kiddushin 50a, where the Gemara says that although one might think that in his heart he opposes writing the *get,* in fact he wishes to comply with the orders of the court.

28. *Sifra (Torat Kohanim) Vayikra,* Parsheta 3:15, p. 5b.

29. The Gemara did not see this additional requirement of "his own free will" as a problem. It held that once one pressures a man into succumbing to the proceedings, such as selling a field of which he wants to remain the owner, he does so "of his own free will." The same would hold true of a man who is forced to give a *get.* Maimonides, in an often quoted passage, says that a man who is forced to give a divorce does so willingly because it stands to reason that although he wants to obey the rabbis, he has been in the clutches of his evil inclination. When forced to act properly, he is actually doing so of his own free will because he rids himself of his evil inclination and every man is interested in doing what is right (*Mishneh Torah,* Hilchot Gerushin 2:20).

To this very day, the requirement that a forced *get* also be of a man's own free will has made it virtually impossible to aid women in their quest for a divorce, given its interpretation by a large number of post-Talmudic decisors (i.e., rabbis—over the centuries—whose decisions of cases expand the corpus of Jewish law). For instance, any attempt on the part of secular legislators to pressure the husband to write the *get* under the threat of a variety of financial sanctions, such as inequitable distribution of assets, is translated by some as impairing his doing so of his own free will.

30. PT Kiddushin 3:11; 64c. The case is one in which a man says that he betrothed a certain woman's daughter but the woman says that it was she herself whom he betrothed (M Kiddushin 3:11). A *get* is desirable so that each of these women is free to marry someone else without the fear of already being married to the first man.

31. The marriage of a *kohen* and divorcee, for instance, takes effect, but is prohibited and therefore subject to rabbinic efforts to terminate it.

32. See Chapter 6.

33. Some texts read that it was erroneous, ברותא. Either way, the *stama,* the anonymous voice of the text, exhibits extreme discomfort in dealing with this assertion.

34. In the Geonic period a number of rabbis write that that is precisely what Jewish women did—they secured a divorce from the secular courts. See Shlomo Riskin, *Women and Jewish Divorce* (New York: Ktav, 1989), 58, 67, 73ff. Many women in Israel today favor resolving divorce matters in the secular courts over the rabbinical courts. It is even possible that when M Gittin 1:5 speaks of *gittin* that are filed in the non-Jewish archives and are signed by non-Jewish witnesses that it is referring to instances in which women went to a secular court to obtain a divorce. See my article, "Pesiqah L'humra B'mishnat Gittin," in *Proceedings of the Tenth World Congress of Jewish Studies,* Jerusalem, August 1990.

35. See Rashi, s.v. *milta d'shehiha.*

36. This means that if one could assume that in all cases he cancels his notification of duress, the *mishnah* in Arakhin would have said they force him until he *gives* the *get.* Since the *mishnah* said that they force him until he *says* he acts voluntarily, this implies that it is necessary for him to repudiate any notification of duress that he had issued. And this, as noted by Tosafot (s.v. *hai man*), became a standard part of the divorce proceedings in the post-Talmudic period, i.e., to nullify prior notifications of duress.

37. Notice, however, that the anonymous voice of the Talmud interprets R. Sheshet's statement in such a way that a *get* given following a notification of duress *is* valid. In this instance, the later redactional addition/interpretation obviates the difficulty by making further demands of him.

38. The same punishments also appear in M Yevamot 10:1. There, too, they are meted out in a case in which the woman acted reasonably, remarrying only after she heard testimony that her husband had died and received permission from the rabbinical court to remarry. See a discussion of the moral problems posed by this *mishnah* in Shamma Friedman, "A Critical Study of Yevamot X with a Methodological Introduction," in *Texts and Studies,* ed. H. Z. Dimitrovsky (New York: JTSA, 1977), 277–282, in particular.

39. The Tosefta appears to be talking about a case in which a Jew with a Hebrew name, who came from Israel, changed his name in the diaspora and then sent a *get* to his wife in Israel with his new non-Hebrew name but without his old Hebrew name. See the first part of T 6:4.

40. So reads the Erfurt ms. The Vienna ms. includes a reference to R. Akiva.

6

Procreation

PRODUCING CHILDREN IS A KEY THEME of the book of Genesis. Three out of four matriarchs spent many years barren and conceived only when God decided it was the right time. Their misery at being childless is expressed in the most extreme manner by Rachel, who says to Jacob, "Give me sons; if not, I will die" (Genesis 30:1). A number of scholars have observed that biblical women were especially invested in making sure that the line continue.[1] Tamar, who tricked Judah into impregnating her (Genesis 38), and Naomi, who masterminded a plan to get Boaz to marry Ruth (Ruth 3), are but two examples.

The topic of procreation is addressed in only one *mishnah* in Tractate Yevamot (6:6), a perfect place for such a passage, given that the broad context is a discussion of how to continue the line of a man who died childless. The immediate implicit message is that men, too, have a strong interest in producing children. This *mishnah* has often been cited by feminists as evidence that the rabbis belittle women, in this instance by devaluing their role in procreation. But careful analysis of this text, in conjunction with associated rabbinic materials in the Tosefta, Bavli, and Yerushalmi, will show that women's exemption from the commandment to procreate stems partly from a patriarchal desire to leave termination of a marital relationship solely in the hands of men and partly from a wish to give women greater control over their personal lives. If so, this *mishnah* treats women neither better nor worse than most others.

Three Questions Arising from the Mishnah

A man may not desist from [the attempt to] procreate [לא יבטל אדם מפריה ורביה] unless he already has children. Bet Shammai says, two sons; but Bet Hillel says, one son and one daughter, for it says, "male and female He created them" (Genesis 5:2).[2]

130

If he took a wife and remained with her for ten years and she did not give birth, he is not allowed to desist [אינו רשאי לבטל]. If he divorced her, she is permitted to marry someone else. And the second husband is allowed to remain with her for ten years. But if she spontaneously aborted [within that period], she counts from the time that she aborted.

A man is commanded to procreate, but not a woman. R. Yohanan b. Baroka says: About both of them it says, "And God blessed them and said to them be fruitful and multiply . . . " [פרו ורבו] (Genesis 1:28). (M Yevamot 6:6)

The *mishnah* opens with the statement that a man may not desist from the act of being fruitful and multiplying—a phrase obviously lifted from Genesis 1—unless he already has children. Bet Shammai sets the requisite number of children at two males but offers no scriptural text or rationale in support of this position.[3] Bet Hillel holds that the obligation can be met by producing one male and one female child and cites "male and female He created them" as proof, suggesting perhaps that man (and woman) imitate God in their creation of human life by producing, as God did, both males and females.

But the *mishnah* does not fully explain what a man who already has two children may desist from. The text cannot be saying that he may unilaterally choose to terminate sexual activity with his wife because elsewhere the Mishnah states (Ketubot 5:6) that he always is required to meet his conjugal obligations to her. It may be saying that once he has the requisite number of sons and daughters he may switch from procreative to nonprocreative sex, meaning that he (or his wife) may choose to use contraceptive devices, drink what the rabbis call "a sterilizing potion" [כוס עיקרים]. Or it can mean that if after having produced two children, he is no longer married, he may marry a woman who is incapable of bearing children or that he may even stay single. The statement remains enigmatic.[4]

The next section of the *mishnah* says that if a husband and wife are still childless after ten years, he is not permitted to desist, apparently from the attempt to procreate. It seems unlikely, however, that this passage would be requiring him to keep trying to have children with the same woman. More likely, it instructs him to try to have children with another woman, either by divorcing this wife and marrying someone else or by keeping this wife and taking a second one.

We thus see that the *mishnah* addresses two parallel issues: what may a man do if he already has children and does not want any more; what should a man do if he does not have any children and still wants—and is in fact obligated—to have some. The same verb, B-T-L (desist), is used in both sections of the *mishnah,* but in neither context is its meaning sufficiently clear.

The *mishnah* further notes that if he divorces the wife who has been barren for ten years, she may marry someone else and that husband, too, may live with her for ten years. That is, the onus of barrenness does not rest on her. If during any ten-year period she spontaneously aborts, the count goes back to zero. Therefore, it is not incumbent upon the second husband—or on the first—to take any action with regard to his own obligation to procreate unless ten totally unfruitful years have passed. This statement makes it clear that one option available to a man who has not fathered children is to divorce his barren wife. But the *mishnah* neither requires divorce nor specifies what other options are available.

The last section of the *mishnah* states explicitly what was assumed all along, namely, that it is he who is obligated to procreate, not she. No proof-text is provided. That this is the first (anonymous) Tanna's position throughout this *mishnah* is evidenced by his discussing only what actions a man may take in the event that no children or two children are born, not any actions that a woman may or must take. The *mishnah* concludes with R. Yohanan b. Baroka's dissenting opinion that both men and women are obligated to procreate and his remarkably explicit prooftext.[5] What remains unclear is the first Tanna's rationale for exempting women from the obligation to procreate. The fact that this entire *mishnah* resonates with references to Genesis 1 deepens the puzzle of the first Tanna's restrictive stance. In Genesis it is clear that men and women are equally bound to populate the earth. Ironically, unlike ritual areas, where exemption often results in abandoning the act altogether, here, even if she is exempt de jure, her de facto participation in the act of bearing children is at least equivalent to a man's.

With these three questions in mind—precisely what action may a man desist from once he has fathered two children, what action he may or should take if no children are born after ten years of marriage, and on what basis did the first Tanna exempt women from the obligation to procreate—we will now look for answers in the parallel material in the Tosefta.

The Tosefta's Approach: Women's Obligation to Procreate

A man may not desist from [the attempt to] procreate unless he already has children.

Children's children are like children. If one [of his two children] dies or becomes castrated he is not allowed to desist.

A man may not live without a woman nor may a woman live without a man. A man is not allowed to drink a sterilizing potion in order to avoid producing children nor may a woman drink a sterilizing potion in order to avoid producing children. A man may not marry a

barren woman, an old woman, an *aylonit* [a woman constitutionally
unsuited for bearing children], a minor, or a woman who is not fit to
have children. A woman may not marry a eunuch even [if he is capable of sexual relations]. . . . (T Yevamot 8:4)

The Tosefta cites the entire first line of the *mishnah* verbatim. It goes on
to say that grandchildren qualify as children; if a man's children died but
left their own children, he is no longer obligated to produce more children
of his own. However, if the child died before having a child of his own or if
he becomes castrated, the parent is obligated to produce more children.
The critical issue is not the child's continued existence but the continuation
of the family line.

The Tosefta then adds that men and women are obligated to marry and
forbidden to make themselves sterile or choose a spouse who is known to
be incapable of procreation. What the Tosefta does not tell us is when
these rules apply: for a person's entire life, or only until he or she has children. But we can deduce an answer. If these rules are to be understood as
applicable always—a man must always be married, his wife must always
be one who can bear children, and he may never drink a sterilizing potion—then what does the Tosefta mean earlier when it says that he may desist from procreative sex once he already has children? Since we have already ruled out the possibility that he may abstain from sexual relations
altogether because he is required to meet his conjugal obligations to his
wife, as the Tosefta also states elsewhere, it follows that the Tosefta intends
for these rules to apply only to men (and women) who have not yet produced children. If so, then I think we have found an answer to the question
of what action a man is permitted to abstain from (or take) once he already
has children. According to the Tosefta, once a man has produced two children and does not wish to have any more, he may drink a sterilizing potion; if he is no longer married, he may choose a second wife who is incapable of bearing children; if he wishes, he need not remarry at all. We will
return later to the topic of women and procreation.

The Tosefta then provides an interesting contrast to the second section
of the *mishnah*.

> If he took a wife and lived with her for ten years and she did not
> give birth, he may not desist; rather, he must divorce her and pay the
> marriage settlement, for perhaps he did not merit being "built up"
> through her [לא זכה ליבנות ממנה]. (T Yevamot 8:5)

Unlike the Mishnah, the Tosefta here spells out what a man is *required*
to do if he has no child after ten years of marriage—divorce his wife. But
the Tosefta's intransigent stand is rather puzzling. Why doesn't it recognize

that there is an alternative course of action, namely, to take another wife without divorcing the first? After all, Mishnah and Tosefta Yevamot are filled with instances in which it is assumed that a man may take more than one wife. Furthermore, the very next line of the Tosefta cites a verse from Genesis (16:3) that says that after Abram lived for ten years in Canaan (in which time Sarai did not give birth), she gave him her concubine saying (v. 2), "Perhaps I will be 'built up'[6] through her." How strange for the Tosefta to learn from the Torah how long it takes to establish that a wife is barren, and even use a poignant phrase about surrogate motherhood first coined by Sarai, but still not recommend what Sarai recommended, that in these circumstances a man take another wife!

This baffling omission leads me to suppose that the Tosefta, throughout its discussion of this topic, holds that women, too, are obligated to procreate.[7] If so, it is easy to understand why at the end of ten years he is required to divorce her and may not simply take a second wife in addition to her: She needs the freedom to find herself another man with whom she can fulfill her obligation to procreate. I can cite two texts in support of this explanation. The first is T 8:4, cited earlier, which states that all the restrictions, like forbidding the use of sterilizing potions, placed upon men who have not yet fathered children, also apply to women. The only reasonable explanation for these restrictions is that the Tosefta holds that a woman, too, is obligated to procreate.

It is interesting that a number of the early versions of the Tosefta, in both manuscript and printed editions, have a different reading of these lines, one that distinguishes between the restrictions placed on men and those placed on women. The text I have been citing so far is the Vienna manuscript, the one that the esteemed Talmudist Saul Lieberman contends is the most reliable.[8] But the Erfurt manuscript, which, he says, was often modified to conform to later Talmudic decisions,[9] has a reading of this paragraph that permits women greater latitude in their behavior, even if they have no children, allowing them to remain single, marry a man incapable of fathering children, and drink a sterilizing potion. These discrepancies may therefore be due to the scribe's deliberately altering the text of the Tosefta in order to make it conform to the Talmudic ruling that women are exempt from the obligation to procreate.[10]

A second text that shows that according to the Tosefta women are obligated to procreate can be found later in chapter 8.

> If he divorced her [because she was barren], she should go and marry another, for perhaps she did not merit being built up through this man. (T 8:6)

If the Tosefta did not think that women were obligated to procreate, why would it concern itself with her immortalization and instruct her to get remarried? Note that the Mishnah at this juncture says "she is *permit-ted* [מותרת] to remarry," whereas the Tosefta says "she *should* remarry" [תלך ותנשא לאחר].

In short, what at first appears as insensitive treatment of women by the redactor of the Tosefta—the requirement that a man divorce his wife after ten years if she did not give birth—is simply the logical outcome of the Tosefta's egalitarian requirement that women, too, procreate. Both hus-band and wife need to find other marital partners if after ten years they have not succeeded in having children together.

Keeping in mind what the Tosefta says, we may be able to answer some of the questions raised by the Mishnah. The first was, why did the Mishnah not spell out what it meant by "desisting" from procreative sex? If we assume that the parallel statement in the Tosefta predates the Mishnah, then we can say that the redactor of the Mishnah knowingly chose to express himself in a vague manner because he did not subscribe to all three options sanctioned by the Tosefta for a man who already had two children: remain single, marry an infertile woman, or use contraceptive de-vices. It is possible that the redactor of the Mishnah, like the amoraic spokesmen in the Gemara (Yevamot 61b ff.), held that a man should al-ways be married.[11] By expressing himself as he did, he did not endorse any one of the Tosefta's leniencies but at the same time did not rule them out. It is also possible that the Tosefta, in this instance, postdates the Mishnah, and if so, the redactors of the Tosefta and the Mishnah agree and the Tosefta is simply spelling out what the Mishnah, for reasons of parsimony of language, left out. Either way, we gather that what a man who has fa-thered children may desist from is not sex but *procreative* sex.

Similarly, the fact that the second section of the Mishnah does not ex-plain what it means when it says that after ten unfruitful years, a husband may not desist from procreative efforts may indicate that the redactor of the Mishnah disagrees with the redactor of the Tosefta. The redactor of the Mishnah could easily have said, as does the Tosefta, that he must divorce his wife and pay the marriage settlement. The fact that he stopped short of saying so suggests that, according to him, divorce is not the only option.[12] This means that he thinks that women are not obligated to procreate and hence need not be divorced for their own sake. Remarkably, the mishnah's "leniency" results from its nonegalitarian stance.

Finally, after discovering in the Tosefta a body of opinion that obligates women to procreate and even deals with the legal consequences of such an obligation, we return even more perplexed to the third query: Why did the redactor of the Mishnah not obligate women to an act that they were, in any event, going to perform? He realized, it seems to me, that relieving women of this responsibility leads to two immediate and, in his opinion, de-sirable results: (1) permitting the use of contraceptive devices by women who have not yet had children and do not want to produce any;[13] (2) forbidding a wife-initiated divorce (with payment of the *ketubah*) for a woman who has not had a child after ten years and seeks the opportunity to have one. That is, by exempting them from this obligation, the Mishnah says that women cannot force a divorce after ten barren years the way men can, nor can they demand, upon marrying a man with children, that he have more. But neither can he force her to have any. What the Mishnah sanctions, in circumstances like these, is for a woman to have no children at all.

The Bavli's Decision to Force Divorce at the Request of a Barren Wife

Support for linking the first Tanna's decision to exempt women from the obligation to procreate with his concerns about wife-initiated divorce and women's use of contraceptive devices appears in both the Bavli and the Yerushalmi. The fact that the Gemara raises both of these issues suggests that they may have been on the mind of the Mishnah's redactor.

––It was stated: R. Yohanan and Resh Lakish, one said that the *halakhah* is in agreement with R. Yohanan b. Baroka [that women are obligated to procreate] and one said it is not. . . .

==What is the decision?

––Come and hear: R. Aha bar Hanina said that R. Abahu said that R. Assi said that a case came before R. Yohanan in the town square of Caesarea [in which a woman who was childless after ten years of marriage was seeking assistance in getting a bill of divorce and payment of the marriage settlement from her recalcitrant husband]. He said, let him divorce her and pay the marriage settlement. Now, should you think that she was *not* obligated to procreate, why would R. Yohanan instruct the husband to pay the marriage settlement to her? [It follows that women are obligated to procreate and the *halakhah* is decided according to R. Yohanan b. Baroka.]

==But perhaps she entered a special plea [and, if so, we cannot learn from here whether the *halakhah* is in agreement with R. Yohanan b. Baroka].

––Like the woman who came before R. Ammi and said to him, "Award me my marriage settlement" [meaning, I want a divorce because I am childless after ten years of marriage]. He said to her, "Leave; you are not obligated [to procreate and so you have no grounds for divorce. You are therefore not entitled to collect the marriage settlement]." She said to him: "In her old age, what will become of that woman [i.e., she herself]"? He responded: "In such a case we certainly force him [to divorce her and pay the settlement]."

--A woman came before R. Nahman [asking for a divorce with payment of the marriage settlement after ten years of marriage and no children]. He said to her: "You are not obligated [to procreate and so you have no grounds for divorce. You are therefore not entitled to collect the marriage settlement]." She said to him: "Does not that woman [i.e., she herself] need a staff in her hand and a spade for burial [i.e., a child]?" He said: "In a case like this, we certainly force [him to divorce her and pay the settlement]." (BT Yevamot 65b)

These three anecdotes, all on the topic of a woman's ability to initiate a divorce for her own sake, imply that a necessary consequence of obligating women to procreate would be that they could dissolve a marriage at the end of ten years if the couple had not produced any children so that she, and not only he, could try to have a child with someone else. To avoid making it possible for a woman to initiate a divorce, it seems to me that the redactor of the Mishnah decided, despite the clear prooftext brought by R. Yohanan b. Baroka, that a woman is *not* obligated to procreate.

If we look closely at the three anecdotes, we see that in the last two, the decisors—R. Ammi, who lived in the land of Israel, and R. Nahman, who lived in Babylonia—held that women were not obligated to procreate but *even so* decided to help them obtain a *get* and collect their marriage settlement. That is, these rabbis felt that they could find in the women's favor even if such a decision went against the rules. Moved by the women's fear of growing old without a child to lean on, they forced her husband to write a *get* and pay the marriage settlement, a rather extreme solution. Had he already fulfilled his obligation to procreate in a prior marriage, this divorce would be of no benefit to him. We see here sympathy for women in difficult straits and a willingness on the part of several rabbis to act boldly and circumvent legal standards in order to meet women's needs. We must remember, though, that the reason the women needed to seek rabbinic assistance is that the power to initiate divorce resided exclusively with men.

It is also instructive to look at the women themselves. In each of these instances, the petitioner does not accept an answer of "no" but keeps trying to get the rabbi to find in her favor. She is clever, resolute, and persistent. And her efforts yield results. These are women who are fighting for the opportunity to become mothers, who discover that being exempted from the obligation to procreate can lead to a frustration of their deep-seated desire. Ironically, it is a wish that society, in most instances, would honor and encourage. In this instance, however, because it involves hardship for a man and in particular may even show—if she succeeds in bearing a child for a different man—that it was he who was infertile and possibly impotent, the rabbis decide, at first, not to release her from her husband. Her ability to describe her situation in poignant terms softens their opposition and brings about a decision in her favor. That women, through their apt argumentation, get men to change their minds, is a favorable assessment of women. In a similar vein, should he and she disagree about his ability to "shoot like an arrow" and impregnate her, the rabbinical judge is instructed to accept her word, because she, not he, is in a position to know if that is so (R. Ammi, BT Yevamot 65a). The Talmud is saying that in this area women should be trusted. I find it impressive that men cede this power to women in a matter of such importance to their self-definition.

The discussion continues with another argument for exempting women from the obligation to procreate:

> Judah and Hezekiah were twins. One was fully formed at the end of nine months [of gestation] and one at the beginning of seven [and so their mother gave birth to each one separately].
>
> Judith, the wife of R. Hiyya [and the mother of the twins], suffered [agonizing] labor pains [because of this unusual twin birth and wanted to stop having children]. She disguised herself, came before [her husband] R. Hiyya, and asked, "Is a woman obligated to procreate?" He answered, "No." She went and drank a sterilizing potion. After some time passed, it became known [that she was avoiding pregnancy]. Her husband said to her, "If only you had given birth to one more bellyful!"

In this story the roles are reversed: R. Hiyya wants to have more children, but Judith, his wife, does not. His very own halakhic decision comes back to haunt him. Had he obligated women to procreate, his wife would have had no choice, even after the difficult birth, but to continue to have more children, which would have been very much to his liking.[14] But because R. Hiyya decided to rule against R. Yohanan b. Baroka, he brings frustration upon himself. When men exempt women from mitzvot, as they do in so many other cases, they do not necessarily anticipate the anguish that they may thus bring, indirectly, upon themselves. Is the Gemara here warning men to think twice before treating women as less than equal in the religious sphere? Since this story ends the discussion of this topic, is the redactor saying that this decision is mistaken? Perhaps.

We should also note that Judith, like the women in the other anecdotes, is clever and resolute. Since she suspected that R. Hiyya would be partial if he knew the identity of the petitioner, she disguises herself, as did the biblical Tamar, also a mother of twins. That is, all the women who appear in the anecdotes in this discussion of women's exemption from the obligation to procreate are women who know how to get their way. Two of them want children and one does not, but the common thread is that they lead the rabbi to issue the response that suits them. They respect Halakhah, but they also know how to achieve a decision in their favor.

Most important, this last anecdote provides us with another answer as to why the redactor of the Mishnah ruled against R. Yohanan b. Baroka: to make it possible for women to make their own decisions about whether to have children. If a woman is not obligated, as we saw with Judith, she may choose to use a contraceptive device. That this is part of the Mishnah's reasoning is also supported by the Tosefta's rule that when a man or woman has already brought children into the world, he or she may choose to drink a sterilizing potion. This statement establishes the connection between the exemption from the obligation to procreate—of women and of men who have already produced children—and the freedom to choose to avoid pregnancy.

The Gemara suggests yet one more way of understanding the Mishnah's decision not to obligate women.

> ==What is the scriptural basis [for exempting women from the obligation to procreate]?
> --R. Ila'a in the name of R. Elazar b'R. Simon said, "Fill the earth and master it" [וכבשה] (Genesis 1:28)—it is man's nature to master [a woman] but not woman's nature [to master a man]." ... [Since וכבשה is spelled defectively, without a "vav," this permits the rabbis to view the verb as in the singular form. If so, the verse is suggesting, given the above context, that a man should conquer a woman.[15] It is not saying that the two of them should conquer "it," the land.] (BT Yevamot 65b)

A little later the Gemara cites another statement by the same Sage:

> --Just as a person is obligated to say those things that the other can "hear," he is similarly obligated *not* to say those things that the other cannot "hear."

The common theme of these two statements is that it makes no sense to obligate someone to perform an act that he is not in a position to perform, that he lacks the means to carry out. Since women are subordinate to men in marriage and are the passive recipients of a man's seed, it seems to me that this sage is saying that it would be cruel and meaningless to obligate women to do that which is not within their power.

The Yerushalmi's Decision
in Support of Childless Women

Like the Bavli, the Yerushalmi attempts to supply a scriptural basis for the Tanna who exempts women from the obligation to procreate. It then discusses the halakhic implications of the exemption.

--R. Jeremiah, R. Abahu, R. Yitzhak b. Merion in the name of R. Hanina: The law is in agreement with R. Yohanan b. Baroka.

--R. Ya'akov b. Aha, R. Ya'akov b. Iddi, and R. Yitzhak b. Hakula in the name of R. Yudan Nesia: If she seeks [to get divorced from a husband with whom she has not been able to have a child in order] to remarry, the law is on her side [הדין עמה].

--R. Lezer in the name of R. Hanina: The law is like R. Yohanan b. Baroka.

--Said to him R. Ba b. Zavda: I was with you [at the time this was stated]; all that was said was that if she seeks to remarry, the law is on her side. (PT Yevamot 6:6; 7d)

It is noteworthy that the Yerushalmi also agonizes over whether a woman is obligated to procreate. A number of Amoraim fix the law according to R. Yohanan b. Baroka, who says she is. A number of others disagree. Even if we accept only the second view, that all that was said was that the law is on the side of a woman who seeks to leave her husband after a period of barrenness in order to remarry, that is still more liberal than the parallel passage in the Bavli. The Yerushalmi does not require a woman to enter a special plea in order for a rabbi to come to her aid. It will help any woman who, because of her desire to bear a child, wishes to end her ten-year-old barren marriage. Note that the Yerushalmi never reaches the conclusion, as does the Bavli, that a woman is exempt from the obligation to procreate. It leaves it as an open question but states clearly that if childlessness brings the couple into conflict, with her wishing to leave him, the law is on her side. This upholds the suggestion that at issue in this *mishnah*, at least according to the Amoraim, is the necessary connection between obligating a woman to procreate and her consequent right to dissolve a barren marriage.

Conclusions

Reading M Yevamot 6:6 together with the parallel passages in the Tosefta and Talmuds reveals that the redactor of the Mishnah could have followed the Tosefta and obligated women to procreate but decided not to because of undesirable anticipated consequences: Such an obligation would permit a woman to sue for divorce and payment of the *ketubah* if she did not give birth to a child within ten years of marriage. It would also limit contraceptive options for women who did not want to bear any children. For these reasons, and possibly because it did not seem appropriate to obligate a woman to do what she was not in a position to carry out, the redactor of the Mishnah favored exemption. There is no denying that this exemption stems from what one may appropriately call a sexist construction of marriage and divorce, one that places men in control of initiating and terminating relationships. Nonetheless, this mishnah clearly regards a woman as more than a baby incubator whose function it is to enable her husband to meet his procreative obligations.[16] Rather, it sees her as a marital partner with her own set of needs, albeit subordinate to her husband. It is significant that the Amoraim in both Talmuds disagree about which view to accept as Halakhah. My guess is that the redactor of the Mishnah, even though he exempted women for any or all of the reasons mentioned above, still experienced ambivalence regarding this issue, as evidenced by his choosing to end the paragraph with R. Yohanan b. Baroka's blatantly egalitarian prooftext, addressed to both Adam and Eve, "Be fruitful and multiply."

Addendum:
The Desirability of Marriage and Children

The rabbis of the Bavli use M Yevamot 6:6 as a jumping-off point to campaign for marriage, not just when a man is young, but throughout his life. They also alter the Mishnah's rule of permission to desist from procreation after a man produces two children and require ongoing attempts throughout his life to have more.

> ==This, [the first line of the *mishnah*,] is suggesting that once he has children, he may desist from having more; but [it does] not [mean that he may desist] from marriage.
> --This supports what R. Nahman said that Samuel said: Even if a man has several children, he may not live without a wife. As it says, "It is not good for man to be alone" (Genesis 2:18). (BT Yevamot 61b)

> . . . As was taught in a *baraita:* R. Joshua says, if he took a wife when young, he should again take a wife when old. If he had children when young, he should again have children when old, as it says: In the morning sow your seed, and when you grow old, do not stay your hand (Ecclesiastes 11:6) . . .
> --Said R. Matena: The law is in agreement with R. Joshua.
> --Said R. Tanhum said R. Hanilai: Any man without a wife is without happiness, blessing, and good. . . .
> --In the West they added: Without Torah and without a wall [to protect him from sin] . . .
> --And R. Joshua b. Levi said: A man must visit his wife [sexually] before leaving on a trip, as it says, "and you will know that there is peace in your tent and you will visit your home and not sin (Job 5:24)."
> We learned in a *baraita:* One who loves his wife as much as himself and honors her more than himself and trains his sons and daughters in

a straight path and marries them off when they mature physically, about him the verse says, "and you will know that there is peace in your tent and you will visit your home and not sin." (62b)

--R. Hiyya's wife used to torment him. [Even so,] whenever he would find something, he would wrap it in his scarf and bring it to her [to please her]. Rav said to him: But she torments you! He responded: It is sufficient for us that they raise our children and save us from sin. (63a-b)

Throughout all the material encouraging marriage, there is a strong sense that, beyond producing heirs, a primary goal of marriage is to protect a man from sexual misadventure. Men know their own weakness and, although possibly tempted to live alone after the death of a wife or a divorce, will find themselves led by their sexual urge into sin. The only solution, according to the Talmud, is contracting a marital liaison. It is true that other benefits of marriage are alluded to, such as the wife's role in homemaking and her offering emotional support and companionship. But they seem to be secondary to a man's urgent need for a sexual partner.

The Talmud comments only briefly on love as a component of marriage. The well-known statement in the above passage—that a man should love his wife as much as himself but honor her more than himself—appears in the immediate context of having sex with his wife before leaving town to fend off improper behavior on her part when he is away. According to the midrashic interpretation, the concluding words of the prooftext from Job, *v'lo teheta*, "and you (or she) will not sin," refer to the wife. If satisfied, she will behave chastely so that when he returns, he will find his home, meaning his wife (M Yoma 1:1), at peace. The formal connection of the next statement about marital love with this preceding one is that the next one, too, is an interpretation of the verse, "and you will know there is peace in your tent . . . ." The passage says that if a husband treats his wife lovingly and respectfully—which means, among other things, that he seeks to satisfy her sexually—he will have peace, not dissension and frustration, in his home or in his wife.[17] The powerful mixture of sexual attraction and romantic love that characterizes the couple's relationship in the Song of Songs does not figure in the rabbinic discussion of marriage, but passing reference is occasionally made to it, such as the poignant closing line of BT Gittin (90b), "If a man divorces his first wife even the Temple altar sheds tears for him . . . for he has betrayed the wife of his youth, his companion and close friend."

We can surmise that the inclusion of so many statements encouraging marriage suggests that men, in perhaps growing numbers, were choosing to remain single. If so, it is possible, once again, that the rabbis sensed a conflict between a life of the mind and a life of the flesh.[18] Since the men who issued these statements were spending long hours in Torah study, they apparently thought that if they stayed single, they would not have to deal either with sexual distraction or with the need to support a family. As the Talmud says elsewhere, in reference to one who first marries and then goes off to study Torah, "with a millstone around his neck, will he be able to study Torah?" (BT Kiddushin 29b).[19] But the sense of most of the Talmudic statements is that it is less distracting to have a wife to go home to, from time to time, than it is to have no wife at all. Unlike Roman thinking on the subject, which valued marriage strictly as a means of producing legitimate heirs and citizens,[20] the Talmud sees marriage as valuable in and of itself, for sexual pleasure and also for a general sense of well-being.[21] This outlook is also at odds with early Christian thinking that valued celibacy over marriage.[22]

It hardly needs to be pointed out yet again that all of the material on marriage looks at it from a man's perspective only. As for women, the rabbis assume that a woman wants and even needs to marry in order to secure protection for herself in a society in which women were vulnerable to abuse or neglect or both when alone. The rabbis summarize this outlook in the pithy statement, "a woman prefers anybody to nobody" [טב למיתב טן דו מלמיתב ארמלו, Kiddushin 41a and elsewhere]. This statement also implies, as we will see in Chapter 7, "Niddah," that women prefer sex with any man to no sex at all.

We also find many statements criticizing those men who do not produce children. The Tannaim in the Tosefta remark that one who does not procreate both denies God and commits murder (T 8:7). They then turn to Ben Azzai, who concedes these points to them, and note that he had no children. He responds, "What can I do, my soul lusts after Torah [חשקה נפשי בתורה]. Let the world be populated by others." And, in fact, M Sotah 9:15 singles him out as an example of diligence and dedication to the study of Torah. Some scholars today say that Ben Azzai's statement suggests that he had homosexual tendencies. If we read this statement in context, we see that such an interpretation is possible but not necessary. It appears in the Tosefta in association with the last part of the *mishnah*, the obligation of men to procreate. The Bavli understands the *mishnah* to mean that beyond procreation, marriage is good in and of itself because, by giving men an opportunity for sexual release, it frees them to study Torah. But Ben Azzai is saying that although others can manage to marry, have sex, produce children, support them, and still study Torah, he is so deeply committed to the study of Torah that he will not allow anything else to take up his time. This can mean that he chose to suppress his libido for the sake of Torah or that long hours of Torah study actually diminished it, as the Talmud relates about R. Sheshet, that he became sterile [איעקר] as a result of going to R. Huna's classes (BT Yevamot 62b).

Women, too, are thought to lose their ability to produce a child if they
remain celibate for a long period of time.

> --When Rabin came [from Israel to Babylonia] he said in the name
> of R. Yohanan: Any woman who waits ten years after [separating
> from] her first husband [before remarrying] will not be able to have
> children.
> --Said R. Nahman, this only refers to a woman who did not intend
> to remarry. But if she intends to remarry, she will be able to give birth.
> --Said Rava to the daughter of R. Hisda [whose first husband,
> Rami bar Hama, had died ten years earlier]: "The rabbis are talking
> about you [קא מרנני רבנן אבתריך]."
> --She said to him, "My mind was on you [for all of these years, i.e.,
> I was thinking of marrying you and so the rule does not apply to
> me]."
> --A woman came before R. Joseph and said to him: "I waited ten
> years after my husband's death and then was able to give birth."
> --He said to her: "My daughter, do not cast aspersions on the
> statements of the Sages [אל תוציאי לעז על דברי חכמים]."
> --She answered: "I had sexual relations with a non-Jew [נבעלתי
> לנכרי]." (BT Yevamot 34b)

The two women who appear in the above passage retort cleverly to the
unfair charges leveled against them. The daughter of R. Hisda was criticized by Rava, the man she took as her second husband and with whom
she then had children, that his rabbinic colleagues suspected her of engaging in sexual activity while a widow and thereby preserving her procreative
capacities. She responded that by thinking about him, which would probably mean sexual thoughts, she was able to maintain her libido and thus her
procreative capacities. The other woman was unfairly suspected by R.
Joseph of mocking the rabbis by doubting the correctness of their observation. But her self-righteous retort, that at the end of ten years of abstinence
she had sex with a gentile and became pregnant, is even more deeply mocking: It is true, she seems to be saying, that sex with a Jewish man after ten
years of abstinence will not activate a woman's libido, but sex with a non-
Jew will.[23] Her comment fits well with the general observation of the rabbis that non-Jewish men, in contradistinction to Jewish men, are sexually
promiscuous and hence more competent. It also suggests that women enjoy
sex, with non-Jewish men in particular.

Notes

This chapter is a revised and expanded version of my article "Women and
Procreation," published in *Tikkun,* November/December 1991.

1. For instance, Adele Berlin makes this point in "Ruth and the Continuity of Israel," in *Reading Ruth: Contemporary Women Reclaim a Sacred Story,* ed. Judith A. Kates and Gail Twersky Reimer (New York: Ballantine Books, 1995), 258.

2. Albeck (336–337) comments on why this verse was chosen over Gen. 1:27, which says the same thing in slightly different words.

3. The Tosefta (Yevamot 8:4) claims that he bases it on the fact that Moses had two sons.

4. Maimonides does address the ambiguity in the Mishnah, interpreting it as follows: "A woman who, after marriage, gives her husband permission to withhold her conjugal rights from her is permitted to do so. When does this apply? When he has children, for in that case he has already fulfilled the commandment to be fruitful and multiply. If, however, he has not yet fulfilled it, he is obligated to have sexual intercourse with her . . . until he has children. . . . " (*Mishneh Torah,* Hilchot Ishut 15:1). Kesef Mishnah *(ad locum)* notes: "Maimonides recognizes that a wife's conjugal rights and the command to procreate are two different and independent obligations."

5. See Jeremy Cohen, *"Be Fertile and Increase, Fill the Earth and Master It," The Ancient and Medieval Career of a Biblical Text* (Ithaca and London: Cornell University Press, 1989), for an analysis and history of interpretation of this verse.

6. JPS translation: "have a son."

7. Cohen (*"Be Fertile and Increase,"* 141) suggests that the logic of R. Yohanan b. Baroka's equal obligation was so compelling that several versions of the Tosefta developed his ruling by including women in the bans on remaining unmarried, and so on. According to Cohen, this fuller version of the Tosefta, as cited above, is a later adapted text. I argue just the opposite—that the fuller version is original and that some mss. were altered to adapt to the Bavli's decision that the law is in agreement with the first Tanna. See note 10.

8. *Tosefta Zeraim,* p. xii.

9. *Tosefta Ki-fshutah,* Moed (xiv). See *Tosefta Ki-fshutah,* Yevamot (69), where Lieberman notes that she cannot even marry a eunuch who is capable of sexual relations but cannot inseminate.

10. Lieberman himself notes (*Tosefta Ki-fshutah,* Yevamot, 68) that this paragraph of the Vienna manuscript may have been written from the perspective of R. Yohanan b. Baroka.

11. Rashi (61b, s.v., *me'ishah lo batil*) comments that the Mishnah's exempting a man from procreation once he has fathered children does not imply that he is exempt from the requirement to marry; however, he may marry a woman incapable of having children.

12. See the fascinating article by Judith R. Baskin, "Rabbinic Reflections on the Barren Wife," *Harvard Theological Review* 82, no. 1 (1989), who concludes (112), based on her reading of aggadic texts, that for cases of childlessness, the rabbis discouraged the available remedy of divorce in favor of trust in prayer.

13. Cf. Rachel Biale *(Women and Jewish Law* [New York: Schocken, 1984], 202–203). See also Baskin, "Rabbinic Reflections on the Barren Wife," 101–114. Baskin surveys a number of views about women's exemption from the obligation to procreate, including the one that it derives from the male-dominated worldview of rabbinic Judaism. See also David Feldman, *Marital Relations, Birth Control, and Abortion in Jewish Law* (New York: New York University Press, 1968), 54.

14. The woman in this anecdote seems to understand the obligation to have children as an ongoing one, beyond just two.

15. Cf. BT Kiddushin 2b: "It is man's nature to woo a woman; it not a woman's nature to woo a man." It is also possible to understand the word *v'khivshuha* וכבשה as saying that a man, but not a woman, is obligated to conquer the land.

16. Judith Wegner, *Chattel or Person?* (New York: Oxford University Press, 1988), 42.

17. The sexual message is implied by the passage's next clause: If he marries off his children when they reach puberty, at which time they begin to experience sexual desire, he will also succeed in maintaining peace in his home.

18. See Daniel Boyarin's comments on this and other related issues, in *Carnal Israel* (Berkeley: University of California Press, 1993), chap. 5, "Lusting After Learning."

19. The passage reads: "We learned in a *baraita*: [If he must make a choice, either] to study Torah or marry, [he should first] study Torah and then marry. If he cannot manage without a wife, let him marry and then study.

– –"Said R. Judah said Samuel: The *halakhah* is, marry and then study Torah.

– –"R. Yohanan said: With a millstone around his neck, will he be able to study Torah?

= ="There is no dispute; this is for us [in Babylonia, to first marry and then study] and this is for them [in Israel, that they should first study and then marry]."

R. Judah in the name of Samuel is actually fixing the *halakhah* according to the minority view of R. Judah (the Tanna), who is the author of the view in the version of the *baraita* in T Bekhorot 6:10. He says that if a man cannot dwell without a wife, he should first marry and only then study Torah. R. Yohanan holds in accord with the anonymous view that one should first study and then marry. As we see above, in the Bavli's version of the *baraita*, there is no apparent dispute. This makes it possible for the *stama* to say that one of the amoraic views applies to Israel and the other to Babylonia.

20. Susan Treggiari, *Roman Marriage* (Oxford: Oxford University Press, 1991), 185.

21. See Michael Satlow, *Tasting the Dish* (Atlanta, Ga.: Scholars Press, 1995), 314, who compares rabbinic texts about the tension between the desire for Torah and the desire for sex with the non-Jewish interest in the relation of philosophy to passion.

22. 1 Cor. 7:25–40.

23. I. Slotki (Soncino translation of the Babylonian Talmud, Yevamot) interprets otherwise: "I had intercourse with a heathen *during* the ten years." I disagree with this interpretation. If she had sex *during* the ten year period, why would it matter that her partner was not Jewish? The fact that she mentions he is a gentile must mean that at the end of ten chaste years only a man like him could reverse the changes in her.

7

Niddah

THE RULES OF FAMILY PURITY require that a husband and wife refrain from sexual relations during her menstrual period and also for some time after, only resuming physical contact after she immerses in a ritual bath *(mikveh)*. Modern scholars usually present these rules in one of two ways: positively, as a strategy for deepening the sexual and also nonsexual aspects of marriage for both husband and wife,[1] or negatively, as a set of rules that is degrading to women, that regards them as objects, and, in particular, finds them repulsive when menstruating.[2] But neither of these two approaches is fully consonant with rabbinic thinking on the subject. The rabbis inherited the rules of the menstruant from the Torah but, as we will see, made significant changes in them. Tracking these changes will help us understand their outlook on the topic of menstrual impurity.

The first thing to note about M Niddah, the Hebrew word for menstruant, is its location: Unlike all the other tractates dealing with women and marriage that appear in the Order of (Married) Women, this one appears in the last division of the Mishnah, called the Order of Purities.[3] The reason is easy to grasp: In the Talmudic period, the topic of the menstruant is primarily one of ritual purity and only secondarily one of marital relations.[4]

Since the word "*niddah*," as used in the Torah and also later books of the Bible,[5] means one who is distanced or banished,[6] some people have suggested that, in the biblical period, a woman was sent out of the camp during her menstrual period to a house of impurity and returned only when the flow of blood stopped. That may have been true. But there is no evidence of such a practice or place in rabbinic literature.[7] On the contrary, there are numerous references to the normal life that a *niddah* leads: For example, she may prepare food for her family, separate hallah,[8] and go out into the public domain on the Sabbath, with wadding to absorb menstrual blood, and not violate Sabbath law (M Shabbat 6:5).[9] Even if the institution of *niddah* in the Bible, and in the Ancient Near East in general, carried with it social or religious implications of isolation, we see that in the Talmudic period that was no longer so.[10]

What is the thrust of this tractate? Like Sotah and Gittin, it is at war with itself. At the same time that it adds new layers of rules to the basic ones presented in the Torah, thus making life more complicated for women and less pleasurable for men and women alike, it speaks out against these stringencies. It erects fences and then tears them down. Since *niddah* is virtually the only issue of ritual purity that is still in practice today, it is clear that this tractate did not move to abolish it altogether. But we will see certain transforming tendencies. It is possible that the tractate's self-contradictory aspects can be explained in terms of the historical development of Halakhah. The Tannaim, whose remarkably lenient views appear from time to time in the Mishnah, are reacting to a prior development of the laws of *niddah* that was excessively stringent and that may have come under attack in their day.[11] The Amoraim, surprisingly enough, reverse the lenient trend and start moving toward stringency.

Niddah *in the Torah*

The basis for the practice of *niddah* separation appears in the Torah. In fact, it is often cited by the rabbis as an exceptionally clear case of a Torah prohibition (M Horayot 1:3; 2:4; M Keritot 1:1).

Leviticus 15 (19–24) tells us that if a woman experiences a flow of blood, she is a *niddah*[12] for seven days;[13] anyone who touches her will be ritually unclean until evening. She passes on ritual uncleanness to objects and from those objects to people. A man who has sex with her will be ritually unclean for seven days. Although verses 21 and 22 talk about the need for immersion for someone who came into contact with any place where the *niddah* slept or sat, the Torah does not explicitly require the *niddah* herself to immerse.

After presenting these rules, the Torah goes on to talk about a related topic, a woman who sees blood for a number of days at a time other than a regular menstrual period (15:25–30). Such a woman, called a *zavah* by the rabbis,[14] is like a *niddah,* contaminating objects with which she comes into contact. If her flow of blood stops, she counts seven days and then becomes ritually pure. On the eighth day she brings a pair of birds to the door of the tent of meeting and gives them to the *kohen* who will offer them for her.

All of these rules need to be understood in the context of the first half of the chapter (15:1–18), which, in parallel fashion to the second half, talks about men's ritual impurity and subsequent return to a ritually pure state. The men under discussion have experienced genital discharges, either because of disease, like a *zav,* or in the normal course of events, like an ejaculant. Once the flow stops, a *zav* counts seven days, washes his clothes, immerses himself, and becomes ritually clean. On the eighth day, he brings a pair of birds to the tent of meeting and gives them to the *kohen* who will offer them before God and atone for him.[15] An ejaculant immerses and is clean by nightfall. The woman into whom he ejected semen must also immerse in water and wait until evening to become ritually pure. The closing verses of chapter 15 talk about the importance of maintaining a state of ritual purity so that one does not make the sanctuary impure, the penalty for which is death.

The verses in other chapters that mention the *niddah* warn against a sexual liaison with her, even though in chapter 15 sex with a *niddah* is not forbidden, only contaminating. Leviticus 18:19 bans it, for no stated reason. Leviticus 20:18 provides a rationale: because he has uncovered the source of her blood, he may not have sex with her. This explanation sounds like male revulsion or fear of menstrual blood. The punishment for sex with a *niddah* is *karet* (v. 29), which is defined by the rabbis as either premature death or excision.

We thus see that the Bible prescribes laws for the *niddah* just like those it prescribes for the *zav,* except that it does not spell out immersion for her, only for those who contract uncleanness by coming into contact with the place where she slept or sat. Can we infer, as do the rabbis, that she, too, certainly needs immersion? Can we assume that the same rituals apply to both the *niddah* and the *zav,* whose need for immersion is explicitly stated? Since the Torah treats them together, as is especially clear in the chapter's closing verses, I think we can draw these conclusions.[16]

Since many people do not read the verses or *mishnah*s about the *niddah* and *zavah* in conjunction with those about the *zav* and ejaculant, they assume that only women can become a source of impurity, and not men. Thus they conclude that these rules treat only women as objects.[17] But that is incorrect. According to the Torah, men, too, need to immerse themselves after a seminal emission. In fact, the purification ritual for the *zavah* is similar enough to that of the *zav* to say that the Torah draws little distinction between men and women as sources of impurity. If anything, the Torah sees the *zav* as more intensely impure than the *niddah* or even the *zavah,* as indicated by the greater number of rules that the Torah spells out for him. The issue in the Bible, therefore, is not gender differentiation with respect to ritual purity but ritual purity and its relation to genital discharges of both healthy and diseased men and women.

Even so, differences between impure men and women developed over time. First, the rules of immersion for the *niddah,* and the ban on sex with her, remained in force throughout the rabbinic period, whereas the rules of the *zav, zavah,* and ejaculant[18] disappeared over time. Second, both Talmuds have Gemara on M Niddah (although the Yerushalmi's Gemara ends at the end of chapter 3), but neither has Gemara on Zavim, or any other tractate in

the Order of Purities. An even more marked difference between the two tractates is that Niddah, in the Mishnah, Tosefta, Bavli, and Yerushalmi, is filled
with halakhic anecdotes, whereas Mishnah and Tosefta Zavim contain none
at all. The asymmetry of material again leads to the conclusion that Niddah
was a set of rules that many people lived by in the rabbinic period, whereas
Zavim, and most other topics of Seder Tohorot, after the destruction of the
Second Temple, were no longer relevant to their lives.

Why did the rules of Niddah alone survive? First, the Torah makes a separate statement banning sex with her, not relating this prohibition to her
ritually impure state. Second, the cross-cultural basis for menstrual separation would have reinforced the rabbinic rules. A fear or revulsion of menstrual blood seems to have been a standard feature of Ancient Near Eastern culture.[19]

Self-Examination and Sexual Relations

We will now turn to M Niddah to examine the rabbis' response to the
Torah's legislation about the menstruant. A key concern of this tractate is
the question of the retroactivity of the transmission of menstrual impurity.
Dealing with this matter is important for several reasons: First, if a woman
finds out after sex that she *may* have been a *niddah* during sex, although
one might think that she and he are both liable for punishment, neither is
liable. Sex with a *niddah* is strictly prohibited by the Torah, but the rabbis,
as we will see, do not erect fences around this law, as they do in so many
other cases. Second, retroactive transmission of impurity will adversely affect her ability to prepare food for her husband. In addition to *kohanim*,
who were required by the Torah to eat sacred food in a state of ritual purity and to avoid contact with the dead, lay Israelites could choose to adopt
some of these same rules. Such people were called *haverim* (associates).
The consequence of this status for associates' wives was that they had to be
ritually pure themselves when preparing food.

> Shammai says, all women confer ritual impurity only from the time
> they see [menstrual] blood; Hillel says: back to the time of their last
> self-examination [פקידה]. But the Sages say: [The law is] according to
> neither this view nor that one; [rather,] she confers ritual impurity ei-
> ther back to the time of the last examination or for the last twenty-
> four hours, whichever is less. . . . (M Niddah 1:1)

The central concept of the entire first chapter is *dayyah sha'atah:* Only
from the time a woman discovers that she is menstruous does she commu-
nicate ritual impurity to whatever she touches, such as food she was
preparing, not retroactively, as of the last time she examined herself. This

concept simply ignores the possibility that she had been *niddah* for some time before she saw blood. Whereas Shammai, one of the earliest Tannaim, establishes this concept, thereby showing his willingness to issue a leniency in this matter, Hillel, his colleague, argues for retroactive defilement as of her last self-examination. In a third, middle opinion, the Sages limit the period of retroactive defilement to twenty-four hours. The rest of the chapter, which develops the concept of *dayyah sha'atah,* clearly accepts the view of Shammai, the most lenient of the three. It would seem to follow that since there is no retroactive transmission of impurity, there is no need for self-examination; the period of ritual impurity begins upon "seeing blood." But M Niddah 1:8 teaches otherwise:

> Even though they said there is no retroactive defilement [for women with regular menstrual periods], she still needs to examine herself regularly [for menstrual blood]. . . . And she must use checking cloths during marital intercourse. . . . And twice [a day] she needs to examine herself, in the morning and at twilight, and also when she prepares for marital intercourse. . . .

This *mishnah* accepts Shammai's leniency of M 1:1 but imposes self-examination as a new stringency. Its purpose is to offset the far-reaching effects of the leniency. By prescribing frequent self-examination, it reduces two eventualities to a minimum: eating "ritually pure" food that was prepared by a *niddah* and engaging in sex with her husband while a *niddah.*

As strict as M 1:8 is, an Amora, in a standard interpretive move, reverses the trend.

> "And twice a day she needs to examine herself . . . "
> --Said R. Judah said Samuel: They taught this only in reference to preparation of ritually pure foods; as for her husband, she is permitted to him *without* [frequent] examination. (BT Niddah 11b)

In this bold statement Samuel limits the *mishnah*'s requirement of regular self-examination to food preparation. As for sexual relations, no immediately prior self-examination is necessary: If she has not yet seen menstrual blood, she may have sex with her husband. Note that his rule opens with the formula, "they only taught this in reference to . . . ," often used by an Amora to limit the scope of a tannaitic statement and to rule otherwise on cases not covered by it. In this instance, Samuel is limiting the *mishnah*'s requirement of self-examination to the case of food preparation alone, even though the mishnah singles out sex as an activity requiring prior examination! Thus, he can introduce a leniency in reference to sexual relations, allowing them to occur unencumbered by prior examination.

The following passages develop this relationship between examination and intercourse:

> --R. Zera asked R. Judah: Need a woman check herself [to see if she is a *niddah*] each time she has sex with her husband?
>
> --He said to him: She should not check herself [לא תבדוק].
>
> --But let her check herself; what of it?
>
> --He will become uneasy and abandon [אם כן לבו נוקפו ופורש] [the sexual encounter altogether]. . . .
>
> --R. Abba asked R. Huna: should a woman examine herself after intercourse [so that if she finds blood her husband will know that he is liable for a sacrifice]?[20]
>
> --He said to him: she should not check herself.
>
> --But let her check herself; what of it?
>
> --He will become uneasy and abandon [future sexual encounters].
> (BT Niddah 12a)

These exchanges between Amoraim indicate an extraordinarily lenient attitude to self-examination. Although frequent examination on her part would practically eliminate the chances of him having sex with a *niddah*, still, the unfavorable outcome would be to reduce the frequency of sex altogether. If they burden the sexual act with examination before and after, the rabbis understand that they will eliminate spontaneity, delay sexual gratification, and ultimately discourage sex. They therefore retreat from the requirement of frequent examination.

Several pages later, at 16b–17a, in conjunction with a statement in M 2:4 about having sex to the light of a candle, to facilitate checking for menstrual blood, we find a lengthy discussion of sex in the daytime. Most rabbis disapprove. R. Hisda, for example, claims that sex in the daytime will cause a man to find something unseemly about his wife. As a result, rather than love her, as mandated by the Torah (Leviticus 19:18)—you shall love your neighbor *rei'a* as yourself (*rei'a* also means lover or wife)—he will come to loathe her. Disagreeing, Rava permits sex in the daytime, as long as the room is darkened. He adds that a scholar may be relied on to use his cloak to block the light.[21]

Again we see strong evidence that sex was considered an activity designed in the first instance for a man's gratification. Since men were heads of household, their needs, according to the rabbis, were more important and pressing than women's. For this reason the rabbis say, perhaps disingenuously, that too close a look at her may dampen his sexual interest. Elsewhere, this same verse is cited as a prooftext by Rav that a man is forbidden to marry a woman without first seeing her, again so that he does not marry her and only afterwards discover that he finds her physically loathsome and thus inappropriate to satisfy his sexual needs (BT Kiddushin 41a). As already noted in Chapter 2, the rabbis frequently encourage a woman to care for her physical appearance in order to maintain her husband's sexual interest in her and thereby his potential for sexual release and pleasure. In rare instances do they suggest that *he* need to act in a certain way to maintain *her* interest.

Note also that all of the above texts assume that the initiator and terminator of the sexual act is he, not she. Even though the rabbis recognized the existence of women's sexual needs and required men to meet them (M Ketubot 5:6, 7), they frowned upon wives' soliciting their husbands (BT Eruvin 100b). According to them, women were meant to respond but not initiate, at least not openly.22

R. Akiva's Intentional Leniencies

A remarkable feature of tractate Niddah is the attempt to minimize the number of cases in which the dry blood stain a woman sees—not at the time of her regular menstrual period—renders her impure.23 If the rabbi to whom she shows the blood stain determines that the blood is uterine, the woman becomes a *zavah*, who must observe clean days corresponding to the blood days, as little as one clean day for one day of blood or, at most, a total of seven clean days. Note that these rabbinic laws differ from the Torah rules stated above. The rabbis interpreted the *zavah* of the Torah as referring to a woman who experiences a flow of blood for at least three days and who must then wait seven clean days before exiting the state of ritual impurity. They then added the notion of a "minor *zavah*," a woman who experiences a flow of blood for only one or two days. She needs to wait only one clean day for each blood day (*shomeret yom k'neged yom*).24

> If a woman sees a bloodspot . . . she may attribute it to anything she can possibly attribute it to. . . . (M Niddah 8:1, 2)

> It once happened that a woman came before R. Akiva and said to him: I saw a blood spot. He said to her: "perhaps you have a bruise [somewhere in your reproductive tract and the blood came from a place other than the womb]?" She answered, "Yes, but it already healed." He then said to her: "Perhaps it could still open up and ooze blood?" She said, "Yes, [it could]." And he declared her ritually clean.

> He then saw his students looking at one another [in surprise at his ruling], and so he said to them: Why is this matter difficult for you to understand? The Sages did not say these things to be stringent but to be lenient [שלא אמרו חכמים הדבר להחמיר אלא להקל], as it says: And a woman from whom blood flows forth . . . (Leviticus 15:19)—this means a flow of blood, not a [dry] blood stain. (M Niddah 8:3)

This set of *mishnah*s is amazingly self-critical. The rabbis are fully aware of their knowing and intentional avoidance of declaring a woman to be ritually impure. R. Akiva goes so far as to place words in a woman's mouth about the origin of a spot in order to dodge the most likely explanation that the blood came from the uterus. His manipulation of the facts so stunned his students that he had to defend his decision by pointing out to them that the rabbis themselves supplemented the core Torah rule of *niddah* with an overlay of bloodstain rules, as presented above (8:1, 2); even so, they did not intend for their own additions to be applied stringently, but leniently. For R. Akiva, this meant that any stain that could possibly be explained as anything other than uterine blood *should* be explained in that way. He is saying that when the Sages introduced legislation regarding blood spots, they did not intend to make their own legislation an institution that in and of itself would be dealt with stringently. The Torah, after all, does not declare a woman to be a *zavah* on the basis of a bloodstain, but only on the basis of a flow of blood. Therefore, as a fence around the Torah, the bloodstain rules were to be applied, but leniently. R. Akiva thus appears to admit that he behaved in a less than intellectually honest way, but he explains his good reason for doing so—not to burden excessively the rules of the Torah, not to interpret them too strictly.

This passage raises serious questions about how one arrives at answers to halakhic queries—with preconceived ideas or in a flexible manner. R. Akiva is closed-minded to any but a lenient answer, but open-minded in his willingness to respond to the reasonable questions of his students. But the *mishnah* also reveals R. Akiva's attitude to the set of bloodstain rules. He is rebelling, I think, against the stringencies imposed by earlier generations of Elders[25] on the rules of the Torah. Not only does R. Akiva thus seek to undermine these stringencies, but so do other Tannaim who rule in similar fashion.[26] Even more so does the *mishnah* itself, which encourages one to attribute a stain to anything except uterine blood. The text presents the bloodstain rules but then immediately proceeds to undermine them. This instance is different from other similar ones in that here, the students, who do not yet know such "hypocrisy," or, in our terms, "nuanced" or progressive thinking, by looking at each other in surprise, call on the rabbinic legislator to justify his actions. Their behavior provokes R. Akiva to issue an astonishingly candid self-justification. He indicates his awareness that his halakhic decision was somewhat predetermined, somewhat independent of the facts of the case, but also his certainty that his behavior was appropriate in this area of law.

Another clear example of this kind of exegesis, issued again by R. Akiva, appears in Zavim, the "sister" tractate dealing with men who become ritually impure by virtue of seminal emissions.

One interrogates the potential *zav* regarding seven matters [to find out if he experienced the emission because of any one of these reasons, and, if so, will remain ritually pure]. . . .

R. Akiva says: even if he ate any food, good or bad, or drank any drink, [we can attribute the seminal emission to that and not declare him a *zav*].

They said to him: But from now on there will be no more *zavim!*

He responded: The responsibility for declaring men to be *zavim* is not on you [אין אחריות זבים עליכם]. (M Zavim 2:2)

It is remarkable that it is again R. Akiva who introduces a transparent leniency. The rules of *zav* were no longer practiced in his day because the Temple no longer stood; therefore his goal was not practical but ideological. Since the issue of the *zav* had attracted numerous stringencies over a period of time, as indicated by the first part of the passage, he felt it necessary to introduce an extreme leniency to halt this process and even reverse it. Such halakhic innovation should not surprise us coming from R. Akiva, known for deriving *halakhot* from parts of words and even individual letters, thus far from the simple meaning of the word or phrase.[27]

This kind of approach gives enormous power to the legislator to shape Halakhah as he sees fit. We might have expected this method to be adopted by those who wish to burden each successive generation with additional stringencies, whereas those who adhere to the simple meaning of the words would more likely produce a set of rules a person can live by. However, the opposite is generally true: By deconstructing and reconstructing words and phrases the interpreter has extensive opportunity to cast things as he thinks fit, which, in the case of R. Akiva above, is the more livable scheme.

In a similar vein, an *aggadah* reports that when Moshe Rabbenu ("our rabbi," so called by the rabbis who saw him in their image) sat in the academy of R. Akiva, he grew anxious because he did not recognize his own Torah in R. Akiva's exposition, but was calmed when he heard R. Akiva say that the law he was deriving, as far afield from the Torah as it may have seemed to Moshe, was still based on the written law (BT Menahot 29b). The question is, why did R. Akiva, on his own, move to reverse the stringent direction in which the laws of *niddah* and *zavim* were developing?[28] It seems that people were provoked by the excessive restrictions of the earlier generations.[29] We find evidence of this in yet another lenient ruling of R. Akiva regarding a *niddah:* allowing her to dress nicely and apply cosmetics even during the week when she is forbidden to her husband. Until R. Akiva's day the Elders[30] prohibited such behavior, for fear it would lead her husband to sexual arousal that he could not contain.[31] But R. Akiva argued in response that a woman who does not make herself attractive—even when a *niddah*—will repel her husband, and he will seek to divorce her (BT Shabbat 64b; Sifra Mezora 9:12).

The inclusion by the redactor of the Mishnah of these two rulings of R. Akiva, and the inclusion by the redactor of the Talmud of that *aggadah*, imply that they are sympathetic to the results-oriented approach to Halakhah.

From Tannaitic Leniency to Amoraic Stringency: The Seven "White Days"

The following *baraita* introduces several more tannaitic leniencies, similar to the kind we saw above. But when the same issues are discussed by the Amoraim, they take a turn to stringency.

> We learned in a *baraita:* If a woman saw blood in conjunction with sexual relations, she may engage in sex a first, second, and third time. From then on, she is forbidden to have sex until she gets divorced and remarried to someone else.
>
> If she married another man and again saw blood in conjunction with sexual relations, she may engage in sex a first, second, and third time. From then on, she is forbidden to have sex until she gets divorced and remarried to someone else.
>
> If she married a third time and saw blood in conjunction with sexual relations, she may engage in sex a first, second, and third time. From then on, she may not have sex unless she first examines herself. [The reason this solution was not adopted earlier, according to the Amoraim, is that one first had to ascertain if the flow of blood was caused by the size of a man's sexual organ or the strength of his thrusting. Since she saw blood in conjunction with sex three times in a row with three different men, we can assume the problem lies with her, not with them.]
>
> How? She inserts a tube, within which rests a painting stick and to the top of which is attached absorbent cotton: If there is blood on the tip of the wadding, it is from the womb; if there is no blood on the tip, this means that it came from the sides [and it is ritually pure].
>
> If she has a bruise "in that place," she can attribute the blood to the bruise.
>
> If she has a regular menstrual period, she can attribute the blood to that. . . . (BT Niddah 65b–66a)

The Tannaim seem to be talking here about a husband and wife who are a poor match for each other, in the physical sense. They recommend divorce in cases in which his activity during sex is too "brutal" for her. The instrument they suggest she use for self-examination is a primitive form of a speculum. As offensive as it sounds to require a woman to use it to determine the nature of the blood she discharged—as much an invasion of privacy as it is—that is also one way of beginning to ascertain the cause of her medical problem.

This *baraita* takes a very "liberal" stand on blood appearing in conjunction with sex. Only when it becomes definite that each time a woman engages in sexual activity blood will appear is she asked to leave her husband. By "liberal," I mean within the framework of accepting the rule that blood of the womb confers ritual impurity and thus forbids sexual activity. This limited liberalism is apparent, in particular, in the last section of the *baraita,* in which all kinds of other explanations are found for the blood, other than having been caused by intercourse, so that the couple may remain married.

Three anecdotes follow about women who see blood in conjunction with sexual relations and come before the rabbis for a decision. Two of the three are dealt with leniently. The Gemara continues:

> – –Said R. Joseph said R. Judah said Rav: Rebbe enacted in Sadot that if she saw blood for one day that she remain [in a state of ritual impurity] for six [more days] in addition to that one day itself [because we assume it is menstrual blood]; if she saw blood for two days that she remain [in a state of ritual impurity] for six days in addition to those two [because the first day may be the end of *zivah* and the second the beginning of *niddah*], but if she saw blood for three days, she must sit for seven clean days [following those three, because she may be in a state of *zivah*].
>
> – –Said R. Zera: The daughters of Israel assumed a stringency upon themselves, that even if they see a blood spot the size of a mustard seed they sit for seven clean days [and not just if they see blood three days in a row and become a *zavah* do they sit for seven clean days]. . . .
>
> – –Said Rava: If they summoned her to get married [at the end of the period of betrothal], she must sit for seven clean days before marrying [Rashi, lest she saw blood because of sexual desire *(ta'avat himmud)*,[32] in anticipating her first sexual encounter].

The first two statements of Rebbe are hard to understand. We can only guess at what they mean. According to Rashi (s.v. *shishah v'hu; shena'im*), Rebbe treats seeing blood for one or two days like a menstrual period and prescribes a total of seven or eight days of separation. The third statement, a standard rule of impurity, notes that seeing blood for three days, apparently not at the time of the expected menstrual period, turns a woman into a full-fledged *zavah* who must then wait seven days before returning to a state of ritual purity, in all a ten-day separation. The days that Rebbe requires her to observe are the seven clean days of the *zavah,* not the seven days of menstrual impurity, and certainly not seven clean days after the seven days of menstrual impurity. In fact, the term "seven clean days," as it appears in the Talmud, refers in *all* instances to the days following *zivah,* not *niddah.*

If we now read R. Zera's statement in the context of the preceding one by Rebbe and the following one by Rava, we see that he is referring to cases of *zivah, not niddah.*[33] His terminology—seven clean days—is the terminology of *zivah.* Were he saying that women added seven white days to the seven *niddah* days, he would have had to be more explicit. Thus, he is *not* saying that Jewish women lengthened the menstrual separation period each month by adding seven white days to the seven days of menstrual impurity, as they have often been blamed for doing,[34] but that they adopted a stringency *in reference to zivah only.* According to the rabbis, a woman becomes a full-fledged *zavah* only if she sees blood for three days in a row. Once the flow stops, she must sit for seven clean days, as prescribed by the Torah. R. Zera is thus saying that Jewish women decided that for *any* irregular bleeding (that is, not at the time of the menstrual period and not necessarily for three days duration), they will sit for seven clean days. Even one tiny spot makes them a full-fledged *zavah.* This is certainly a stringency, but not one that approaches the level of stringency to which many have thought R. Zera refers.[35]

It is of interest that M 4:1 already makes a reference to women invoking stringencies (or leniencies) of their own in matters of seeing blood. It says that the Kuthean women, a rabbinic name for the descendants of the Samaritans, and considered partly Jewish, would sit seven days if they saw any blood whatsoever, whether or not it proved to be menstrual blood, and thus necessary.[36] It is also true that women refused to go to the *mikveh* when angry with their husbands, as did the wife of the exilarch Abba Mari (67b).[37] The rabbis seem to have sensed that in the area of *niddah* women had taken matters into their own hands.[38] Did the rabbis view this with equanimity or not? It is hard to say.

Since the statement by R. Zera is not the origin of the "white days," the name for the seven days added to every menstrual separation period, then where do they come from? Aside from one reference to them in BT Shabbat 13a, in an anecdote in which a pious and scholarly man died young because he did not observe the seven white days as scrupulously as the seven days of menstrual impurity,[39] the standard assumption throughout the Talmud is that menstrual separation is seven days only. In fact, when an Amora seems to suggest that a *niddah* count seven white days after the blood flow has stopped, the Gemara immediately asks, "What need has a *niddah* for counting [seven white days]?" and replaces the word *nid-*

dah with *zavah* (69a). Is there any evidence of white days following a menstrual period aside from that story? Not explicit evidence, but there is one suggestive reference.

In discussing the possibility of immersion in a *mikveh* in the daytime, the following statement appears:

> --Said R. Pappa to Rava and Abaye: Now that the *rabbis* have made all *niddot* into doubtful *zavot* [Rashi, and require them to count seven clean days after the seven *niddah* days], let them immerse on the seventh day [of the clean days; Rashi, this would be acceptable for a *niddah* because she could immerse any time after her seven days of impurity; and a *zavah* is permitted to immerse in the daytime].
> ==Because of R. Simon's dictum [they may not]. . . . (BT Niddah 67b)

R. Pappa refers here to a significant change in the rules of *niddah:* The rabbis consider all menstruants to be doubtful *zavot,* which means that they must sit for seven clean days when the flow of blood stops. Thus they may not immerse on the night following the last blood day, but rather at the end of seven additional white days. R. Pappa is saying that the rabbis eliminated the distinctions between a *niddah,* who sees blood for about seven days in a row, and a *zavah,* who sees blood for three days in a row not at the time of her menstrual period. This change is remarkable and far-reaching: both *niddot* and *zavot,* according to these rabbis, will have to sit seven clean days after the blood stops. We thus see that it was men and *not* women who extended significantly the monthly menstrual separation period, in many instances doubling it from seven to fourteen days!

It seems clear that the addition of the seven clean days to the seven days of menstrual impurity was made in the latter half of the amoraic period. There are no tannaitic references to it. We know that men imposed the stringency, probably because it did not make sense to them to differentiate between the *zavah* and the *niddah,* because the light irregular bleeding of many a *zavah* was being treated so much more stringently than the regular and longer flow of a *niddah.*[40]

This entire segment, then, begins with what I consider to be leniencies regarding a woman who sees blood in conjunction with sex. The rabbis do not decide to prohibit such a woman from ever having sex again just because they fear that the man who sleeps with her may violate a rule of the Torah. Instead, they provide ways for her to continue having sex. They finally suggest that she always examine herself and, based on the outcome and the associated leniency of interpretation of the results, either continue or discontinue sex. Following several related anecdotes, the *sugya* takes a sharp turn toward stringency. R. Zera mentions women's self-imposed stringency, and Rava decides to declare every bride, once the wedding date is set, a *zavah*.[41] The trend seems to be that as time passes, the rules of *niddah* become more strict. It is possible that the surrounding Zoroastrian culture pushed the rabbis in this direction.[42] Studies show that the tendency to deal strictly with this area of Jewish law continued and even grew stronger in the post-Talmudic period.[43]

Behavior During the Week of Niddah

When M Shabbat 2:6 says that women who are not careful about *niddah* deserve to die in childbirth, it is probably referring to a woman who had sex with her husband on a day she saw blood. Similarly, M Ketubot's law (7:6) that a woman should be divorced and forfeit her *ketubah* if she had sex with her husband while she was a *niddah* seems to refer to the simple requirement of separating from him for seven days. As M Keritot 1:1 says, there are thirty-six transgressions in the Torah for which one is punished with *karet*: one who has sex with his mother, his father's wife, or, among others, a *niddah*. The rule prohibiting sex with a *niddah* is therefore clear and, like the other forbidden liaisons, needs no further elaboration. In fact, the Tannaim do not give it any. To what extent a married couple can interact with each other, socially and possibly physically, when she is a *niddah*, comes up for discussion only among Amoraim.

We should also note that M Niddah's omission of this and other key topics indicates that this tractate is primarily concerned with one thing and one thing only: blood that does or does not confer ritual impurity—coming from a *niddah*, a *zavah*, a woman who spontaneously aborts, and a woman who gives birth. There are many anecdotes about women who come to rabbis to find out the ritual consequences of the blood they saw. But M Niddah shows very little interest in the home life of the couple when she is a *niddah*. Although scattered references to this topic are found in the Gemara—not in Tractate Niddah, but elsewhere—there is no sustained discussion of it anywhere. This lack of material leads me to believe that the laws of *niddah*, as they were observed in the early amoraic period, when ritual purity for the preparation of food was no longer an issue in Babylonia,[44] were a simple matter of refraining from sexual relations for the week of the blood flow. As we saw above, with the addition of the seven white days, a turn toward stringency began at some time in the later amoraic period.

We will now look at a well-known passage on the subject of the interaction between a husband and a wife who is a *niddah*. Talking about the household chores that a woman must perform for her husband, the rabbis say that even if she has a full complement of servants, there are still some small tasks that she herself should carry out for him.

--Said R. Yitzhak bar Hananya said R. Huna: Even though they said that she sits in a *katedra* [an easy chair, if she has servants who will perform all the housework for her], she still mixes his wine, makes his bed, and washes his face, hands, and feet.

--Said R. Yitzhak b. Hananya said R. Huna: All the labors that a woman performs for her husband, a *niddah* performs for her husband, except for mixing the wine, making the bed, and washing his face, hands, and feet.

--Rava said: That only means in his presence; but if done not in his presence, we have no problem [with her mixing and serving the wine and making the bed].

"Mixing the wine:"

--Samuel's wife changed it [her regular practice, and handed the wine to him] with her left hand [and thus did not transgress R. Huna's rule that a *niddah* does not serve wine to her husband].

--Abaye—she [his wife] would put it on the mouth of the barrel.

--Rava—on the pillow.

--R. Pappa—on the stool.[45](BT Ketubot 61a)

Were the rabbis concerned about the possibility of a *niddah* transmitting ritual impurity to her husband, they would have spoken of her inability to prepare food for him when a *niddah*. Here, all she may not do is mix his wine in his presence, which implies, says Rava, that she may mix it for him *not* in his presence. As R. Huna notes above, all other household labors, such as baking and cooking, are permitted. Furthermore, when not a *niddah,* she is specifically bidden to perform these three "special" tasks herself—mixing his wine, making his bed, and washing his face, hands, and feet, apparently because they create a sense of sexual intimacy. Therefore, when she is a *niddah,* the reason she may not perform these tasks is that they are likely to lead to sexual arousal on his part. Each of the four women mentioned above, when a *niddah,* either handed wine to her husband in a different way from usual or left it for him to drink without handing it to him directly.[46] Notice that it was the women themselves who figured out how to serve him his wine when a *niddah* but still fulfill the letter of the law of not doing so in a sexually intimate manner. We thus see that a wife who is a *niddah* is not hampered in any way from carrying out her household duties. As for the couple's relationship with each other when she is a *niddah,* not only is sex per se forbidden, but even, this source indicates, any kind of activity that would lead to sexual arousal.[47]

What also emerges clearly from this passage is one aspect of the nature of the relationship between a husband and wife in general, not just when she is a *niddah*: She is to serve him, cater to his needs, and perform even the small gesture of washing his face, hands, and feet. (This is still a practice of many women in the Middle East today.) He is not asked to do any of these tasks for her. According to the Tosefta (Kiddushin 1:11), washing the face, hands, and feet is one requirement of the honor due parents. By extension, a wife is to treat her husband as someone superior to her, deserving of her respect.

Niddah's *Benefits to Men:*
Sexual Strategies for Giving Birth to Sons

In discussing the period of ritual impurity following a spontaneous abortion, R. Ishmael and the Sages debate the issue of when the fetus forms (M Niddah 3:7). All agree that there is no fetus to speak of for the first forty days of gestation. R. Ishmael holds that a male is formed by the forty-first day and a female by the eighty-first. But the Sages say that all fetuses, male and female alike, are formed by the forty-first day.[48]

This *mishnah* triggers a lengthy aggadic discussion (30b–31a) on pregnancy, fetal development, sex during pregnancy—recommended only in the last trimester, when, the rabbis believed, it was good for both mother and fetus—and birth.[49] The *sugya* then turns its attention to strategies for sex determination of the fetus.

> We learned in a *baraita*: . . . if a woman gives forth seed first [i.e., if she reaches orgasm before he does],[50] the outcome will be a son. If a man gives forth seed first, the outcome will be a daughter. . . .
> --Said R. Katina: I could have made all my children males.
> --Said Rava: If someone wants only sons, he should engage in repeated intercourse [in the same night].
> --Said Rebbe: A woman conceives close to the time of her menstrual period. . . .
> --Said R. Yohanan: A woman conceives close to the time of immersion [in the *mikveh*]. (BT Niddah 31a-b)

Even though the strategy of satisfying a woman first is suggested for men's sake, to produce sons, rather than for women's, it is still beneficial to women. It is hard to say if men who wanted sons would follow this recommendation, but those who formulated it certainly were strongly encouraging men to satisfy their wives.

R. Katina boasts that he could have had all sons (but did not!). By this he means that he was so skilled that he could postpone reaching climax at will, an endorsement of the *baraita*'s advice on how to produce sons. Rava proposes that repeated intercourse in the same night is another strategy for producing sons, thereby implying that he is able to do so himself, also evidence of his virility.[51] Note that this same rabbi says elsewhere in the tractate that repeated intercourse in the same night is permitted, without worrying in the interim if the woman has seen menstrual blood (16b). In a similar self-congratulatory vein, later in the tractate (64b), Samuel describes his own sexual agility, saying, "I can perform several acts of intercourse [with a virgin] without causing her any bleeding!"

Why do the rabbis make these self-congratulatory comments? Not only to make a halakhic point. More likely they represent a form of locker room talk, or male bonding. Given the discussion of women's bodies, menstrual blood, and sexual restrictions, it is not surprising that talk of personal sexual accomplishments follows. Even so, elsewhere we see them express the opposite feelings: intense anxiety about their ability to please women sexually and fear of humiliation. One of the starkest statements on rabbinic sexual anxiety is the following:

> "Do not cook in a pot your friend has already cooked in."
>
> To what does this refer? [To a man who married] a divorcee in the lifetime of her [ex-]husband.
>
> For it has been stated: If a divorced man marries a divorced woman, there are four people in bed. If you like, even marriage to a widow [is not recommended], because not all "fingers" are the same. (BT Pesahim 112a-b)

Rashi (s.v. *she-ayn*) explains this cryptic reference: Since not all male sexual organs are the same size, sex [with her second husband] may not be as good as sex with her first, and she will come to belittle him.[52] It is hard to imagine a more insecure statement on the part of men with regard to their own sexual abilities, especially in the correlation between a woman's sexual pleasure and the size of a man's penis. However, speaking openly about these matters among themselves enables men to deal with anxieties and expectations.

Another aspect of men's insecurity is the fear that their inability to satisfy their wives will lead their wives to seek more satisfying relationships with other men. Then, in the ultimate act of deception, the wives will attribute the illegitimate child to their husband.[53] Legitimacy is a universal concern of ancient society.

There are a number of other places in the Talmud where advice is given for producing sons. In BT Shevuot 18b, R. Yohanan says that if a man refrains from sex with his wife close to the time of her menstrual period, he will produce sons. R. Elazar says that if he sanctifies himself during the sexual act (which means, according to Rashi,[54] that he behaves modestly), he will produce sons. The existence of so many statements of this sort indicate that men, and probably also women (as we will see), had a clear preference for sons over daughters.

In all these instances the rabbis exploit a man's wishes in order to get him to behave in ways they deem worthy. They dangle the reward of sons in front of his eyes so that he will observe the laws of *niddah* scrupulously, engage in sex in a sanctified manner, allow himself full sexual expression, but also see to it that his wife reaches orgasm. That they needed to admonish men about these forms of behavior may suggest that it is precisely these matters that men neglected. Although eschewing them did not constitute transgression of the law, the promise of a reward might get men to change.[55]

The *sugya* continues with a series of questions and answers, located here because several address the topic of *niddah*. The most important source for our purposes is the one that explains why a couple is required to separate for one week each month.

> R. Simon b. Yohai's students asked him:
> 1. Why does a woman who gives birth have to bring a [sin] offering?
> —because she swears she will never have sex again;
> 2. Why seven unclean days following the birth of a boy and fourteen following the birth of a girl?
> —because everyone is happy at the birth of a boy, and so she relents after seven days, and sad at the birth of a girl, and so she only relents after fourteen.
> 3. Why does the Torah say that circumcision is on the eighth day [and not sooner]?
> —so that it won't happen that all are happy and the parents of the boy are sad [Rashi: For the first seven days they are forbidden to engage in sexual relations because she is ritually impure[56]].
> 4. . . . R. Meir used to say, why does the Torah separate a *niddah* for seven days?
> —so that her husband will not come into constant contact with her and thereby come to loathe her [מפני שרגיל בה וקץ בה]; so that she will be to her husband like a bride entering the *huppah*.
> R. Dostai b'R. Yannai's students asked him:
> 5. Why do men chase after women and not women after men? . . .
> 6. Why do men face down [during sex] and women face up?
> —Each according to the manner of creation [since she was created from him, she looks up at him; since he was created from the ground, he looks down at it].
> 7. Why does a woman become appeased[57] but not a man? . . .
> 8. Why is a woman's voice pleasing but not a man's? . . . [58] (BT Niddah 31b)

The first four questions are serious ones about Torah rulings. Three are almost feminist in tone: Why a sin offering after giving birth? Why the excessive period of ritual impurity after the birth of a girl? Why separate a wife from her husband for seven days a month (implying that fewer would be more reasonable)? But the answers are not feminist: One should punish a woman for vowing never to have sex again; boys are preferred over girls; were it not for the week of separation each month, husbands would find wives repulsive—it is the separation that allows him to maintain sexual interest in her.

Questions five to eight are more frivolous than one to four and not Torah based in the same way. But they complement the first four by describing men's endorsement of the sexual status quo: Men initiate sexual relationships with women; men assume the superior position during sex.

When we examine R. Meir's explanation of *niddah* separation in this context, we are not surprised that his answer is sexual, because this question, like the others in this series, is sexual and not biological. But his answer is also sexist. The theme of the entire unit is the superiority of and preference for males. Therefore, R. Meir's statement, read in context, does not say that a couple that practices the rules of family purity, as they are now called, will enhance their sexual satisfaction and intimacy, an acceptable rationale for following them often cited today. Rather, in context, R. Meir is saying that, like other rules of the Torah that benefit men, so does this one, in that the separation will enhance a man's pleasure when his wife is once again permitted to him. According to this logic, the woman's sexual pleasure is an incidental derivative of the man's. Thus, although it may be true that both he and she benefit sexually as a result of the monthly separation, the genesis of this notion is sexist.

Niddah *as Didactic Construct*

The commandment of *niddah* serves, as noted above, as a prime example of a mitzvah clearly stipulated by the Torah, unlike so many others that the rabbis themselves introduced. Because of *niddah*'s role as a paradigm, the rabbis issued rulings about it that they constructed for didactic purposes only. These rulings cannot, therefore, be considered practical instruction. The reason that it is necessary to identify and document this phenomenon is that a passage like the following could easily be understood as saying that women, in the eyes of the rabbis, were no more than sex objects.

The following passage from M Shevuot deals with the punishments levied on a court for issuing mistaken teachings. It uses the example of *niddah* to illustrate the principle of the doubling of punishment.

> . . . What is the positive mitzvah regarding a *niddah* for which the rabbinical court, if it issued a mistaken ruling about it, must bring a sacrifice [called *par he'elem davar shel tzibbur*]?

> If a man was engaging in sex with a woman who was ritually clean
> and she said to him, I just now became ritually unclean, and he imme-
> diately withdrew, he is liable, because withdrawing [erect] gives him as
> much pleasure as entering [erect]. [If the court instructed him to be-
> have in this manner, it incurs a liability.] (M Shevuot 2:4)

> ==What should he do?
> – –Said R. Huna in the name of Rav: Dig his nails into the ground
> [i.e., bed] and wait until it [his penis] dies [i.e., until he loses the erec-
> tion]. (BT Shevuot 18b)

When read in context, we see that this *mishnah* has two goals. The secondary one is to teach that the ban on sex with a *niddah* is so extreme that if
she became a *niddah* in the course of sexual relations, he must terminate the
encounter in a way that minimizes his physical pleasure. But the primary goal
is to teach something else, namely, that in addition to the negative rule—do
not draw near to a *niddah*—there is a positive one as well, that a man must
separate himself from her if already involved with her. The surrounding
*mishnah*s make similar claims for other mitzvot. Although it is not obvious
that this doubling is what the Torah had in mind,[59] it is a standard technique
of the rabbis to increase the number of Torah admonitions in order to double
the corresponding punishments for behavior that they were especially interested in eradicating. Therefore, to demonstrate the existence of a positive
mitzvah associated with the ban on relations with a *niddah,* they needed to
create a case illustrating it—not an easy task at all. For this reason they constructed a scenario that, to the reader, may seem preposterous. Nevertheless,
the rabbis had little choice. Only by reading this *mishnah* in context can one
understand it in this way, and even, to my mind, understand it at all.

Again, it is hard not to notice the male perspective from which this rule,
and many others, are written. In this case the woman is little more than an
object or prop, conveniently present for his sexual gratification and conveniently *niddah* in order to generate halakhic tension. But since this *mishnah,* as already noted, is more interested in teaching the principle of a double punishment for a serious transgression than a particular halakhic rule,
it need not consider the effect of its rule on all the parties to the act. In this
instance of insensitivity to women, is it apologetic to say that all that is relevant is the halakhic principle? I do not think so. The likelihood of such a
case arising is so slight, and the possibility of seeking a rabbinic opinion
before sexual disengagement is so logistically complicated, that this source
can only be viewed as a didactic construct and not practical advice.

Immersion

M Niddah makes no reference to immersion at the end of a menstrual period. In fact, when the Mishnah mentions immersion, it refers to other

cases, such as the immersion of a *kohen* before eating sacred food or the immersion of utensils in order to render them ritually pure. Only a few passages, in other tractates, refer to the immersion of a woman at the end of her menstrual period.

> A *niddah* who . . . went down and immersed. . . . If she put her hair in her mouth, or made a fist, or pursed her lips tightly, it is as if she has not immersed. (M Mikvaot 8:5)

The Tannaim here assume that women must immerse at the end of the menstrual period and state several specific restrictions. But they seem to have found no need to elaborate on the details of this ritual. This silence probably means that women knew what to do. Unless the rabbis were changing the rules or adding to them, there was no need to spell things out.

The Amoraim, however, do discuss issues related to the immersion of a *niddah*. Three topics merit much attention: whether a *niddah* may immerse in the daytime or only at night, what constitutes an interposition that invalidates the immersion (because some part of her body did not come into contact with the water), and how close to the time of immersion is it necessary for a woman to wash her hair (66a–68a).[60] One of these, a discussion of the time of immersion, is relevant to our discussion of the development of the laws of *niddah* in the amoraic period.

> --Said Rav: A *niddah* who immerses herself on time [at the end of the seventh day], only immerses herself at night. But one who immerses not on time [only later], may immerse either in the daytime or at night.
>
> --R. Yohanan said: Whether she immerses on time or not, she only immerses at night, because of the possibility of misleading her daughter [סרך בתה, who may mistakenly immerse on the seventh in the daytime, Rashi].
>
> --And even Rav retracted, as reported by R. Hiyya bar Ashi in the name of Rav: A *niddah*, on time or not on time, only immerses at night. . . .
>
> --R. Iddi arranged in Naresh for women to immerse on the eighth day [in the daytime] because of the lions.
>
> --R. Aha b. Jacob [did the same] in Papponia because of thieves.
>
> --R. Judah [did the same] in Pumbedita because of the chill.
>
> --Rava [did the same] in Mehoza because of *abula'ei* [אבולאי].[61]
>
> --Said R. Pappa to Rava and Abaye: Now that the rabbis have made all *niddot* into doubtful *zavot* [and require them to count seven clean days], let them immerse on the seventh day [in the daytime]. . . . (BT Niddah 67b)

This small section illustrates two important points, one of which, the addition of seven clean days to the *niddah* separation, is discussed above. The other is the alteration of an already determined *halakhah*. In this case, since it was considered dangerous for women to go out at night in order to immerse, the rabbis of a long list of Babylonian towns declared it permissible for them to immerse in the daytime of the eighth (or any later) day. As the Talmud recounts, daytime immersion was at first permitted by Rav but later abandoned by him in favor of the more stringent position, proposed by R. Yohanan, a rabbi in the land of Israel. This led, in the course of time, to difficulties in Babylonia, leading many rabbis to revert back to the more lenient opinion.

This is a rather interesting case of the real needs of the people, in this case women, serving to influence the course of halakhic development. The stringency that was exported from Palestine to Babylonia had to be abandoned because of the difference in life circumstances.

Conclusions

Unlike many other issues surveyed in these chapters, *niddah* moves from leniency to stringency, but not evenly and not without contradictory trends. The rabbis seem to be affected by the fact that the *niddah* is grouped in the Torah with the *zav* and *zavah*. And since it is hard for them to distinguish between a flow of blood during a menstrual period and at other times, they erase the Torah's distinction and mesh the two institutions: Any uterine blood, seen at any time during the month, necessitates, with the termination of its flow, a set of seven white or clean days. On the one hand, this absolute rule simplifies matters enormously, in that a woman need not distinguish between the blood of *niddah* and *zivah*. On the other, the rule moves in the direction of stringency by maximizing the number of days each month during which a woman is forbidden to engage in sexual relations with her husband. Three distinct time periods seem to have occurred in the development of the laws of *niddah*: early tannaitic stringency, later tannaitic and early amoraic leniency, and later amoraic stringency, beginning about the time of R. Zera.

The leniencies found in these chapters are more prominent than the stringencies. The requirement of cumbersome self-examination is limited to the issue of the preparation of ritually pure food, which itself disappeared not later than the amoraic period and most likely sooner. For sexual relations, excessive self-examination was eliminated. Great efforts are made to call the blood that a woman sees not menstrual and not *zivah*, but simple pure blood that came from a source other than the womb. Anecdotes affirm that the rabbis actually ruled leniently in these matters. Moreover, R. Akiva seems bent on easing some of the rules of *niddah* and *zav*, possibly because of people's rejection of the stringent excesses of previous generations. Such a phenomenon can be seen in other rulings of R. Akiva and also in tractate Shabbat, in which the old prohibitions of moving utensils from one place to another on the Sabbath are relaxed by the later Tannaim.[62]

It is also noteworthy that all of the texts talk about the *niddah* in her own home, preparing food for the family or refraining from engaging in sexual relations with her husband. There is no reason to believe that her state as a *niddah* or *zavah* in any way affected her dealings with the world outside her home. There is no mention of her inability to enter a synagogue or to perform any rituals. The picture that is drawn of a *niddah* is of a woman who lives her life rather normally, goes out as much as she does at any other time, engages in the same activities and chores, but separates sexually from her husband for seven days a month.

In the course of time, when eating food in ritual purity was no longer relevant, the only parts of the laws of *niddah* that remained were the menstrual separation, the added days, and immersion. Aside from immersion, these laws affect men in the same way they affect women in a monogamous society, which rabbinic society apparently was.[63] That is, although this tractate is about women, the trajectory of the rules includes men almost as much as women. The longer she is considered ritually impure, the longer the period of abstinence from sexual activity for both of them.

What does all this say about a woman's body? Not necessarily that men considered it an object. Rather, biblical religion regarded genital discharges, from men and women alike, with fear or revulsion. The cult of purity seems to transcend gender. Minor differences are established between men's and women's purification rites and even their ability to transmit impurity, but in general, ritually unclean men and women are treated in a similar manner. The situation of relative parity changed in the rabbinic period. *Niddah* remained a topic of practical relevance but *zav* became a subject of theoretical interest only. Even if we ascribe the beginnings of *niddah* to a blood taboo (and the beginnings of *zav* to a semen taboo), it later was transformed into a set of rules governing food preparation for those who chose to eat only ritually pure food and a way of regulating sex for married couples. *Niddah*, at the beginning of the rabbinic period, or in the prerabbinic period, was thus a less sexist institution than it was at the end, both because the rules of *zav* became inoperative over time and also because additional layers of rules, many of them stringencies, were superimposed on the biblical core throughout the rabbinic period.

Since the topic of sex came up fairly frequently in this tractate, it is also important to note that the standard assumption here is that a man initiates sexual activity for his own pleasure. A woman's being a *niddah* stands in the way of his gratification. Women's needs are acknowledged and men are instructed to satisfy them, but only, for the most part, as an incidental outcome of meeting his own sexual needs. None of this is surprising in a patriarchal culture. As for the theory that the rules of *niddah* were instituted in order to deepen marital sexual pleasure for both husband and wife, we see that this is not wholly true. Enhancing a man's sexual pleasure in marriage is an after-the-fact rabbinic explanation for the Torah's mandated menstrual separation. That women, too, benefit from the separation was not mentioned by the rabbis.

It is also possible that an interest in promoting procreation underlies some of the legislation on this topic. The likely result of bringing a couple back together after a one or two week separation, exactly at the time that she is most fertile, is increased opportunity for conception. It is not clear that the rabbis knew these facts in a precise manner, but some of them pointed to a correlation between these biological phenomena.

Notes

1. For instance, Rachel Biale, *Women and Jewish Law* (New York: Schocken, 1984), 172–173 and n. 12.

2. Judith Wegner, *Chattel or Person?* (New York: Oxford University Press, 1988), 163–165, claims that the rabbis see the menstruant as both object and person.

3. One manuscript of the Talmud (Munich 95) places Niddah at the end of the Order of Women, for reasons that, I think, are obvious.

4. See Michael Satlow, *Tasting the Dish* (Atlanta, Ga.: Scholars Press, 1995), 296ff.

5. E.g., Ezek. 22:10; Lam. 1:8.

6. The JPS translation of the state of *niddah* is "impurity." Baruch A. Levine says that the word *niddah* itself, from the root N-D-H—to cast or throw, connotes, not impurity, but the physiological process of the flow of blood (*JPS Torah Commentary, Leviticus,* 97). Tirzah A. Meachem, "Mishnah Tractate Niddah with Introduction: A Critical Edition with Notes on Variants, Commentary, Redaction and Chapters in Legal History and Realia" (in Hebrew), Ph.D. diss., Hebrew University of Jerusalem, 1989, says that *niddah* means "distanced." In time it became a name for the woman herself and then a metaphor for sin and impurity in general (150–152). The Brown, Driver, and Briggs (BDB) lexicon says that it means excluded or expelled.

7. Lawrence H. Schiffman, "Laws Pertaining to Women in the Temple Scroll," in *The Dead Sea Scrolls: Forty Years of Research,* ed. Devorah Diamant and U. Rappoport (Leiden: E. J. Brill, 1992), 210–228. One version of M Niddah 7:4 talks about *bet ha-tumot* and another about *bet ha-temeiot.* Schiffman understands this text as referring to special houses for menstrually impure women. Yedidya Dinari, "The Customs of Menstrual Impurity: Their Origin and Development," *Tarbiz* 49 (1979–80): 302–324, S.J.D. Cohen, "Menstruants and the Sacred in Judaism and Christianity," in *Women's History and Ancient History,* ed. Sarah B. Pomeroy (Chapel Hill: University of North Carolina Press, 1991), 273–299, and Schiffman, all argue that isolation of the *niddah* used to be practiced in the prerabbinic or early rabbinic period but that there is no clear evidence that any Jewish group in

the rabbinic period isolated the *niddah*. Even in the Christian Bible there is no evidence that a *niddah* was isolated.

8. Ravina (BT Bekhorot 27a).

9. That a *niddah,* in some Jewish groups, does not enter a synagogue, is a post-Talmudic development. See S.J.D. Cohen, "Menstruants and the Sacred in Judaism and Christianity," who discusses the post-Talmudic Baraita D'Niddah and its tendency toward stringency and superstition.

10. Cohen (ibid.) says that there is no sign that the purity system was intended to discriminate against women or to exclude them from the sancta: "Women were marginal altogether in the rabbinic Judaism of late antiquity and the Middle Ages, and the rhetoric of impurity only served to strengthen and justify an order which already existed and which, until recently, both men and women accepted" (299).

11. See *Sifra (Torat Kohanim)* end of Mezora, and BT Shabbat 64b, cited below.

12. The Torah uses the word *niddah* (Lev. 15:19) to denote a woman's state— either of impurity or of experiencing a blood flow—not the woman herself. The use of *niddah* to mean menstruant is a rabbinic innovation that is rooted in the Torah's language.

13. Note that the Torah does not require a woman to experience a blood flow for all seven days to be a *niddah.* Even if blood flows for fewer days, she is a *niddah* for a full week.

14. Although the Torah distinguishes between two kinds of blood flow, the normal and the abnormal, it does not give women experiencing either of these phenomena a name. The rabbis, using the terms or roots appearing in the biblical verses, call the menstruant a *niddah* and the woman experiencing an abnormal flow of blood a *zavah.* This latter condition may be referring to one of many gynecological conditions, for example, pelvic inflammatory disease. As we will see later, the rabbis call a man who experienced a seminal emission a *ba'al keri,* based on the biblical term *mikreh laylah* (Deut. 23:11), nocturnal emission.

15. Judith Wegner notes that the phrase "before God" is missing in the expiatory rites of the *zavah.* A woman, she says, can approach God only indirectly ("Leviticus," in *The Women's Bible Commentary,* ed. Carol A. Newsom and Sharon H. Ringe [Westminster: John Knox Press, 1992], 42).

16. *JPS Bible Commentary, Leviticus* (97). Levine writes that it is clear that although the requirement of immersion is not spelled out in vv. 20 and 23, only in 21–22, it is also to be applied to the *niddah* herself. He notes that for an abnormal impurity, such as *zav* or *zavah,* a rite of expiation is required, above and beyond bathing and laundering (98). Jacob Milgrom (*Anchor Bible, Leviticus*) notes the chiastic structure of the chapter, a sign of its literary unity and probably of the consistency of purification ritual.

17. Rosemary Ruether, "Feminist Interpretation: A Method of Correlation," in *Feminist Interpretation of the Bible,* ed. Letty M. Russell (Philadelphia: Westminster Press, 1985), says that in a male-dominated society, "Menstruation and childbirth are interpreted to them [women] as pollution over against a male-controlled sacred sphere" (113).

18. As we will see later, the rules of the *zavah* merged with the rules of the *niddah.* In BT Berakhot 22a the rabbis report that men found the requirement that an

ejaculant immerse before the study of Torah to be a burden. In the amoraic period it was canceled. See also BT BK 82a-b for a discussion of the ejaculant's immersion.

19. According to Levine (*JPS Commentary, Leviticus,* 223), *zav* lost its relevance because it was related to the cult. The practice of *niddah* did not, because it had other applications related to human reproduction that became a major focus of rabbinic purity law. Dinari says that there is a folk opinion that a *niddah* has destructive powers; for this reason it was common among ancient peoples to distance her. No such powers were ascribed to the *zav*.

20. This is the second version of his question. The first was found to be faulty.

21. There are several places in the Talmud in which a Torah scholar [תלמיד חכם] is trusted to engage in activities that are forbidden to others. Taking interest on a loan from a gentile is another one of them (BM 71a).

22. Although R. Samuel b. Nahmani in the name of R. Yonatan does encourage a woman to initiate sex with her husband, promising her extraordinarily fine children if she does so, men do not seem to have generally favored it (Nedarim 20b). The contradiction between his recommendation that women initiate and the conflicting one that they not initiate—one who does so is called aggressive [חצופה]—is resolved by the anonymous voice with the statement that she should not initiate or solicit but indicate that she is sexually interested (Rashi, s.v. *d'meratzya*). Men are warned not to force sex on their wives with the opposite threat, that if they do so they will produce disreputable children (BT Eruvin 100b). Connecting desired or undesired behavior with how one's children turn out seems to have been a common rabbinic rhetorical tactic. This tells us that people accepted the notion that their behavior, particularly during sex, affected their children's future. If so, this technique would have been useful in influencing men to conform to certain behavioral patterns. See Satlow, *Tasting the Dish*, 303ff. It is also possible to view these statements as a way of saying that how a man treats his wife sexually will be as public as the character of their children (Susan E. Shapiro, personal communication, January 15, 1997).

23. The blood stain a woman sees not at the time of her regular period may result from many different conditions, one relatively common one being *mittelschmerz,* midovulatory spotting. The rabbis' tendency to be lenient with stains of this sort and not require sexual separation of husband and wife is consistent with preserving her ability to conceive. However, we cannot be sure that the rabbis had precise knowledge of when ovulation took place. Leniency in these matters is also consistent with the desire not to limit the opportunity for sex and to preserve her ability to prepare ritually pure food for her husband.

24. See David C. Kraemer, "A Developmental Perspective on the Laws of Niddah," *Conservative Judaism* 38, no. 3 (Spring 1986): 26–33, for a discussion of the rabbis' understanding of the laws of *niddah* and *zavah*.

25. A legacy of the past, as indicated in a number of Dead Sea Scrolls. See discussion of R. Akiba's rulings at the end of this section.

26. T Niddah 6:17: "She [the *niddah*] attributes it to anything she can [possibly] attribute it to. It once happened that R. Meir attributed the stain to red eye salve; Rebbe attributed it to the sap of the sycamore." Note that R. Meir is R. Akiva's protégé.

27. See Y. N. Epstein, *Mevo'ot Lesifrut Hatannaim* (Jerusalem: Magnes Press, 1957), 521–542; Ephraim E. Urbach, *The Halakhah, Its Sources and Development* (n.p.: Yad Latalmud, 1986), 104–105, esp. n. 42.

28. Examples of stringency in the laws of Niddah are the rules of self-examination, dating back at least to Hillel and Shammai, and, as already mentioned, the bloodstain rules (8:1, 2). Examples of stringency in the laws of *zav* are implied in M Zavim 2:2 and stated in 2:1 and elsewhere in the tractate.

29. See T Moed Qatan 2:10,14 for two more examples of R. Akiva's easing earlier restrictions. The issues are drinking certain potions, apparently with medicinal properties, on the intermediary days of a festival, and sitting on a gentile's merchandise display bench on the Sabbath, presumably because it would appear that a Jew was doing business on the Sabbath. One gets the impression, from these passages and others, that R. Akiva represents a liberalizing force in the history of Halakhah.

30. Heb., *zekenim harishonim.*

31. Cf. *Aboth de Rabbi Nathan A,* chapter 2 (Schechter ed., 8), where only the rules of a *niddah* disfiguring herself appear, without mention of R. Akiva's leniency.

32. This kind of secretion is dealt with in BT Niddah 20b. The rabbis thought that women secrete blood as a result of sexual yearning. There they decide that it does not make her impure; here, they decide that it does. Meachem, "Mishnah Tractate Niddah with Introduction," explains this blood as an attempt by the rabbis to overlay male physiology onto the female body, assuming that there is a female analogue to erection and ejaculation. The rabbis saw menstrual blood as an equivalent of semen. See 188–190 for an excellent analysis of this entire topic.

33. Meachem (ibid., 176) and S.J.D. Cohen ("Menstruants and the Sacred in Judaism and Christianity," 278–279) interpret R. Zera as saying that what the women did was consider *any* blood they saw, menstrual or otherwise, to be blood of *zivah,* and hence requiring seven clean days. I do not find that warranted by the words of R. Zera himself. There is no need to attribute to R. Zera two restrictive practices—seven clean days of the full-fledged *zavah* for seeing even one bloodspot of a minor *zavah* (which would require only one clean day) and seven clean days after every menstrual period—instead of one restrictive practice. The context of R. Zera's comment is the seven clean days of the *zavah.* Rebbe was apparently saying that seeing blood for one or two days may be considered menstrual blood and will not require seven clean days, only that she count seven *niddah* days. But seeing blood three days in a row, presumably not at the time of one's expected menstrual period, necessitates counting seven clean days. It is only a little later, as we shall see, that the rabbis erase all differences between the *zavah* and *niddah.*

34. R. Biale (*Women and Jewish Law,* 153) says that women turned to their own stringency and ceased to rely on rabbinic experts.

35. That R. Zera was understood as also referring to menstrual blood, and hence to a longer monthly separation, is already suggested by Rashi and Rambam: "*Even a niddah counts seven clean days;* for the women adopted a stringency upon themselves, like the statement of R. Zera" (Rashi, BT Niddah 67b, s.v. *safeq zavot shavinhu*).

"The daughters of Israel accepted upon themselves the following additional stringency, that if she sees even a small blood spot she will sit seven clean days, *even if she saw this blood at the time of niddah.* Since she saw the blood for one or two or seven days or more, when the blood stops she counts seven days like a full-fledged *zavah* and then immerses herself on the night of the eighth day. . . . " Rambam (Hilchot Issurei Biah 11:4)

I think it clear that both Rashi and Rambam extend R. Zera's statement to include the case of *niddah*, even though there is no need to do so. See note 33.

36. Alternatively, that they would count the last of the three days of *zivah* as the first of the seven clean days (BT Niddah 33a).

37. Rashi (s.v. *d'kut*) explains that she had a fight with him and did not want to go to immerse.

38. See also the relevant anecdote from PT Ketubot (2:5; 26c) cited at the end of the Conclusion.

39. The following story (BT Shabbat 13a-b) does not appear to be mainstream Halakhah. It is the only "tannaitic" reference to white days. The term for white days, *yemei libbun*, appears nowhere else in the Talmud.

"Tana d'vei Elijah: A certain disciple who studied much died young. His wife looked for an answer to his premature death. None was forthcoming. Elijah [he is only mentioned explicitly in the parallel versions, which will be referred to] visited her one day and asked her how her husband behaved toward her when she was a *niddah*. She said, he did not even touch her little finger. And in her white days? He ate and drank with her and slept with her in physical contact. And yet he never thought of engaging her in sexual activity. And Elijah said to her, thank God for killing him, for he paid no respect to the Torah, which says, 'Do not draw near to a woman who is in a menstruous state' (Lev. 18:19).

――"When R. Dimi came [from the land of Israel], he said: [They slept in only] one bed [and the husband thought that that was sufficient, but it was not].

――"In the West they said that R. Yitzhak bar Yossi said: A garment separated the two of them [and that was not sufficient]."

Meachem, "Mishnah Tractate Niddah with Introduction" (186), claims that this story has to postdate R. Zera, which means that she does not consider it a tannaitic source. The version of the story found in Aboth D'Rabbi Nathan B (chap. 2, p. 9, Schechter ed.) has a slightly different wording. Instead of "*niddah* days" and "white days," Elijah asks her about the "first days" and the "last days." Such a reading need not mean that women were observing seven white days after the seven *niddah* days but that they were distinguishing between the early days of the seven, in which there is a blood flow, and the later days of the seven, in which there may not have been any flow at all. Alternatively, if the term does refer to seven additional white days, it may represent pietistic behavior in the tannaitic period or later. Note also that the victim is a Sage and the wise man is Elijah, the prophet (Cohen, electronic communication, November 22, 1996).

40. See BT Niddah 69a, where a serious critique is issued against treating lighter cases more strictly than serious ones. See next note.

41. S.J.D. Cohen suggests that Rava's ruling may not be a stringency at all but a way of guaranteeing an interval between the agreement to marriage and the marriage itself, during which time the bride could change her mind. Calling her a *zavah* gives the delay halakhic enforceability (electronic communication, November 22, 1996).

42. I first learned this point from the undergraduate thesis of Lauren Eichler (Princeton University, 1994). For further discussion see Meachem ("Mishnah Tractate Niddah with Introduction," 190) and BT Shabbat 110a and Pesahim 111b.

43. See S.J.D. Cohen, "Menstruants and the Sacred in Judaism and Christianity," and note 9, this chapter.

44. In Palestine, preparing and eating food in ritual purity continued into the amoraic period. I. Ta Shma, "Niddah," *Encyclopedia Judaica* (12:1145).

45. Some see in this passage a discreet way for a woman to inform her husband that she is a *niddah* (R. Biale, *Women and Jewish Law,* 160). This is not what the passage is saying.

46. Rashi (s.v. *mihlefa lei*) says that she did it in this manner in her white days, implying that she did not serve him wine at all in the seven *niddah* days. Cf. Tosafot s.v. *mahlefa d'bithu.*

47. See BT Sanhedrin 37a for a statement about the permission for a *niddah* to be alone with her husband, despite the ban on sex between them. The Gemara notes that even a hedge of roses is sufficient to restrain people from violating Jewish law.

48. See David Feldman, *Marital Relations, Birth Control, and Abortion in Jewish Law* (New York: New York University Press, 1968), who comments on the implications of this belief for therapeutic and elective abortion (251–294). See also my article "Abortion: Where We Stand," *United Synagogue Review* 42, no. 2 (Spring 1990).

49. Permission for sex during pregnancy is a rather clear indicator that sex is permitted for its own sake. This was a matter of debate among the Dead Sea sects. See Lawrence H. Schiffman, *Reclaiming the Dead Sea Scrolls* (Philadelphia: JPS, 1994), 129.

50. The word in the Talmud, *le-hazri'a* (to give forth seed), refers to orgasm and not just ovulation. This definition is suggested by R. Yitzhak, who says that if a man holds himself back from release until the woman "gives forth seed" first, the offspring will be male (BT Niddah 31b).

51. In Eruvin 100b repeated sexual intercourse in the same night is frowned upon. But the contradiction between what is said there and what Rava says here is resolved by the anonymous Talmudic voice in terms of securing his wife's consent.

52. Rashbam comments (s.v. *she-ayn*): since sex with the second husband is not as pleasing to her as with the first, she will come to hate him. A minor but telling difference in formulation.

53. In BT Yevamot 118b, Resh Lakish says that it is better for a woman to live with anybody than nobody. In that context, he is saying that a woman would rather be married, even to a lower-class man, than live alone. In other words, having sex with a coarse man is better than living alone and having no sex at all. The *sugya* ends, and the chapter ends, with a tannaitic statement: "And all women who marry coarse men will conduct extramarital affairs, become pregnant, and then attribute the offspring to their husbands." Does this mean that women will behave in such a deceitful manner because men like this will not know any better or that these men will not know how to satisfy their wives sexually and their frustration will push them to find satisfaction elsewhere? Is this a statement about women or about men? Cf. BT Nedarim 91a-b, where women are portrayed as having extramarital sex but as acting as if it happened without their knowledge and, thus, without any intention on their part.

54. S.v. *hameqadesh atzmo.*

55. See Satlow, *Tasting the Dish*, 7ff., for a fascinating discussion of the various legal and nonlegal techniques that the rabbis used in order to persuade people to comply with norms and mores of private activities that the rabbis were not in a position to enforce. See also his discussion of eugenics, 303ff.

56. S.v. *shelo yihyu*.

57. BT Niddah 66a: To become appeased means to accept an offer of marriage. This statement apparently means that it is easier to gain a woman's consent to a proposed match than it is to gain a man's.

58. It seems that all eight of these questions relate to sex and birth of children. The only one that appears to deviate from this topic is the seventh, but if it means to appease for marriage and sex, then it fits in.

59. It was the rabbis themselves who decided that there was also a positive mitzvah associated with the *niddah*; it is not explicit in the Torah. We read in M Horayot 2:4, "What is the positive mitzvah associated with a *niddah*? To separate oneself from her [פרש מן הנדה]. What is the negative mitzvah? Do not draw near to a *niddah* [לא תבא אל הנדה]." Shevuot 18b attempts to derive it from the Torah itself, citing and expounding on "ותהי נדתה עליו" (Lev. 15:24). But the verse hardly supplies us with a source for the positive rule of "separate from a *niddah*."

60. It seems likely that the rabbis are referring to pubic hair.

61. This word has a number of interpretations. See the Jastrow dictionary. One possible interpretation is "city gates" or those who loiter there.

62. T Shabbat 14:1; BT Shabbat 123b; PT Shabbat 17:5; 16a. See Yitzhak Gilat, *The Teachings of R. Eliezer Ben Hyrcanos and Their Position in the History of the Halakha* (Tel Aviv: Bar Ilan University, 1968), chap. 1.

63. Tal Ilan (*Jewish Women in Greco-Roman Palestine* [Tübingen: J.C.B. Mohr, 1995], 86–88) suggests that polygamy was not common among the poorer classes but was common among the well-to-do.

8

Inheritance

INHERITANCE LAW IN THE BIBLE is an outstanding example of discrimination against women: In most cases, men inherit all, women nothing.[1] It is likely that this distinction made sense in the time of the Bible, given the patriarchal and tribal nature of society and the emphasis on possession of land. By passing land from one generation of men to the next, the tribe maintained its holdings.[2] The rabbis, heirs to the biblical system of law but living in a different set of social and economic realities, found these rules inappropriate for their times. As Reuven Yaron notes, the rabbis introduced changes because of "the unsatisfactory state of the law of succession, as far as daughters and widows were concerned."[3] A close reading of their statements on the subject reveals that while still adhering to the letter of the biblical law, they, in essence, transformed it. They did not alter it to the extent that women inherited equally with men. But they did award a woman a sizable portion of her father's wealth and they made it possible for him to choose to give her any amount he wanted. Their principal strategy was to encourage fathers *in their lifetime* to give their daughters large gifts, which, although technically not "inheritance," nonetheless helped right the gender imbalance. In this area of law, more than in most, the rabbis seem halakhically self-aware, with respect to both their goal of giving a woman a portion of her father's estate and their realization that they needed openly to behave contrary to what the Torah dictates.

I am not suggesting that it was the rabbis who first decided to give women a share of their fathers' and husbands' wealth. In the ancient world, two sums of money were associated with women leaving home to get married: the bride-price paid by her husband to her father and the dowry given by her father to her for use in her own home (although her husband was entitled to any income accruing from it). The bride-price, assuming her father kept it for her should she ever return home,[4] allowed her to "inherit" a portion of her husband's estate. The dowry allowed her to "inherit" a portion of her father's estate. So, even in the Bible, provided these two payments were made, a woman was not excluded totally from the circle of heirs. We also have evidence, from the time of the Bar Kokhba rebellion (about 130 C.E.), contained in documents found in the Judaean desert, that giving large dowries to daughters when they married, apparently as a way of circumventing biblical inheritance law, was common practice.[5] As for the Greco-Roman world, women could inherit from husbands, fathers, and all other male relatives.[6]

The reason that inheritance law comes closer than any other area in Jewish law to eradicating significant differences between men and women may have to do with the beneficiary's being a daughter, not a wife. In the rabbinic period little change can be noted in the law that wives do not inherit from husbands, although husbands are sole heirs of wives. Despite men's preference for sons over daughters, they seemed to love their daughters once they had them.[7] And part of loving them was being concerned about their future, which meant, among other things, awarding a daughter a not-insubstantial share of her father's assets. It is also true that inheritance is primarily a monetary matter, not a marital or ritual issue. Change is therefore easier.[8]

Inheritance Law in the Bible

We read in Numbers 27 (1–11) that when a man dies, his property passes to his sons. Only if he leaves no sons does it go to his daughters. If there are no daughters either, the property goes to his brothers on his father's side, then to his father's brothers, and so on. The rules of intestate succession are agnatic, which means that the estate is to remain in the hands of the decedent's relatives on his father's side. He is the agnate of his own sons and daughters.

I do not think that the Bible could make a clearer statement of the disenfranchisement of women with respect to the transfer of property from one generation to the next. Daughters inherit nothing, except in those cases in which there are no sons.

What triggered the Bible's presentation of inheritance laws was the claim of Zelophehad's five daughters. He died in the desert, and these women, anxious to keep their father's name from being blotted out, are the first to raise the issue of daughters' inheriting when there are no sons—not exactly a feminist demand. After acknowledging the validity of their limited request (Numbers 27:7), God dictates to Moshe a full set of inheritance laws. Some time after this victory, the men of Menasseh complain that they stand to lose because the general tribal holdings will be diminished if the women marry out of the tribe (36:1–4). After God bids Moshe to tell them that they, too, like the women, are making a valid point, God calms their fears by limiting the women's choice of mate to men in their own tribe (35:6). Thus, these five women lose a measure of freedom, even though they succeed in saving their father's name. On this note the book of Numbers closes, suggesting, perhaps, a major theme in human relationships—how to solve problems so that no one feels that he loses when the other gains.

It is remarkable that the same scene is replayed in the Mishnah.

> ... If someone died and left sons and daughters: If the estate is large, the sons inherit and the daughters are maintained [i.e., given basic needs] from it; if it is small, the daughters are maintained from it and the sons go begging on the doorstep. Admon[9] objected: Just because I am a male, should I suffer a loss? [בשביל שאני זכר הפסדתי]
> Said Rabban Gamliel: I favor Admon's opinion. (M Ketubot 13:3)

Admon's cry of anguish, "Since when should a *man* find himself discriminated against?" is ironic in the one instance in Jewish inheritance law in which women are favored over men. His cry resonates with that of the men of Menasseh. Both complaints are validated—the men of Menasseh's by God and Admon's by Rabban Gamliel. More dramatic terms would be hard to find to express the strong resistance of men to giving women greater rights.

It seems to me that since Admon formulated his sense of injury in such general terms, he is talking about more than just the situation at hand. He is likely to be responding to the trend of rabbinic inheritance law, and marriage and divorce law too, to give women more and more benefits, often at the expense of men's. Since Admon was an early Tanna, we cannot say for certain that he had already witnessed considerable change. But he may have seen that the introduction of the *ketubah* granted women extensive privileges that they did not have before that time.

Returning to the Bible, we find one more fascinating reference to this matter. At the very end of the book of Job, when it is stated that he had a second set of children, seven sons and three daughters, and the names of only the daughters are given, the narrator goes on to say that "their father gave them a parcel of land [נחלה] among their brothers" (Job 42:15). The meaning is rather clear: Despite women's disenfranchisement by biblical inheritance law, Job awarded his daughters, in his lifetime, a share of his real assets![10]

Dowry as a Share of a Woman's Father's Wealth

Although the Mishnah accepts the biblical rule that sons inherit all and daughters nothing, it speaks at length of the monetary arrangements accompanying marriage, in particular, the sums of money that a woman brings to her marriage.[11]

If the father of the bride stipulates that he will give his daughter's husband a sum of money [a dowry] . . . (M Ketubot 6:2)

If she stipulated to bring in [a dowry] of 1,000 dinarim [zuz], then he [the husband] stipulates [in the *ketubah*], in corresponding fashion, that he owes her 1,500 [because he will invest these moneys and make them increase; it is the principal plus profit that he obligates himself to return to her upon dissolution of the marriage]. . . . (M 6:3)

If a father marries off his daughter without stipulating [a dowry], he may not give her less than 50 zuz. If he stipulates that he will give her nothing, . . . the groom must provide her with the clothing she needs before she leaves her father's home. And similarly one who marries off an orphan, he should not give [her a dowry of] less than 50 zuz. If there is communal money available, he should give her a dowry according to her station in life [לפי כבודה]. (M 6:5)

If a minor orphan[12] was married off by her mother or brothers with her consent,[13] and they *wrote*[14] her [a dowry] of only 100 or 50, when she matures she may claim from them what was fitting for her to receive.

R. Judah says: If [a man] married off his first daughter, the second should receive [after his death] what he gave the first [in his lifetime]. But the Sages say: Sometimes a man is rich and grows poor or poor and grows rich; rather, one assesses the value of his property and gives her a dowry accordingly. (M 6:6)

It is clear from these *mishnah*s, 6:5 in particular, that a father is expected to give his daughter a sum of money upon her marriage. If he refuses, it is the groom's responsibility to provide her with a trousseau before she leaves her father's home. Furthermore, it makes no difference what the husband does with the dowry money, as long as he accepts responsibility for it and returns it to her when the marriage dissolves. M 6:6 and also 6:5 indicate that the amount of the dowry is to vary with the relative wealth of the father. The larger his holdings, the larger a dowry he is expected to grant her.[15]

The Tosefta draws a closer connection between dowry and inheritance.

If a man dies and leaves sons and daughters, and the estate is large, the sons *inherit* and the daughters are *maintained and given a dowry* from it [ניזונות ומתפרנסות]. How do the sons inherit? . . . (T Ketubot 6:1)

How are the daughters maintained and given a dowry? One does not say, if their father were alive, he would have given them such and such; rather we see how much girls like them [i.e., of similar socioeconomic status], receive as a dowry and this is what we give them. (T 6:2)

Rebbe says: Each one takes one tenth of the assets. R. Judah says: If he married off his first daughter, the second should receive [after his death], what the first received. (T 6:3)

These *baraita*s determine that dowry and also maintenance, the ongoing day-to-day support,[16] are a daughter's due from her father's estate after his death. T 6:1 speaks of these moneys in parallel fashion to the son's inheritance, implying thereby that it is her inheritance, even though it may not be called such. T 6:2 adds that the size of this dowry should be determined by the father's economic standing and the standard practice of other men in similar situations. T 6:3 presents the most liberal view of all, that of Rebbe, who holds that each daughter is to receive one tenth of her father's assets upon marriage. All agree, in other words, upon a way to give daughters a share of their father's estate in the event that they have brothers who inherit: Call it *"parnasah"* and make it large enough so that what a daughter gets is comparable to what a son gets. Those who say that it is not a fixed amount, but either commensurate with his economic standing or one tenth of his assets, clearly make the analogy between a daughter's dowry and a son's inheritance.

Both Talmuds seized upon this proportionate way of assessing a dowry after a father's death.

— — . . . But did not Rava say . . . the *halakhah* is according to Rebbe [that each daughter takes one tenth of the assets] . . .

. . . [We learned in a *baraita*:] Rebbe said: A daughter who is maintained by her brothers [after their father's death] takes one tenth of the assets [as a dowry]. They said to Rebbe: According to you, someone who has ten daughters and a son, the son will receive nothing once the daughters [all take their dowry]! He said to them: This is what I mean, the first takes one tenth of the assets, the second [takes one tenth] of what the first one left, the third [takes one tenth] of what the second one left, and then they all divide it up evenly [and in this manner the son will have an inheritance of about one third of the estate]. . . .

We learned in a *baraita*: If daughters either mature before they marry or marry before they mature, they lose their maintenance but not their dowry—the opinion of Rebbe. R. Simon b. Elazar says, they even lose their dowry [if they mature before they marry]. What can they do? They can "hire" husbands and claim their dowry [prior to maturing so that they do not lose it].

— —Said R. Nahman: Huna told me that the *halakhah* is according to Rebbe. . . . (BT Ketubot 68a)

The first of these two *baraita*s notes, once again, the conflict between sons and daughters. It is like the first paragraph of the Tosefta in that it stipulates that daughters collect their dowry from the estate, but specifies, as does T 6:3, that each is entitled to one tenth. The question almost asks itself: What about the sons? Is not their share significantly diminished if so much is given to the daughters? The answer is that there will always be something left for the sons, even if each daughter claims one tenth; moreover, a son's share will be larger than a daughter's because a daughter receives less than a proportionate share of the assets. If we take a case in which there are three daughters and seven sons (like Job's second family), and an estate of 1,000, the first daughter gets 100, the second daughter one tenth of what is left, 90, and the third daughter one tenth of what is then left [.10(810)], 81. This leaves 729 to be divided among seven sons—so each will get a share of about 104, which is larger than the share of any one of the daughters, with the gap between a son's and a daughter's share growing as each successive girl takes her due. If there is one daughter followed by nine sons, there is full equality—each child will get one tenth. If there are nine daughters and one son, the last of the girls will get a share of 43, whereas the son will get what remains, 389. If the daughters then divide up their shares evenly, as also recommended by Rebbe, each will get about 68.

As the last part of the quoted passage indicates, according to Rebbe the dowry is protected: The daughters cannot lose it when they mature, even though they lose their right to maintenance at that time. Since R. Simon b. Elazar holds otherwise, he recommends that if a girl whose father died did not marry before reaching maturity, she should "hire" herself a husband in order to claim her dowry. In other words, she should circumvent disenfranchisement of her share of the estate by staging a betrothal.

It is hard to understand why the definition of a dowry as one tenth of a father's assets appears in Rebbe's name in the Tosefta, the Bavli, and the Yerushalmi (PT Ketubot 6:6; 30d), but not in the Mishnah. The Mishnah requires that a father give a daughter no less than 50 or 100 zuz and the same to her sister who marries after their father's death. Although it does say that a daughter can later demand what she deserves, she is not initially entitled to the one tenth fixed by the other texts. The Mishnah also presents R. Judah's view that the second daughter should get what the first one got and the Sages' view that after the father's death, the dowry is determined according to his wealth. But these are still not so generous a grant, in most cases, as the rule of one tenth.

We also see, from the opening line of Ketubot 68a, that the Amoraim fixed the law according to Rebbe's rule that a dowry after the father's death is one tenth of his estate. For a family in which there were many children, the share that each daughter received would vary with the size of the estate but would in most cases be smaller than that of a son.[17] The important point is that it was no longer accurate to say, once a dowry after a father's death was pegged at one tenth—*a relative share and not a set amount*—that sons inherited and daughters did not.[18]

I do not think it possible to overestimate the significance of the rule of giving a girl a dowry of one tenth of her father's estate. This is probably as outright a rejection of the Torah's rule of a daughter's exclusion from inheritance as one can find.[19] The question is, Why did the rabbis adopt this liberal principle, clearly at the expense of sons? There are two answers: because they loved their daughters and also because they could see ahead to the day when their daughters' sons would inherit from their mother what she "inherited" from them, the grandfathers. We can find evidence for this outlook on the part of fathers of the bride in the enactment of the *ketubat bnin dikhrin* (the *ketubah* of the male offspring). M Ketubot 4:10 stipulates that should a woman predecease her husband and he inherit her assets, then, upon his death, the dowry that she brought into the marriage will be inherited only by the sons that she had with him and not by his sons from another wife. The Gemara comments:

> --Said R. Yohanan in the name of R. Simon b. Yohai: Why did they institute the *ketubat bnin dikhrin?* So that a father would seize the opportunity to "write" for [i.e., give to] his daughters [a share of his wealth] *just as* he "writes" for his sons [כדי שיקפוץ אדם ויכתוב לבתו כבנו].
>
> ==Can it be that the Merciful one says [in the Torah] that sons inherit and daughters do not and the rabbis come and enact that daughters *do* inherit?
>
> ==This too is from Scripture, for it says: "Take wives and produce sons and daughters and take wives for your sons and give your daughters to men in marriage" (Jeremiah 29:6)—the verse makes good sense in reference to sons, for it is within a father's power to find them wives. But his daughters, is it within his power to marry them off? This verse, therefore, comes to teach that he should clothe her and bedeck her and give her something [of substance, i.e., a dowry] so that men will seize her and marry her [דקפצי עלה ואתו נסבי לה].
>
> ==How much [does he give her as a dowry in his lifetime]?
>
> --Said Abaye and Rava: Up to a tenth of his estate. (BT Ketubot 52b)

This passage explicitly equates dowry and inheritance. When it says that a man should write, that is, give,[20] his daughter in the same generous way that he gives his son, the reference is to the inheritance he leaves his son. The dowry he gives to his daughter in his lifetime becomes the way in which he can pass on to her a share of his wealth. Interestingly, this passage already assumes that a man wishes to give such a share to his daughter and is designed to teach something else, namely, that if a father fears that what he gives her will, in the course of time, pass on to some other man's grandsons, then the rabbis guarantee, by means of this *ketubah* stipulation, that his assets will go only to his own grandsons.

Since the Gemara understands R. Yohanan's statement to be saying that dowry is a surrogate inheritance, it has no choice but to go on and ask: How can it be that the rabbis rescind or transform the Torah's explicit provision that daughters do not inherit when there are sons? The weak scriptural support that they bring to support a daughter's "inheritance" reveals that this rule is not even hinted at in the Torah. In fact, the opposite is true: The rabbis clearly intend to circumvent the Torah's disenfranchisement of women in inheritance law.[21] The Gemara's barely relevant Jeremiah prooftext indicates that this is an after-the-fact attempt to support a bold legislative initiative. The message of this passage, stated very bluntly, is that rabbis may come along and introduce legislation that frustrates Torah law, provided their goal is worthy. The argument in BT Gittin 33a (see Chapter 5) that the rabbis were *not* legislating against the Torah when they restricted a man's freedom to cancel a *get*, was more convincing. Here, it is clear that they *are* legislating against the simple Torah rule that daughters do not inherit for the purpose of keeping the Torah in line with social justice.[22] The Gemara, however, cannot make this point openly, only obliquely.

We cannot fail to notice that this dowry rule of one tenth significantly improves women's rights and even their status. Although the practice of fathers giving dowries to daughters was common in the ancient world, dowries given after a father's death in this kind of proportion probably were not, as evidenced by the rabbinic debate on this point. It would seem that Rebbe introduced the proportional one-tenth rule to make sure that a wealthy girl did not get too little and a poor girl too much of her father's estate. The one catch in this computing system is that a woman whose father died and who does not marry will never be able to claim her "inheritance," unless she follows R. Simon b. Elazar's advice (Ketubot 68a) and "hires" for herself a husband.

Gifts in Contemplation of Death

In addition to the dowry, there is yet another manner in which a man can choose to give part of his estate to his daughter. Since he cannot name her as an heir, he can make her a gift in contemplation of death and in this way transfer part of his estate to her. Reuven Yaron, who has written extensively on this subject, comments that such a gift is one that "is finally irrevocable only on the donor's death." Since it takes effect upon death, and not before, it was in substance identical to bequeathing an inheritance but in form radically different. Such a gift roughly corresponds to the Roman *donatio mortis causa*.[23]

1. If a man says, "So-and-so my firstborn will *not* receive a double share [of my estate] or "so-and-so my son will *not* inherit along with his brothers," he has said nothing because he has stipulated against the Torah.

2. If he divides up his estate among his sons by the word of his mouth and assigned more to one son and less to another, or gave the firstborn an equal share with his brothers, his words stand [because these are gifts in contemplation of death and not an inheritance].

But if he said, "as an inheritance," he has said nothing [i.e., he cannot deny his firstborn a double share nor give one son more than another].

If he wrote either at the beginning, or in the middle, or at the end, "as a gift," his words stand.

3. If a man says, "so-and-so will inherit me" in a case in which he has a daughter, or "my daughter will inherit me" in a case in which he has a son, he has said nothing because he has stipulated against the Torah. R. Yohanan b. Baroka says: If he said so about someone who is fit to inherit from him, his words stand; but about someone not fit to inherit from him his words do not stand.[24] . . . (M Baba Batra 8:5)

The second section of this *mishnah* provides a strategy for circumventing the Torah's rules of intestate succession that favor a firstborn over other sons and sons over daughters. If a father makes a gift in contemplation of death to anyone he wishes, provided he *does* say it is a gift and does *not* say it is an inheritance, his words stand.[25] The third section of this *mishnah* addresses the issue of a man's freedom to distribute his assets as he sees fit. Note that this *mishnah* shows him how to circumvent the Torah: Since he cannot openly and explicitly stipulate against the Torah, he can achieve exactly the same end, that is, distribute his assets as he wishes, by adopting the strategies outlined or maybe even recommended here by the rabbis. It seems to me that the author of this paragraph, as made evident by his examples, opposes the bias in favor of a firstborn son and against daughters.

The Yerushalmi also seems to oppose special rights of the firstborn.

– –R. La gave all the brothers an equal share [השווה את הבכורה לאחין], even the firstborn.[26]

– –Said R. Haggai: Is there not a verse that says that he may not favor [the son of the beloved wife over the firstborn son of the despised wife but must give him a double portion (Deuteronomy 21:16)]?

– –Said R. Lezer: In the name of the worship service! He has the power to [deny him his double portion], but he is not permitted to do so [from the outset, העבודה שיכול אלא שאינו רשאי]; [instead,] he can give it as a gift [i.e., he can distribute the estate equally to all sons as gifts, not as inheritance]. (PT Baba Batra 8:4; 16b)

This passage reinforces the legal strategy for redistribution. It records a rabbinic decision in which the firstborn is treated no differently from the other brothers, all of whom received the same share of their father's estate. When asked to explain how R. La could arrive at such a decision, given that the Torah stipulates otherwise, R. Lezer responds that the testator distributed his assets as gifts, not as inheritance.

Again, it seems extraordinarily clear that in this case one has to circumvent Torah law in order to do what one thinks is right, that is, give an equal share to all of one's sons. A double share for the firstborn was no longer justified in many rabbis' eyes. Calling the inheritance "gifts" rather than "inheritance" becomes the simple solution.

This passage in the Yerushalmi is important because it tells us that an actual case was adjudicated in this manner. Moreover, the statement is clearly made that there is nothing wrong with wanting to do things differently from what the Torah recommends, provided one adopts the appropriate legal strategy. The Torah's inheritance laws have become the default position, available for a man who does not wish to deal with his estate in any other way. But if he is not satisfied with that manner of distribution, the door is open to many other possibilities.[27]

The issue of a daughter's disenfranchisement, in addition to generating halakhic controversy, stirred political debate as well. According to M Baba Batra 8:2, an heir's direct descendants stand in for him if he dies before inheriting from his own progenitors. For instance, if a man dies leaving a daughter and a son's daughter, the granddaughter inherits all, because she stands in for her father, the decedent's son. The decedent's daughter inherits nothing. This particular rule, which seems to defy common sense in that a person who is two generations removed takes precedence over one who is one generation removed, with both being of the same gender, subjected the rabbis to much criticism.

> We learned in a *baraita:* . . . for the Sadducees said, let the decedent's own daughter inherit together with his son's daughter! Said R. Yohanan b. Zaccai [in defense of the *mishnah*'s rule] . . . (BT Baba Batra 115b)

> The Sadducees say that the son's daughter and the [decedent's own] daughter are both equal [in their right to inherit from the decedent]. For they say: "If the daughter of my son, who derives standing from my son, inherits from me, then my own daughter, who derives standing from me, how much the more so should she inherit from me!" (PT Baba Batra 8:1; 16a)

This passage, in which the Sadducees mock the illogical rulings of the rabbis, indicates that the bias against women in inheritance law was not only an academic matter but also part of the public political discourse. R. Yohanan b. Zaccai may have been able to provide a technical halakhic answer to defend the rabbis' position, but the Sadducees' claim takes the moral high ground: How can you disenfranchise daughters in favor of granddaughters?

The discussion of daughters' taking a share along with sons triggered a similar query about wives.

> – –R. Abba sent [a letter] to R. Joseph b. Hama: If a man says, let my wife take a share like that of my sons, she takes a share like one of the sons.
> – –Said Rava: Provided it is [a share] of the assets he owns now [at the time that he made the statement] and that it includes any sons born to him later. (BT Baba Batra 128b)

> – –Said R. Judah said Samuel: If a man assigns all of his assets to his wife, he has only appointed her a guardian [and not an heir, לא עשאה אלא אפוטרופא]. . . . (131b)

Since the first statement appears in conjunction with M Baba Batra 8:5, about the distribution of assets as one sees fit and not according to the Torah's scheme, R. Abba is proposing a strategy for enabling wives to inherit from husbands. Rava qualifies it somewhat. Other statements on this topic appear a few pages later, again implying that wives' disenfranchisement was considered problematic by the rabbis and that they took steps to resolve it. In a sense, the inheritance of the wife has been guaranteed by the promise made in the *ketubah*. But in the Baba Batra cases, a husband is interested in enfranchising his wife in a proportional way, at the expense of his other heirs. Although there is much more discussion of daughters' inheritance than wives', it is not unreasonable to conclude that by the end of the amoraic period, men—and also women—who followed rabbinic law had the freedom to bequeath their assets to whom they wished, not necessarily favoring a firstborn or leaving out daughters and wives.

Disposition of a Mother's Estate

The Mishnah (Baba Batra 8:4) introduces a topic not found in the Torah—disposition of a mother's estate. The question is: Do the sons take all, leaving their sisters nothing, as the Torah legislates for a father's estate, or given the Torah's silence, are the rabbis free to decide on their own how to adjudicate this matter? By reading a series of rather complicated texts in chronological order, we will find that the topic remained controversial and unresolved for several centuries.

The same goes for sons and for daughters regarding inheritance [אחד הבן ואחד הבת בנחלה], except that a [firstborn] son takes a double share of his father's estate but not of his mother's, and a daughter is maintained from her father's estate, but not from her mother's. (M Baba Batra 8:4)

This *mishnah* is hard to understand. First, what is the "same" for sons and daughters with respect to inheritance? The standard interpretation[28] is that when there are no sons, daughters divide up the father's estate in the same way that sons do. The words "the same" are distorted in this interpretation, however, for in most instances daughters, who get nothing, are not the same as sons. Second, once an equality is stated regarding sons and daughters, we would expect the Mishnah's "except that" to introduce some exception to that rule of equality, that is, some way in which sons and daughters differ *from each other*. Instead, the Mishnah states two differences in law between the father's and the mother's estate, one that holds true for sons and one that holds true for daughters.[29]

To resolve these difficulties, we turn to the parallel passage in the Tosefta.

Just as a son takes precedence over a daughter in the [distribution of the] father's assets, so too he takes precedence over a daughter in the [distribution of the] mother's assets; R. Elazar b'R. Yossi says in the name of R. Zechariah b. Hakazzav, and a similar [statement was made by] R. Simon b. Judah of Kfar Ibus in the name of R. Simon: The same goes for a son and the same goes for a daughter, they are *equal* in their [inheritance of] the *mother's assets*. (T Baba Batra 7:10)

What we see here is quite striking: The first (anonymous) Tanna holds that sons always take precedence over daughters in inheritance, whether it be in the father's estate as dictated by the Torah or in the mother's estate, whose laws can be learned by analogy from the father's estate. But a number of Tannaim, disagreeing with the anonymous Tanna, claim absolute equality for sons and daughters when it comes to disposing of a mother's estate. This may be the only issue of privilege in rabbinic literature regarding which full equality of women and men is recommended.

Unlike the Mishnah's phrasing "the same goes for sons and the same goes for daughters regarding inheritance," which, as we have noted, is an opaque formulation, here the rule of sons' taking precedence over daughters in the disposition of both a father's and mother's estate is spelled out clearly as an advantage that sons have over daughters. An even greater contrast between the Mishnah and the Tosefta is the use in the Tosefta, by a named Tanna, of the phrase "the same goes for sons . . . the same goes for daughters . . ." with respect to a rule that treats sons and daughters *exactly the same:* the distribution of their mother's estate. Thus, the Tosefta's use of this phrase is perfectly clear, whereas the Mishnah's is ambiguous. So, if we assume that the Tosefta's paragraph is older than the corresponding *mishnah,* then, when the redactor of the Mishnah selected this passage for inclusion in his collection, he reworked it in order to impose his own, *less* egalitarian point of view on it. However, he sacrificed clarity in order to make his point. To show that sons should be awarded *all* of their mother's estate, without losing even part of it to maintenance for their sisters or to the firstborn's extra share, not only did he omit all mention of R. Zechariah b. Hakazzav and the others, but he co-opted their linguistic formulation for his own rule, even though it does not frame the rule very well. That is, not only does the redactor of the Mishnah fix the *halakhah* contrary to the Tannaim of the Tosefta and omit all reference to their dissent, he even takes over their phraseology for his own purposes.[30]

We thus see that the issue of disposing of a mother's estate was debated by many generations of Tannaim, beginning with R. Zechariah b. Hakazzav, who lived in the time of the Temple and favored equality, and ending with the redactor of the Mishnah, in about 200 C.E., who ruled against equality. Remarkably, the controversy continued well into the amoraic period. After citing a version of the Tosefta's *baraita,* one that includes the view of R. Zechariah b. Hakazzav, the Gemara brings three anecdotes:

––R. Nitai was thinking of ruling in a case [of brothers and sisters arguing over the disposition of their mother's estate] like R. Zechariah b. Hakazzav. Said to him Samuel: Like whom? Like Zechariah? Zechariah is nothing [אפס זכריה]!

––R. Tavla issued a ruling in accordance with R. Zechariah b. Hakazzav. Said to him R. Nahman: What is this? He said: R. Hinena b. Shelemya has said in the name of Rav, the *halakhah* is in accordance with R. Zechariah b. Hakazzav. He said to him: Retract, or I will take R. Hinena b. Shelemya out of your ear!

––R. Huna b. Hiyya was thinking of ruling in a case [that came before him] in accordance with R. Zechariah b. Hakazzav. Said to him R. Nahman: What is this? . . . (BT Baba Batra 111a)

We learn from these three passages that in the amoraic period the issue of disposing of a mother's estate was far from settled. Although R. Zechariah b. Hakazzav is not mentioned in the Mishnah, three early amoraim wish to rule like him. His view is made known to them, it seems, from the *baraita.* It is quite unusual for Amoraim to rule according to a Tanna whose opinion contradicts the one view presented in the Mishnah.

In each of the three cases, in which we may assume sisters were suing brothers for an equal share of their mother's estate, a little known Amora wishes to find in their favor and is squelched by a prominent colleague. What motivated these Amoraim to want to rule in favor of a daughter's right to inherit? It seems to me that it can be nothing other than a sense of fairness. In a matter about which the Torah is silent, these three men decide that a mother's estate should be divided equally between her sons and daughters.

The Yerushalmi parallel (Baba Batra 8:1; 16a) highlights this controversy. It quotes the *baraita* from the Tosefta, with the dissenting view of R. Zechariah b. Hakazzav, and then says that R. Joshua b. Levi, a first-generation prominent Amora, rules the same as he. Here, too, an Amora rules the same as a Tanna whose view is *not* included in the Mishnah. The Yerushalmi then reports that a case came before R. Yannai of Capodoccia, a fourth-generation Amora, involving a woman who was apparently suing her brother for half of their mother's estate. He and his three colleagues, R. Huna, R. Judah b. R. Simon b. Pazi, and R. Aha, together decided the case according to the Mishnah and thus overturned the ruling of R. Joshua b. Levi that followed R. Zechariah b. Hakazzav and favored women. They note that their colleagues outside of the land of Israel mistakenly rely on R. Joshua b. Levi's leniency. The Yerushalmi then cites three Amoraim, each of whom names an early master who rules *against* R. Zechariah.[31] Here, as in the Bavli, early sympathy for R. Zechariah is replaced by later strenuous objection to his opinion. This ongoing controversy, generation after generation, makes it clear that the injustice continued to bother the rabbis. Equity in this matter seems to have been an attractive idea to them.

Both Talmuds include yet more material on this subject. Following these brief incidents, we find a lengthy anecdote from the early amoraic period in which two rabbis debate the related issues of a woman's disenfranchisement and a firstborn's double enfranchisement.[32]

The two main protagonists are the aged R. Yannai, a student of R. Judah the Prince, and R. Judah Nesia, a grandson of R. Judah the Prince and a Prince himself.[33] The core of the vignette is an exchange between the two masters. R. Judah Nesia asks R. Yannai for a scriptural source for the law that a son takes precedence over a daughter in a mother's estate. He responds that Numbers 36:8, when talking about women's inheritance, mentions "tribes" in the plural. This grammatical form implies that the rules of inheritance for a father's tribe are comparable to the rules of inheritance for a mother's—just as a son takes precedence over a daughter in the disposition of a father's estate, so does he take precedence in the disposition of a mother's. R. Judah Nesia challenges the analogy: "If so, then just as a firstborn son takes a double share of his father's estate, he should likewise take a double share of his mother's estate," a conclusion contrary to the one stated in M Baba Batra 8:4. R. Judah Nesia is thus suggesting that we either give a son both advantages—precedence over a daughter in the disposition of a mother's estate and also a firstborn's double share of a mother's estate—or else neither. Other positions, like the one R. Yannai espouses, are not logically sound. Upon hearing this, R. Yannai mutters to his assistant, "Help me get up; this man does not wish to learn."

This story is very perplexing. That R. Judah Nesia finds fault with R. Yannai's derivation suggests that R. Judah is not pleased with the rule that favors sons over daughters, even though at the outset he appears to accept it when he asks for its scriptural basis. I say this because R. Yannai's derivation is no different from other rabbinic derivations of law from Scripture. Thus, R. Judah's challenge is not mere finding fault with the application of a hermeneutical device but more likely an objection to the Mishnah's ruling. Moreover, R. Judah's retort can be construed as a criticism of the rule of a firstborn's double share, a law that offends moral sensibilities in the rabbinic period much the same way as the disenfranchisement of daughters. The end of the story is its most ironic part: R. Yannai accuses R. Judah Nesia of being closed-minded when, in fact, it is he himself who is unable to entertain the possibility of equal inheritance for women and men. In neither the Bavli nor the Yerushalmi version does R. Yannai respond directly to the critique. As soon as he hears R. Judah's suggestion that women should inherit from their mothers and that firstborns should not receive a double share, R. Yannai abruptly ends the conversation and prepares to leave.[34]

It is noteworthy that in the Yerushalmi version, after R. Judah Nesia listens to R. Yannai's analogy, he suggests that this verse, in fact, teaches the reverse: Just as a daughter has an equal share with a son in her mother's estate, so too should she have an equal share with a son in her father's estate! That is, R. Judah Nesia expresses his dissatisfaction with sons' taking precedence over daughters not only in a mother's estate but even in a father's estate, a position that is blatantly at odds not only with the Mishnah but also with Scripture!

Conclusions

We have seen, in this survey, the considerable turbulence on the subject of women's inheritance in both the tannaitic and the amoraic periods. The rabbis exhibit a growing opposition to disinheriting women, despite the Torah's prescriptions. The Tannaim say, almost explicitly, that a person can behave totally differently from what the Torah prescribes, distribute his wealth as he sees fit, provided that he does not violate the letter of the law. As long as the assets that a father gives to a daughter are given as a dowry or as a gift in contemplation of death, it is legitimate for him to assign her a substantial share of his wealth. This area, more than marriage, divorce, or ritual, is one in which the rabbis felt women deserve to be given more rights than the Torah allows. It differs from the others in that men's dignity is not at stake, nor is their relationship with their wives. What is at stake is their relationship with their daughters, with an eye toward prospective grandsons. Inheriting a share of a father's estate is a boon to women because many assets may have accumulated after they had married and received a dowry.

Chapter 8 of Baba Batra, which deals with inheritance, seems subversive in its principal message: It dwells on rabbinic opposition to many of the Torah's rules of intestate succession, not just the disenfranchisement of women. Though the rabbis raise women's issues in many different places in the chapter, they also challenge a firstborn's rights to a double share and the lack of the testator's freedom to disinherit Torah mandated heirs.

As we have seen, the rabbis make many significant changes in the rules of distribution of assets. But we also find resistance to change for the benefit of women, most notably in the Mishnah's rejection and omission of R. Zechariah b. Hakazzav's suggestion of equality in the disposition of a mother's estate. It seems that men will go just so far. Perhaps the notion of equality, even in one limited area, was too much for them to consider. Nevertheless, the amoraic debate on this topic, in both Palestine and Babylonia, with so many rabbis from so many generations taking part, suggests that at least a minority valued and promoted equality for women.

Notes

1. The one exception is that if there are no sons, the daughters inherit all (Num. 27:8).

2. In a matriarchy, however, passing land from one generation of women to the next would have worked equally well.

3. Reuven Yaron, *Gifts in Contemplation of Death in Jewish and Roman Law* (Oxford: Clarendon Press, 1960), 18.

4. Cf. Gen. 31:15: Rachel and Leah say about Laban, their father, "We are like strangers to him; he sold us [in marriage] and has eaten our money." They presumably mean that he was supposed to keep at least part of the bride payment for them. See the *Anchor Bible, Genesis*, commentary by E. A. Speiser, 245.

5. In reporting on Greek documents found in the Judaean desert, Hannah Cotton suggests that a deed of gift that a woman received from her father upon marriage implies that such a document was the only way to ensure that she received part of his estate. This would correct the inequities of the rules of inheritance. "Women's Documents from the Judaean Desert," lecture, Israel Museum, May 19, 1996.

6. Yaron gives additional reasons for the introduction of gifts in contemplation of death, beyond the unsatisfactory state of the law with regard to daughters and widows: the desire of people who had accumulated wealth to dispose of their prop-

erty as they saw fit; growing contact with the Hellenistic world, where such free-dom had long been established (*Gifts in Contemplation of Death*, 18). He suggests that the introduction of the changes occurred about 100 B.C.E.

7. See statements on fatherly love, BT BB 141a. See also Yaron (*Gifts in Contemplation of Death*, 16), who cites an Aramaic document from Elephantine, Egypt, from 404 B.C.E., in which a father bequeaths half a house to his daughter Yehoyishma "in affection, because she did maintain me when I was old in days."

8. See note 22.

9. The Mishnah says that Admon, a judge in Jerusalem at the end of the period of the Second Temple, issued seven rulings. This is the first.

10. Athalya Brenner points this out in her edited volume, *A Feminist Companion to Wisdom Literature* (Sheffield: Sheffield Academic Press, 1995), 57–58. She calls it the deconstructive nature of the epilogue.

11. The noun *parnasah* (dowry) does not appear in the Mishnah or in the Tosefta but that is what is being described. The verb *lefarnes* suggests that fathers who marry off a daughter are to give her a sum of money as a dowry. The expression *pasak lah* means, according to Albeck, that he stipulated for her to receive a certain amount as a dowry. The Mishnah also uses the phrase *katvu lah* (Ketubot 6:6), "they wrote for her," which means that they—her mother or brothers—gave her such-and-such items for a dowry. This equivalence of writing and giving is extremely important in the analysis of the passage in BT Ketubot 82b (in Chapter 3) about the transformation of the *ketubah* from an advance to a deferred payment. The "writing" may refer to a written record of the dowry for which the husband accepts responsibility or to a written promise by the father to pay up upon marriage, not before. See also BT Ketubot 52b, further on in this chapter, where the term "to write," as used by R. Yohanan, means "to give." See notes 14 and 15.

12. In rabbinic usage the word *orphan* connotes a person who has lost either one parent or both.

13. M Yevamot 13:2; Albeck, "her knowledge" (59).

14. "Write" and "give" appear to be interchangeable in this context. Writing refers to the document outlining the husband's receipt of the moneys and his acceptance of responsibility for them. See next note.

15. As time passed, the groom's obligation to return the dowry to the bride at the termination of the marriage, as well as to pay her the additional sums that he owes her, were all written up in the *ketubah* itself. Cotton ("Women's Documents from the Judaean Desert") doubts that the common practice of Jews at the time of the Bar Kokhba rebellion was to specify two sums, a dowry and also a "bride price." She finds evidence of a dowry only. It was written into the *ketubah* as an obligation that the husband accepted upon himself to repay upon dissolution of the marriage.

16. Although a father is not required to maintain his daughters in his lifetime, once he dies, the daughters' maintenance is to be drawn from his estate, lessening thereby the amount inherited by the sons. An easy model to imagine is that the sons inherit the real property, and the daughters, until they either mature or marry, are maintained from the income of the inherited assets. See M Ketubot 4:6, 11, and associated materials in the Bavli and Yerushalmi.

17. One can construct cases in which there are about twice as many sons as daughters and thus a daughter's share is greater than a son's.

18. The Yerushalmi also fixed the law according to Rebbe's rule of one tenth:

--"R. Zeira asked R. Nahman b. Jacob and R. Ammi bar Pappi: Which tanna holds the principle of [assigning] one tenth of the assets [for the dowry]?

--"Said to him R. Zeira in the name of R. Jeremiah: Assigning one tenth of the assets for the dowry is the opinion of Rebbe.

"[As we learned in a *baraita:*] They asked Rebbe: If there were ten daughters, and the first took one tenth, and the second took one tenth, . . . then there would be nothing left for the son. He answered them: The first takes one tenth and leaves, and the second takes one tenth of what is left. . . . It turns out that the ten girls take a little less than two thirds and the son takes a little more than one third . . . " (PT Ketubot 6:6; 30d).

What interests the Amoraim here is the rule of one tenth. Some are apparently not familiar with the passage in the Tosefta that presents Rebbe's view in contradistinction to R. Judah's. But they seem to know of the principle and are informed that Rebbe issued it and defended it. Like the Bavli, the Yerushalmi adopts this principle as its standard. See the rest of the discussion in the Yerushalmi in which the rabbis decide to rule like R. Hanina, who gives a second daughter, after her father's death, one tenth of his assets.

19. Cotton ("Women's Documents from the Judaean Desert") makes precisely this point in reference to the deeds of gift found in the archives of Babatha and Salome Komais. She theorizes that these deeds were written by fathers upon the marriage of daughters, with the specific purpose of circumventing the Torah's disenfranchisement of women. In other words, there is evidence, from about 130 C.E., that women were given large dowries, presumably for the fathers to give them in this way a share of the wealth. We also have evidence from these archives of husbands making large gifts to wives.

20. See notes 11, 14, 15.

21. See note 19.

22. There is extensive rabbinic discussion of the possibility of ruling against the Torah, in particular in monetary matters. See, for example, M BM 7:11 and associated Gemara.

23. Yaron, *Gifts in Contemplation of Death,* 1.

24. There is much discussion in the Bavli about whether or not the *halakhah* is in accord with R. Yohanan b. Baroka. His view, that as long as the person to whom one transfers the inheritance is a Torah heir, the redistribution is allowed, has enormous implications for daughters. However, a tannaitic source in the Bavli (130a) says, in the name of R. Ishmael the son of R. Yohanan b. Baroka, that his father did *not* have in mind to bequeath to a daughter and disinherit sons. The extensive discussion of whether the law follows R. Ishmael leads me to believe that it was precisely this issue—favoring a daughter over sons—that divided the rabbis over the generations. The Yerushalmi also discusses this matter extensively (PT BB 8:5; 16b).

25. The oral statement of a dying man is considered to have the force of a written will.

26. Either R. La divided up his own estate in this manner or he so divided up someone else's estate.

27. See BT BB 126b ff. The anecdotes suggest that the firstborn's special privileges were still granted in the amoraic period.

28. Albeck, Baba Batra, 145.

29. Ibid. addresses this problem by adding the following points: A firstborn daughter does not take a double share, neither of her father's assets nor of her mother's; a son is not maintained either from his father's estate or from his mother's. In this way, the Mishnah makes sense in that it compares sons and daughters in reference to *nahalah*, interpreted as the sum total of the father's and mother's estates. The problem with this interpretation is that it does not arise from the text itself but is superimposed onto the text.

30. See Y. N. Epstein (*Mavo Lenusach Hamishnah*, 2nd ed. [Jerusalem: Magnes Press, 1964], 660) for a similar analysis of this *mishnah*. Epstein considers the connecting phrase "except that" [אלא ש——] to be an arbitrary way of connecting the two disparate parts of the *mishnah*, the second of which also appears in M Bekhorot 8:9.

31. R. Joshua b. Levi (!), R. Yohanan, R. Hoshaia.

32. BT BB 110a; PT BB 8:1; 16a.

33. The story begins with a brief interchange that informs the reader of preexisting hostility between the two rabbis. R. Yannai is told by his assistant that the man approaching them is dressed in fancy clothes. When R. Judah draws near, R. Yannai fingers the cloth of R. Judah's cloak and makes a disparaging comment. Before any conversation takes place, R. Yannai has already indicated his disdain for R. Judah Nesia's wealth and position.

34. Note that it is someone who is reputedly wealthy and well connected who is in favor of expanding women's inheritance rights and also limiting those of the firstborn. Both of these changes move in the direction of fairer distribution of assets. It is also interesting that R. Judah Nesia is pictured by R. Yannai at the very beginning of the anecdote as arrogant, and yet it is R. Yannai who dismisses him summarily without responding to the point that he raised.

9

Testimony

THE TOPIC OF WOMEN'S EXCLUSION from giving testimony is a sensitive one today. Since the time of the Talmud, women have been barred by Jewish law from serving as witnesses, both at courtroom trials, to establish the facts of the case, and at religious rituals, to witness a ceremony like marriage. When pondering this exclusion, we can hardly avoid thinking that for the rabbis to have deemed women untrustworthy witnesses, they must have severely devalued their intellectual capacities.[1] To find out if this is so will not be easy. Since no Talmudic tractate deals solely with the subject of giving testimony, we will have to collect statements on the subject from many different tractates and then examine each one on its own and in relationship to the others.

That women may not testify in civil and criminal cases is axiomatic in the Mishnah. No statement explicitly prohibits them, but indirect statements abound, such as "whatever testimony a woman is unfit to give, they—for example, dice rollers and those who lend money on interest—are also unfit to give" (M Rosh Hashanah 1:8), and the complementary statement in T Sanhedrin 5:2, "but testimony that a woman is fit to give, they are fit to give." Although two witnesses are generally required by Jewish law, in some cases only one is necessary and that one may be a woman. A number of these cases have critical consequences for the Jewish community. For example, in order to establish a man's death and permit his wife to remarry, a woman's testimony may be accepted. Also, in order to determine that a woman in captivity was not raped and could therefore return to her *kohen* husband,[2] a woman's testimony may be accepted.

One popular explanation for women's exclusion from giving testimony in civil and criminal cases is that summoning them to a courtroom for interrogation is an assault on their dignity. Women are, in fact, reliable, but a verse teaches that a woman's dignity is best preserved in the recesses of her own home (Psalms 45:14).[3] This explanation, as appealing as some may find it, is a distortion of the Talmud's own statements on the subject. As we will see later, the Talmud implies that the need to give testimony in a courtroom *overrides* a woman's need to stay at home—not a surprising conclusion for jurists to reach.

A second popular theory is that the Talmud considers women to be emotional and intellectually shallow, and hence unreliable.[4] This theory, also, is problematic. If the rabbis thought these things about women, why would they allow them to testify in cases, such as those mentioned above, in which false testimony could, in the long run, ruin many innocent individuals? If a witness lies, the woman for whom he or she testifies may enter into, or resume, a sexual relationship forbidden by the Torah.

Based on a close reading of relevant texts, I have developed an alternative explanation that effectively accounts for the particular inclusions and exclusions: Women, although reliable in and of themselves, could not testify in most civil and criminal cases because, when married, they were beholden to their husbands and likely to be influenced by them in how they reported what they saw. That is, a woman could not testify because her subordinate status was likely to compromise her ability to tell the truth. Women as women were reliable. However, when they found themselves under the control of men, as wives necessarily would, they were not free to tell the truth. Another consequence of their subordinate status was that they could not testify in cases concerning men, their superiors, lest they compromise men's dignity. If these arguments are correct, then why, in a limited set of cases, was their testimony acceptable? In those cases the rabbinical judges were attempting to resolve the indeterminate marital status of other women. In such circumstances, the rabbis accepted all available *fit* individuals as witnesses.

We will now see how this theory emerges from the words of the text themselves.

Women's General Reliability

The theme of chapter 15 of M Yevamot is the testimony of women. The first several *mishnah*s describe a woman testifying about her own marital status. The focus then shifts to cases in which other women testify on her behalf.

> If a woman and her husband went abroad, and there was peace between them and peace in the world, and she came back [alone] and said, "My husband died," she is permitted to get remarried. Even to her *levir* [if she had produced no children].
>
> If there was peace between them but war in the world, or conflict between them but peace in the world, and she came and said, "My husband died," she is not believed [for if the world was at war, she could be

mistaken about his death; and if they were at war, she had reason to fabricate a report of his death so that she could marry someone else].

R. Judah says: She is not to be believed unless she showed up weeping and wearing torn clothing [as a sign of mourning]. They [the Sages] retorted: The same holds for both women [either weeping or not weeping]; they may remarry. (M Yevamot 15:1)

According to this passage, a woman who reports her own husband's death is believed and permitted to remarry, as long as there is no obvious reason for her to have fabricated the report or to have been mistaken. That is, a woman's testimony about her own husband's death is accepted by the majority of the Sages, even though her lying could lead to an adulterous relationship and the production of children of impaired lineage.

R. Judah is more skeptical than the others. The only women he will believe are those who show up emotionally distraught and wearing torn clothing, clear evidence that they are mourning their husband's death. Note, however, that although he is less trusting of women, he still accepts their testimony if certain behaviors support it.

The next two *mishnah*s show that the issue of accepting a woman's testimony was debated even by the earliest schools of rabbis, Bet Shammai and Bet Hillel:

[The rabbis of] Bet Hillel say: We only heard this to be so [that her testimony is accepted about the death of her husband] if she had just come in from the harvest, in that same province [i.e., not from abroad], and it is like what once happened.

Said to them Bet Shammai: The same is true for a woman who just came in from the harvest [of grain], or of olives or of grapes, or [even] from somewhere else. The Sages [in an earlier case] spoke of the harvest [of grain] because of an incident that actually occurred [but they were not limiting their ruling to such circumstances].

[Upon hearing this, the rabbis of] Bet Hillel changed their minds and ruled like Bet Shammai. (M 15:2)

[The rabbis of] Bet Shammai say: She may remarry and collect her *ketubah* [from the estate of the first husband on the basis of her own testimony]. [The rabbis of] Bet Hillel say: She may remarry but may *not* collect her *ketubah*.

Said to them Bet Shammai: Since you permit the sexual liaison [i.e., remarriage], which is a more stringent matter, why do you not permit [the collection] of money, which is a more lenient matter?

. . .

[Upon hearing this, the rabbis of] Bet Hillel changed their minds and ruled like Bet Shammai. (M 15:3)

The rabbis of Bet Shammai, despite the general rule that a woman may not testify, accept her testimony as to her husband's death, initially in a much wider set of circumstances than do the rabbis of Bet Hillel. That is, they establish the acceptance of her testimony as a principle, not just an exceptional case. They similarly accept her testimony for the purpose of the monetary aspects of the marriage settlement. Although Bet Hillel at first objects to this logical implication, Bet Shammai convinces them that the ability to remarry and the right to her *ketubah* money must go hand in hand. Usually considered the stricter of the two schools, Bet Shammai in this case rules more leniently, and also in general, in legislation affecting women.[5]

Since *mishnah*s 2 and 3 come from an earlier period of time than does *mishnah* 1, *mishnah* 1 must already assume Bet Shammai's rule that a woman is believed even if she comes from abroad. But the rabbis of *mishnah* 1 circumscribe it by eliminating a number of cases from consideration. They impose the restriction of "did she have reason to lie?" According to them, the restriction would take effect if she and her husband were at war with each other or if there were any reason to think that she was mistaken. R. Judah goes even further by requiring evidence of mourning on her part. But his colleagues reject his proposed stringency, as Bet Shammai rejected Bet Hillel, viewing it as an unreasonable limitation on the acceptability of women's testimony. We thus see that women's testimony was established early in the tannaitic period, over the opposition of Bet Hillel, and reestablished later in a slightly restricted form.

In *mishnah* 4, the rabbis go on to allow all to testify that her husband died, the "all" including other women but excluding those who, the rabbis say, are not to be trusted to give testimony regarding her: her mother-in-law, her mother-in-law's daughter (i.e., her sister-in-law), her co-wife, the woman married to her husband's brother, and her husband's daughter (from another wife). The rabbis assume all these women to be inimically disposed toward her and likely to fabricate a death report for the purpose of wreaking havoc on her life. Unfortunately, we have no way of knowing if these observations corresponded to the social realities of the time.[6]

The rules stated by the last *mishnah* of the chapter point to some general principles:

. . .

For a woman is not believed when she says, "my *levir* died," so that she would be allowed to remarry [without levirate release]; nor [is she believed] if she says, "my sister died," so that she would be allowed to enter into his house [i.e., marry her sister's husband]. A man is not believed when he says, "my brother died," so that he would be allowed to marry his brother's wife, nor "my wife died," so that he would be allowed to marry his wife's sister. (M Yevamot 15:10)

The reason these claims are not accepted is that in each of these cases the person who is making the claim has a reason to lie—to be able to marry a particular person to whom he or she has taken a fancy. In the first case, a woman is not believed as to her *levir*'s death because women were suspected of trying to avoid levirate marriage. She would be believed, however, in reporting on her husband's death.

Since the rabbis single out only these people as being predisposed to lie, they must assume that other claimants, whom they declare believable, have no reason to lie. To state this more generally: These exceptions imply that the underlying issue for this entire chapter is reliability. People are considered reliable, *men and women alike,* when they testify to someone's death. Only when they have clear reason to lie are they not considered reliable. Without the motivation to marry someone in particular or, in the case of a bad marriage, to get remarried to anyone, people are considered truthful. Corroboration of the fact that the rabbis considered women truthful will be found in the next chapter of Yevamot.

Allowing a Woman to Testify About a Man's Death

The very last *mishnah* of the entire tractate presents the halakhic history of the rule of allowing one witness to establish the fact of a man's death and, moreover, allowing that one witness to be a woman.

> Said R. Akiva: When I went down to Nehardea to intercalate the year [i.e., to add an extra month[7]] I met Nehemiah, Ish [a resident of] Bet Dli, who said to me, "I have heard it is only R. Judah b. Bava who permits a woman in Palestine to remarry on the evidence of one witness."
> I [Akiva] said to him: "That is right."
> He [then] said to me: "Tell them, in my name, [for] you know how hard it is to travel in these dangerous times, that I have a tradition from R. Gamliel the Elder that one may permit a woman to remarry on the evidence of one witness."
> And when I, [Akiva], came and told this to R. Gamliel, he rejoiced at [hearing] this and said, we now have a colleague for R. Judah b. Bava [i.e., someone who rules as he does].
> As a result [of this interchange], R. Gamliel remembered that [several] men had been killed at Tel Arza and R. Gamliel the Elder had permitted their wives to remarry on the evidence of one witness.
> And it became standard practice [הוקבע] to permit a woman to remarry on the evidence of hearsay testimony, of a male slave, of a woman, of a female slave.
> [But] R. Eliezer and R. Joshua say: One may not permit a woman to remarry on the evidence of [only] one witness.

R. Akiva says: Not on the evidence of a woman, a male slave, a female slave, or relatives. . . . (M Yevamot 16:7)

This *mishnah* is rather unusual in that it gives a detailed, even dramatic report of how a particular change in law came about. Although this is the closing *mishnah* of the entire tractate, it is the basis for much that is presented earlier in chapters 15 and 16. Its first, larger message is that the motivation for the change in Halakhah was the dilemma of women whose husbands had been killed but whose deaths had not and could not be legally established by two witnesses. The predicament of these women moved the rabbis to relax standards of testimony, to require only one witness instead of two. Note the unusual use of "rejoice" to describe R. Gamliel's response to hearing the report that a second rabbi, his own grandfather, had relaxed the rules of testimony. Note also that the tractate ends on a positive note, showcasing a *mishnah* of great depth and sensitivity. By placing this passage at the end, rather than somewhere in the middle, the redactor indicates the special value he attaches to it. As noted in Chapter 5, tractates often conclude with inspirational homilies.

The second message is that the halakhic change came about slowly, through the building of consensus. A good reason was not enough to make this change; there also needed to be a critical mass of rabbis who were willing to adopt it. The younger Rabban Gamliel was interested in this change but reluctant to act without the support of at least two colleagues. Nehemiah Ish Bet Dli was also interested in this change and took action to see it implemented. By the time the new rule became standard practice, it had become more liberal—hearsay testimony, as well as the testimony of male and female slaves and women, were acceptable.

Why does the Mishnah give such a detailed description of the evolution of this rule? Probably so that it could not be challenged, given its radical nature. As things stand, five rabbis—Nehemiah Ish Bet Dli, R. Akiva, R. Judah b. Bava, Rabban Gamliel the Elder, and Rabban Gamliel—all hold that one may permit a woman to remarry on the basis of only one witness. Two object, R. Joshua and R. Eliezer, and one, R. Akiva, who helped to establish the new practice, places restrictions on it that no one else places. This wide variety of views, together with the report of a historical triggering event, would make it impossible for anyone to claim later that this rule was adopted without proper deliberation.

We should further note that the redactor of the Mishnah has already incorporated this rule in a number of the paragraphs of chapters 15 and 16, as has the redactor of the parallel material in the Tosefta.[8] If we read the rest of the chapter, we see that there is a tendency on the part of the rabbis to accept the weakest possible evidence, even a disembodied voice (M 16:6), in order to release a woman from the grip of her dead husband.

One could argue, at this point, that relaxing the rules of testimony in this case is a function of rabbinic compassion, not belief in women's reliability. In order to extricate a woman from an indeterminate marital state, which meant living without a husband and not being allowed to find another, and to protect women from unsolicited and unwanted sexual advances by men, the rabbis relaxed the rules of testimony in a number of cases and required only one male witness instead of two. Furthermore, one could suggest, the rabbis invited women and also slaves to testify only after they had broken the two-witness paradigm. The logic of the halakhic change would run as follows: Although one man is less reliable than two, and women and slaves are not reliable at all, in certain situations that would lead to solving women's marital difficulties, their testimony is deemed acceptable.

I would respond that in this case and in others that we will look at shortly, the rabbis unquestionably relaxed the standards of testimony because of their desire to help women. But that is true only insofar as the testimony of one male witness is concerned, because one male witness is still considered a fit witness, although not as reliable as two. It is virtually inconceivable to me that if the rabbis held women and slaves to be generally unreliable, they would have permitted them to testify in this case and others. If so, the compassion of the present would be outweighed by the difficulties of the future. If the female witness were to lie or make a mistake and the man were not dead, the rabbis would be permitting a woman to remarry even though she is still married to her first husband, a consequence that they fear and that they take measures to avoid. It therefore makes much more sense to say that they allowed the one required witness to be even a woman because they knew women were reliable, just like men. However, because of differences in social status, they allowed women to testify only for other women, such as those in marital straits. As we will see shortly, there are *no* instances in which a woman may testify on behalf of a man.

Non-Jewish slaves were also considered reliable by the rabbis but also could not testify because of secondary social status. The lack of distinction between a male and a female slave makes clear that "slave" status, not gender, was the issue that could either disqualify or qualify them, depending on the case.[9] Just as the rabbis would have considered it wrong to send a man to be executed on the basis of testimony given by a slave, so would they have considered it wrong to execute or even punish a man on the basis of testimony given by a woman, who had greater social standing than a slave but was still not a full-fledged member of society. Children, another low status group, are *not* allowed to testify in any of these cases because of immaturity. A child's word is accepted only when offered spontaneously, as in M Yevamot 16:5.

Women Testifying on Behalf of Women

The following *mishnah*s provide additional instances in which women testify on behalf of, or against, other women. These passages, together with the fact that there are no instances in which women testify for or against men, support the theory that social status plays a role in setting qualifying standards for witnesses.

> ... All are fit to bring a *get* [from abroad to Palestine and testify that in their presence it was written and signed], except for a deaf-mute, mentally impaired person, minor, blind person, and non-Jew. (M Gittin 2:5)
>
> ... As long as when he [i.e., the messenger] accepted the *get* and when he delivered it his faculties were normal, he is a fit bearer. (M 2:6)
>
> Even the women who are not trusted when they say, "Her husband died," [such as her mother-in-law] are trusted to bring her a *get* [from abroad]. ... What is the difference between [testifying about] a *get* and about [a man's] death? The document proves [the truth of their claim].
> [Even] the wife herself may bring her own *get* from abroad, provided she says, "In my presence it was written and signed." (M 2:7)

These *mishnah*s assign the bearer of the *get* a legal function above and beyond delivering the *get:* He or she must testify that it was written and signed in his presence. The reason is clear: Should there later be questions about the validity of the *get,* it need not be sent abroad to be validated. The Mishnah allows women as well as men, and even the woman with whom and to whom the *get* was sent, to serve as bearers of the *get* and hence as its witnesses. The criterion for serving as a bearer is reliability. People of sound mind and lacking an incentive to lie, be they male or female,[10] are reliable. Again, these *mishnah*s imply that women are essentially reliable when they offer testimony in a court of law.

> If one witness says that she was defiled [i.e., was unfaithful to her husband] and one witness says she was not, or if one *woman* says she was defiled and one *woman* says she was not, she would have to drink [the bitter waters, because the witnesses cancel each other out and her guilt remains in doubt].
> If one says she was defiled and two say she was not, she would have to drink [because two cancel out one and her guilt remains in doubt].
> If two say she was defiled and one says she was not, she would not have to drink [because the testimony of two is accepted and a woman

who is known to have been unfaithful may not be tested by the waters]. (M Sotah 6:4)

If one witness says, "I saw the killer," and another says, "No, you didn't," or if a *woman* says, "you saw the killer," and another [*woman*] says, "No, you didn't," they would break the neck of the calf [because the witnesses cancel each other out and the murderer's identity remains in doubt; see Deuteronomy 21:1–9 and Chapter 1, "Abolishing the Ordeal"].
If one witness says, "I saw [the killer]," and two say, "You did not," they would break its neck.
If two say, "We saw [him]," and one says to them, "You did not," they would not break the calf's neck [because the ritual is only implemented if the murderer's identity is in doubt]. (9:8)

These *mishnah*s imply that if only one witness, *male or female*, testifies that the woman was defiled or who the murderer of the unidentified corpse is, this one witness cancels the ordeal of the bitter waters or the ritual of breaking the calf's neck. Considered with other statements the rabbis made on these subjects (some of which we saw in Chapter 1), which indicate that they were interested in avoiding implementation of both of these rituals, these relaxed standards of testimony are not surprising. As for the woman suspected of infidelity, in the *mishnah*'s final case of two witnesses versus one, in which she does not drink, it was to her benefit not to endure public humiliation. However, it was not to her benefit to be dismissed without a *ketubah,* a prerogative given to the husband in such a case (M Sotah 6:2).
Given these limitations on women's ability to serve as witnesses, it is remarkable that the Mishnah mentions women as testifying in a case of *eglah arufah,* a religious ritual, but one that is associated with a capital case. To prevent a calf from having its neck broken unnecessarily and the entire ritual from being performed unnecessarily, the rabbis accept a woman's testimony. Note that there is no man on trial.

If two women were taken captive and one says, "I was taken captive but was not defiled" [i.e., raped], and the other also says, "I was taken captive but not defiled," they are not believed [because each has a reason to lie, i.e., the desire to resume life with her husband, a *kohen*]. But if they testify about each other, they are believed [i.e., they are not thought to be in collusion, with each one agreeing to testify or lie for the other]. (M Ketubot 2:6)

For the passage to be consistent with the rules of the preceding *mishnah,* one has to assume that the first part of this *mishnah* presents a case in which there is independent knowledge of the women's captivity.[11] Therefore, because each woman has a reason to lie, neither is believed as to her own state of purity. In the second part, there is no independent knowledge of their captivity. Each woman testifies that the other was taken captive but that she was not defiled. Because of the principle "the same mouth that forbade [her to return to her *kohen* husband] is the mouth that permits her [to return to her *kohen* husband]," both halves of her testimony—that the other woman was taken captive and that she was not raped—are accepted. This passage teaches us that in a case of alleged rape during captivity only one witness is necessary to clear a woman and that the one witness may be a woman.

Note that all of these *mishnah*s conform to what I have said: Women's testimony is accepted when they testify on behalf of (or against) other women. One could again suggest that the rabbis introduced this leniency out of sympathy for women in various predicaments, not out of the belief that women are reliable. The anonymous voice of the Talmud says exactly that in reference to women returned from captivity—that the rabbis were lenient because of the sympathy they felt for them (BT Ketubot 27b). I would once again respond that if women were known to fabricate testimony, in the long run they could seriously harm the woman on behalf of whom they were testifying. I do not think that the rabbis would help a woman at one time only to hurt her later. Rather, they were trying to help women in various difficult circumstances and found it easy to do so in this case because one woman was testifying about another woman, a person with similar subordinate status. There is no reason not to accept her testimony. A woman is a reliable witness. Here the issue of one male witness does not arise for historical reasons: A woman in captivity, it seems, was held with other women and only they would know if she had been defiled. In one poignant instance, though, a *kohen*, R. Zechariah b. Hakazzav, attempted to testify on behalf of a woman, his wife, saying that she had not been defiled, because "he had held her hand in his the entire time that enemy forces occupied Jerusalem." If his testimony were accepted, the two of them could resume normal marital life. It was not accepted, however, on the grounds that a person may not testify for his own benefit (M Ketubot 2:9).

All these passage suggest that the rabbis consider women to be reliable but accept them as witnesses only for other women. I know of no case in the Talmud in which a woman testifies about a man, such as to establish his priestly lineage, a matter that, according to some rabbis, requires only one witness (M Ketubot 2:7, 8). The word *eid*, meaning witness, as it is used in the Mishnah (see M Sotah 6:4 and 9:8), refers only to a *male* witness. The one exception to this rule is found in T Ketubot (2:3), in which R. Simon b. Gamliel, after stating in the name of R. Simon b. Hasegan the requirement of only one witness to establish priestly lineage, goes on to permit even a woman to offer such testimony about a man.[12] This statement appears nowhere else in rabbinic literature. Although the redactor of the Mishnah included the first part of R. Simon b. Gamliel's statement in the Mishnah (M Ketubot 2:8), it seems that he deliberately decided not to include the second part, in which a woman is allowed to testify about a man.

The Social Status Argument for Women's Exclusion

The strongest and clearest statement of the rule that social status played a role in setting reliability standards for witnesses appears in the following complicated set of passages. We will see that even when women's testimony *is* accepted in a court of law, should one man testify to the contrary, the rabbis value the women's statements less than the man's. The most reasonable explanation of this distinction is the higher social status of men.

> 1. If one witness says that he [i.e., her husband] died, and she remarried, and then [another] one comes and says that he did not die, she need not leave [her second husband].
> 2. If one witness says that he died, and then two say he did not, even if she had [already] remarried, she must leave [her second husband].
> 3. If two say, "he died," and one says, "he did not die,"—even if she had not yet remarried, she may go [ahead and do so]. (M Yevamot 15:4)

> If one *woman* says that he died and one *woman* says that he did not die . . .
> If one [male] witness says that he died and one says that he did not die, or if one *woman* says that he died and one *woman* says that he did not die, she may not remarry. (15:5)

These *mishnah*s deal with contradictory testimony, before the fact of remarriage and even after. Women are mentioned only in M 15:5 and once again are not included in the word *eid* (witness). The formulation of the last part of this *mishnah*—two separate clauses, one dealing with male witnesses and one with female—leads the reader to believe that although women may testify about a man's death, they may not testify in the same hearing as men and their testimony may not cancel a man's. However, the rabbis of the Yerushalmi (Yevamot 15:6; 15b) state the contrary, claiming that they have a tannaitic source that explicitly indicates that a man and a woman may testify against each other in the same case, and if they contradict each other, the testimonies cancel each other out.

The Bavli develops the issue of female witnesses versus male witnesses. It attempts to explicate the novel point made by the second section of M 15:4, repeated herein.

"If one witness says that he died and then two say he did not, . . .
she must leave [her second husband]."

==But this is obvious! [It is a well-known principle] that the testimony of one cannot stand up against the testimony of two! [And the
mishnah need not have reiterated this rule!]

==No, what [the *mishnah*] is discussing here is unfit witnesses
[פסולי עדות], and it is in accord with the teaching of R. Nehemiah.

As was taught in a *baraita:* R. Nehemiah says, Wherever the
Torah[13] accepted the testimony of [only] one witness [instead of two],
[we] decide the case according to the majority [of the witnesses]. [We]
regard *two women* [whose testimony contradicts that of] *one man* as
two men [who contradict] *one man* [and decide the case *according to
the two women*]. (BT Yevamot 117b)

The principle stated here is that once a woman is allowed to testify, the
rules that apply to her are the same as those that apply to a man.
According to R. Nehemiah, and the *mishnah* that, the Gemara claims, in-
corporates his view, a male witness does not count more than a female one.
Since this rule was not obvious, it needed to be stated explicitly by the
mishnah. Therefore, two women, both of whom in general are unfit witnesses, are believed in a case where they contradict the testimony of one
male witness. Since they are regarded as if they were two men who testified, the two women override the one man. If the man testifies that a certain man died and they testify that he is still alive, the woman in question
must leave her second husband.

The parallel source in the Tosefta is worded somewhat differently,
enough to make one wonder if the Bavli had an agenda of its own and for
that reason, when citing this *baraita,* deliberately changed its formulation.
We will first compare the Bavli's and Tosefta's versions of this *baraita* and
then return to the Bavli to see yet another version of this same source.

. . . If one woman says that he died and two women say that he did
not die, the two women are like one man [and they cancel each other
out]. (T Yevamot 14:1)

According to the above statement, women who testify are *not* treated
like men. Two women versus one woman are regarded as one person versus one person, and if the woman in question had already remarried by the
time that the contradictory set of witnesses appeared, she need *not* leave
her second husband, unlike the *mishnah* that says that she must. However,
if she had not yet remarried, she no longer has permission to do so.

R. Nehemiah says: Wherever the rabbis declared a woman's testimony fit, it is like a man's; all goes according to the majority of wit-

nesses. *Two women* [who contradict the testimony] of *one woman* are like two men [who contradict the testimony] of one man [and we decide according to the majority]. (14:1)

If we read the *baraita* as is, even though Lieberman notes that the text is garbled,[14] we see that R. Nehemiah is disagreeing with the previous view. He says that if two female witnesses later contradict one female witness, they override her, and the woman in question must leave her second husband. But note the critical change in wording: Instead of two women testifying contrary to what one *man* said, as in the *baraita* in the Gemara, the Tosefta speaks of two women testifying contrary to what another *woman* said. By implication, if two women testify against one man, their testimony does *not* override his but only cancels it. The woman in question need *not* leave her second husband. If they overrode it, the woman in question would have to leave her second husband.

We may now ask: Which version is correct or original? Is R. Nehemiah's "go according to the majority" principle saying that two women supersede one *man*, or only that two women supersede one *woman*? The text of the *baraita* in the Tosefta supports only the weaker of these two conclusions. The first version of the *baraita* in the Bavli supports the stronger one, but the second version, as we will now see, supports only the weaker conclusion—that women can supersede women but not men.

== . . . If a fit witness [i.e., a man] came first [and said her husband died], then, even if 100 *women* come and contradict him, they add up to only one witness, [and so she may stay married]. The [above] *mishnah*, however, deals with a case in which a woman [i.e., a generally unfit witness] came first [and testified that the man died, and his wife remarried, and then two women came and testified that he was still alive. In such a case she must leave her second husband.]

==And [we] explain R. Nehemiah thus:

R. Nehemiah says: Wherever the Torah accepted the testimony of [only] one witness, we decide [the case] according to the majority of the witnesses. They regarded *two women* against *one woman* like two men against one man.

==But two women against one man, it is like one versus one. (BT Yevamot 117b)

This passage makes distinctions between men and women as witnesses *even in cases* in which the standard rules of testimony are suspended and women's testimony is accepted. Note that women's testimony is accepted either to permit a woman to remarry or to dissolve her second marriage. The testimony of one or more women can also cancel a man's testimony.

But two or more women cannot overturn what one man has said and send a woman out of her second marriage, even though two men can! Note that the second version of R. Nehemiah's statement replaces the word "man" with "woman," so that there is no case in which women's testimony overrides a man's.

The Yerushalmi *sugya* (PT Yevamot 15:6; 15d) also cites and interprets R. Nehemiah's statement. It concludes that when one woman testifies and then several women contradict her, the several women override her. But, it adds, even if one hundred women were to contradict one male witness, they could not override him, only cancel him. The Yerushalmi, therefore, like the second view of the Bavli, understands R. Nehemiah to be limiting his majority principle to instances in which women testify against other women. When many women contradict one man, R. Nehemiah would count it only as one versus one, as does the concluding anonymous note in the Bavli.

We thus see that the issue underlying R. Nehemiah's statement, whichever version we accept, is *not* women's reliability, because in these cases their testimony is acceptable. If so, for what reason may two women *not* override the testimony of one man and, for instance, dissolve a second marriage, given that they can override the testimony of one woman and also cancel the testimony of one man.[15] The explanation that seems to be most reasonable is a social one: Some rabbis could not accept the notion that women's testimony could override men's. They could accept women contradicting men and, as a result, canceling men's testimony; but they could not tolerate the idea that women could supersede men and replace men's testimony with their own, even if there were two women to one man. That would be compromising a man's dignity. It is remarkable that even when the two-witness paradigm is broken and women's testimony is accepted, a vestige of men's superiority survives intact. Many scholars of the Talmud who study this section fail to note this point.[16]

If this concern for men's dignity is at the root of R. Nehemiah's statement, or even is only the concern of the Yerushalmi and Bavli in their interpretations of his statement, then a social basis for the general exclusion of women from giving testimony is possible and even likely. This passage strongly suggests that the rabbis valued women's testimony less because women's status is lower, not because they are less reliable. It follows that what disqualifies women from giving testimony in most civil and criminal cases is their social inferiority in comparison to men.[17]

A final note: The significance of the first version of R. Nehemiah's statement in the Bavli in which two women *do* override one man should not be downplayed. Although the second version ultimately took precedence and is supported by the version of the *baraita* in the Tosefta and the Yerushalmi, the existence of the first indicates that some rabbis subscribed to the notion that women's and men's testimony should be valued equally in those cases in which women may testify. It is tempting to speculate that the existence of variant readings is a function not simply of faulty transmission but of the prejudices of the transmitter.[18]

A Second Rationale for Women's Exclusion

There is one more text in the Talmud that suggests why a woman may not, in general, offer testimony in a court of law. The reason is related to the social status argument we have discussed, but it is worded much more starkly.

> One who saves [something] from a river [that washed it away], or from troops, or from robbers: If the owners despaired [of getting it back], the one who saved it may keep it.
>
> And similarly a swarm of bees [that left one field and moved to another], if the owners despaired [of retrieving them], the bees belong to the one [who owns the field where they landed and relocated].
>
> Said R. Yohanan b. Baroka: Women and children are believed when they say, "The swarm originated over there [and the new owner must return them]." (M Baba Kama 10:2)

The subject under discussion is movement of property out of the owner's possession by forces beyond his control, such as a flood, a robber, or self-propulsion. To what extent is the finder obligated to return the property to the original owner? So long as the owner did not despair, the Mishnah obligates the finder to return it. But R. Yohanan b. Baroka suggests an additional criterion of return: If there is evidence as to where the property originated, then even if this information comes from women or children, it is accepted, and the new owner must give back the property that "arrived on his doorstep."

This is the only case in the Mishnah in which a woman or a child may testify regarding a monetary matter.[19] In this instance the woman or child is not taking away from someone something that he owns but rather not allowing him to take possession of a windfall, making sure that the original owner gets his property back, even if he has already despaired. Why R. Yohanan b. Baroka accepts women's testimony in this case is hard to know. Perhaps he does not regard it as testimony, as suggested by the Bavli (BK 114b). In order to make this rule consistent with the rest of the Mishnah, the possibiliiy is raised that the information provided by the women or children was not testimony but only spontaneous remarks and hence acceptable. Such remarks have special status in Jewish law.

T Ketubot, when discussing the kinds of testimony accepted from an adult about things he saw when he was a child, cites R. Yohanan b. Baroka's statement and then qualifies it.

When is this so [that one may accept the testimony of women and children]? If they gave their testimony on the spot. But if they left and came back, they are not believed; perhaps they gave [this testimony] *because they were seduced or frightened* into doing so, [מתוך הפתוי ומתוך היראה]. (T Ketubot 3:3)

Women (and children) are not here considered trustworthy witnesses because others may seduce or even almost force them into saying something other than what they know to be true. That is, their dependent status makes them vulnerable to persuasion and intimidation. A woman's reliability is compromised, not by her mental or emotional faculties or weakness, as so many have argued for so long, but by her subordinate status, by her being open to pressure because of her need to rely on others for sustenance and protection. She is beholden to the men in her life. They may push her to testify to their benefit. The rabbis of the Yerushalmi, when commenting on the associated *mishnah* in Ketubot, quote this passage from the Tosefta. They thus imply their agreement with its rationale (PT Ketubot 2:10; 27a). This is clear evidence of a social status argument for not accepting women's testimony.

Even with this restriction, R. Yohanan b. Baroka still allows a woman to give testimony in a monetary matter. However, he is the only one to do so. According to the other views in the *mishnah,* the swarm belongs to the new owner even if a woman knows to whom it originally belonged. This is an instance in which suppression of evidence leads to monetary loss, if the evidence is reliable. However, these other rabbis apparently think that a man cannot be deprived of a windfall on the basis of what a woman says. As suggested in the Tosefta, although a woman on the spot can be assumed to be telling the truth, once she leaves and returns, it is possible that someone, most likely the man to whom she is subordinate, will influence her to report it differently. Therefore, according to these rabbis, the monetary loss would not be on the part of the original owner but on the part of the new owner.

Why did R. Yohanan b. Baroka view this case so differently from other monetary matters? As already mentioned, possibly because he does not consider the woman's statement to be testimony. Possibly because his view of women and children is somewhat different from that of the others. Note that he alone, in the Mishnah, holds that women are obligated to the mitzvah of procreation, as are men (M Yevamot 6:6).

Other Cases in Which Women May Testify

Two more cases of women giving testimony are of special interest.

We learned in a *baraita:* A midwife is believed when she says [in delivering twins], "this one came out first, this one came out second."

In what circumstances? That she did not leave and come back. For if she left and came back, she is not believed. . . .

We learned in a *baraita*: A midwife is believed when she says [upon assisting at two births at the same time in the same place], this one is a *kohen* and this one a levite. . . . In what circumstances? That no one challenged her. But if someone challenged her, she is not believed. (BT Kiddushin 73b)

It is obvious that in these cases no man is present and thus a woman must act as witness. Various restrictions independent of gender are added: She needs to have been continuously present at the births, and there cannot be another person present at the births who challenges her. She is not believed if these conditions are not met.

The underlying assumption here seems to be that a woman can be relied upon to testify truthfully in a situation of this sort. Once again the case is a woman testifying about another woman (and the children to whom she gave birth). And once again we can conclude that women must have been considered fit witnesses, or they would not have been allowed to testify in this important case. Her testimony here has far-reaching implications in terms of the ritual of redemption of the firstborn, the firstborn's right to a double portion of his father's estate, and priestly privileges.[20]

The second text (BT Ketubot 85a) appears in a series of anecdotes about the imposition of oaths in the courtroom. It is both the latest text presented here and one of the very few that relates an actual event on the topic of women and testimony.

The Gemara reports that Rava ordered that an oath be administered to a certain female litigant who was appearing before him in court. Rava's wife, identified in the text as the daughter of R. Hisda,[21] told him that the woman was not to be trusted to take an oath. Rava accepted his wife's testimony[22] about the woman and instead asked the other litigant to take an oath. The legal consequences of this transfer of an oath, according to Rashi,[23] are that the male claimant would be authorized to collect the money from the suspect woman. If this woman had taken an oath, she would not have had to surrender the money. The testimony of Rava's wife, therefore, had immediate practical results. A second anecdote follows in which R. Pappa, like Rava's wife, seeks to discredit someone else, a man, but Rava does not accept R. Pappa's testimony, because, Rava says, the words of only one witness are not valid. R. Adda bar Mattanah, also present at the time, asks Rava, if that is so, why did he accept his wife's testimony but not R. Pappa's? Rava answers that he knows his wife to be reliable [קים לי בגווה], whereas he cannot say the same for R. Pappa.

Here, again, a woman is believed regarding another woman. Would Rava have accepted his wife's report had she given him information about a man? It is hard to say. What is the redactor telling us by juxtaposing these two anecdotes and, in particular, by reporting that Rava trusted a woman but not a man, at that time a junior colleague but later on a prominent sage? Is this a veiled critique of women's exclusion from testifying in Jewish law or just a jab at R. Pappa? Note that Rava is the rabbi who permitted women to initiate betrothal and participate in the ceremony.[24]

The Scriptural Derivation of Women's Exclusion

Having marshaled evidence in support of the social status argument for women's exclusion from giving testimony, I want now to show that the privacy argument, mentioned in the opening statement of this chapter, is based on a misreading of the Talmud.

The following passage is famous today because many use it to promote the view that women belong at home and for that reason may not testify in civil and criminal cases. But those who do so are not paying close attention to the logic of the text. When understood properly, it does just the opposite: It rejects the privacy argument as the basis for women's exclusion from giving testimony. It fails to supply any other, however.

> The oath of adjuration may be administered to men but not to women, to persons not related [to the litigants] but not to relatives, to those fit and not to those unfit to give testimony [because of a history of civil violations]. (M Shevuot 4:1)

Administering an oath of adjuration to potential witnesses is a strategy developed by the rabbis, based on a verse in the Torah (Leviticus 5:1), to force those who have information about a case to come forward and give it. The oath affirms that the man who takes it is not concealing any information. If he did know something, it is assumed that he would rather testify than lie under oath. The oath was intended for use in monetary claims cases only.

There are three categories of people in this *mishnah* who may not take this oath because they are unfit to testify: relatives, because they presumably love (or hate) the litigant; those who are suspect regarding money; and women. This grouping implies that women, like the others, cannot be relied upon to tell the truth. But the reason is not evident. The Gemara tries to find one, or at least to provide a scriptural basis for women's exclusion. The following passage is long, somewhat repetitive, and difficult. But it is necessary to work our way through it in order to be in a position to interpret the last part, dealing with women's privacy needs, accurately.

> From where [in Scripture] do we learn that women may not serve as witnesses?

It was taught in a *baraita:* "And the two *men* [who are engaged in a dispute] shall stand [before God, the *kohanim,* the judges, and so on" (Deuteronomy 19:17)]—this verse speaks of witnesses [and teaches that they must be male].[25] But perhaps it speaks of litigants, not witnesses, [and, if so, does *not* exclude women from giving testimony]. When it continues and says "who are engaged in a dispute," it refers to the litigants. Therefore, the preceding words "and the two men shall stand" must refer to the witnesses.

If you wish [I will provide an alternative prooftext that limits testimony to men]; here (Deuteronomy 19:17) it says "two" and there (Deuteronomy 19:15) it says "two"; just as there it refers to witnesses, so too here, the word "two" refers to witnesses [and the word "men" in this verse further teaches that they must be male].

==Why does the *baraita* give an alternate derivation? [What is wrong with the first?]

==Should you claim that since it does not say "*and* the ones who are engaged in a dispute" [and without the word "and" it is possible that] the entire phrase refers to the litigants [and thus teaches nothing about women's exclusion from giving testimony, therefore the baraita provides a second proof, based on a textual analogy, that women may not serve as witnesses.] . . .

It was taught in another *baraita:* "And the two men shall stand"— this verse speaks of witnesses [and teaches that they must be male]. But perhaps it speaks of litigants, and not witnesses? [Not so.] Do you think that only men come [to court] as litigants, and not women? [Since women also come to court as litigants, the words "the two men" most likely refer to witnesses and teach that they must be male.]

If you wish [I will provide an alternative prooftext that limits testimony to men]; here (Deuteronomy 19:17) it says "two" and there (Deuteronomy 19:15) it says "two"; just as there it refers to witnesses, so too here, the word "two" refers to witnesses [and the word "men" in this verse further teaches that they must be male].

==Why does the *baraita* give an alternate derivation? [What is wrong with the first?]

==Should you claim [that the words "and the two men shall stand" reasonably refer to litigants being male, and not to witnesses being male, because men come to court to litigate and] women *do not,* [because to maintain their dignity they stay at home,] as it says, "The glory of the princess is in the recesses of her home" (Psalms 45:14), [then one cannot learn from this verse that women are not fit to serve as witnesses. Therefore the *baraita* provides an alternative derivation].
. . . (BT Shevuot 30a)

This lengthy passage attempts to derive women's exclusion from testimony three times over (only two have been cited), in three separate but similar tannaitic teachings. Each of the three teachings presents a derivation of the restriction, a critique of the derivation, and then an alternative derivation. The three alternative derivations are identical. Such interpretive abundance is not common in the Talmud. That the rabbis work so hard to find a derivation leads one to suspect that there is no clear scriptural basis for this ruling.[26]

The last paragraph of the passage is of particular interest. If it is true, the argument goes, that women, in order to protect their dignity, do not come to court as litigants, then the entire statement "and the two men who are engaged in a dispute shall stand" refers to litigants only. It thus contains no superfluous expression that could refer to witnesses and from which we could derive that women are disqualified. The *baraita* goes on to find a different verse to teach that women may not testify.

The first thing to notice about this section is that the verse about privacy, "The glory of the princess . . . ," is *not* introduced in order to explain why women cannot testify but why women may choose not to appear as litigants, why they may send a man in their place. The second thing to notice is that if maintaining a woman's privacy and dignity were, in fact, also a reason not to testify, then the Gemara would have said so and would not go on to find a different verse to exclude women from testifying. But since the *baraita,* as understood by the Gemara, continues with an alternate scriptural derivation of the rule that women may not testify, it clearly does *not* think that privacy considerations, and the verse from Psalms, restrict a woman from giving testimony. We must also keep in mind that testimony can only be given in person, not as hearsay or secondhand, whereas a female litigant, at least in a monetary matter, need not appear in court but can be represented by someone else.[27] By not invoking the privacy argument in conjunction with testimony, the Gemara is saying that the requirement to testify in court *supersedes* the societal need to protect a woman's privacy—an observation that most people who read this passage fail to make.[28]

It is ironic that although the anonymous voice of the text says, regarding litigancy, that women may or should stay home and be represented by someone else,[29] we find many instances in the Talmud in which women did come to court to press their claims. The notion of women's privacy that appears in this passage is thus not consistent with life as lived by women in the amoraic period.[30]

The parallel passage in the Midrash Halakhah sheds further light on this matter.

"The two men" (v. 17): I can only learn from here that men may come to court as litigants. What about a man and a woman, a woman and a man, and two women with each other? "That are engaged in a dispute"—in whatever way [meaning any pair of litigants, regardless of gender, may face each other in court].

Could it be that a woman is fit to give testimony? It says here "two" (v. 17) and it says there "two" (v. 15); just as here [in reference to litigants] it [i.e., "two"] implies men but not women [because to include women as litigants it was necessary to utilize an additional phrase], so too there [in reference to witnesses, v. 15] it means men but not women [and no superfluous phrase comes to include them]. (Sifrei Devarim 190[31])

The midrash makes a clear distinction between the permissibility of women's serving as litigants and women's serving as witnesses. A woman can serve as a litigant even when the other litigant is a man. Gender does not seem to be an issue when it comes to seeking redress in the courts as a litigant. Does this not suggest that gender *is* an issue regarding testimony, that the rabbis felt it inappropriate for a woman to testify against a male witness, and either against or for a male defendant?

Conclusions

A review of all of these passages on testimony highlights the difficulty of the issue. Had the rabbis excluded women totally, we would have much more easily understood their motivations. The mix of inclusions and exclusions, however, perplexes the reader and demands a far more nuanced explanation than simply saying that the rabbis did not consider women trustworthy. The theory presented here—that social status issues play a role in rabbinic thinking about women and testimony—seems to offer the most reasonable reading of all the sources on the subject.

We may be tempted to credit the rabbis with a fundamental concern for women's welfare. For this reason they allowed women to testify in certain cases. However, we must keep in mind that as real as their concern for women's welfare may have been, they were able to express it in those cases without great difficulty because the testimony they accepted from women was offered on behalf of other women only. No men were involved. It is not surprising that social structures, patriarchy in this case, should play a role in developing the rules of fit witnesses. In fact, it would be surprising if men in a dominant position regarded those whom they controlled, women and slaves, as equal to them in rights and privileges and in a position to be immune to pressure.

Having said all this, I still think that credit is due the rabbis, not so much for making the exceptions to women's exclusion from giving testimony, but for openly admitting that they relaxed standards. It is true that the Talmud asks about the wisdom of lowering standards of testimony if, in the long run, fabricated testimony will create even greater difficulties for the woman of indeterminate marital status. It gives three answers to its own question. (1) Because the rabbis deal so harshly with a woman who remarried on the basis of a false death report, they treat her leniently at the outset, when the report is first heard, easing the criteria for its reliability (BT Yevamot 88a). (2) They say that women are known to substantiate matters before they remarry and only marry if they are sure they are no longer tied to the first husband (BT Yevamot 93b). (3) The rabbis say that since people know that the truth will eventually emerge, they are not likely to lie (BT Yevamot 93b).

I find these answers unsatisfactory. It makes no sense to me to treat a woman leniently at the outset if what awaits her later is a harsh punishment. No woman wants to think that she is subject to a game of chance: Some women who remarry on the basis of the testimony of "unreliable" witnesses will regain stability in their lives, but others will be condemned to ongoing suffering. In addition, the notion that a woman is expected to be the final arbiter of her own fate, to go beyond what the judges require and somehow determine if the witnesses are lying or not, is a concept foreign to good jurisprudence. It seems to me that the Gemara offered these explanations as its best defense against the inherent immorality of the Mishnah's rulings in these matters, which punish her for a crime she did not commit. By shifting the burden to the woman herself, the Gemara removes all blame from the courtroom judges and from its own authors, the legislators.[32]

Precisely because these explanations for the relaxation of standards make so little sense, we have to look once again at all the relevant materials to see if some other explanation would fit the texts better. The notion that women and slaves in and of themselves are reliable goes a long way to resolve the difficulties. Since they testify truthfully, just like men, the likelihood of their leading a woman astray is very small. Therefore, when the rabbis deviated from the general rule of a woman's being socially unfit to testify, and permitted her to do so on behalf of other women, they did not lower the standards of testimony any more than when they decided to allow only one man to testify.

I think that the lower social status of women is the only explanation that reasonably accounts for the mix of inclusions and exclusions. Had R. Nehemiah not made his statement about the inability of women to override men, and had R. Yohanan b. Baroka not made his statement about women's vulnerability to persuasion, we would have made plausible proposals but not had proof positive of the difference between men and women on the witness stand. Given all the texts, we see that the rabbis value women's testimony but, at the same time, because of their patriarchal mind set, could not treat women's testimony in the same way as men's.

Notes

1. Judith Wegner (*Chattel or Person?* [New York: Oxford University Press, 1988], 120) writes that the Sages acknowledge a woman's mental and moral capacities by allowing her to testify in a variety of cases and that they thus equate her mental capacities to those of a man. But Wegner does not address the vast number of cases in which a woman may not testify. Ilan (*Jewish Women in Greco-Roman Palestine* [Tübingen: J.C.B. Mohr, 1995], 163–165) writes that the Sages in general disqualify a woman from serving as a witness, but many exceptions arose because of actual custom and practice. She cites Josephus, writing in the first century C.E., who says that women were disqualified by Jewish law because of their light-headedness and brazenness. The one passage in the Dead Sea Scrolls that seems to say that women may give testimony is far from clear. See Eileen M. Schuller, "Women in the Dead Sea Scrolls," *Annals of the New York Academy of Sciences*, 1994, 123–124.

2. As noted in Chapter 3, a lay Israelite is required to take back a wife who was raped. A *kohen* is forbidden to do so.

3. In his *Encyclopedia Judaica* article "Witnesses" (16:586), Israel Supreme Court Justice Haim Cohen, when explaining why a woman is disqualified from testifying, cites the Talmudic statement that appearing in court would be an affront to her dignity. This means she is a private individual. Gershon Holzer ("Women's Testimony in Jewish Law" [in Hebrew], *Sinai* 67 [1970]:94–112) writes that there are two principal reasons why a woman is disqualified from testifying: (1) that her special and *highly regarded* (my italics) [מכובד] social status expresses itself in modesty and discretion, so that she cannot appear in public places like a court of law; (2) that women are light-headed and lazy and therefore not likely to report things accurately.

4. See note 3.

5. *The Literature of the Sages*, pt. 1, ed. Shmuel Safrai (Philadelphia: Fortress Press, 1987), 194–195.

6. Note that these first four *mishnah*s all assume, without saying so explicitly, that in this case only one witness is necessary and that the one witness may be a woman, even the wife herself.

7. The Jewish calendar is both lunar and solar. Every two or three years an extra month is inserted in order to align it with the solar calendar and to make sure that the festivals are celebrated in due season, Pesah in the spring, and so on.

8. M Yevamot 15:1–5, 16:5; T Yevamot 14:1, 7.

9. See M Yevamot 16:7, M Ketubot 2:9, M Sotah 6:2.

10. Even those who may have reason to lie, such as the female relatives listed in M Yevamot 15:4, will not do so in a case in which the *get* would prove them wrong. See "Women's General Reliability."

11. Albeck, 94.

12. His statement ends: "And not that a woman should come to court but that she should say 'give it [priestly lineage, *terumah* (priestly dues)] to him.'" Lieberman (*Tosefta Ketubot*, 62) comments that this means that she need not testify in court. Rather, one may rely on her just as one does in matters of forbidden food. One manuscript does not include the words "and not that a woman should come to court but," which suggests, perhaps, that this phrase is a later addition.

13. See the textual emendation recommended by Shamma Friedman, "A Critical Study of Yevamot X with a Methodological Introduction," in *Texts and Studies*, ed. H. Z. Dimitrovsky (New York: JTSA, 1977), 338–339. He points out that the words "the Torah accepted the testimony" [האמינה תורה] are not likely to be correct, because the Torah never made such a statement about one witness. The correct version is in the Tosefta, which says that "the rabbis declared fit" [הכשירו חכמים].

14. Lieberman, *Tosefta Yevamot*, 168.

15. Similarly, if two women say he died and then one man says he did not die, if she had not yet married, she may go ahead and do so. These are the circumstances of the last part of M 15:4.

16. It has been my experience that when I tell knowledgeable people about this distinction, they tell me I have misunderstood the text; when I show it to them "in the words," they concede the point.

17. Women could not testify in civil cases, even if the litigants were women. For a possible reason, see "A Second Rationale for Women's Exclusion."

18. See, for example, BT Kiddushin 80b, Tosafot, s.v. *ki hahee*.

19. M Keubot 2:10 lists instances in which an adult may testify about what he saw as a child. See next paragraph in text.

20. See T Kiddushin 5:8; T Niddah 6:8; T BB 7:2 (the basis for the citation from BT Kiddushin 73b above).

21. See another anecdote involving this woman at the end of Chapter 6.

22. That her statement about the female litigant is to be taken as testimony is made clear later in the text when Rava refers to it as such.

23. S.v. *le-shevuah ashekenegdah*.

24. See Chapter 3, "Women's Initiation of Betrothal."

25. The plain sense meaning of v. 17 is that if two men seek justice in a court of law and a false witness testifies against one of them (v. 16), his ploy will be uncovered by the judges. The two men referred to are litigants, not witnesses. V. 15 states the rule that two witnesses—not just one—are necessary in order to establish factual truth in a court of law.

26. The Yerushalmi also derives from Scripture that women may not serve as witnesses (Shevuot 4:1; 35a). It first learns from a textual analogy of two verses (Deut. 19:17 and Num. 11:26) that women and children may not serve as judges. Several Amoraim, R. Yossi b. R. Bon and R. Huna in the name of R. Yossi, then deduce from the same two verses as the *baraita*s in the Bavli that women may not serve as witnesses.

27. See Tosafot s.v. *kol kevudah*.

28. See PT Yoma (1:1; 38d) for a story in which a women's modest dress leads to the outstanding accomplishments of her sons. Ps. 45:14 is quoted there to indicate that women should dress modestly, both in public and in private. It does not imply that a modest woman should stay at home.

29. The anonymous speaker perhaps bases his statement on BT Ketubot 97b, "R. Yohanan says: No man wants his wife to be degraded in a court of law." This can be taken to mean that men want women to be represented by others.

30. The notion of women not litigating in court appears to have been fabricated by the anonymous voice of the text in order to explain why a second prooftext had to be brought. The anonymous speaker provides an explanation that is possible, but is not necessarily the general case.

31. Finkelstein ed., 230.

32. See Friedman's insightful discussion of all these issues, "A Critical Study," in particular 277–282.

10

Ritual

TEXTUAL STUDY AND PUBLIC PRAYER are two major foci of Jewish activity today. Both are performed in a communal setting, and until recently, both have been dominated by men. Since the rabbis developed these forms of worship, with their associated rules of inclusion and exclusion, we may reasonably infer that they did not accord importance to women's spiritual or intellectual life, that they actively sought to maintain women at the margins. As for study, this conclusion is warranted. Many Jewish women today—although enrolled in Jewish schools—are not allowed to study Talmud. In traditional circles, women may still not be ordained as rabbis. As for public prayer, however, we must be careful not to confuse today's religious realities with those of the second to fifth centuries. Given that Judaism in the time of the Talmud was not focused on synagogue life—Judaism in Israel today still is not—we must investigate the question: How did the rabbis view women's need for or connection to a wide variety of ritual acts? For what reasons did they either obligate women to perform, or exempt or prohibit them from performing, these acts?

Many account for women's exemptions and exclusions with the claim that women's demanding domestic role would conflict with the discharging of ritual responsibilities, or that women, by nature, are private, and men public. But the rabbinic statements themselves do not support those claims and distinctions. On the contrary, the powerful argument for the differing levels of ritual responsibility, arising from a close reading of the words of the texts themselves, is that women occupy secondary social status in comparison to men, an argument utilized in Chapter 9 to explain women's exclusion from testimony. This status will not only explain women's pattern of exemptions but also their inability to assist men in the discharge of their ritual obligations. Even so, as time passed, the rabbis imposed on women more and more ritual obligations. These additions are proof of the rabbis' increasing recognition of women's spiritual needs and of the fact that excluding women from active Jewish observance could undermine their commitment to Jewish life in general. Finally, we will see that the very same rabbi who obligated men to recite daily, "Blessed be God for not making me a woman," explains this blessing not as a misogynist gibe but as a statement of men's gratitude for their higher level of ritual obligation. He does not go so far as to say that this level of obligation derives from men's status as head of household, although a later rabbi implies exactly that. As we saw in the chapters on *sotah*, divorce, *niddah*, and inheritance, here, too, we will find evidence of struggle and conflict: Some rabbis favored greater ritual involvement for women and some lesser. The former triumphed.

Women's Ritual Obligations: A Chronological View

The key passages on the topic of women and ritual obligations are not found in any of the tractates dealing with ritual, but, surprisingly, in Kiddushin, the tractate dealing with betrothal. Since we know that the redactor of the Mishnah acted with intention in his arrangement of material, we may assume he had a reason for locating the two sets of rules adjacent to each other. To discover that reason, we will first look at these passages on their own and then interpret them within their literary and legal context.

As already noted in Chapter 3, the first six *mishnah*s of chapter 1 of Kiddushin discuss the acquisition by men of a whole range of goods, from a wife, at one end, to slaves, cattle, and real estate, at the other. The striking similarity between the methods of betrothing women and those of purchasing slaves and fields suggests that wives were owned by their husbands as property. In what appears to be a radical break in the flow of material, *mishnah*s 7 and 8 discuss a different topic altogether: obligations to perform mitzvot, first the obligations of fathers (or parents) and children to each other, and then the ritual obligations of women and men. In a concluding aggadic flourish, *mishnah*s 9 and 10 talk about the reward that accrues from performance and the punishment that is incurred by lack of performance.

> All obligations[1] of the son on the father [כל מצות הבן על האב], men are obligated but women are exempt.
> And all obligations of the father on the son [וכל מצות האב על הבן], both men and women are obligated. (M Kiddushin 1:7a)

It is hard to know what the two key phrases mean—the "obligations of the son on the father" and the "obligations of the father on the son." Each can be interpreted in more than one way, either as the obligations a father has to his son or those that a son has to his father. In a sense, one has to work backwards: Since women are exempted in the first clause but obligated in the second, it seems more reasonable in an ancient authoritarian society to exempt them from obligations to their children than to their parents. "Father" and "son" in the first clause are to be understood literally but in the second as referring to parents and children.[2]

The parallel passage in the Tosefta defines the two difficult phrases, presenting them in the same order as in the Mishnah but reversing the meaning:[3]

> What is the obligation of the son on the father [מצות הבן על האב]? He must feed him, give him drink, dress him, cloak him, take him out and in, and wash his face, hands, and feet. The same applies to both men and women, except that a man has the means at his disposal [to accomplish these tasks] whereas a woman does not [אין ספק בידה לעשות], because *she is under the control of others* [שיש רשות אחרים עליה].
>
> What is the obligation of the father on the son [מצות האב על הבן]? To circumcise him, redeem him [from a *kohen,* if he is a firstborn], teach him Torah, teach him a trade, and marry him off. And some say, to [teach him to] swim in the river. (T Kiddushin 1:11)

We see that, according to both the Mishnah and the Tosefta, men and women alike are obligated to care for parents. The Tosefta, however, goes on to qualify the daughter's obligation: She is, for the most part, exempt, because both she herself and her financial assets are controlled by others, that is to say, her husband.[4] The Tosefta thus establishes a connection between a *woman's subordinate social and marital status* and her *ability to fulfill mitzvot*: When married, she is not in control of her time or money and will, therefore, not be able to care for her parents. It is possible that the redactor of the Mishnah chose to say that she is "obligated," without qualification, because he disagrees with the opinion expressed in the Tosefta. Even if in many cases it will not be possible for a married daughter to take care of her parents, the redactor still says she is obligated. It would seem that as the father of a daughter, the redactor wants to require her to take care of him, even though as the husband of a wife, he will have to allow her to cater to her parents' needs at the expense of his. The reason, according to the Gemara, that a father, but not a mother, is obligated to his son is that if a woman is not obligated to perform a specific ritual act for herself, such as redemption of the firstborn, she is not required to perform it for others (BT Kiddushin 29a).

In its discussion of the second clause of the *mishnah,* women's obligation to care for parents, the Gemara quotes the above passage from the Tosefta and then continues:

> ––Said R. Iddi b. Abin said Rav: If she gets divorced, the two of them—[a son and a daughter]—*are equal.* (BT Kiddushin 30b)

R. Iddi bar Abin in the name of Rav is making an exception to the exemption: Although the Tosefta does not obligate a married woman to care for parents, he obligates a woman who became single to do so, because she is no longer controlled by a man.

The Yerushalmi develops this idea further:

> The same goes for a man, the same goes for a woman. A man has means at his disposal, but a woman does not have means at her disposal, because she is under the aegis of others. If she is widowed or divorced, she becomes like one who has the means.[5] (PT Kiddushin 1:7; 61a)

The Yerushalmi makes the same point as the Bavli in essentially the same words but includes the exceptions to the exemption, the widow and the divorcee, within the *baraita* itself, rather than presenting them as an Amora's addition. The freedom of action that these rabbinic texts attribute to the divorced or widowed woman echoes Numbers 30:10, where the only women who must keep the vows they take are those who do not have a husband or father who could cancel them. The Torah thus recognizes that women have religious needs, but it subjects their religious behavior to the approval of the man under whose control they happen to be.

The connection between women's freedom to perform mitzvot and their marital status assists us in interpreting the second part of *mishnah* 7. It, too, compares women's and men's obligations, this time with respect to ritual.

> And all positive mitzvot that are time-bound, men are obligated but women are exempt. And all positive mitzvot that are not time-bound, the same holds for men and for women, they are [both] obligated.
>
> And all negative mitzvot, whether or not time-bound, the same holds for men and for women, they are obligated. . . . (M 1:7b)

This *mishnah*, the only one that presents general rules of ritual obligation for women, obligates women and men equally to three of the four categories of mitzvot: positive mitzvot that are not time-bound and negative mitzvot, both time-bound and not time-bound. Women are exempt only from time-bound positive mitzvot. We can begin to find out why by examining the associated passage in the Tosefta.

> What is [an example] of a positive time-bound mitzvah? *Succah* [dwelling in a booth on the festival of Succot], *lulav* [waving palm branches on the festival of Succot], and *tefillin* [donning phylacteries each morning].
>
> What is [an example] of a positive non-time-bound mitzvah? Returning a lost object [to its owner], sending away the mother bird when tak-

ing the young, erecting a railing on a roof, and *tzitzit* [wearing fringes on the corners of the garment]. R. Simon exempts women from *tzitzit* because it is a positive time-bound mitzvah. (T Kiddushin 1:10)

Why are women exempt from the positive time-bound mitzvot listed here? The most popular explanation is that performing these mitzvot would interfere with a woman's ability to meet her domestic responsibilities, in particular to care for her children.[6] But this answer assumes that the performance of positive time-bound mitzvot must occur in a highly specified window of time. It also assumes that no one else could share her domestic responsibilities, freeing her for whatever time was necessary for the performance of the mitzvah.

These two assumptions are false. First, because a woman in Talmudic society lived with her husband's family,[7] she would probably have had no trouble getting help with domestic chores from a mother-in-law, sister-in-law, or even from her own children. Second, this domestic explanation creates a false distinction between men's and women's daily responsibilities. When the *mishnah* was articulated, mitzvot that took much time were unlikely to be appropriate for either men or women, because each had many daily tasks to perform. Life was hard for all but the upper class of society. That women would find it more difficult than men to find time to pray the morning prayers between 6 and 10 A.M. does not make sense: If they did not have servants, the husband and wife would each have vast responsibilities. If they did have servants, each would have the opportunity to devote time to prayer. Third, the domestic explanation does not account for the fact that many mitzvot, such as the requirement to hear the shofar blasts on Rosh Hashanah or light the Chanukah candles, take very little time, can be performed within a wide block of time, and can be performed at home. But the most pointed critique of the domestic theory of exemption is that one of the most time-consuming of all mitzvot, prayer—the set of eighteen petitionary blessings that had to be recited twice or even three times daily—is obligatory not just upon men but also upon women (M Berakhot 3:3)!

Another popular, contemporary explanation of women's exemption, that the rabbis felt it was not necessary to obligate them to perform key ritual acts because they are on a higher spiritual level than men and thus do not need them, also does not make sense. Let alone that there is no evidence of such a difference between men and women, the obligation of women to many mitzvot, even positive time-bound ones such as prayer and Grace after meals, seriously challenges the notion that the rabbis felt that women do not need mitzvot. In fact, a major theme of the Torah is the requirement for a Jew to perform ritual acts as a sign of acceptance of the terms of God's covenant.[8] The essence of the Mishnah and Gemara is the elaboration of those mitzvot and their application to both men *and women.*

The answer, therefore, has to be sought elsewhere. Why are the rules about women and mitzvot found in this particular place in the Mishnah, right after the rules of acquiring a wife? Their juxtaposition suggests that a woman who is acquired by a man becomes obligated to him primarily. He controls both her time and her money. Once married, she would not have the opportunity to fulfill religious obligations unless her husband allowed her to do so. She thus cannot be *independently* obligated to perform them.[9] This explanation tallies with the Tosefta's statement of why a woman is exempt from caring for her parents, which is mentioned in the first half of the same *mishnah*. That others control her is a fact of married life with far-reaching consequences.[10] It is also true that performance of some of these mitzvot announces to the world that a person is free and independent, in charge of himself. R. Joshua b. Levi says that a slave who dons tefillin is a free man (BT Gittin 40a). Were a woman to don tefillin, she would be proclaiming to all that she is no longer subordinate to her husband. The rabbis could not permit her to take such a step.

The rule of women's exemption can be understood in yet another, related way. A more literal rendering of the Hebrew phrase *mitzvot aseh she-hazeman gerama* is that these mitzvot are ones that will come your way no matter what, independent of the circumstances of your life. As the seasons, the *zemanim*, roll around, the time for eating the paschal lamb, hearing the shofar blasts, and sitting in a *succah* will certainly arrive.[11] The category called *mitzvot aseh shelo hazeman gerama*, non-time-bound positive mitzvot, in contrast, will not necessarily come your way, ever. If you do not own a home, you will not be obligated to build a railing on the roof; if you do not find someone's lost object, you will not have an opportunity to return it; if you do not come across a nest with a mother bird and young, you will never have the opportunity to send away the mother and keep the young. A woman is thus exempt from those active mitzvot that a Jew will surely find himself executing in the course of the Jewish day, week, and year, but is obligated to those that may never come her way. Why?

The Talmud mentions the phrases "positive time-bound" or "non-time-bound" mitzvot *only* in connection with women. That is, this distinction was created solely for the purpose of distinguishing between women's ritual obligations and her exemptions. It was not a category that had any other use. For men, who are obligated to perform all positive mitzvot, there is no significance to this distinction. Had there been some other meaning to this categorization of mitzvot, not relating to women, I would have to concede that their exemption could flow from some other reason. If, for the sake of argument, time-bound positive mitzvot required the expenditure of money, then we could explain women's exemption as flowing from her lack of control of financial assets. But since this distinction was devised only to create a category from which women are exempt, the reason for the exemption has to lie in the meaning of the phrase itself, namely, that these are the key mitzvot of marking Jewish time. It is not that they take time.

Women were exempted from the essential ritual acts of Judaism, those that year in and year out mark Jewish time, in order to restrict their performance to men, to heads of household; only people of the highest social standing, according to the rabbis, does God consider most fit to honor or worship Him in this important way. This hierarchical arrangement is reminiscent of Temple protocol. Only *kohanim*, the individuals of highest social standing, as evidenced by their more stringent rules for marriage, ritual purity, and physical fitness (Leviticus 21), could serve as Temple functionaries.[12] The point is that those who serve God must themselves be especially worthy. In rabbinic society this meant that only males were fitting candidates for the time-bound positive commandments, the highest form of ritual act. Women are exempt, although not forbidden, because they are individuals of lower social standing, who, therefore, honor God less when serving Him. This status argument, a variation of the previous one that women are controlled by men, is, in my opinion, a reasonable explanation of women's exemption. The location of the rules of ritual performance in the tractate about betrothals and the meaning of the defining phrases themselves are the clues.

The next *mishnah* in the chapter, although it concerns Temple sacrifice rather than time-bound mitzvot, will, when read together with its associated Gemara, sharpen our understanding of this one. It is part of the same group of *mishnah*s.

> Laying on of hands [on the head of the sacrificial animal], waving [the *minhah* sacrifice], bringing it close [to the altar], . . . , sprinkling the blood, receiving [the blood from the neck of the animal to be sacrificed]—[these acts] are to be carried out by men but *not* by women [נוהגים באנשים ולא בנשים],[13] except for the *minhah* [offering] of the *sotah* and the *nezirah* [person who vows not to drink wine or cut (his or) her hair for a specified period of time], that the women themselves wave. (M Kiddushin 1:8)

To begin with, this *mishnah* teaches that laying on of hands on the animal to be offered and waving the *minhah* sacrifice may be performed by lay Israelite men but not lay Israelite women. The third activity, bringing the animal to the altar, and all those that follow, may be performed only by *kohanim*, not even lay Israelite men. Since the Torah itself makes clear that men but not women may serve as Temple functionaries, why need the *mishnah* state that these rituals may be carried out by the sons of Aaron, the *kohanim*, but not by the daughters of Aaron? On what basis could one have thought that priestly women were allowed to function in the Temple that the *mishnah* found it necessary to rule it out?[14] Since it is clear that not even Israelite men can perform any of the activities beyond the first two, this *mishnah* must be addressing only *kohanot,* women of the priestly clan. Does this passage imply that a question arose in those days about the eligibility of women serving in the Temple and therefore the rabbis issued this set of prohibitions?

I do not think so. The *mishnah*'s repeated references to women's absolute exclusion from Temple ritual may lead us to a deeper understanding of M 1:7b (about women's ritual exemptions): It is *only* Temple practices that are forbidden to women, none of the other ritual activities. Reading M 1:8 and M 1:7 in reverse order makes their purposes clear. M 1:8 is saying that every single Temple activity is not only not obligatory upon women, but even forbidden to them. M 1:7 goes on to say that the rituals that were able to survive the destruction of the Temple, such as shofar, lulav, and *succah,* are obligatory upon men, but not women. But it does not forbid women from participation, as it does with respect to the Temple service. It allows them to choose to engage in these activities. The associated Gemara, BT Kiddushin 36a, derives from verses, several times over, that women are forbidden to participate in the offering of sacrifices in the Temple. It is standard practice in Midrash Halakhah to derive or state the same teaching, again and again, in order to emphasize thereby the legitimacy of the derived conclusion. The same is true of M 1:8 here.

This significant difference between the rabbis' treatment of women's participation in Temple ritual and post-Temple Jewish ritual strongly suggests an alteration in their basic outlook: Although in post-Temple Judaism women are not obligated to participate in key religious rituals, they are no longer forbidden to do so. Moreover, the many exceptions the rabbis made to these exemptions, as we shall see, give further evidence that the rabbis considered women to be religiously needy. To say it in different words: The rabbis recognized that the practice of Judaism after the destruction of the Temple had to differ significantly from the practice of Judaism during the time of the Temple. So, along with the radical restructuring of Jewish ritual practice that brought the celebration of the Sabbath and holidays from the Temple into the home and from the *kohen* to the lay Israelite, the rabbis also opened the door to greater participation by women.[15] Rather than compare exemption to obligation, it is more useful to compare exemption (M 1:7) to prohibition (M 1:8). Women could not actively participate in the Temple service, as noted in M 1:8, but they did gain permission (M 1:7) and even acquired obligation to participate in some key rituals in the new configuration of Jewish practice.

From Exemption to Obligation

A careful look at tannaitic and amoraic statements about women and mitzvot shows that the rabbis made more and more exceptions to the rule of women's exemption, obligating them, as time passed, to more and more time-bound positive mitzvot.

The most important exception to the rule of exemption appears in M Berakhot 3:3.

Women, slaves, and minors are exempt from Shema and tefillin *but obligated to prayer,* mezuzah, and Grace after meals.

It is easy to see that this *mishnah* disagrees with M Kiddushin 1:7. It obligates women to prayer, a clear example of a positive time-bound mitzvah, the boundaries of which this very tractate of Mishnah spends much time delineating.[16] That women are obligated to Grace after meals is not surprising because it is not a time-bound positive mitzvah; it need only be performed if a person ate, in particular if he ate the amount of food that necessitated a full Grace (M Berakhot 7:2). Mezuzah, too, is a non-time-bound positive mitzvah.

The Tosefta lists other positive time-bound mitzvot that obligate women that are not found in the Mishnah: They are required to eat matzah (unleavened bread), the paschal lamb, and bitter herbs (T Pesahim 2:22); they are required to bring the *simhah* sacrifice to the Temple on the three pilgrimage festivals, a remarkable requirement in view of the fact that the Torah requires only men to be seen three times a year at the Temple (T Hagigah 1:4). In fact, the rabbis themselves construct the entire notion of the requirement of a *simhah* sacrifice and also women's obligation to bring it.[17] It is possible they have the future in mind, or the past—the fact that women in the time of the Temple did bring festival sacrifices[18]—but more likely the *simhah* obligation is a statement on their part that women should be ritually involved, although not to the same extent as men. That is, they create for women an imaginary obligation of the past, not grounded in any verse, in order to suggest that women are obligated to be involved in religious ritual, even though certain exemptions still apply. They are not free to choose to become involved. Note also that the Torah itself requires women to be present at the reading of the entire Torah to the people, once in seven years on the holiday of Succot (Deuteronomy 31:12).

When the anonymous voice of the Gemara wonders how the *mishnah*'s rule of women's exemption from positive time-bound mitzvot can be taken at face value, since there are so many exceptions to it, we find the following answer:[19]

--R. Yohanan said: We do not learn from general rules even if the exceptions are listed. (BT Kiddushin 34a)

This Amora is saying that one may not apply a general rule to all cases, even if it begins with the word *hakol,* meaning "this rule applies to all," and even if it lists (all) exceptions. For the rule under discussion, women's exemption from positive time-bound mitzvot, the *mishnah* lists no exceptions. According to R. Yohanan, the Mishnah's statements are not prescriptive rules but generalizations of particular instances: Many cases, therefore, are consistent with the stated rule but many others are not. The Mishnah does not bother to list all exceptions that we learn from other rabbinic texts.

This unusual array of rules and exceptions can also be explained differently. The numerous references in the Mishnah to women and individual mitzvot, such as their exemption from *succah* (M Succah 2:8) and from *re'iyah* (appearing at the Temple on the pilgrimage festivals, M Hagigah 1:1) and their obligation to prayer (M Berakhot 3:3) are unnecessary because the rules of M Kiddushin 1:7 cover all cases and therefore obviate the need for a separate listing. The presence of all these bits of information may point to an underlying rabbinic debate about the nature of women's religious obligations, some thinking she should have more and some less. An analogy to the rules about children and ritual obligations will help clarify this point.

The rabbis seem to have had two ways of looking at a minor's obligations. One is that as he reaches each developmental stage, more mitzvot are required of him, such as when old enough to talk, his father must teach him "*Shema yisrael*" (the first verse, T Hagigah 1:2). The other is that when a child reaches puberty, later defined as thirteen for boys and twelve for girls, and not before, all the mitzvot apply.[20] The Mishnah seems to lean in the latter direction but still includes some examples of the first approach: A child who is able to shake a lulav has to do so (M Succah 2:8); or, a child who is able to go up to the Temple on his father's shoulders, or holding his hand, has to do so (M Hagigah 1:1). The Amoraim accommodate these two approaches by distinguishing between a child who has reached the age of education, who is obligated to the mitzvot, and one who has not, who is thus exempt.[21] However, theirs is not the simple explanation for this phenomenon. It is more likely that the Mishnah is preserving evidence of the existence of two competing approaches.

As for women, the Mishnah also presents evidence of two approaches: For some Tannaim, a woman's obligations and exemptions are derived from the rules of M Kiddushin 1:7; for others, each case is dealt with separately. This second approach probably mandates a higher level of obligation.

These differences notwithstanding, in the amoraic period, we see marked movement in the direction of greater obligation.

> --Said R. Joshua b. Levi: Women are obligated to read the megillah, because they too were part of the miracle [of deliverance].[22] (BT Megillah 4a)

––Said R. Joshua b. Levi: Women are obligated to drink the four cups [of wine that punctuate the Pesah seder], because they too were part of the miracle [of deliverance]. (BT Pesahim 108b)

––Said R. Joshua b. Levi: Women are obligated to light the Chanukah lamps, because they too were part of the miracle [of deliverance]. (BT Shabbat 23a)

==[The reason that women are obligated to pray is that] prayer is petitions.
––Said R. Ada b. Ahavah: Women are obligated to recite Kiddush [on the Sabbath], as stipulated by the Torah. . . .
––Said Rava: Anyone who is bound by the Sabbath restrictions is similarly bound by the Sabbath ritual acts. (Berakhot 20b)

––Said R. Elazar: Women are obligated to eat matzah on Pesah, according to the Torah; for anyone who is bound not to eat *hametz* (leavened products), is similarly bound to eat matzah. (BT Pesahim 43b)

In all these instances, Amoraim are imposing upon women new obligations to perform ritual acts—*all positive time-bound mitzvot*—that M Kiddushin 1:7 would have exempted them from.[23] In each case, a reason is given. By the end of the amoraic period, women are locked into observance of the key rituals of Pesah, Chanukah, Purim, and, to a large extent, the Sabbath. I think this development is strong evidence that the rabbis recognized the importance of making religious practice more central to the lives of women.

Their statement about women's obligation to pray is especially revealing. The same *mishnah*—Berakhot 3:3—*exempts* women from reciting the paragraphs of the Shema but *obligates* them to prayer. Since both relatively lengthy rituals are pillars of the morning service, *shaharit,* it is hard to understand the distinction. The Gemara cited explains that even though it would follow from the rules that she should be exempt, she is obligated to prayer because "prayer is petitions," meaning, that a woman is the best advocate before God for herself and for those for whom she prays. It follows that the rabbis understood and accepted the fact that people, both men and women, need to turn to God to ask for help, and that the most effective way of doing so is by oneself. As the Yerushalmi (PT Berkahot 3:3; 6b) says in reference to obligating women to prayer: each and every person needs to ask for mercy himself (or herself). This argument does not apply, however, to the recitation of the Shema, a set of verses constituting a confession of faith and an acceptance of the yoke of the mitzvot. Only men are obligated to recite these theologically significant words twice daily.

Women Discharging the Responsibilities of Men

The corollary of imposing ritual obligations on a woman is allowing her to
discharge the obligations of others—recite Grace after meals for men, read
the megillah for men, and so on.

The Mishnah makes only one explicit statement on this topic: someone
who is *not* obligated to a certain mitzvah may *not* discharge the responsibilities of others who are obligated (Rosh Hashanah 3:8). The immediate
context in M Rosh Hashanah is that a deaf-mute, minor, or mentally impaired man may not blow the shofar for anyone obligated to hear the
blasts because those people themselves are not obligated to hear them. This
means that obligation is a necessary condition for being able to discharge
the responsibilities of others. Is it also sufficient?

The Mishnah (Berakhot 3:3) obligates women to recite Grace after
meals but then excludes them from the quorum of three who together will
recite Grace and the call to Grace, the *zimmun* (M Berakhot 7:2). In this
case a woman is obligated but, nevertheless, may not join men in the mu-
tual discharge of this responsibility.[24] It seems, then, that one can be obligated and still not be able to discharge the responsibilities of others. An
obligation is thus a necessary but not a sufficient condition for the eligibility to perform rituals for others. What else is needed?

A variety of texts on the topic of women and minors assisting men with
reciting sacred texts and leading public prayer suggests that the individual
reader's social status also matters. The Gemara cites a *baraita* that says
that anyone who affronts the dignity of the congregation, like a woman or
a child,[25] may not represent it—may not read from the Torah in public—
even though that person is technically eligible (BT Megillah 23a).[26] The
idea of public honor also seems to underlie the same *mishnah*'s other rules:
that a minor *kohen* may not bless the congregation[27] and that a person
dressed in rags, with his body exposed, may not read from the Torah in
public, pass before the ark, or recite the priestly blessing.

The Tosefta presents the clearest statement of all on the role that dignity
plays in determining who may discharge which mitzvah for whom.

A minor may translate for an adult [who is reading from the Torah
in public] but it is beneath his dignity [אין כבודו] for an adult to translate for a minor. (T Megillah 3:21)

The reason that the dignity of an adult is compromised in translating for
a minor is that translation is a lesser role than reading from the Torah itself. Differing from all the other tannaitic sources, this one does not leave it
up to the reader to conclude that social status is a factor in determining
who may discharge ritual responsibilities for whom, but says so explic-

itly.[28] Younger people command less respect than older people. Age, like gender, matters.

Finally, some passages curse any man who needs to depend on women, slaves, and minors to assist him in discharging his ritual responsibilities.

> If a slave or a woman or a minor recites *Hallel* (Psalms 113–118, recited on festivals) for him, he must repeat everything that they say [since he is obligated to this mitzvah and women and minors are not]. And let him be cursed. If an adult man was reciting *Hallel* for him, he answers hallelujah [after each verse or section of a verse]. (M Succah 3:10)

> Come and hear [the following tannaitic source]: ... A son recites Grace after meals for his father, a slave for his master, and a wife for her husband. But the Sages said: Let a man be cursed if his wife or child recites Grace for him.[29] (BT Berakhot 20b)

When we read these two sources in conjunction with each other, we see that it is not merely because a man is unlearned that he should be cursed. If his ignorance were the object of condemnation, it would not matter who recited Grace after meals or Hallel for him. He is cursed only if the person who assists him is of lower social status; when an adult man assists him in reciting Hallel, he is not cursed.[30] This distinction within the law suggests that it is not fitting for a head of household to be dependent for the execution of religious ritual on those who are dependent on him. The curse is invoked not just because he should have learned the prayers or blessings but also because he finds himself or has placed himself in circumstances that compromise his dignity.

This wide array of rules leads us to a general conclusion: In addition to being obligated, the one who functions on behalf of others—be it one or many—must be someone who does not affront their dignity, who occupies the same social standing. In the ancient world women were on a lower social rung than men and for that reason could not assist them in discharging their ritual obligations. Even women's obligation to various mitzvot could not cancel out the problem of their lower social status.

Women's Voluntary Performance of Mitzvot from Which They Are Exempt

We noted above that the ban on women's participating in the Temple worship service implies that the exemption of women from the performance of religious ritual is only that and nothing more. This means that women may choose to perform these acts on a voluntary basis. The question then arises whether women can perform them even if they break some law in the process, a law that men, who are obligated, are allowed to break in the

course of performing a mitzvah. For instance, can a woman blow the shofar for herself on Rosh Hashanah, on a voluntary basis, if, in the course of
doing so, she violates the rule of *shevut*, complete cessation from work?

BT Hagigah 16b helps us to answer these questions.

> Speak to the people of Israel. . . . And he shall lay his hand [on the
> head of the sacrifice] (Leviticus 1:2, 4)—the men of Israel perform lay-
> ing on of hands; the women of Israel may not.
>
> R. Yossi and R. Simon say: The women of Israel may perform the
> laying on of hands on a voluntary basis.
>
> Said R. Yossi: Abba Elazar told me that once we had a calf desig-
> nated as a *shelamim* sacrifice and we brought it to the women's
> gallery, and the women performed laying on of hands, not because the
> women were *obligated* to do so, but in order to give them *spiritual sat-
> isfaction* [נחת רוח].

In this remarkable anecdote, the rabbis invite women to lay their hands
on the head of an animal sacrifice, not because they thought women were
required to do so, but in order to allow women to express themselves religiously, to derive spiritual satisfaction. The rabbis' motivation is a moving
detail in and of itself.

The Gemara goes on to note that, in its opinion, the issue was more complicated than at first meets the eye. In the course of laying their hands on the
animal, if they did so with full force, the women would be breaking a different rule: performing work or activity on an animal that has been designated
as *heqdesh*, Temple property. Interpreting the story so that the women are
not committing this infraction, the Gemara reduces women's activity to let-
ting their hands "float" on the head or the back of the animal. This interpretation, however, does not seem to be the simple understanding of this anecdote, or others like it. The story suggests, rather, that minor rules may be
broken even for voluntary performance of mitzvot, because allowing people,
that is, women, to express themselves religiously supersedes a minor infraction of the law. According to T Rosh Hashanah 2:16, women, although not
obligated to blow the shofar on Rosh Hashanah, may choose to do so for
themselves, even though blowing a shofar for someone not obligated to do
so would be considered a violation of the day. Post-Talmudic commentators
learn from these examples that not only may women choose to perform
these ritual acts, they may also recite the accompanying blessings—which in-
fuse the ritual act with religious meaning—even though one might think that
in doing so they invoke God's name in vain. Again, rabbis bend the rules in
order to afford women spiritual satisfaction. We thus see that this anecdote,
in which the rabbis valued women's spiritual lives, came to have critical halakhic significance.[31]

"Blessed Be God for Not Making Me a Woman"

The discussion of women and ritual would not be complete if we did not make reference to perhaps the most sexist Jewish ritual practice. The statement, "Blessed be God for not making me a woman," which in the post-Talmudic period entered the daily morning service,[32] seems to express an intensely disparaging attitude to women. Many cite this blessing as evidence of rabbinic misogyny.[33] Reading it in context may deepen our understanding of its intended meaning and the thinking that led to its adoption in the daily liturgy.

> R. Judah says, [there are] three things a man must say every day, blessed [be God] for not making me a gentile; blessed [be God] for not making me a boor; blessed [be God] for not making me a woman.
>
> Not a gentile, because gentiles are not worthy in God's eyes (Isaiah 40:17); not a boor, because a boor does not avoid sin; not a woman, because women are not obligated by the mitzvot. (T Berakhot 6:18; PT Berakhot 9:1; 13b, with minor variations)

The context of this passage in the Tosefta is a discussion of the blessings a Jew recites before performing a mitzvah, such as putting on *tzitzit* or tefillin. Note that the very same rabbi who argues for daily recitation of these blessings then goes on to explain why each is recited. He finds nothing wrong with women as women; the issue for him is that they are not obligated to perform mitzvot in the same way that men are.[34] Were this second half of the passage, justifying the recitation of the blessing, issued today, we would call it apologetics—a deliberate attempt to explain away a serious rabbinic bias against women. But it is the same man who issued both statements back then. He instituted the recitation of these three blessings and then went on to rationalize each one. What did he mean by his statement that men should thank God for not being created as women because of women's exemption from mitzvot? Is he acknowledging men's superiority over women but trying to attribute it—and perhaps limit it—to men's more demanding ritual lives, a rather benign way of perceiving superiority?

If the triad were not of his making, if it rather were something that people were known to say anyway—and there is much evidence that this was so[35]—then his deeming it obligatory to recite each day, together with his "religious" interpretation, would mean that he is deliberately trying to modify people's outlook, to get them to see women in less negative terms. If so, he may be saying that women are not unworthy in God's eyes like gentiles, nor are they sinners like boors. Rather, the reason that men thank God for not being created as women is that men see themselves as more religiously worthy because God makes more ritual demands of them. That is, it is possible, if not too likely, that R. Judah was aware of the misogynist or triumphalist underpinnings of the popular statement about women and was trying to counteract them with his argument about mitzvot.[36]

Reading the Bavli's commentary on the *baraita* leads to a different interpretation. The first part, R. Judah's statement that one is required to recite these three blessings every day, also appears in BT Menahot 43b. The second part, the presentation of the rationales for the three blessings, is omitted. The context in the Gemara is a discussion of mitzvot and, in particular, R. Meir's requirement to recite one hundred blessings every day. An amoraic discussion of R. Judah's three required blessings follows:

> We learned in a *baraita*: R. Judah[37] used to say, a person is obligated to recite three blessings every day, and they are: that He made me Jewish,[38] that He did not make me a woman, that He did not make me a boor.[39]
>
> --R. Aha b. Jacob heard his son reciting, [Blessed be God] that He did not make me a boor. He said to him: To such an extreme? [Rashi: Is this not a show of arrogance?]
>
> --Should I instead thank God for not making me a slave? I cannot, because a slave is like a woman [and that blessing is already part of the liturgy]!
>
> --[No,] a slave is lower than a woman [עבד זיל טפי]. (BT Menahot 43b)

This rabbi's son interprets R. Judah's blessings in a sexist manner, namely, that men are thankful that they are not socially inferior like women, who, in this statement, are compared to slaves—either occupying the same low level (according to the son) or one only slightly higher (according to the father). It would seem that the Bavli's omission of the second part of R. Judah's statement—about women and mitzvot—made this alternate interpretation of the first part possible; the rabbi and his son seem to know only the first part. This is a third interpretation of R. Judah's blessing about women. When men express gratitude for being created as men, they are not saying that women by nature are defective, as thought by the Greeks, or that they are inferior because they have fewer religious demands made upon them, as suggested by R. Judah, but that they occupy lower social status.

However, if we think further, we may consider this interchange not a third interpretation of R. Judah's blessing but a nuanced reading of the second. The father and son may be saying that not obligating women to the time-bound positive mitzvot is a function of their lower social status, because, as we saw above, it may result from their not being full-fledged members of the religious community. It is thus possible that R. Aha and his son *did* know the second part of R. Judah's statement, but that they saw exemption from ritual acts as a *consequence* of low social status and not vice versa.

If we now return to R. Judah and assume, like R. Aha b. Jacob, that he had women's social status in mind, his statement is even more remarkable. It is as if he is saying, Never mind the fact that women's exemptions flow from lower status; the real reason a man should thank God for not being a woman is *not* his higher status but his greater level of ritual obligation. Since obligation to ritual is what matters, men should be thankful for their better, although more demanding, lot in life. Is this a way, perhaps, for the Tanna to comfort the men of his day for the large number of ritual demands placed on them? Is he casting the obligations in a positive light? Is he making a life of obligation more desirable—even though more difficult—than a life of exemption? The entire section seems to be an attempt on the part of the rabbis to "sell" their system to the populace by promising protection from sin as a reward for fulfilling the mitzvot and, in particular, by bolstering a man's ego for his special level of obligation: A Jewish man's superiority flows from his being commanded by his Creator.[40]

Conclusions

A close reading of many texts has shown us that the reason women are exempt from positive time-bound mitzvot is that only the full-fledged members of society are obligated to perform the ritual acts that define Jewish practice, those that need to be performed year in and year out. It would be compromising the dignity of God and of the heads of household to include others in this obligation. It is they who don special garb, like tefillin; it is they who must daily confess faith in God, reenact the great moments of Jewish history at Passover, Shavuot, and Succot, and celebrate the New Year by hearing shofar blasts. A woman's exemption from these acts has nothing to do with her household and child-rearing chores. She is simply a lesser person in the grand scheme of things, subordinate to her husband and ready to take orders from him. In a patriarchal society, key religious acts are turned over to the patriarchs, the men, and not the subordinates, the women and children.

During Talmudic times, this hierarchical distinction was in the process of becoming blurred. The rabbis began to increase women's obligations, imposing on them a variety of mitzvot relating to the holidays and the Sabbath. They recognized that women, like men, needed to express themselves religiously, open a direct line of communication with their Maker, and also that women were significant members of Jewish society—not as significant as men, but significant nonetheless.

It seems to me that the issue of who is obligated and who is exempt, and whether it depends on biology, sociology, physical or mental capacity, are all issues that the Talmudic rabbis were struggling with. For this reason, in many tractates we find competing statements as to which segments of the population are obligated and which exempt from fulfilling the particular act under discussion. Two things become clear from surveying rabbinic literature: There were no generally accepted rules of ritual obligation that one could turn to for answers; there was a wide variety of opinion on these matters. In most cases, only one opinion was included in the Mishnah so that the rules of obligation and exemption were set accordingly for generations to come. It was left for the Bavli and Yerushalmi to fill in the wider range of opinions, occasionally changing what the Mishnah had to say, either by citing a *baraita* that disagreed with the Mishnah or by giving a rationale.

Why is it important to recognize this struggle? Because it is an advance over the Torah's outlook on women and mitzvot: It acknowledges women's changing status. The Torah rarely obligates women directly. It addresses itself to men who then relay it to the women who are in their charge. The Ten Commandments are a good example. It is men who are commanded not to commit adultery with someone else's wife and not to lust after her or anything else that belongs to their fellow man.[41] Similarly, the requirement to appear at the Temple three times a year is directed to men. Although women were obligated to live Jewishly, it was their husbands who were in charge of seeing that they did so. Like children, they were not independently obligated.

That the rabbis find it necessary, in most tractates, to deal with the question of whom the law obligates means that they thought in terms other than those found in the Bible. They must have been interested in including, at least some of the time, groups that were not included in the Bible, such as women, or even groups not mentioned at all, such as the physically handicapped. Even if the rabbis declare women exempt, they have still advanced over the Torah, which, for the most part when discussing mitzvot, does not mention women at all.

Notes

1. The word in Hebrew, *mitzvat* (not *mitzvot*), appears throughout in the singular. I have translated it in the plural.

2. The word בן in the first clause, on the subject of parental obligations to children, refers to sons only because a father has no obligations to his daughters, but בן in the second clause refers to both sons and daughters and their obligations to their parents; אב in the first clause refers to fathers only, but אב in the second clause refers to both mothers and fathers, since honoring parents, as defined by the Torah, includes both mothers and fathers.

3. For the Tosefta, obligations incumbent on the son to perform for the father are called "obligations of the son on the father" rather than "obligations of the father on the son," as in the Mishnah. The same reversal holds true for obligations incumbent on the father to perform for the son: For the Tosefta, these are "obligations of the father on the son," whereas for the Mishnah they are "obligations of the son on the father." It is easily noticed that the Tosefta reverses the order for the two kinds of obligations: It discusses those that fall on children to perform for parents first and the obligations of parents to children second. The Mishnah, at least according to the Tosefta and Bavli, does the opposite. That is, even though both works present the Hebrew phrases in the same order, the Tosefta interprets them in one way and the Mishnah in another.

4. One manuscript of the Tosefta (Erfurt) reads "husband" instead of "others." That is most likely an interpretation or clarification.

5. Rashi notes (s.v. *sippek*), that her husband could object. To what? To her spending her time in this way. Tosafot (s.v. *sheyesh reshut*) comment that even though she must turn over her earnings to her husband, the problem is not lack of means but lack of access: How can one obligate a married woman to care for her father and mother when she lives elsewhere, with her husband?

This comment of the Tosafot is similar to the argument raised above: Rather than say that others control her and she is not free to spend her time caring for her parents, the Tosafot say that the issue is that she is not living close enough to her parents to be able to care for them.

6. Shmuel Safrai, in his article on women's obligation to the mitzvot, "Mehuyavutan shel Nashim Bemitzvot Bemishnatam shel Hatannaim," *Bar Ilan Yearbook for Jewish Studies and Humanities,* 5755 26/27: 227–236, concludes that since women, according to the rabbis, were present at Sinai, they would have been obligated by the mitzvot. It is their heavy domestic schedule that precludes them from performance. Therefore, the *mishnah* about women's obligations and exclusions is a summary of what women found themselves capable of doing. It reflects social reality already in practice; it is not a set of rules for determining which mitzvot obligate women and which do not. I see no textual evidence for such an interpretation. Safrai is deriving social realities from a legal text.

7. For example, BT Pesahim 87a says that on the first festival after she gets married a woman is very anxious to go back to her father's home to celebrate. This implies that she lived with her husband's family. See also the *baraita* in BT Ketubot 82b, which understands divorce as a woman's leaving her father-in-law's home and returning to her father's home. See also M Eruvin 8:5, which makes reference to a man's going to spend the Sabbath with his daughter who lives in the same city but not in his house.

8. See, for instance, Deut. 11:13–21. This paragraph is part of the Shema and recited twice daily by men.

9. *Abudarham Hashalem* (Jerusalem: Usha Press, 1340/1963), 25. Abudarham says that since a wife was subservient to her husband, were she obligated, she would have to choose between pleasing God and pleasing her husband. See the article by Noam Zohar, "Mah Bein Ish L'ishah," *Et La'asot,* no. 1 (Summer 1988): 103–112, in which the author sees social status as a crucial factor in determining the level of obligation to the mitzvot.

10. It is only in the modern world that we dismiss such logic because we are not comfortable with the idea that religious obligations are contingent upon, or vary with, social position. Furthermore, that men, in the rabbinic period, controlled women in marriage is a notion that many people in the modern period are not willing to state openly.

11. See Jay Rovner, "Rhetorical Strategy and Dialectical Necessity in the Babylonian Talmud: The Case of Kiddushin 34a–35a," *HUCA* 65 (1994): 200–201. See, in particular, n. 48, and the references to Jacob Neusner's phrase, "dependent on the time [of the year]."

12. This male hierarchy is also reminiscent of the community organization of the Dead Sea sects. Only men could undergo initiation rites and become full-fledged members. Women were present in these communities, but not obligated nor permitted to participate in communal rites in the same way as men. See Lawrence H. Schiffman, *Reclaiming the Dead Sea Scrolls* (Philadelphia: JPS, 1994), pt. 2, "The Community at Qumran."

13. The verb לא נוהג \ נוהג means "applies to/does not apply to" or "may be practiced by/may not be practiced by." It does not mean "customarily performed by." See, for instance, M Shevuot 4:1, "The oath of adjuration may be administered to men but not to women," which uses the same verb, [נוהגת [באנשים ולא בנשים. For another example of this usage, see T Hagigah 1:4.

14. Cf. Tosafot (s.v. *haqabbalot v'hazaot*), who ask a similar question, "Why is it necessary to list the Temple activities that women may not perform; cannot one deduce these rules simply from the fact that women could not be Temple functionaries—only Aaron and sons were fit?" Although my answer differs from theirs, they, too, are troubled by the superfluity of most rules of this *mishnah*.

15. Tal Ilan (*Jewish Women in Greco-Roman Palestine* [Tübingen: J.C.B. Mohr, 1995], 176–184) argues the opposite. In the period of the Temple, she says, women were actively involved in Temple life, bringing sacrifices and coming to pray. In the laws of the Mishnah, which, according to her, reflected actual practice in the post-Temple period, there is a sharp reduction in women's participation. I do not accept this analysis. One should not compare laws about obligations and exemptions to historical evidence of women's participation. Moreover, if, in this case, law reflects social and religious reality, why not say the same for other laws as well and thereby reach the conclusion that women, in the rabbinic period, were reciting the set of eighteen blessings at least twice a day? By suggesting—without basing her argument in the words—that this *mishnah* reflects historical reality, she undermines her entire thesis that laws and historical evidence are not to be confused with each other, and that most Jews were not living strictly according to the law as the Tannaim presented it. Judith Wegner (*Chattel or Person?* [New York: Oxford University Press, 1988], 147ff.) says that the framers of the Mishnah went beyond Scripture in banning women outright from many mitzvot or exempting them in theory and discouraging them in practice. She, too, makes assumptions that do not have a basis in the text.

16. The *stama d'gemara* in Berakhot 20b suggests that prayer obligates women because, although one might think this mitzvah is time-bound, it is not. That is not the simple explanation of the *mishnah*'s rule. It seems to me that the *stama* fabricated this answer in order to respond to the question it raised about why the

Mishnah obligates women to this mitzvah. See my article "Women and Prayer: An Attempt to Dispel Some Fallacies," *Judaism*, Winter 1993.

17. All the Torah requires is that a man not come empty-handed to the Temple on the pilgrimage festivals. It is the rabbis who determine that he must bring three kinds of sacrifices: *olot re'iyah, shalmei hagigah*, and *shalmei simhah*.

18. See the article by Chana Safrai, "Women and Processes of Change in the Temple in Jerusalem," in *A View into the Lives of Women in Jewish Societies*, ed. Yael Azmon (Jerusalem: Mercaz Shazar, 1995), 63–76.

19. The Yerushalmi asks the same question (Kiddushin 1:7; 61c).

20. T Hagigah 1:3; M Niddah 6:11. This view is somewhat at variance with that of Yitzhak Gilat, "Ben Shelosh Esreh Lemitzvot," *Mehkerei Talmud* 1 (Jerusalem: Magnes Press, 1990), who writes that the word *minor*, קטן, does not have a set meaning in tannaitic literature. He says that there is no fixed age at which a minor becomes obligated to perform mitzvot. As for legal acts that require knowledge and/or consent, such as vows, M Niddah 5:6 talks about intellectual maturity. Even at the end of the tannaitic period there is a debate about the age of maturity, some saying boys mature earlier and some saying girls do (BT Niddah 45b). In the amoraic period, Gilat says, there was a move toward standardization. He thus sees no evidence of conflicting opinions but rather of development over time.

21. BT Hagigah 4a. See also BT RH 33b; Megillah 19b; Succah 28b; Arakhin 2b.

22. M Megillah 2:4 says that all except for a deaf-mute, minor, or a mentally impaired individual are eligible to read the megillah, the Book of Esther, in public for others, though R. Judah disagrees and considers a minor a fit reader. The *mishnah*'s silence with respect to women implies that it holds that they are included in the cohort of fit readers. It is possible that this is what led R. Joshua b. Levi, in the time of the Gemara, explicitly to obligate women and permit them to read the megillah for others (BT Megillah 4a).

23. T Pesahim 2:22 obligated women to eat matzah. The Mishnah did not.

24. According to BT Berakhot 20b, at issue is whether women's obligation to recite Grace after meals is from the Torah, like men's, or from the rabbis. Only if it is from the Torah may she recite the Grace after meals for men. This question is left hanging. See my article "Women and Prayer," n. 19.

25. However, M Megillah 4:6 says the opposite, that a minor *is* allowed to read from the Torah and Prophets (the *haftarah*) in public. Since a child has lower social status than an adult, it would seem that what allows him to read from sacred texts in public is the need for capable readers. According to Albeck (Moed, 366), it was a custom to honor a smart child with the *haftarah* reading. It is also true that a male minor is on his way to becoming a fit adult reader.

26. When this *baraita* appears in the Tosefta, it says that "all count in the seven Torah readers, even a child, even a woman, but one does not call upon women to read in public" (T Megillah 3:11). The passage gives no reason for not calling upon women even though it has just said that they are eligible. It is the Gemara's version of this *baraita* that says explicitly that women may not read in public, although technically eligible, out of concern for *the dignity of the congregation* [כבוד הצבור] (BT Megillah 23a). This is probably an explanatory addition. See my article "Women and Prayer," 102, n. 24.

27. Rashi (s.v. *v'eyno noseh et kapav*) says that it is degrading [גנאי] for the congregation to be blessed by a minor.

28. A similar statement is made later in the same chapter, T Megillah 3:30, that a person who is inappropriately dressed may not read from the Torah, "because it is not dignified [אין כבוד]."

29. Compare the parallel in T Berakhot 5:18. After saying that women are not obligated and may not recite Grace for others, the Tosefta continues and says, "In fact they said, a woman recites Grace for her husband, a son for his father, and a slave for his master." No second clause curses men for relying on women.

30. Rashi, in Succah 38a (s.v. *v'tavo lo me'erah*), calls women, slaves, and minors "despicable representatives" [שליחים בזויים].

31. See Tosafot RH 33a, s.v. *ha R. Yehudah;* and Maimonides, *Mishneh Torah,* Hilchot Tzitzit 3:9. See my article "Women's Voluntary Performance of Commandments from Which They Are Exempt" (in Hebrew), *Proceedings of the Eleventh World Congress of Jewish Studies* (Jerusalem), 1994.

32. The proposed alternative blessing for women in the Orthodox prayer book is "that he made me according to His will [שעשני כרצונו]." Other proposals include casting the blessing in positive language, "that God has made me in His image *[be'tzalmo].*" A fascinating Renaissance alternative blessing was discovered by George Jochnowitz (". . . Who Made Me a Woman," Commentary, April 1981, 63). He writes that in the vernacular in southern France, we find: "Blessed are Thou . . . who made me a woman."

33. For example, Wegner (*Chattel or Person?* 153) says that this kind of exemption and exclusion diminishes the status of women.

34. He is not saying that women are not obligated by any but by time-bound positive mitzvot, like succah and tefillin. See Lieberman, *Tosefta Ki-fshutah,* Berakhot, 121.

35. Diogenes Laertius (*Lives,* Loeb ed., chap. devoted to Thales, 35) remarks that it was stated in the name of Socrates that there were three blessings for which he was grateful to Fortune: "first, that I was born a human being and not one of the brutes; next, that I was born a man and not a woman; thirdly, a Greek and not a barbarian." See Lieberman, *Tosefta Ki-fshutah,* Berakhot, 120, for a full treatment of this subject. See also Ilan, *Jewish Women in Greco-Roman Palestine,* 176, n. 1.

36. Even his statements about gentiles and boors can be viewed as an improvement on popular ideas about these people. Common to all three statements is the status of the group vis-à-vis the mitzvot.

37. The text of the printed edition reads "R. Meir." That is a mistake. His name was picked up from the previous statement. The correct name, as indicated in the marginal notes in the printed Talmud, is R. Judah.

38. The parallel versions in the Tosefta and Yerushalmi say, "that He did not make me a gentile," שלא עשני גוי. The Bavli's positive formulation is a correction in response to censorship. The version that entered the daily prayer book is the one that appears in the Tosefta. The Conservative prayer book has adopted the positive formulation.

39. Note also that the blessing "has not made me a boor" has been replaced with "has not made me a slave." The reason for this change is found in the continuation of the passage.

40. Cf. Ilan (*Jewish Women in Greco-Roman Palestine*, 177), who argues that were it not for this statement of R. Judah, we would not know that a life of religious obligation for women is desirable. Mitzvot for women, she says, are presented as punishments(!), such as for Eve's causing Adam to sin.

41. Even though linguists would argue that the masculine singular is unmarked in Hebrew, a gendered language, and could therefore be addressing a woman as well as a man, still, the seventh and tenth commandments reveal that the unit as a whole is directed to men.

Conclusion

There is nothing absolutely ideal; ideals are relative to the lives that entertain them.

—*William James*

$\mathcal{A}$s a Talmudist, I have tried, throughout this book, to read the sources in as accurate a fashion as possible, applying to them the comparative and contextual analytical techniques described in the Introduction. As a feminist, I have tried to ferret out from these texts the thinking about women, their social status, their relationship to men, and the impact of rabbinic law on them. In addition, I have tried to point out the flaws in the two reigning theories, namely, that the rabbis—in grossly oversimplified terms—either hated women or else loved and respected them. The situation, to my mind, is much more complicated: On the one hand, the rabbis operated in a patriarchal framework and continued to treat women as secondary to men; on the other, they instituted many significant changes to benefit women. Although at any given moment in time Jewish law assigns women fewer rights and lower status than men, not always treating them as well as surrounding cultures, when we trace developments in Jewish law over time we see distinct movement, in a wide variety of legal and social institutions, from lesser status for women to greater.

Our examination of ten key issues and institutions of rabbinic law revealed:

1. that marriage, which used to involve the purchase of a woman by a man from her father, became, in rabbinic times, a form of "social contract" entered into by the prospective bride and groom
2. that divorce, which used to be the prerogative of men only, became possible for a woman, with the assistance of a rabbinical court, who could "force" a *get*
3. that women's exemption from the obligation of procreation was not designed to devalue their role in procreation but rather to deny

them an opportunity to sue for divorce after ten years of a barren marriage; even so, when put to the test, on a case-by-case basis, childless women were given the right to divorce their husbands

4. that women's exclusion from the right to give testimony does not imply intellectual incapacity or emotional excess but is a function of their lesser social status; thus, women could testify on behalf of other women

5. that the law of the wayward wife, the *sotah,* which punished innocent as well as guilty women, but never men, was interpreted in a way that made it impossible to implement

6. that women's disenfranchisement with respect to their father's estate turned into partial enfranchisement when the rabbis established a dowry of a one-tenth share of the father's net worth

7. that it was not women but men who added the extra seven "white" days to the seven-day sexual separation of husband and wife each month

8. that, according to the Talmud, women, in general, do not actively seduce men, but that men are involuntarily aroused in the presence of women, and, for that reason, may not spend time alone with them

9. that the biblical model of compensating the victim's father for the loss of her virginity in a case of rape was abandoned in favor of a model of assault and battery, with compensation determined accordingly, and paid, in certain instances, to the victim herself

10. that women's exemption from time-bound positive mitzvot was replaced in the course of time with selective obligation, a move consistent with the transformation of Judaism in the post-Temple period from a Temple-based to a home-based religion

I was able to arrive at these conclusions, most of which differ significantly from those presented in other books on the subject, because I read sources contextually, examining each together with associated rabbinic materials from the same time period and from others, either earlier or later. It is all too easy, if one reads texts out of context or plucks them from here and there to arrive at a different set of conclusions altogether. Although disparaging, even misogynistic, statements about women can be found in the Talmud, there is no textual evidence that the differential treatment of women and men derives from these attitudes. Rather, the explanation for the legal bias in favor of men is that the rabbis inherited and worked within a patriarchal society. In such a society, women occupy a subordinate social status.

It is therefore remarkable that in virtually every major area, as we have noted, the law was moving in the direction of extending to women more rights. Why did the rabbis make these changes? They were not feminist or proto-feminist. I can only speculate that a growing self-awareness on their part, a growing discomfort with patriarchal privilege, a deepening moral critique of society drawn from the words of the Torah themselves, greater familiarity with surrounding cultures, and even pressure brought by the people themselves, such as by women seeking divorce relief from gentile courts—all of this led to change.

Did the rabbis invent these new, enlightened rules themselves, or did they simply adapt them from Aramaic common law or Greco-Roman law? Does it make any difference if, in fact, they are "borrowed"? Since so many ancient law codes are reworkings of earlier codes and practices, and since so many similarities exist between rabbinic law and other ancient systems, there is reason to believe that a significant part of what we see in the Talmud was already standard practice. But that does not diminish the accomplishments of the framers of rabbinic law. What I have been particularly interested in showing is that, from generation to generation, individuals introduced modifications into transmitted texts and that these modifications, when taken together, add up to a larger picture of improving people's lives, women's in particular. Even if the rabbis did not invent the *ketubah* or the dowry or the wife-initiated divorce, they chose to incorporate them into the rabbinic scheme of things.

Moreover, since within their own circles they debated fine points of law, it follows that it was not necessary for them to accept, uncritically, the common practice of the people. The fact that in many areas they chose to depart from it suggests that they did not simply adopt cultural norms but filtered them through their own religious and legal patterns of thinking, accepting only those practices that appealed to their (patriarchal) sense of justice and devotion to God.[1] That is, showing that some rabbinic legislation was not invented by them but rather taken over by them does not disprove that the rabbis acted deliberately to improve women's social and legal position. It actually strengthens that point. For even though the rabbinic system of law, like most others, is based on previous ones, it, nonetheless, deliberately made changes that it saw fit to make. We also saw, in many instances, uneven development over time: The Tosefta ruled leniently, the Mishnah stringently, and then the Bavli and Yerushalmi leniently, like the Tosefta.

We should also note that the consequence, if not the intention, of much of the legislation we looked at was to protect women and strengthen marital bonds. For instance, although the rabbis themselves probably recognized that the monthly sexual separation of husband and wife derived from a biblical revulsion of menstrual blood, they also understood that the result of such a separation was to maintain his sexual interest in her and also hers in him. Similarly, obligating only men to procreate and exempting women was probably a way to prevent women from initiating divorce, but the outcome was to make it possible for women to choose to have children or not. In a world of high incidence of maternal mortality, this choice may have been important to women. Even the paragraphs that barred men from being alone with women and fathers from sleeping in bodily contact with young daughters, although intended to protect men from sexual transgression, also served to protect women and children from sexual abuse.

What also came to light in the course of reading the Talmudic materials were many passages in which men explicitly or implicitly express anxiety about their own abilities. For so long, we have heard men's dismissive critique of women, for their garrulousness, jealousy, vanity, light-headedness, sexual promiscuity, to name a few of their supposed defects. Now that women are studying the Talmud, they may find new parts that will be of special interest, such as those in which men describe themselves as weak or foolish or fearful, qualities not usually associated with them. Here and there the men let their guard down and reveal some of their own insecurities. The presence of these materials, as scattered as they are, suggests that the Talmud's composite picture of men is probably different from what most of us think.

It is significant that nearly every woman appearing in these chapters is portrayed by the Talmud in positive terms. When women come to court, they make reasonable requests of the rabbinical judge and are appropriately accommodated by the decision he renders. Many of them appear clever, resolute, and possessing clarity of vision. On occasion, they shame men who are lacking in some of these very same qualities. The fact that the Talmud, overall, portrays individual women favorably indicates that the rabbis were willing to recognize merit and talent even in those who were subordinate to them.

Returning now to our original question at the beginning of this book: How do we, today, respond to the fact that the rabbis of the Talmud treated women in a less than equal manner, since we find such discrimination distressingly unethical? Can we accept their legislation if we reject their social agenda? In my opinion, yes. An important finding of this study is that Jewish law changes over time, albeit slowly, and that the key legal institutions at the end of the rabbinic period looked very different from the way they looked at the beginning. Or, to put it more conservatively, the rabbis fleshed out the institutions of Jewish law in ways that one could not have predicted by reading the relevant Torah verses. It is true that they did not achieve or even seek equality for women. But, since they were moving consistently to give women more "rights," I suggest that we not judge them too harshly. The changes they made and, in particular, *the direction in which they were headed*, makes them fitting precursors for us. As we face our own problems with the practice of Judaism today, we can turn to the rabbis of the Talmud for solutions. They laid the groundwork and pointed the way.

I would like to end this book in the same way that it began, with a story about men and women and their complex set of interrelationships.

> --Samuel wanted to have sex with his wife.
>
> She said to him, "I am ritually impure [and hence not available]."
>
> But the next day, [without having immersed in a *mikveh*], she said to him, "I am now ritually pure."
>
> He challenged her: "Yesterday you said you were *impure* and today you are *pure?*"
>
> She answered: "Yesterday I did not have enough strength [for sex, לא הווה בחיילי היי שעתא. Today I do.]"
>
> He went and asked Rav [if he should believe her that she is pure].
>
> Rav said: "Since she gave a reasonable explanation [מתלא] of her behavior, she is believed." (PT Ketubot 2:5; 26c)

This anecdote turns marital dynamics upside down. It is well known that issues of ritual purity restrict a woman's sexual availability. For this reason no husband can ever be sure that when he wants sex with his wife, she will be able to accommodate him. But we find here a new limiting factor: a woman's ability falsely to claim ritual impurity when not in the mood for sex. It would seem that Samuel's wife could simply have said "no" but decided instead that the easiest and most effective way to resolve the matter was to offer a "religious" excuse. Rav tells Samuel to accept her lie as "truth" because she gave what he calls a reasonable or plausible explanation for telling it—not wanting to engage in sex with her husband! He thus supports women's ability to exercise power over men in this way. The ultimate outcome is that the purity rules, which some say treat women like objects, in this case give a wife a measure of control over the couple's sex life.

The Babylonian Talmud's version of this anecdote brings other truths to light.

> --Samuel asked Rav: If a woman says she is ritually impure and then [the next day] says she is ritually pure, what is the law? [Is she to be believed when she says, without any intervening immersion in a *mikveh*, that she is pure? May her husband proceed to have sexual relations with her?]
>
> He said to him: . . . if she gives a reasonable explanation [for lying], she is believed [when she says she is ritually pure].
>
> Samuel listened to Rav say this forty times(!) and still could not bring himself to act upon it. (BT Ketubot 22a)

It is remarkable that in this version of the incident, Samuel asks Rav precisely the same question that he asked in the other one, but without any reference to his personal circumstances. By not locating Samuel's query within an anecdote, the redactor does not allow any real woman's voice to be heard in this exchange. As a result, the charm and certainly the bite of the story are lost. The issue of a wife thwarting her husband's sexual drive because she was not interested in sex at the time, although probably implied, is not brought to the surface. Samuel is the main character in this version, and his extraordinary (or perhaps excessive) piety, the note on which the story ends, is singled out for praise. By introducing these changes, the redactor has censored the story, rewriting it in a way that preserves the legal conundrum but makes the rabbi look righteous rather than foolish (or foolishly righteous).

Returning to the first version, we may now ask: Why did men choose to incorporate this story into the Talmud? The simple answer is that it is an apt illustration of a rabbinic rule of evidence, "if someone gives a reasonable explanation of the lie one told, he or she is believed." A better answer is that the deliberate, even savvy inclusion of anecdotes like these shows that the Talmudic rabbis do not take themselves too seriously. They exhibit a liveliness of outlook and an openness to self-critique. Moreover, the redactor may have deliberately injected a feminist message, namely, that clever, resourceful women may take patriarchal structures designed to subordinate women and utilize them instead for their own empowerment within rabbinic law itself. In the Talmud, women seemed content with gaining a measure of control within a patriarchal system. Today, armed with the knowledge that Jewish law is open to change, women are likely to seek to become full-fledged members of the Jewish community.

Notes

1. This same point is made by Reuven Yaron (*Gifts in Contemplation of Death in Jewish and Roman Law* [Oxford: Clarendon Press, 1960], 19). He says that although there was considerable Hellenistic influence on the laws of disposition of one's estate, the Hellenistic legal institutions were not accepted indiscriminately.

Glossary

aggadah (adj. aggadic) the portion of rabbinic literature that is nonprescriptive and often homiletical; it can take the form of a scripturally based teaching or an independent rabbinic pronouncement

agunah (pl. *agunot*) Hebrew for anchored woman; a wife who is not living with her husband, either because his death cannot be properly established or because he withholds a bill of divorce from her, but not free to remarry

Amora (pl. Amoraim; adj. amoraic) a rabbi who lived during the years 200 to 500 C.E., in either Babylonia or Palestine, and participated in the discussions and analysis of tannaitic and biblical traditions

Aramaic a northwestern Semitic language used throughout the Ancient Near East in late antiquity in which many important Jewish texts, including parts of the Talmud, were written

b., b' (in a rabbi's name) Hebrew or Aramaic, standing for *ben* or *bar*, meaning "son of"

baraita (pl. *baraitot*) a tannaitic teaching not included in the Mishnah but remaining outside of it; such teachings are often cited in the Gemara

Bavli short for Talmud Bavli, the Hebrew name for the Babylonian Talmud

bet din Hebrew for court of law

betrothal the first stage of Jewish marriage; can be dissolved only by a divorce but does not allow the couple to live together

Bet Hillel, Bet Shammai Hebrew for the House of Hillel, the House of Shammai; these schools of rabbis, each following the philosophy of an illustrious founder, flourished in the first century C.E.; in most matters of Jewish law, the House of Hillel rules more leniently than the House of Shammai

bogeret Hebrew for a young woman who has reached physical and mental maturity and legal independence

boshet payment for shame, such as that inflicted by a rapist on his victim

bride-price the money paid by the groom to the father of bride in exchange for taking his daughter in marriage

251

Chanukah   Festival of Lights, celebrating the deliverance in the time of the Hasmoneans (about 165 B.C.E.) from the hellenizing strictures of the Syrian king Antiochus

Deuteronomy   the fifth book of the Bible

dinar   the smallest silver coin in use in Palestine and Babylonia; equivalent to a zuz

dowry   the money, real estate, or other goods that a father gives his daughter upon her marriage; the wife retains title, but the income from the assets accrues to the husband

eglah arufah   Hebrew for the ritual of breaking a calf's neck if an unidentified corpse is found not far from a population center (Deuteronomy 21:1–9)

erusin   Hebrew for betrothal, a term deriving from the Bible and later replaced by the rabbinic term *kiddushin*

Exodus   the second book of the Bible

Gemara   Aramaic for tradition(s); the extensive analysis of and commentary on the Mishnah by Amoraim and post-amoraic anonymous rabbis; term is used interchangeably with Talmud

Genesis   the first book of the Bible

get (pl. *gittin*)   Hebrew for bill of divorce

Grace after meals   set of blessings recited after a meal

haftarah   Hebrew for a reading from the Prophets, a part of the Sabbath and festival liturgy

halakhah   Hebrew for prescriptive legal statement

Halakhah (adj. halakhic)   the body of Jewish law supplementing biblical law

Hallel   Hebrew for Psalms 113–118, part of the festival liturgy

karet   a form of punishment mentioned in the Bible, defined by the rabbis as excision from the Jewish people or premature death

kenas   Hebrew for the fifty silver shekels that a rapist must pay the father of his victim

ketubah   Hebrew for marriage settlement, the moneys that the groom promises to pay the bride upon dissolution of the marriage by death or divorce; the *ketubah* document is signed at the wedding and given by the groom to the bride

Kiddush   from Hebrew for sanctification, specifically referring to the blessing over wine that ushers in the Sabbath

kiddushin   rabbinic term for betrothal; see betrothal

kohen (pl. *kohanim*)   the highest Jewish caste; the sons of Aaron, who served as priests in the Temple

Kutheans   descendants of the original Samaritans who created a syncretistic religion, accepting only some parts of Scripture; viewed by the rabbis as partly but not fully Jewish

levir   Latin for husband's brother

levirate marriage   the Biblical requirement that the widow of a childless man marry his brother—her *levir*—in order to produce an heir for the deceased (Deuteronomy 25:5–9)

Leviticus   the third book of the Bible

ma'ariv   name of the daily evening prayer

mamzer (pl. *mamzerim*)   Hebrew for people of impaired lineage who are ineligible to marry a fit Jew; offspring of an incestuous or an adulterous union

megillah   Hebrew for scroll, often a reference to the Book of Esther, read on the holiday of Purim

mezuzah   a manuscript of specific biblical verses, affirming God's sovereignty and the obligation to observe mitzvot, that is affixed in a special case to the doorpost of a Jewish home

Midrash Halakhah   the collections of tannaitic teachings that line by line derive new laws from Scripture

mikveh   Hebrew for ritual bath; used for purification after a menstrual period and for conversion to Judaism

minhah   a meal offering brought to the Temple; also the name for the afternoon prayer

Mishnah (adj. mishnaic)   the six orders of Jewish law compiled by R. Judah the Prince and published orally around 200 C.E.; subdivided into tractates, chapters, and paragraphs, each of which is called a *mishnah* (pl. *mishnah*s)

mitzvah (pl. mitzvot)   Hebrew for commandments, often referring to ritual acts but also to meritorious deeds

na'arah   Hebrew for a girl between the ages of twelve and one day and twelve and one-half and one day

niddah   Hebrew for a menstruant

Numbers   the fourth book of the Bible

ordeal of the bitter waters   ritual performed on a woman whose husband suspects her of infidelity

parnassah   Hebrew for dowry

patriarchy   a social configuration in which the patriarch, a man, is head of household and in control of his wife (or wives), children, and slaves *pegam*   Hebrew for payment by a rapist for the loss of virginity and for personal injury; amount varies according to social circumstances

perutah   smallest copper coin in use in Palestine and Babylonia

Pesah   spring festival commemorating the Exodus from Egypt

Purim   holiday celebrating deliverance from the Persian king Ahasuerus and his adviser Haman, who sought to annihilate all Persian Jews

rabbi(s)   Hebrew for "(my) teacher"; the name for the men—teachers, legislators, and judges—who shaped the texts of the Talmudic period

rabbinic period   the period during which the rabbis flourished, from about the first century B.C.E. to about the seventh century C.E.

Rashi   acronym of name of R. Shlomo Yitzhaki of Troyes, France, 1040–1105, author of an important, extraordinarily clear, line-by-line commentary on almost all tractates of the Babylonian Talmud; also author of an important commentary on the Torah

Rav   Abba Arikha, a first-generation Babylonian Amora

Rava   R. Abba, a prominent fourth-generation Babylonian Amora

Rebbe   shortened name for Rabbi Judah the Prince, the imputed editor of the Mishnah

Rosh Hashanah   Jewish New Year holiday

separate hallah   the action of separating a portion of unbaked dough for a priestly gift

shaharit   name of the daily morning prayer

Shema   the central Jewish prayer consisting of various key passages from the Torah; includes a confession of faith and statement of acceptance of the commandments; recited morning and night

shofar   Hebrew for ram's horn, sounded on the Jewish New Year.

simhah   Hebrew for rejoicing; a name for one of the sacrifices to be brought to the Temple on the three pilgrimage festivals

sotah   Hebrew for wayward wife

stama d'gemara   the anonymous voice of the text; the stratum in the Babylonian and Palestinian Talmuds that weaves together the earlier tannaitic and amoraic statements

succah   Hebrew for the booth in which one dwells on the festival of Succot

Succot   the harvest festival in the fall

sugya   Aramaic for a unit of Talmudic discourse

tallit   prayer shawl, worn today by men and also women for the *shaharit* service and by the prayer leader for most services; in the rabbinic period, a sheetlike outer garment

Talmud (adj. Talmudic)   a collective name for the Mishnah and Gemara, the literary results of the rabbinic discussions of Jewish law and tradition

Tanna (pl. Tannaim; adj. tannaitic)   the spokespersons of the tannaitic period, ending about 200 C.E., whose views are found in the Mishnah, Tosefta, Midrash Halakhah, and the *baraitas* found in the Talmud

tefillin   Hebrew for the phylacteries donned by Jews during morning prayers but worn, in the Talmudic period, for most of the day; cubical compartments of leather affixed to the arm and forehead with leather thongs, containing biblical passages that emphasize God's sovereignty and the obligation of the Jew to observe God's commandments

tikkun ha-olam   Hebrew for enactments to repair the social order

Torah   Hebrew for teaching; refers to (1) the five books of Moses; (2) all Jewish study, the entire religious and ethical and cultural literature of Judaism

Torah reading   the public reading each Monday, Thursday, Sabbath, festival, and fast day of a portion of Scripture

Tosafot   Hebrew for additions; critical and explanatory glosses on the Babylonian Talmud written by a school of rabbis in France and Germany in the twelfth and thirteenth centuries

Tosefta (adj. Toseftan)   the companion volume to the Mishnah, dating from the same period and organized in the same fashion, containing material that supplements and complements the mishnaic teachings; some Toseftan teachings predate the Mishnah

tosefet ketubah   Hebrew for the additional moneys that a groom may promise a bride in the *ketubah*, over and above the statutory amount

tractate   a volume of Mishnah or Talmud

usufruct (Hebrew, *perot*)   use of the profit gained from the property of another; herein, the income of a bride's dowry that accrues to the husband

vow   a promise to God to engage in or refrain from a certain kind of behavior or to regard a certain object as forbidden, usually in exchange for God's granting the petitioner's request

Yerushalmi   short for Talmud Yerushalmi, the Talmud composed in Palestine, completed about a century earlier than the Talmud Bavli

Yom Kippur   Day of Atonement, a fast day with the theme of repentance

zav, zavah   Hebrew for a man or woman suffering from a genital discharge; for women the discharge is usually blood seen at a time other than the menstrual period

zivah   legal condition of one suffering from a genital discharge

zuz   smallest unit of silver currency; same as dinar

Bibliography

Primary Sources

Aboth de Rabbi Nathan. Ed. Solomon Schechter. New York: Feldheim, 1945.

Abudarham Hashalem. Jerusalem: Usha Press, reprinted 1962.

Anchor Bible: Genesis, commentary by E. A. Speiser; *Leviticus,* commentary by Jacob Milgrom. New York: Doubleday, 1967, 1991.

Bereshit Rabbah. Ed. J. Theodor and Ch. Albeck. Jerusalem: Wahrmann Books, 1965.

A Dictionary of the Targumim, The Talmud Babli and Yerushalmi, and the Midrashic Literature. Ed. Marcus Jastrow, 1903. Reprinted, New York: Judaica Press, 1985.

The JPS Torah Commentary: Leviticus, commentary by Baruch A. Levine, 1989; *Numbers,* commentary by Jacob Milgrom, 1990; *Deuteronomy,* commentary by Jeffrey H. Tigay. Philadelphia: Jewish Publication Society, 1996.

Mishneh Torah. Maimonides.

Mekhilta d'Rabbi Ishmael. Ed. H. S. Horovitz and I. A. Rabin. Frankfurt, 1931; reprinted Jerusalem: Wahrmann Books, 1970.

Seder Elijah Rabbah and Zuta. Ed. Meir Ish Shalom. Vienna, 1904; reprinted in Israel, 1969.

Shishah Sidrei Mishnah. Ed. Hanokh Albeck. Jerusalem: Mosad Bialik; Tel Aviv: Dvir, 1952–1958.

Sifra (Torat Kohanim). Ed. I. H. Weiss. Vienna, 1862; reprinted New York: Om, 1946.

Sifrei Bemidbar. Ed. H. S. Horovitz. Leipzig, 1917; reprinted Jerusalem: Wahrmann Books, 1966.

Sifrei Devarim. Ed. Louis Finkelstein and H. S. Horowitz. Berlin/New York, 1939; reprinted New York: JTSA (Jewish Theological Seminary of America), 1969.

Talmud Bavli.

Talmud Yerushalmi.

Tanakh, The Holy Scriptures: The New JPS Translation according to the Traditional Hebrew Text. Philadelphia: JPS, 1988.

The Temple Scroll. Ed. Yigal Yadin. Jerusalem: Israel Exploration Society/Institute of Archaeology of the Hebrew University of Jerusalem, 1983.

The Tosefta: Zeraim, Moed, Nashim, Nezikin. Ed. Saul Lieberman. New York: JTSA (Jewish Theological Seminary of America), 1955–1988.

Tosephta. Ed. Moshe Shmuel Zuckermandel. Jerusalem: Wahrmann Books, 1963.

Secondary Sources

Adler, Rachel. "I've Had Nothing Yet So I Can't Take More," *Moment* 8 (September 1983).

Archer, Leonie. *Her Price Is Beyond Rubies: The Jewish Woman in Graeco-Roman Palestine.* Journal for the Study of the Old Testament Series, 60 (Sheffield, UK: Sheffield Academic Press, 1990).

Baskin, Judith R. "Rabbinic Judaism and the Creation of Woman." In *Judaism Since Gender,* ed. Miriam Peskowitz and Laura Levitt. New York: Routledge, 1997.

_____. "Rabbinic Reflections on the Barren Wife," *Harvard Theological Review* 82, no. 1 (1989).

Berlin, Adele. "Ruth and the Continuity of Israel." In *Reading Ruth: Contemporary Women Reclaim A Sacred Story,* ed. Judith A. Kates and Gail Twersky Riemer. New York: Ballantine Books, 1995.

Biale, David. *Eros and the Jews.* New York: Basic Books, 1992.

Biale, Rachel. *Women and Jewish Law: An Exploration of Women's Issues in Halakhic Sources.* New York: Schocken, 1984.

Boyarin, Daniel. *Carnal Israel: Reading Sex in Talmudic Culture.* Berkeley: University of California Press, 1993.

Brenner, Athalya, ed. *A Feminist Companion to Wisdom Literature.* Sheffield: Sheffield Academic Press, 1995.

Cohen, Haim, "Witnesses." *Encyclopedia Judaica* (16:586).

Cohen, Jeremy. *"Be Fertile and Increase, Fill the Earth and Master It": The Ancient and Medieval Career of a Biblical Text.* Ithaca, N.Y.: Cornell University Press, 1989.

Cohen, Shaye J. D. "Menstruants and the Sacred in Judaism and Christianity." In *Women's History and Ancient History,* ed. Sarah B. Pomeroy. Chapel Hill: University of North Carolina Press, 1991.

Cotton, Hannah. "Women's Documents from the Judaean Desert." Lecture, Israel Museum, May 19, 1996.

Dinari, Yedidya. "The Customs of Menstrual Impurity: Their Origin and Development," *Tarbiz* 49 (1979–80).

Elon, Menahem. *Jewish Law: History, Sources, and Principles.* Philadelphia: Jewish Publication Society (hereafter, JPS), 1994.

Epstein, Y. N. *Mavo Lenusach Hamishnah,* 2nd ed. Jerusalem: Magnes Press, 1964.

_____. *Mevo'ot Lesifrut Hatannaim.* Jerusalem: Magnes Press, 1957.

Feldman, David. *Marital Relations, Birth Control, and Abortion in Jewish Law.* New York: New York University Press, 1968.

Friedman, Shamma. "A Critical Study of Yevamot X with a Methodological Introduction." In *Texts and Studies,* ed. H. Z. Dimitrovsky. New York: JTSA (Jewish Theological Seminary of America), 1977.

_____. "Tosefta Atikta . . . ," *Tarbiz* 62, no. 3 (5753/1992–1993).

Frymer-Kensky, Tikvah. "The Bible and Women's Studies." In *Feminist Perspectives on Jewish Studies,* ed. Lynn Davidman and Shelly Tanenbaum. New Haven: Yale University Press, 1994.

Gilat, Yitzhak. "Ben Shelosh Esreh Lemitzvot," in *Mehkerei Talmud* 1, ed. Yaacov Sussmann and David Rosenthal. Jerusalem: Magnes Press, 1990.

_____. *The Teachings of R. Eliezer Ben Hyrcanos and Their Position in the History of the Halakha*. Tel Aviv: Bar Ilan University Series of Research Monographs, 1968.

Goitein, S. D. "Women as Creators of Biblical Genres," *Prooftexts* 8, no. 1 (January 1988).

Goodblatt, David, "The Babylonian Talmud." In *The Study of Ancient Judaism*, pt. 2, ed. Jacob Neusner. New York: Ktav, 1981.

Halivni Weiss, David, "The Use of קנה in Connection with Marriage," *Harvard Theological Review*, 1964.

Hauptman, Judith, "Abortion: Where We Stand," *United Synagogue Review* 42, no. 2 (Spring 1990).

_____. "An Assessment of Women's Liberation in the Talmud," *Conservative Judaism* 26, no. 4 (Summer 1972).

_____. *Development of the Talmudic Sugya: Relationship Between Tannaitic and Amoraic Sources*. Lanham, Md: University Press of America, 1988.

_____. "Feminist Perspectives on Rabbinic Texts." In *Feminist Perspectives on Jewish Studies*, ed. Lynn Davidman and Shelly Tanenbaum. New Haven: Yale University Press, 1994.

_____. "Images of Women in the Talmud." In *Religion and Sexism*, ed. Rosemary Ruether. New York: Simon and Schuster, 1974.

_____. "Pesiqah L'humra B'mishnat Gittin," *Proceedings of the Tenth World Congress of Jewish Studies*, Jerusalem, August 1990.

_____. "Women and Prayer: An Attempt to Dispel Some Fallacies," *Judaism*, Winter 1993.

_____. "Women and Procreation," *Tikkun*, November/December 1991.

_____. "Qiyum Meratzon Shel Mitzvot Aseh Shehazeman Geraman Al Yedei Nashim," *Proceedings of the Eleventh World Congress of Jewish Studies*, Jerusalem, 1994.

Holzer, Gershon, "Women's Testimony in Jewish Law" (in Hebrew), *Sinai* 67 (1970).

Ilan, Tal. "A Window onto the Public Domain—Jewish Women in the Time of the Second Temple" (in Hebrew). In *Eshnav Lehayeihen Shel Nashim B'Hevrot Yehudiot*, ed. Yael Azmon. Jerusalem: Mercaz Shazar, 1995.

_____. *Jewish Women in Greco-Roman Palestine: An Inquiry into Image and Status*. Tübingen: J.C.B. Mohr, 1995.

Jochnowitz, George. ". . . Who Made Me a Woman," *Commentary*, April 1981.

Kraemer, David C. "A Developmental Perspective on the Laws of Niddah," *Conservative Judaism* 38, no. 3 (Spring 1986): 26–33.

Levine, Amy-Jill, ed. *"Women like This": New Perspectives on Jewish Women in the Greco-Roman World*. Atlanta, Ga.: Scholars Press, 1991.

Lieberman, Saul, *Greek and Hellenism in Jewish Palestine*. Jerusalem: Bialik, 1962.

_____. "How Much Greek in Jewish Palestine?" *Texts and Studies*. New York: Ktav, 1974.

_____. *Tosefta Ki-fshutah: Zeraim, Moed, Nashim, Nezikin*. New York: JTSA (Jewish Theological Seminary of America), 1955–1988.

Meachem, Tirzah Z. "Mishnah Tractate Niddah with Introduction: A Critical Edition with Notes on Variants, Commentary, Redaction and Chapters in Legal History and Realia" (in Hebrew). Ph.D. diss., The Hebrew University of Jerusalem, 1989.

Neusner, Jacob. *Method and Meaning in Ancient Judaism*. Brown Judaica Series, no. 10. Missoula, Mont.: Scholars Press, 1979.

_____. *Judaism: The Evidence of the Mishnah*. Chicago: University of Chicago Press, 1982.

Neusner, Jacob, ed. *The Study of Ancient Judaism*, pt. 1. New York: Ktav, 1981.

Pardes, Ilana. *Countertraditions in the Bible: A Feminist Approach*. Cambridge: Harvard University Press, 1992.

Peskowitz, Miriam. *Spinning Fantasies*. Berkeley: University of California Press, forthcoming.

Peskowitz, Miriam, and Laura Levitt, eds. *Judaism Since Gender*. New York: Routledge, 1997.

Plaskow, Judith. *Standing Again at Sinai*. San Francisco: Harper and Row, 1990.

Riskin, Shlomo. *Women and Jewish Divorce*. New York: Ktav, 1989.

Rovner, Jay. "Rhetorical Strategy and Dialectical Necessity in the Babylonian Talmud: The Case of Kiddushin 34a–35a," *HUCA (Hebrew Union College Annual)* 65 (1994).

Ruether, Rosemary. "Feminist Interpretation: A Method of Correlation." In *Feminist Interpretation of the Bible*, ed. Letty M. Russell. Philadelphia: Westminster Press, 1985.

Safrai, Chana. "Women and Processes of Change in the Temple in Jerusalem." In *A View into the Lives of Women in Jewish Societies*, ed. Yael Azmon. Jerusalem: Mercaz Shazar, 1995.

Safrai, Shmuel. "Mehuyavutan shel Nashim Bemitzvot Bemishnatam shel Hatannaim," *Bar Ilan Yearbook for Jewish Studies and Humanities* 26/27 (5755/1994–1995).

Safrai, Shmuel, ed. *The Literature of the Sages*, pt. 1. Philadelphia: Fortress Press, 1987.

Satlow, Michael L. *Tasting the Dish: Rabbinic Rhetorics of Sexuality*. Atlanta, Ga.: Scholars Press, 1995.

_____. "'Wasted Seed,' the History of a Rabbinic Idea," *HUCA (Hebrew Union College Annual)* 65 (1994).

Schiffman, Lawrence H. "Laws Pertaining to Women in the Temple Scroll." In *The Dead Sea Scrolls: Forty Years of Research*, ed. Devorah Diamant and U. Rappoport. Leiden: E. J. Brill, 1992.

_____. *Reclaiming the Dead Sea Scrolls*. Philadelphia: JPS, 1994.

Schuller, Eileen M. "Women in the Dead Sea Scrolls," *Annals of the New York Academy of Sciences*, 1994.

Ta Shma, I. "Niddah." *Encyclopedia Judaica* (12:1145).

Treggiari, Susan. "Divorce Roman Style: How Easy and How Frequent Was It?" In *Marriage, Divorce, and Children in Ancient Rome*, ed. Beryl Rawson. Oxford: Clarendon Press, 1991.

_____. *Roman Marriage: Iusti Coniuges from the Time of Cicero to the Time of Ulpian*. Oxford: Oxford University Press, 1991.

Urbach, Ephraim E. *The Halakhah, Its Sources and Development.* n.p.: Yad Latalmud: 1986.

Valler, Shulamit, *Women and Womanhood in the Stories of the Babylonian Talmud.* Tel Aviv: Hakibbutz Hameuchad, 1993.

Wegner, Judith, *Chattel or Person? The Status of Women in the Mishnah.* New York: Oxford University Press, 1988.

_____. "Leviticus." In *The Women's Bible Commentary*, ed. Carol A. Newsom and Sharon H. Ringe. Westminster: John Knox Press, 1992.

_____. "Philo's Portrayal of Women—Hebraic or Hellenic?" In *"Women like This:" New Perspectives on Jewish Women in the Greco-Roman World*, ed. Amy-Jill Levine. Atlanta, Ga.: Scholars Press, 1991.

Weinfeld, Moshe. *Deuteronomy and the Deuteronomic School.* Oxford: Oxford University Press: 1972.

Yaron, Reuven. *Gifts in Contemplation of Death in Jewish and Roman Law.* Oxford: Clarendon Press, 1960.

Zakovitch, Yair. "The Woman's Rights in the Biblical Law of Divorce," *Jewish Law Annual* 14 (1981).

Zohar, Noam. "Mah Bein Ish L'ishah." *Et La'asot,* no. 1 (Summer 1988).

Index of Texts Discussed

General Index

Abortion, 175(n48)
  and definition of childless marriage, 131
  spontaneous, 160
Adler, Rachel, on rapist's responsibility, 99(n17)
Adultery, 16, 22, 23, 25, 29(n1), 86
Age
  legal consequences of, 89, 92, 100(n28)
  maturity, 100(nn 26, 27)
  obligation to mitzvot by, 230, 241(n20)
  respect for, 233
  of women at marriage, 96, 101(n47)
Agunot, attempt to reduce number of, 111
Akiva, R., leniencies, 173(n29)
  over women's blood stains, 153–156
Annulment, marriage, 102, 110–114, 121
Appearance
  niddah dressing nicely, 155–156
  rabbis encouraging women to care for physical, 51, 153
Archer, Leonie, on rabbis view of women, 30
Asceticism, sexual, 41–43
R. Ashi, 9*ba'al keri*, 171(n14)

Baraitot, definition of, 8–9
Barrenness, onus of, 132
Baskin, Judith
  on childless women praying, 145(n12)
  on studies of women and rabbinic Judaism, 13(n13)
  on women's exemption from procreation, 145(n13)
Behavior
  immodest, 59(n50)
  mother's modest dress and sons' accomplishments, 219
  problems with men's regarding wives, 19
Behavorial standard, betrothal formula phrase used as, 59(n50)
Ben Azzai
  on childlessness, 143
  on teaching daughter Torah, 22, 23, 43, 57(n33)
Ben Sira, belief on women's sexuality, 48–49, 58(n43)
Beruriah, 57(n26)
Bestiality, 34, 37, 56(n17)
Betrothal, 68–73, 121
  formula, 59(n50), 128(n23)
  groom reciting formula, 71, 76(n21)
  initiated by women, 72–74, 213
  as purchase, 69, 70, 71
  staging to claim estate share, 182
  through third party, 72–73
  women's consent to, 69–71, 76(n20)
  women not participating in ceremony, 72
Betrothed woman, designated *zavah*, 174(n41)
Biale, David, on rabbis view of women, 30

272